VULNERABILITIES
TO DELINQUENCY

VULNERABILITIES TO DELINQUENCY

Edited by
Dorothy Otnow Lewis, M.D., F.A.C.P.
Professor of Psychiatry
New York University School of Medicine
New York
and
Clinical Professor of Psychiatry
Yale University Child Study Center
New Haven, Connecticut

SP MEDICAL & SCIENTIFIC BOOKS

New York

SPECTRUM PUBLICATIONS, INC.
175-20 Wexford Terrace, Jamaica, N.Y. 11432

Library of Congress Cataloging in Publication Data
Main entry under title:

Vulnerabilities to delinquency.

    Includes index.
    1. Juvenile delinquency. 2. Criminal psychology.
3. Criminal behavior, Prediction of. 4. Psychobiology.
I. Lewis, Dorothy Otnow.
RJ506.J88P79   364.2'4   80-22362
ISBN 0-89335-136-9

To Gillian and Eric

Contributors

JONATHAN E. ALPERT
Yale University School of Medicine
New Haven, Connecticut

DAVID A. BALLA, Ph.D.
Yale University Child Study Center
New Haven, Connecticut

BARBARA BARD, Ph.D.
Department of Human Services
and Special Education
Central Connecticut State College
New Britain, Connecticut

DENNIS P. CANTWELL, M.D.
Neuropsychiatric Institute,
University of California
Los Angeles, California

ROBERT CANCRO, M.D.
Department of Psychiatry
New York University School of Medicine
New York, New York

DONALD J. COHEN, M.D.
Departments of Psychiatry,
Psychology, and Pediatrics
Yale University Child Study Center
New Haven, Connecticut

GILBERT H. GLASER, M.D.
Department of Neurology
Yale University School of Medicine
New Haven, Connecticut

DOROTHY OTNOW LEWIS, M.D.
Department of Psychiatry
New York University School of Medicine
New York, New York
and
Yale University Child Study Center
New Haven, Connecticut

AKE MATTSSON, M.D.
Division of Child and Adolescent Psychiatry
New York University School of Medicine
New York, New York

SARNOFF A. MEDNICK, Ph.D
Social Science Research Institute
University of Southern California
Los Angeles, California

MARK PICCIRILLO
Yale University School of Medicine
New Haven, Connecticut

JONATHAN H. PINCUS, M.D.
Department of Neurology
Yale University School of Medicine
New Haven, Connecticut

ERNESTO POLLITT, Ph.D.
School of Public Health
University of Texas
Houston, Texas

B.J. SAHAKIAN, Ph.D.
Laboratory of Neuroendocrine Regulation
Massachusetts Institute of Technology
Cambridge, Massachusetts

SHELLEY S. SHANOK, M.P.H.
Department of Psychiatry
New York University School of Medicine
New York, New York

BENNETT A. SHAYWITZ, M.D.
Departments of Pediatrics and Neurology
Yale University School of Medicine
New Haven, Connecticut

Acknowledgments

I wish to thank the American Journal of Psychiatry and the Journal of the American Academy of Child Psychiatry for permitting me to use in this book some of the data previously published in these journals. I also wish to thank the Law Enforcement Assistance Administration for their support in our studies of violent juvenile offenders.

I would like to thank Mariann Giammarino for her assistance in preparation of the manuscript.

I am especially grateful to Thomas Cooney, Jr. and Sol Chafkin of the Ford Foundation. Their continuing support and encouragement made it possible to embark on our studies of medical factors associated with delinquency and to follow through in these especially fruitful areas of investigation. Without them much of the work reported in this book would not have been accomplished.

My love and thanks to Esther Anderson for creating an environment in which the work could take place, and to Gillian and Eric Lewis for their patience during the long months of writing.

Special thanks and love go to Melvin Lewis whose wisdom, knowledge and editorial skills enhanced the book.

Foreword

During the decade or so following World War II psychiatry was grossly oversold to the general public in the United States. People were given to believe that a variety of social ills and discomforts could be healed by skillful psychiatric intervention. There seemed to be no problem which could not be conceptualized as psychic in origin, including war, poverty, criminality, violence, and a variety of more mundane concerns. Clearly, these mental "illnesses" should respond to proper "treatment." As so often happens following a "hard sell," the initially convinced customer is left with a significant level of disappointment, if not rage. Thus it was with psychiatry, which could not deliver the cornucopia of benefits that were promised, and in fact found great difficulty in even reducing the anguish of the chronically psychotic. After riding off madly in all directions, psychiatry did grievous if not mortal injury to its credibility. More recently, reality has begun to intrude in psychiatric practice and research. There is a return to scientific method and a substitution of data for opinion. The neural sciences are proceeding at a breath-taking pace and are beginning to integrate experience as well as biology into highly sophisticated models of illness. It would be ironic indeed if now the field were to begin to deliver on the promises made and false hopes created such a painfully short time ago.

During the worst period of overselling, the models used by psychiatry were excessively if not exclusively social in nature. While the *tabula rasa* theory of neonate development was denied in theory, it was often used in practice. Schizophrenia could clearly be caused by poor mothering, and certainly lesser "mental" problems such as juvenile delinquency and violence represented no challenge to a mother who wished to turn out such a child. One could not merely call these colleagues sexist, because women were well represented among the theorists, and mothers were imagined to be profoundly powerful. In this mythology fathers barely appeared and had virtually no influence on the development of their children, let alone the behavior of their wives. Following fertilization fathers played little if any significant role in the development of the child. Interestingly enough, any illiterate peasant would know better and reject such a naive developmental approach, but the intellectual community once again was unable to see the obvious.

Psychoanalysis, particularly as expounded by Freud, was initially less exclusively social and placed considerable emphasis on constitutional factors which operated in a manner that was not totally dependent upon social experience. Freud in particular saw many psychological outcomes as determined by biologic factors, but certain of his followers were less biologic in their orientation and placed greater emphasis on intrapersonal and interpersonal events. The basically neurologic and heavily physiologic approach of Freud became almost totally social in its orientation in America and no longer served as a counterbalance to social psychology and learning theory.

During the same time that psychiatry was dominated by social models of both normal development and illness there were a handful of individuals who tended toward biologic reductionism. They tended to see behaviors as predetermined in a Calvinistic sense and inevitable in their expression. These people did not offer a viable alternative to the excessively social model, and in fact, by their very reductionism and pessimism, served to foster the same model which they rejected. If the choice was between the explicit hope of the social model and the implicit hopelessness of this so-called biologic model, most young practitioners would and did opt for the former.

There have been a number of revolutions described in psychiatry in recent years, some of which have actually occurred. Perhaps the most important of these can be characterized as the Quiet Revolution. With very little fanfare and no media coverage, psychiatry has become increasingly biopsychosocial in its thinking. Genetic, biochemical, and physiologic factors are discussed as commonly as intrapsychic, interpersonal, and cultural factors. Psychiatrists are ever more comfortable in assuming the interface role between behavior and biology, which role is dictated by the nature of that which they have chosen to study. Psychiatrists are increasingly able to talk to patients in terms of their experience and to nonpsychiatric colleagues in terms of science — all of this without self-consciousness. If there has ever been a revolution in the field, it is this one. Finally, psychiatry has come to realize that all illnesses, and not merely mental illnesses, are biopsychosocial. The mental illnesses are a special case but do not differ fundamentally in their nature. Psychological, social, and cultural factors play as much of an etiopathogenic role in a disease such as cancer as they do in a disease such as depression.

This volume in many ways is testimony to the extent to which this revolution has already taken place. It is entitled *Vulnerabilities to Delinquency*, and in fact carries out the promise of its title remarkably well. The dream of Adolf Meyer to create a true psychobiology is only now beginning to be realized. He could not have anticipated the form, let alone the specific parameters, which would be included in our present understanding. The recent knowledge of neurochemistry could not have been anticipated by Meyer, but is well represented in this volume. Different authors bring very different perspectives to the same or related problems. Some utilize animal models while others work with people. Some are more concerned with electrical activity in the brain and others with nutritional status. The vast majority of these chapters reflect, however, the effort to integrate, in a sophisticated manner, both psychologic and biologic variables into a relatively comprehensive picture of the problem being studied.

What emerges repeatedly in a most sobering fashion is the relative clinical neglect received by these troubled young people. They have been labeled as deviants, and the label has assumed an explanatory power which is both remarkable and unrealistic. Young people with epileptic disorders and/or psychotic illnesses have had their problems undiagnosed and untreated. The maudlin aphorism that "there is no such thing as a bad boy" has served to injure many children who have received "education" in the place of medical treatment. There is a particularly interesting chapter by Lewis and Shanok illustrating how unconscious and perhaps even conscious bias operate to support the inadequate diagnosis, disposition, and treatment of minority adolescents. The disparity between the rhetoric and the actual care given these young people is remarkable. It is hoped that the pendulum will not overswing in the opposite direction and yield a curious dialectic in which the field will excessively neurologize and biologize to the exclusion of psychological and social awareness. The probability is high, however, that this will occur because it has been the history of ideas as seen in human beings. It appears most difficult for people to operate with complex models that borrow from different disciplines. It is much easier to substitute one oversimplification for another. Perhaps the most exciting promise of this volume lies in its relative freedom from polemic and oversimplification. Time will tell whether rationality is intruding and this book is illustrative of a real change emerging, or whether the hope is premature.

While the volume does represent an edited effort, eighty percent of the chapters are contributed by Lewis and Shanok. For this reason, there is much more consistency in theme and style than is usually the case in an edited volume. It would be more accurate to say that Lewis has invited a few people to develop several areas in which she did not feel particularly qualified. This has led to a much more readable and consistent book than otherwise would have been possible.

The multidisciplinary approach taken in the study of the complex problems of violent and delinquent adolescents is of even greater promise than any of the results obtained thus far. The work presented in this volume ranges from interesting to genuinely exciting. What is of more importance, however, is the philosophy of the approach, which is far more comprehensive and integrative than has been the usual custom in psychiatry in the past. When reading these chapters, this author is reminded of Freud's vision of neurophysiology and psychoanalysis being merged and the subsequent dream of Meyer for a scientifically-based psychobiology. It would be going beyond the data to say that the dream has been fulfilled, but it is more than mere optimism to say that the content of the dream is becoming more lucid.

Robert Cancro, M.D.

Contents

Part I

Some Neuropsychiatric Factors

CHAPTER ONE

Psychobiological Vulnerabilities in Perspective

DOROTHY OTNOW LEWIS

Long, long ago—well, actually, not so long ago—poor people, crazy people, and criminals were intentionally housed together. Although it would be nice to assume that this practice expressed an unconscious recognition that these ostensibly different populations had similar kinds of disorders and required similar care and treatment, it is more likely that they simply posed the same kinds of problems for society and elicited the same hostile feelings. Hence, they were dealt with similarly.

Recently, as will be seen in the following chapters on hyperkinesis, neurological disorders, psychosis, and race, strong evidence has been accumulated suggesting that, at least as far as children are concerned, those incarcerated and those sent to state hospitals are remarkably similar in many respects. They not only suffer from similar kinds of neuropsychiatric disorders, but they also tend to behave in similarly antisocial, often violent, ways. That they are cared for, or rather housed, in different institutions may prove to be a reflection more of bias than of need.

Ironically, in the past, when psychiatric patients were distinguished and separated from criminals and the rest of the poor, it would have been hard to determine which population was better off, the prisoners or the patients. (Such, of course, is often still the case!) The kinds of therapeutic interventions provided to psychiatrically disturbed patients were often no less brutal than the punishments meted out to prisoners. One might hazard a guess that both kinds of treatment were equally effective.

3

Several of the most incapacitating neuropsychiatric disorders—schizophrenias, epilepsies, depressions, and attentional disorders—have recently been ameliorated, though not cured, by various combinations of medical, psychological, educational, and environmental interventions. The antisocial disorders, on the other hand, have proved particularly resistant to the kinds of interventions advocated and implemented for their treatment. The wealth of data in the following chapters leads one to suspect that therapeutic failure in the case of antisocial behavior may result, at least partially, from our reluctance or inability to differentiate and treat the different vulnerabilities within each individual offender that contribute to his or her aberrant behaviors. It would therefore be inaccurate to conclude that the lack of psychosocial rehabilitation following incarceration reflects a total lack of knowledge regarding the etiology and potential treatments for antisocial behavior. Equally misleading is the assumption that current treatment programs and practices within correctional institutions reflect in any way what could be done, given our understanding of the interaction of biological, psychological, and social factors in the generation of delinquency.

The following chapters contain data already available about *some* of the biopsychosocial factors that have been found to be associated with delinquency. Much of this information is relevant to future program planning. Unfortunately, the movement from basic knowledge, to medical and psychological practice, and then to large scale social implementation, is extraordinarily slow.

The purpose of this book is to make available to doctors, lawyers, social scientists, teachers, probation officers, legislators, and—above all—to those directly involved in the care of the thousands of youngsters incarcerated in correctional institutions some of the newest knowledge about the possible biopsychosocial vulnerabilities that contribute to delinquency. We hope that this knowledge will then be used wisely and cautiously, as we seek to improve the care and treatment of children.

CHAPTER TWO

Delinquency and Psychotic Disorders

DOROTHY OTNOW LEWIS

In this chapter we shall examine some of the increasingly strong evidence of an association between psychotic symptomatology and some antisocial behaviors in children. Because the literature on juvenile offenders is sparse and the majority of serious adult offenders have juvenile records, we shall also examine some of the adult literature as well as that pertaining to juveniles. It should be stressed from the outset that we are not discussing all of juvenile delinquency. Rather, we are exploring evidence that a proportion of juveniles whose antisocial behaviors bring them to the attention of the courts suffer from the kinds of impaired thought processes, judgment, reality testing, and impulse control characteristic of psychotic disorders. Unlike the flamboyantly obvious signs and symptoms of acute schizophrenia, the disorders to be discussed are not necessarily easily recognized and immediately discernible. In fact, signs and symptoms are often sporadic and fluctuating in intensity. Moreover, they often tend to be obscured by blatant antisocial behaviors. For these reasons, psychotic symptomatology in many delinquent children usually goes unrecognized and untreated, or incorrectly treated.

This exploration of the relationship between delinquency and psychosis sprang from the clinical observation that many delinquent children referred to a juvenile court clinic in the early 1970s manifested clear signs and symptoms of psychotic disturbances (Lewis et al., 1973). In fact, of the first 40 children referred to the court clinic, 10 demonstrated psychotic symptomatology.

Examples of the kinds of psychotic symptomatology noted were as follows: one child attempted to throw a sibling out the window in response to a hallucinated voice; another heard the voice of a dead friend and followed it to the roof of a building; and several children felt continually under attack by imagined people or forces and felt the need to carry weapons ranging from razors to .22 caliber guns. We reported all 10 cases in detail, aware that the assessment of psychotic symptoms may vary, and we were careful to designate psychotic only the most clearcut symptoms such as recurrent hallucinations and pervasive paranoid ideation.

Our more recent clinical experience, doing meticulous psychiatric, neurological, and psychological evaluations of violent delinquents in a securely closed setting serving the entire state of Connecticut, has been consistent with our previous findings at the court clinic. In fact, the prevalence of paranoid ideation and of auditory and visual hallucinations in our current population of violent juveniles is far greater than in the court-clinic-referred children. Furthermore, there is clinical evidence to suggest that psychotic symptoms in several cases influenced the violent behaviors for which the children were incarcerated.

For example, one juvenile of normal height, weight, and with average good looks repeatedly attacked women, declaring that women "looked at (him) funny" when he walked down the street, making him angry. Another juvenile who attacked and sexually assaulted a smaller child whose sled he had taken totally reversed the situation in his mind and justified the attack, saying, "The other kid was following me." Yet another youngster left the office at the conclusion of a psychiatric interview accompanied by the examiner, wheeled around, and punched the first person he saw. When asked why he did this, he indicated that the boy behind him had just called his mother an obscene name. In spite of the fact that there were numerous witnesses to the attack, the assailant could not be convinced that not a word had been spoken. Another assaultive youngster was described by his mother as being so suspicious he secreted knives all around his room, under his pillow, in his closet, on shelves, and over the door frame.

We also found that many of the parents of the delinquent children we evaluated suffered from serious psychopathology other than sociopathy or alcoholism. For example, one mother was noted to converse animatedly with a nonexistent companion as she sat in the waiting room. Her husband, a former prison inmate and psychiatric hospital patient, locked his children in a room and sprayed mace under the door as a method of discipline. Another father, released from a psychiatric hospital just prior to the birth of his son, threw the infant across the room into his crib and, at night, burned the arms and legs of his other children with cigarette butts. One father who, at the time he was interviewed, appeared agitated and paranoid, terrorized his family, beating his epileptic delinquent son in order to exorcise the devil. He believed that church attendance twice daily and regular beatings would rid his son of the demonic forces possessing him.

Our clinical observations of parental psychotic symptomatology led us to examine more systematically the possible association of parental schizophrenia and delinquency. Our initial epidemiological studies indicated that the parents of delinquent children were significantly more likely to be psychiatrically hospitalized and/or treated than a demographically comparable sample of the general population (Lewis et al., 1976; Lewis and Balla, 1976). We also found that psychiatrically treated fathers tended to marry psychiatrically treated mothers, and that fathers with criminal records also seemed to gravitate toward psychiatrically treated women (Lewis and Balla, 1976). While we found that parents of delinquent children were often treated at more than one facility and that diagnosis of the same individual differed at different times and in different institutions, it was of some interest that the most common diagnosis attributed to fathers who had been both incarcerated and psychiatrically hospitalized was schizophrenia and not sociopathy or alcoholism as one might expect.

Having ascertained the higher prevalence of psychiatric hospitalization in the parents of delinquents than in the general lower socioeconomic population, we wonder whether the converse situation would hold true. That is, did psychiatrically hospitalized parents, particularly schizophrenic parents, tend to have delinquent children? In a study comparing the prevalence of delinquency in the children of schizophrenics with the prevalence of delinquency in the children of demographically similar non-schizophrenics, we found that schizophrenics were at significantly greater risk of having a child known to juvenile court than demographically comparable non-schizophrenics (Lewis and Balla, 1976). Regardless of whether the populations compared were black or white, male or female, schizophrenics were more likely than non-schizophrenics to have a child known to juvenile court, the significance of differences varying according to the size of the samples.

It seemed reasonable, on the basis of our clinical and epidemiological work, to speculate that something about serious parental mental illness (perhaps specifically schizophrenia) brings about the conditions within a home and creates the vulnerabilities within certain children that are conducive to the development of delinquency. These clinical and epidemiological findings, while suggestive of an association between parental schizophrenia and children's delinquency, must be interpreted with caution in that they fail to establish whether other kinds of parental psychiatric disorders, such as depressive illness, also predispose certain children to delinquency. However, our own studies, seen in the context of the work of other investigators in the field, suggest the possibility that a predisposition to the kind of psychotic symptomatology we presently associate with schizophrenia, combined with a variety of environmental factors, some known and others yet to be understood, are in many instances related to the development of delinquency in some of the children of schizophrenics.

LITERATURE SUGGESTING THAT THERE IS NO ASSOCIATION BETWEEN DELINQUENCY AND PSYCHOSIS

Just as there is a growing body of knowledge pointing toward an association between some antisocial behaviors and serious psychopathology other than sociopathy, so there is a large compendium of literature purporting to demonstrate that no association exists between the two phenomena. There are investigators who have asserted with conviction that there is no greater prevalence of psychosis in the delinquent or criminal populations than in the population at large. Wyrsch (1955) reported schizophrenia, the paradigm of psychosis, to be rarely found either in a population of criminals or in their first degree relatives. McGee (1960) reported that of 21,000 inmates in California prisons and 9,000 parolees, no more than 600 were diagnosed psychotic. Kloek (1968) reported that only one of the 500 delinquents he studied was flamboyantly psychotic, although 30 of Kloek's 500 subjects were thought possibly to suffer from schizophrenia. Similarly, Cloninger and Guze (1970a, 1970b) and Guze et al. (1969) reported that schizophrenia was rarely to be found either in the criminal populations they studied or in the first degree relatives of criminals. Schuckit et al. (1977), in a diagnostic study of 199 male accused felons, reported that antisocial personality, alcoholism, drug abuse, organic brain syndromes, and affective disorders were characteristic of their psychopathology. Schizophrenia was not diagnosed, although of the three prisoners diagnosed as suffering from organic brain syndrome, one was described as "jailed after his paranoid delusions led him to threaten a neighbor with a knife" (p. 120); the second was arrested after "behaving in a strange manner in a public place, (being) . . . confused and suspicious" (p. 120); and the third "had been psychiatrically hospitalized seven times in 9 years for the repeated acute onset of psychoses." He, too, was arrested due to "aggressive and unusual behavior resulting from his paranoia" (p. 120). Gibbons (1970) went so far as to assert that all of the evidence he reviewed failed to support a picture of psychologically maladjusted delinquents.

LITERATURE SUGGESTING THE EXISTENCE OF AN ASSOCI- ATION BETWEEN PSYCHOSIS AND DELINQUENCY

Although clinical investigators have had difficulty categorizing the psychiatric disorders encountered in the delinquent and criminal populations, many researchers who have immersed themselves in the day-to-day diagnosis and treatment of antisocial individuals have been impressed by the severity of the psychopathology they have encountered.

Healy (1920), in an early study of 823 delinquent children, con- cluded that in 455 cases, "mental abnormalities and peculiarities" were a "main factor" contributing to delinquency. Of the 455 delinquents with serious psychiatric abnormalities, Healy reported that 80 were con- sidered psychotic and 60 epileptic. Unfortunately, terms such as "mental abnormalities and peculiarities," and even "psychosis" and "schizophrenia," were usually ill-defined, making evaluation and replication of findings an almost impossible task.

The vague descriptive terms often used to characterize the psycho- pathology of delinquents and criminals are not necessarily a reflection of sloppy clinical observation or research design. Many extremely delin- quent or criminal individuals, albeit seriously maladaptive in their behaviors, fail to manifest consistently the hallmarks we have come to associate with psychosis. They are not always delusional, hallucinating, or rambling and illogical. Nevertheless, many delinquents and criminals manifest these kinds of symptoms sporadically and have been recog- nized as suffering from more seriously disabling psychiatric disorders than simply neurotic, characterologic, or drug-related problems. To quote Oltman and Friedman (1941), many criminals "exhibit emotional and psychological states which cannot be included in any of our cur- rently accepted psychiatric groups. . . . Many present a borderline state of mental health. . . ." (p. 16). They go on to say, "The term 'psycho- pathic personality' has not been satisfactory inasmuch as it has out- grown its usefulness for all but a small proportion of criminals. . . . In the majority of cases the criminal's life from childhood on is one of conflict and maladjustment in all spheres." (p. 40.)

Frustrated himself with the discrepancy he observed between the clearly psychotic behaviors of many of his criminal subjects and their failure to fit neatly the diagnostic criteria for schizophrenia, Kloek (1968) concluded, "More and more I feel that there is a very remarkable and sometimes bewildering lack of adequacy of the conceptual frames currently used in psychiatry." (p. 20). Musing on the difficulties distinguishing between violent acts engendered by psychotic disorders and those resulting from ordinary human aggression, he went on to say, "Because imperfection is omnipresent in man, and yielding to human imperfection is closely connected with the notion of guilt, social inadequacy will be accepted as pathological only if there are clear standards to distinguish it from common human imperfection." (p. 20). Only recently have some of the so-called borderline states alluded to by Oltman and Friedman (1941) been related systematically to our increasing knowledge of schizophrenia (Heston, 1970, 1977; Rosenthal, 1968). The association of borderline psychotic states with delinquency will be discussed subsequently in our consideration of the family studies of schizophrenic individuals.

Ten years after Kloek bemoaned the limitations of psychiatric diagnosis, particularly as applied to delinquency and criminality, there are still no hard and fast, universally accepted criteria for distinguishing uncontrollable psychotic violence from ordinary human aggressiveness. There is little agreement even among psychiatrists regarding the competency, reality testing, and capacity for impulse control of a given individual accused of a violent act. Case studies based on clinical interviews and relying predominantly on subjective impressions rather than quantifiable measures are often unconvincing. They control neither for examiner skill and/or bias nor for the patient's ability to feign insanity. Thus even our own clinical reports (Lewis et al., 1973; Lewis and Balla, 1976) of psychotic symptomatology in delinquent populations, often containing verbatim dialogue, must nevertheless invite skepticism. One psychiatrist's diagnosis of schizophrenia is another's diagnosis of adjustment reaction of adolescence. Perhaps the most useful function of clinical reports is the impetus they provide to conduct more objective epidemiological investigations.

There is a growing body of epidemiological literature calling attention to the possible association of some antisocial behaviors and psychosis. Follow-up studies of children presenting initially with antisocial behaviors, inordinate aggressiveness, and officially documented delinquency suggest that these kinds of presenting symptoms are among the most ominous for future social adaptation. Morris (1956), in his follow-up study of 66 children with behavior disorders, found that by adulthood, 13—almost 20%—had been diagnosed schizophrenic. Childhood behaviors manifested in this group included truancy, stealing, lying, cruelty, disobedience, destructiveness, and temper tantrums; behaviors traditionally recognized as symptomatic of psycho-pathology other than psychosis. Lee Robins (1966), in her 30-year follow-up study of children with antisocial behaviors, found that 30% of children formerly diagnosed antisocial were, in adulthood, diagnosed psychotic. In fact, only 19% of the antisocial children she studied were considered on follow-up to be psychiatrically healthy. More recently, a 25- and 30-year follow-up study (Balla et al., 1974) revealed that by age 35, over 11% of children known to juvenile court had received psychiatric treatment, the majority requiring hospitalization. Since outpatient treatment was readily available to the study sample, hospitalization was taken as an indication of severity of psychopathology.

Evidence of an association between juvenile delinquency and psychosis can also be found in retrospective studies of the childhood behaviors of psychotic adults. Fleming (1967) reported a multiplicity of antisocial childhood behaviors such as stealing, running away, and sexual misconduct in the histories of individuals who subsequently became schizophrenic. Mednick and Schulsinger (1968) too reported notable behavior problems in the past histories of children who sub-sequently became overtly psychotic. In a retrospective study of 500 psychotic criminals, Silverman (1946) found "abnormal behavior traits in childhood predominantly of an aggressive nature—incorrigibility, and petty thievery" in the histories of 22% of his subjects and "behavior disturbance of a less aggressive character—truancy, lack of affection for others, unreliability, restlessness, and nervousness" (p. 309) in an additional 16.8%. Nameche et al. (1964), studying the histories of hospitalized schizophrenics seen during childhood at the Judge Baker Guidance Center, found that many had presented initially with anti-social behaviors including stealing, running away, and "sexual acting out." More recently, Watt and his colleagues (1970, 1972) reported that unsocialized aggression was characteristic of pre-schizophrenic males, while inhibited behavior characterized pre-schizophrenic females. In an extensive review of the literature on the behavioral antecedents of adult schizophrenia, Offord and Cross (1969) concluded that "adult schizo-phrenia should be divided into two major groups, those who have dif-ficulty in childhood or early adolescence and those who do not." They point out that retrospective studies based on child guidance clinic records are skewed toward finding antisocial antecedents to schizo-phrenia because the less disruptive pre-schizophrenic children will not be brought to the attention of clinics and court. One might argue, however, that the more antisocial disruptive pre-psychotic youngsters, whether or not they are over-represented in the literature, are certainly of greatest concern to society.

ANTISOCIAL BEHAVIOR AMONG PSYCHIATRIC PATIENTS

Evidence that discharged psychiatric patients tend to manifest their problems of adaptation in antisocial behaviors is confusing. Zitrin and his colleagues (1976) have reviewed evidence on both sides of the controversy. In their recent paper, "Crime and Violence Among Mental Patients," they cite early studies in New York State (Ashley, 1922; Pollock, 1938) and in Connecticut (Cohen and Friedman, 1945) suggesting that discharged psychiatric patients have lower arrest rates than the general population. More recently, Guze and his colleagues (1974), in a study of psychiatric outpatients, reported that schizophrenic patients were rarely the perpetrators of serious antisocial acts.

In contrast to the above studies, Rappeport and Lassen (1965), looking at arrest rates for crimes against persons, found that discharged male psychiatric patients had significantly higher arrest rates than nonpatients, particularly for the crime of robbery. In their study of discharged psychotic patients, Giovannoni and Gurel (1967) found that their subjects had significantly higher arrest rates for serious crimes such as robbery, assault, and homicide than did the general population. Most of the former patients had been diagnosed schizophrenic and had histories of alcohol abuse. Consonant with their findings were those of Paull and Malek (1974), who reported evidence that schizophrenic patients are frequently arrested for major and minor infractions of the law. Similarly, Hafner and Boker (1973) reported that schizophrenic patients were more likely than other psychiatric patients to commit violent crimes.

Zitrin and his colleagues (1976) studied the arrest rates, quality of offenses, and diagnoses of a large sample (867) of patients admitted to the psychiatric division of Bellevue Hospital over a two-year period. They found that 23.3% of the psychiatric patients had been arrested at least once during the two years before or the two years after their admission to the study. Of the 23.3% of arrested patients, 13.5% had been charged with nonviolent offenses, 9.8% with violent offenses. In the entire sample of 867 patients as well as in the group arrested for violent crimes (85), almost 50% were diagnosed schizophrenic. Those schizophrenic patients arrested for offenses involving actual bodily harm also had a mean number of arrests for all offenses greater than any of the other diagnostic groups. Analyzing the data from a different perspective, Zitrin found that of the entire group of 867 patients, only 10% of schizophrenic patients were arrested for violent offenses, compared with 16% of alcoholics, 30% of drug-dependent patients, and 5% of patients with other diagnoses. Of note, however, was the finding that many of the schizophrenic patients were also abusers of alcohol and drugs. Comparing the Bellevue sample with the rest of the urban United States reveals that psychiatric patients in the study had greater arrest rates for major crimes such as murder, rape, robbery, aggravated assault, and burglary than did residents of the urban areas of the country. Furthermore, the rates of arrest for serious crimes except murder and robbery for the sample of mental patients were higher than the rates for their community, an area of the city noted for its high crime rate. Zitrin and his colleagues concluded, "The commonly held belief that the mentally ill commit fewer crimes than the general population is not supported by our study. Indeed, the arrest records of these 867 psychiatric patients from the Bellevue Hospital catchment area show that their rates of arrest for criminal behavior, including violent offenses, are higher than corresponding rates in their community." (p. 47).

Of special relevance to the study of delinquency and psychosis was the relative youthfulness of the psychiatric patients arrested for violent offenses compared with those arrested for nonviolent offenses. Violent offense rates climbed steadily throughout adolescence, reaching a peak in the mid-twenties. More of the patients in the nonviolent offense group were in the 30- to 40-year age interval. The Zitrin study is certainly consonant with our own findings of an association between severe, often psychotic psychopathology and extreme violence in incarcerated adolescent juveniles (Lewis et al., 1979b).

FAMILY STUDIES SUGGESTIVE OF AN ASSOCIATION BETWEEN PSYCHOSIS AND ANTISOCIAL BEHAVIORS

Among the greatest contributions to our understanding of the association of delinquency and schizophrenia are the studies of the families of schizophrenic individuals. As early as 1937, Bender reported delinquent behaviors in the children of schizophrenics. Since then there has been a growing body of knowledge suggesting that genetic factors play an important role in the development of schizophrenia and possibly in the development of schizophrenia-like maladaptive disorders. Studies of the concordance of schizophrenia in monozygotic and dizygotic twins (Rosenthal, 1971; Pollin and Stabenau, 1968); studies of the prevalence of schizophrenia in foster home-reared or "adopted-away" children of schizophrenics (Heston, 1966); and studies of the prevalence of schizophrenia in the first-degree relatives of schizophrenic individuals (Mednick and Schulsinger, 1968) strongly point to genetic factors in schizophrenia. In a review of the current research in this area, Heston (1977) reported that the estimated concordance rate for schizophrenia among monozygotic twins was 45%; concordance between siblings, 8%; and between a schizophrenic parent and a child, 12%. He reported that if both parents were schizophrenic, a child's chances of becoming schizophrenic ranged from 25% to 50%. None of these percentages, varying as they do, point to a simple genetic explanation of schizophrenia.

Heston, Rosenthal, Mednick and Schulsinger, and others who have studied the families of schizophrenics have noted that an unusually high percentage of first-degree relatives suffer from severe psychopathology other than flamboyantly obvious schizophrenia. While Rosenthal (1971) refers to a "schizophrenic spectrum" of disorders, Heston (1970) refers to the group of seriously psychiatrically disabled relatives of schizophrenics as "schizoids." In Heston's words, "I use the term schizoid as a name for the schizophrenic-like disabilities seen in relatives of schizophrenics, or for the individual manifesting such disabilities." He goes on to explain, "The schizoid exists, and he sometimes shows as much impairment psychiatrically as a typical schizophrenic. Several problematic behaviors have been associated with the schizoid. Among males, antisocial behavior has been found commonly enough to warrant the older subdesignation, 'schizoid psychopathy.'. . . Entries in the police records of the schizoid psychopaths in my study reflected impulsive, seemingly illogical crimes such as arson, unreasoning assault, and poorly planned theft [p. 250]." Although well-marked hallucinations and delusions were not part of the picture, Heston called attention to "micropsychotic episodes" when the schizoid individual was more obviously bizarre in his behavior and thinking than at other times.

The behaviors described by Heston were similar to, though more disruptive than, those reported by Mednick and Schulsinger (1968) as characteristic of the prepsychotic children of schizophrenic mothers. These children, prior to their overt psychosis, were disruptive in class, posed disciplinary problems, and were domineering and aggressive.

The behaviors and symptoms reported by Heston, Mednick, and others to be characteristic of preschizophrenics and of relatives of schizophrenics are similar in quality to the behaviors and symptoms we have observed in many delinquent children. They are especially characteristic of some of the more aggressive and recidivistic offenders we have evaluated.

SOCIAL, MEDICAL, AND PSYCHODYNAMIC FACTORS CONTRIBUTING TO PSYCHOTIC AND ANTISOCIAL BEHAVIORS

The strong, and what we consider convincing, evidence that genetic factors influence the development of schizophrenia and the schizophrenic spectrum disorders of adaptation, which include some forms of delinquency, does not by itself explain either schizophrenia or delinquency. Most children of schizophrenics are probably neither delinquent nor schizophrenic, and most delinquents do not have schizophrenic parents. Clearly, social, physical, and psychodynamic factors influence the ways in which an inherited vulnerability will be expressed. Our own finding that black schizophrenics in our community were more likely than white schizophrenics to have a court-involved child points to a probable social factor or factors that influence some of the children of black schizophrenics to express their feelings and thoughts in antisocial ways. Moreover, as will be seen in the chapter on race bias, our society tends to treat disturbed black children more punitively than disturbed white children. Rosenthal et al. (1968) reported that the psychiatrically disturbed first-degree relatives of schizophrenics in Denmark, unlike the individuals in Heston's study, did not become antisocial. They tended instead to manifest frankly schizophrenic disorders, what were considered borderline schizophrenic disorders, paranoid ideation, and so-called "schizoid" tendencies.

Rosenthal's study is noteworthy both because it reported severe borderline psychotic disorders in the relatives of schizophrenics and because it highlighted the probable influence of social factors on the overt expression of vulnerabilities. Rosenthal et al. (1971) stated, "We should pay close attention to this difference between Heston's study and ours because it suggests that whether an individual with the assumed diathesis that we are talking about becomes psychopathically antisocial or not is determined in overriding fashion by environmental factors. And it suggests that such factors are much more prevalent in the United States than in Denmark." (p. 386). Many of the violent delinquent children we have evaluated manifest paranoid symptoms similar to those described by Rosenthal. That they then frequently act on these paranoid delusions in antisocial dangerous ways suggests that their environments either encourage the overt expression of these kinds of delusions or fail to inculcate the need to suppress the expression of such impulses.

In addition to possible genetic vulnerabilities to maladaptive behaviors, there is evidence that physical trauma, particularly physical trauma to the central nervous system of biologically vulnerable children, can contribute to distorted thinking and maladaptive behaviors. Pollin and Stabenau (1968) have reported that perinatal factors affect the expression of schizophrenia itself and that in cases of monozygotic twins discordant for schizophrenia, most often the twin of lower birth weight, or who had sustained perinatal trauma, or who had experienced early central nervous sytem disorders such as encephalitis, was the twin who became schizophrenic.

Rosenthal (1968) too speculated on the possible contribution of trauma to the central nervous system to the overt antisocial manifestation of a child's vulnerability to schizophrenia. Puzzled at the difference between the antisocial behavior of the children in Heston's American study and the more overtly psychotic symptoms of children in his own Scandinavian study, Rosenthal remarked, "It is also possible that prenatal factors among Heston's hospitalized mothers may have somehow contributed to psychopathy in their children." (p. 386).

Our own clinical and epidemiological studies of the medical histories of delinquent children (Lewis and Shanok, 1977), particularly our studies of the medical histories of extremely violent delinquents (Lewis et al., 1979a), indicate that seriously delinquent children, many of whom manifest vulnerabilities to disorganized thinking, have been subjected to serious central nervous system trauma from birth, throughout childhood, and on into adolescence. One can hypothesize that the perinatal problems, head and face injuries, and severe physical abuse at the hands of psychiatrically impaired parents combine to elicit psychotic thought processes and maladaptive antisocial behaviors that might otherwise have remained dormant in these psychiatrically vulnerable youngsters.

Finally, one cannot dismiss the effects of psychodynamic factors on the modes of expression of a vulnerability to schizophrenia. The fact that for years psychodynamic factors were stressed almost exclusively in the genesis of both schizophrenia and antisocial behaviors (Lidz and Lidz, 1949; Bateson et al., 1956; Singer and Wynne, 1965; Johnson and Szurek, 1952) indicates their importance. Often, psychodynamic factors are so obvious that unfortunately no other factors are considered or dealt with. The model of parental violence, the experience of emotional neglect, the endurance of actual physical torture by parents, and the extreme difficulties in communication in schizophrenic families—all are factors that influence the ways in which a psychiatrically vulnerable child's disorder will be expressed.

Finally, the combined effect of social, physical, and psychological traumas on psychologically vulnerable children of schizophrenics in our society is probably responsible in great measure for the especially antisocial and sometimes dangerous fashion in which some of them manifest their problems. Sometimes this combination of social, physical, and psychodynamic factors is sufficient to engender antisocial behavior. We would suggest only that in our society, the psychologically vulnerable child of a schizophrenic parent may be even more likely than his less vulnerable peers to respond in a disorganized fashion to stress, and to behave in maladaptive and antisocial ways.

A major issue facing child psychiatry today concerns the need for mental health professionals to recognize the childhood behavioral precursors of serious adult psychopathology, pathology often manifested by dangerous antisocial behaviors. In spite of the many indicators pointing to the malignant outcome of childhood antisocial behaviors, and the evidence that childhood neurosis has a relatively benign prognosis (Robins, 1966), an inordinate amount of psychiatric treatment is devoted to neurotic problems. It is difficult to convince mental health professionals and society as a whole of the need to focus attention on the study of the etiology and treatment of delinquency. How does one convince a profession founded on weekly office- or clinic-based psychotherapy to turn its attention toward the diagnosis and treatment of a population of resistant, hostile, often violent, financially unremunerative children and families? The irony of the situation springs from the fact that meticulous diagnostic study of individual children in the delinquent population often reveals eminently treatable disorders.

REFERENCES

Ashley, M. C. (1922). Outcome of 1000 cases paroled from the Middletown State Hospital. *N.Y. State Hosp. Quart.*, 8:64–70.

Balla, D. A., Lewis, D. O., Shanok, S. S., Snell, L., and Henisz, J. (1974). Subsequent psychiatric treatment and hospitalization in a delinquent population. *Arch. Gen. Psychiat.*, 30:240–245.

Bateson, G., Haley, J., Weakland, J., and Jackson, D. D. (1956). Toward a theory of schizophrenia. *Behav. Sci.*, 1:252–264.

Bender, L. (1937). Behavior problems in children of psychiatric and criminal parents. *Psychol. Monogr.*, 19:22–247.

Cloninger, C. R., and Guze, S. B. (1970a). Female criminals. *Arch. Gen. Psychiat.*, 23:554–558.

Cloninger, C. R., and Guze, S. B. (1970b). Psychiatric illness and female criminality. *Am. J. Psychiat.*, 127:303–311.

Cohen, L. H., and Friedman, H. (1945). How dangerous to the community are state hospital patients? *Conn. Med.*, 9:697–700.

Fleming, P. (1967). Emotional antecedents of schizophrenia. Read at the First Conference on Life History Research in Psychopathology, Teacher's College, Columbia University.

Gibbons, D. C. (1970). *Delinquent Behavior.* Englewood Cliffs, NJ: Prentice Hall.

Giovannoni, J. M., and Gurel, L. (1967). Socially disruptive behavior of ex-mental patients. *Arch. Gen. Psychiat.*, 17:146–53.

Guze, S. B., Goodwin, D. W., and Crane, J. B. (1969). Criminality and psychiatric disorders. *Arch. Gen. Psychiat.*, 20:583–591.

Guze, S. B., Woodruff, R. A., and Clayton, P. J. (1974). Psychiatric disorders and criminality. *JAMA*, 227:641–642.

Hafner, H., and Boker, W. (1973). Mentally disordered violent offenders. *Soc. Psychiat.*, 8:220–229.

Healy, W. (1920). *The Individual Delinquent.* Boston: Little Brown & Co.

Heston, L. L. (1966). Psychiatric disorders in foster home reared children of schizophrenic mothers. *Brit. J. Psychiat.*, 112:819–825.

Heston, L. L. (1970). The genetics of schizophrenia and schizoid disease. *Science*, 167:249–256.

Heston, L. L. (1977). Schizophrenia. *Hosp. Pract.*, 12:43–49.

Johnson, A. M., and Szurek, S. A. (1952). The genesis of antisocial acting out in children and adults. *Psychoanal. Quart.*, 21:323–343.

Kloek, J. (1968). Schizophrenia and delinquency. *Int. Psychiat. Clin.*, 5:19–34.

Lewis, D. O., and Balla, D. A. (1976). *Delinquency and Psychopathology.* New York: Grune & Stratton.

Lewis, D. O., Balla, D. A., Sacks, H., and Jekel, J. (1973). Psychotic symptomatology in a juvenile court clinic population. *J. Am. Acad. Child Psychiat.*, 12:660–675.

Lewis, D. O., Balla, D. A., Shanok, S. S., and Snell, L. (1976). Delinquency, parental psychopathology, and parental criminality. *J. Am. Acad. Child Psychiat.*, 15:665–678.

Lewis, D. O., and Shanok, S. S. (1977). Medical histories of delinquent and nondelinquent children. *Am. J. Psychiat.*, 134:1020–1025.

Lewis, D. O., Shanok, S. S., and Balla, D. A. (1979a). Perinatal difficulties, head and face trauma, and child abuse in the medical histories of serious youthful offenders. *Am. J. Psychiat.* 136:419–423.

Lewis, D. O., Shanok, S. S., Pincus, J. H., and Glaser, G. H. (1979b). Violent juvenile delinquents: psychiatric, neurological, psychological, and abuse factors. *J. Am. Acad. Child Psychiat.* 18:307–319.

Lidz, R. W., and Lidz, T. (1949). The family environment of psychiatric patients. *Am. J. Psychiat.*, 106:332–345.

McGee, R. (1960). Proc. Symp. Mentally Abnormal Offender, Atascadero State Hospital Symposium, Dept. of Mental Hygiene, Sacramento, CA (p. 15).

Mednick, S. A., and Schulsinger, F. (1968). Some premorbid characteristics related to breakdown in children with schizophrenic mothers. *J. Psychiat. Res.*, 6:267–291.

Morris, A. H., Jr., Escoll, M. D., and Wexler, R. (1956). Aggressive behavior disorders of childhood. *Am. J. Psychiat.*, 112:991–997.

Nameche, G., Waring, M., and Ricks, D. (1964). Early indicators of outcome in schizophrenia. *J. Nerv. Ment. Dis.*, 139:232–240.

Offord, N. R., and Cross, L. A. (1969). Behavioral antecedents of adult schizophrenia. *Arch. Gen. Psychiat.*, 21:267–283.

Oltman, J. E., and Friedman, S. (1941). A psychiatric study of 100 criminals with particular reference to psychological determinants of crime. *J. Nerv. Ment. Dis.*, 93:16–41.

Paull, D., and Malek, R. A. (1974). Psychiatric disorders and criminality. *JAMA*, 227:641–642.

Pollin, W., and Stabenau, J. R. (1968). Biological, psychological, and historical differences in a series of monozygotic twins discordant for schizophrenia. In: *Transmission of Schizophrenia*, D. Rosenthal and S. S. Kety (eds.). Oxford: Pergamon Press, pp. 317–332.

Pollock, H. M. (1938). Is the paroled patient a menace to the community? *Psychiat. Quart.*, 12:236–244.

Rappeport, J. R., and Lassen, G. (1965). Dangerousness-arrest rate comparisons of discharged patients and the general population. *Am. J. Psychiat.*, 121:776–783.

Robins, L. (1966). *Deviant Children Grown Up.* Baltimore: Williams & Wilkins.

Rosenthal, D. (1971). A program of research on heredity in schizophrenia. *Behav. Sci.*, 16:191–201.

Rosenthal, D., Wender, P. H., Kety, S. S., Schulsinger, F., Welner, J., and Ostergaard, L. (1958). Schizophrenics' offspring reared in adoptive homes. In: *Transmission of Schizophrenia*, D. Rosenthal and S. S. Kety (eds.). Oxford: Pergamon Press, pp. 377–391.

Schuckit, M. A., Herrman, G., and Schuckit, J. J. (1977). The importance of psychiatric illness in newly arrested prisoners. *J. Nerv. Ment. Dis.*, 165:118–125.

Silverman, D. (1946). The psychiatric criminal. *J. Clin. Psychopath.*, 8:301–327.

Singer, M. T., and Wynne, L. C. (1965). Thought disorder and family relations of schizophrenics, IV. *Arch. Gen. Psychiat.*, 12:201–212.

Watt, N. F. (1972). Longitudinal changes in the social behavior of children hospitalized for schizophrenia as adults. *J. Nerv. Ment. Dis.*, 155:42–54.

Watt, N. F., Stolorow, R. D., Lubensky, A. W., and McClelland, D. C. (1970). School adjustment and behavior of children hospitalized for schizophrenia as adults. *Am. J. Orthopsychiat.*, 40:637–657.

Wyrsch, J. (1955). *Gerichtliche Psychiatrie.* Bern: Paul Haupt.

Zitrin, A., Hardesty, A. S., Burdock, E. I., and Drossman, A. (1976). Crime and violence among mental patients. *Am. J. Psychiat.*, 133:142–149.

CHAPTER THREE

Hyperactivity and Antisocial Behavior Revisited: A Critical Review of the Literature

DENNIS P. CANTWELL

ABSTRACT

This chapter reviews evidence that the hyperactive child syndrome is connected with the development of delinquent, antisocial behavior in childhood, adolescence, and later life. The evidence comes from childhood histories of adults with antisocial disorders, from post facto and prospective follow-up studies of hyperactive children, from family studies of both hyperactive children and antisocial personalities, and from treatment studies. In addition, the possible mechanisms of the association between hyperactivity in childhood and delinquent behavior are considered. These include: the persistence of a physiological abnormality; genetic, familial, and environmental factors; and educational failure.

INTRODUCTION

Persistent antisocial delinquent behavior in childhood and adolescence is one of the most significant predictors of serious psychiatric and social impairment in adult life (Robins, 1966; Kohlberg et al., 1972). This chapter will review the evidence suggesting that one common psychiatric disorder of childhood, the hyperkinetic syndrome, is strongly associated with the development of antisocial behavior in childhood, adolescence, and later life.

A pertinent starting point is a discussion of the terminology involved. "Antisocial personality disorder," also synonymously described as "sociopathic personality" or "sociopathy," is a psychiatric diagnosis which should be limited to adults. The essential features of this disorder are a history of continuous and chronic antisocial behavior in which the rights of others are violated. The onset is generally before the age of 15 and the persistence of antisocial behavior occurs after the age of 18 and into adult life. There is also a failure to sustain good job performance over a period of several years, although this latter aspect is not often evident in women or self-employed men who have not been in a position to demonstrate this feature.

Early childhood signs of this personality disorder include such antisocial behavior as lying, stealing, fighting, truancy, and resistance to authority. In adolescence one may see unusually early or aggressive sexual behavior and excess use of alcohol and drugs. In general, these kinds of antisocial behaviors continue into adulthood, although there is a suggestion that after the age of 30 or 35 the more flagrant aspects tend to diminish with time, particularly sexual promiscuity, fighting, vagrancy, and criminal behavior.

This diagnosis is not made when the antisocial behavior is symptomatic of other mental disorders such as schizophrenia, schizoaffective, paranoid disorder, or severe mental retardation. However, there often are signs of personal distress in these individuals including complaints of inability to tolerate boredom, depressive symptoms, tension, and feelings that others are against them. There are some suggestions that these interpersonal difficulties and dysphoria may persist in adult life, past the time when the more flagrant aspects of antisocial behaviors have dissipated. These individuals also have a marked impairment in the capacity to sustain lasting, close, warm, and responsible relationships with family, friends, or sexual partners.

Antisocial personality disorder occurs much more commonly in males than females and also begins earlier in males. The prevalence of antisocial personality in American males is about three percent, and in American females less than one percent. The disorder also tends to run in families. The fathers of both males and females with antisocial personality disorder tend to have the same diagnosis. There is also a tendency toward associative mating, so that the offspring of women with antisocial personality disorder are at a high risk for having both parents with the disorder. Moreover, there seems to be a familial relationship with alcoholism and hysteria (Briquet's Syndrome).

This familial and clinical relationship has led some investigators to postulate that antisocial personality, alcoholism, and hysteria form part of an "antisocial spectrum" (Cloninger and Guze, 1973). The essential feature of Briquet's Syndrome (hysteria) is a pattern of recurring and multiple somatic complaints for which medical attention is sought and no organic cause can be found. This pattern begins before early adulthood and has a chronic but fluctuating course. The complaints are often presented in a dramatic, vague, or exaggerated way, and many of the medical symptoms are of the "pseudo-neurologic," conversion type (blindness, paralysis, aphoria, etc.).

In contrast to antisocial personality disorder, this disorder is much more common in females than it is in males. The association of alcoholism, sociopathy, and hysteria has been noted by a number of other authors. Forrest (1967) has presented data indicating the presence of significant antisocial behavior and alcoholism in some patients with hysteria. Robins (1966) found that 20 of 76 girls referred to a child guidance clinic because of aggressive antisocial behavior were given a diagnosis of hysteria when they were seen as adults. Many convicted female felons present a mixed picture of hysteria in antisocial disorder (Cloninger and Guze, 1970, 1973). In a series of studies, these authors found a familial link between males with antisocial personalities and alcoholism and females with hysteria. First-degree male relatives of males with antisocial personality had increased prevalence rates for alcoholism and antisocial personality, while their female relatives had increased prevalence rates for hysteria. Similarly, systematic family studies of first-degree relatives of women with hysteria reveal increased prevalence rates for sociopathy and alcoholism in their male relatives and for hysteria in their female relatives. Finally, a pattern of associative mating seems to emerge, that is, males with alcoholism and antisocial personality disorder tend to marry females with hysteria, and females with hysteria tend to marry males with alcoholism or antisocial personality disorder. Thus, their children are exposed to "double doses," both environmental and genetic, of the factors that lead to psychiatric disorder in childhood.

Since children are developing personalities, it is inappropriate to give a diagnosis of antisocial personality, or for that matter, any personality disorder to a child. There are a group of disorders called "conduct disorders" which are similar in clinical picture to antisocial personality in adults. The essential feature of the group of disorders called conduct disorders is repetitive and persistent patterns of antisocial behavior that violates the rights of others, which is beyond the ordinary pranks and mischief of children and adolescents. Three categories of conduct disorders are generally described: an undersocialized conduct disorder with an unaggressive subtype and an aggressive subtype, and a socialized conduct disorder. The basis for the distinction between the socialized and unsocialized types is the presence or absence of the establishment of adequate social bonds to others. Within the undersocialized group a distinction between the aggressive and unaggressive types is made by the presence or absence of a pattern of aggressive antisocial behavior. The essential features of the undersocialized conduct disorder (aggressive type) are a failure to establish a normal degree of affection, empathy, or bonding with others; a pattern of aggressive antisocial behavior; and behavior difficulties at school. The essential features of the undersocialized conduct disorders (unaggressive type) are likewise, a failure to establish a normal degree of affection, empathy or bonding with others; behavior difficulties at school; and a pattern of non-aggressive antisocial behavior. The pattern of aggressive antisocial behavior seen in the aggressive subtype includes: chronic lying, bullying, stealing, vandalism, physical aggression, extortion, and breaking and entering. The unaggressive type has a lack of this bold, openly aggressive behavior unless it is directed against children who are decidedly younger or decidedly weaker. The pattern of behavior manifested by these children includes stealing, lying, superficial friendliness of a manipulative type, a repetitive pattern of running away from home overnight, staying out late, and chronic disobedience including avoiding confrontations. Lying is very generally self-protective and manipulative. These children are felt likely to become hangers-on or fringe members of a delinquent group. Both of these types are felt to be more frequent in children of parents with antisocial personality disorder. The natural history of the severe forms of both types includes the development of antisocial personality in later life.

In contrast, the essential features of the socialized type of conduct disorder are a pattern of antisocial behavior; affection, empathy, or bond with others; and behavior difficulties at school. The antisocial behavior occurs outside of the home but may be displayed in the home, and there are always behavior difficulties at school such as truancy, destructiveness, and aggression. Children with the socialized form of conduct disorder do have age appropriate friendships and are likely to show concern for the welfare of their friends or companions. This is what distinguishes them from the unsocialized type. Although the data are not universal in this respect, it is felt that the course is more variable with this type and seems to be more favorable than that of the under-socialized type of conduct disorder. There does appear to be a connection with some form of adult antisocial personality as well. All forms of conduct disorders are much more common in males.

One of the common psychiatric disorders of childhood is the hyperkinetic syndrome. A variety of names have been attached to this disorder, including: hyperkinetic reaction, hyperactive child syndrome, minimal brain damage, minimal brain dysfunction, minimal cerebral dysfunction, and minor cerebral dysfunction. These names reflect different etiological views of this disorder although the clinical descriptions of the children who have been described by these various terms are very similar. The official term for this disorder in the new diagnostic and statistical manual for mental disorders, DSM III (American Psychiatric Association, 1979) will be Attention Deficit Disorder with Hyperactivity. The reason for this is that it has become clear that attentional difficulties are prominent and virtually always present among hyperkinetic children, and data seem to indicate that although excess motor activity may diminish in adolescence, difficulties in sustained attention persist in a substantial proportion of children previously diagnosed as hyperkinetic or hyperactive.

In the remainder of this paper the term Attentional Deficit Disorder with Hyperactivity (ADDH) will be used to describe this disorder. The children who have this condition display excessive motor activity for their age as well as attentional difficulties and impulsivity. In school they are described as having a short attention span, as being impulsive and distractable and failing to follow through on instructions and complete work, and as being disorganized and inattentive. The vast majority of these children have no known neurological disorder present, and about five percent of the cases are associated with *known* organic bnormalities. One disorder begins in early life, and, although the course is not fully known, the data do suggest that attentional difficulties, academic problems, and social difficulties may persist into adolescence and adult life.

Recently Wender and his colleagues at the University of Utah have described a significant number of adult patients with personality disorder diagnoses who seemed to be "hyperactive children grown up" (Wood et al., 1976).

The focus of this chapter will be a critical review of the literature addressing itself to two questions: (1) Is there a relationship between ADDH in childhood and antisocial behavior in adolescence and later life? (2) What is the nature of that relationship?

EVIDENCE FOR ASSOCIATION BETWEEN ADDH AND ANTISOCIAL BEHAVIOR

Childhood Histories of Adults with Antisocial Disorders

There are a number of studies of adults with antisocial behavior and alcoholism indicating that a significant percentage probably were hyperkinetic as children. Quitkin and Klein (1969) found that most of their adolescent and young adult patients who were impulsive and destructive as adults were considered to have a mild to moderate hyperkinetic syndrome as children. The data of Shelley and Reister (1972) support this finding. Data from the Cambridge Summerville Youth Study (McCord and McCord, 1960) and the Oakland Growth Study (Jones et al., 1960) indicate that alcoholic adults were often described as restless, aggressive, and impulsive children.

Wood and his colleagues (1976) identified 15 adult psychiatric patients at the University of Utah clinic who were believed to have been hyperkinetic children. Four of these were given a diagnosis of definite or probable antisocial personality as adults. West and Farrington (1974) have shown in prospective studies of delinquency that delinquents-to-be are distinguished from their peers many years before their delinency begins. Some of the symptoms which help distinguish the predelinquents from their controls are those suggestive of the presence of the hyperkinetic syndrome.

In summary, data from childhood histories of adults with antisocial disorders indicate that the presence of symptoms of the hyperkinetic syndrome in childhood may be a predisposing factor to the development of antisocial disorder.

Post Facto Follow-up Studies of ADDH Children

Two retrospective (or post facto) follow-up studies of hyperkinetic children followed into adulthood have been published. In the first systematic study of hyperkinetic children, Menkes and her colleagues (1967) followed up 14 (11 males and 3 females) of 18 children seen in the Johns Hopkins Child Psychiatry Outpatient Department between 1937 and 1946. The follow-up interval ranged from 14 to 27 years, while the ages of the patients at follow-up ranged from 22 to 40 years. At follow-up, four were psychotic and in institutions and two were retarded and totally dependent on their families. Of the eight who were self-supporting at follow-up, four had spent some time in institutions such as jail or juvenile halls.

In a similar study, Borland and Heckman (1976) examined 20 men who had been diagnosed as hyperkinetic 20 to 25 years previously at the Lehigh Valley Child Guidance Clinic in Allentown, Pennsylvania, and compared them to their brothers. Four of the 20 were given a diagnosis of antisocial personality as adults, while none of their brothers was given a psychiatric diagnosis or had seen a physician for emotional or psychiatric problems. The hyperkinetic group changed jobs much more frequently than their brothers, and at the time of follow-up had not reached the socioeconomic status of either their brothers or their fathers.

In a recent study, Morrison (*Am. J. Psychiat.*, in press) compared 48 adult psychiatric patients, 27 men and 21 women, who had received a diagnosis of hyperactivity as children with two groups of patients in his private practice who had not received this diagnosis. The first comparison group was matched for age and sex but not for socio-economic status. The second comparison group was matched for age, sex and socio-economic status. The ex-hyperactive patients more often had a diagnosis of substance abuse as adults, either alcoholism or drug abuse. Twice as many of the ex-hyperactive adults received a primary diagnosis of alcoholism. Secondary alcoholics were also counted and the difference increased even more.

Personality disorders of all types were more common in the grown-up hyperactive subjects than in either comparison groups. Five of the ex-hyperactive adults were antisocial personalities as adults, as compared with only one such diagnosis in the group matched for social class and none in the group not matched for social class. Twenty-three of the ex-hyperactive subjects had a primary diagnosis of either personality disorder, or drug or alcohol abuse. This was twice as frequent as either of the two comparison groups. It was also noteworthy that the grown up hyperactives were less likely than patients in either of the comparison groups to have an adult diagnosis of affective disorder. In summary then, even when patients were matched for age, sex and social class, from the same private practice, those subjects who had been hyperactive in childhood showed more personality disorder (especially antisocial personality disorder), more alcoholism, and less affective disorder.

All of these post facto studies of grown up ADDH children suggest a strong relationship with antisocial behavior in later life.

Prospective Follow-up Studies of Hyperkinetic Children

Prospective studies by Weiss et al. (1971) at the Montreal Children's Hospital, by Mendelson et al. (1971) at the St. Louis Children's Hospital, and by Hussey et al. (1974) in Vermont all support the notion of a link between the hyperkinetic syndrome and antisocial behavior in later life. Weiss and her colleagues reported on the status of 64 hyperkinetic children (60 boys and 4 girls) four to six years after their initial referral, when the children had been 6 to 13 years old. At follow-up 25% had a history of antisoical behavior, with 15% having already been referred to the courts. Mendelson et al. interviewed the mothers of 83 children who were between the ages of 12 and 16 years. All of these children had been diagnosed as hyperkinetic two to six years earlier at the Children's Hospital in St. Louis, Missouri. Antisocial behavior of a rather marked degree was a frequent finding at follow-up. Twenty-two percent of the children had long histories of such behavior and were considered likely to be sociopathic as adults. Nearly 60% had had some contact with the police, 17% on three or more occasions. Nearly 25% had been referred to the juvenile court. A variety of antisocial symptoms were present in a large number of the children at the time of follow-up: 51% were involved with fighting and stealing, 33% had threatened to kill their parents, 15% had set fires, 7% had carried concealed weapons, 5% exhibited significant drug abuse, and 15% were having significant problems with excessive drinking. Two-thirds were considered by their parents to be incorrigible. The picture emerging from this study was one of children who had had difficulty conforming to rules, whether the rules were set by society or by their families.

Hussey et al. (1974) reported on 84 hyperkinetic children, 9 to 24 years of age, who had been followed from 8 to 10 years. School dropout from this hyperkinetic population 8 to 10 years after they had initially been seen was five times higher than that expected for the state of Vermont as a whole, and the group was 20 times more likely to be institutionalized in a facility for delinquent youths than the general population.

Thus three different types of studies (childhood histories of adult patients with antisocial behavior, post facto follow-up studies of hyperkinetic children, and prospective follow-up studies of hyperkinetic children) all strongly support the idea that there is a link between the presence of the ADDH syndrome in childhood and significant antisocial behavior in adolescence and later life.

Family Studies

In a systematic psychiatric examination of the biological parents of 50 hyperkinetic and 50 matched normal control children (Cantwell, 1972), 16% of the fathers of hyperkinetic children were given a diagnosis of sociopathy and 30% were diagnosed as alcoholic; 8% of the mothers of hyperkinetic children were diagnosed as alcoholic and 16% were given a diagnosis of hysteria or probable hysteria (the criteria of Feighner et al., 1972, for the diagnosis of hysteria were used). Eight (16%) of the fathers of hyperkinetic children were thought to have been hyperkinetic as children and six of these were given a diagnosis of alcoholism as adults. One was given a diagnosis of sociopathy, and one had an undiagnosed psychiatric illness with heavy drinking as one of the major symptoms. Two (4%) of the mothers of hyperkinetic children were thought to have been hyperkinetic as children and as adults one was felt to be a hysteric and one was given a diagnosis of probable hysteria.

In a similar study Morrison and Stewart (1971) systematically evaluated parents of 59 hyperkinetic and 41 normal control children: 20% of the fathers of the hyperkinetic children were given a diagnosis of alcoholism and 5% were diagnosed as antisocial personality; 5% of the mothers of the hyperkinetic children were diagnosed as alcoholic and 10% were given a diagnosis of hysteria. Nine fathers of the hyperkinetic children appeared to have been hyperkinetic in childhood. As adults five were diagnosed as alcoholic, one was an antisocial personality, and two were heavy drinkers. Of three previously hyperkinetic mothers, one qualified for a diagnosis of both alcoholism and hysteria.

These two family studies suggest that the hyperkinetic syndrome does run in families and is transmitted from parents to children. They also suggest that the hyperkinetic syndrome in childhood predisposes to the development of alcoholism, sociopathy, and hysteria in adulthood.

The studies reviewed above suggest that the parents and siblings of males with antisocial personality and of females with hysteria have an excess of the same psychiatric conditions found in the parents of hyperkinetic children. In view of the sex differences in antisocial personality and hysteria, Guze proposed that antisocial personality in males and hysteria in females may be manifestations of the same underlying pathological process (Cloninger and Guze, 1973). The data reviewed here suggest that the presence of the hyperkinetic syndrome in childhood may be part of this underlying process.

One caveat to these family studies is that ADDH children often have an associated conduct disorder. There was no effort in either of these studies to specifically exclude ADDH children who may have had an associated conduct disorder. In fact, a number of them probably did. Thus, one hypothesis might be that the association with certain specific types of psychopathology in family members may be with the conduct disorder rather than with the ADDH syndrome per se. Limited information is available on this subject. In a recent study (Stewart et al., 1978), 16 boys with hyperactivity alone, 27 boys who were hyperactive and had an unsocialized aggressive conduct disorder, and 17 psychiatric controls were compared. Their data suggest that fathers of the hyperactive boys who also had a conduct disorder had a higher prevalence of antisocial personality than the fathers of the purely hyperactive boys and the fathers of the psychiatric controls. Also, alcoholism was more common in the first group of fathers than among the psychiatric controls. But the fathers of the "pure" hyperactive boys tended to have an intermediate prevalence of alcoholism. These data suggest that future family studies of the ADDH syndrome should separate out those ADDH children who also have an associated conduct disorder.

Treatment Studies

Another theoretical way of linking two syndromes is observing that they have a similar positive response to a particular form of therapeutic intervention. The effectiveness of stimulant medication in the treatment of ADDH children is well known (Barkley, 1978). Fifteen studies of children treated with amphetamine, involving 915 subjects, revealed that 74% were improved and 26% were unchanged or worsened. Similarly, in fourteen studies with methylphenidate, involving 866 subjects, a 77% improvement rate was obtained. And in two studies involving 105 subjects with magnesium pemoline, 73% improved. The results obtained with placebo in eight of these studies involving 417 subjects revealed that only 39% improved while 61% were unchanged or worse. Clearly the stimulants are the psychopharmacological agents of choice for this disorder.

It is less well recognized that certain youths with antisocial delinquent behavior also are responsive to stimulant medication. As early as 1947, Hill reported a positive response for some delinquents to amphetamine therapy (Hill, 1947). Eisenberg et al. (1963), in a well-controlled study conducted in a residential training school for delinquent boys, demonstrated a statistically significant reduction in symptoms among subjects given amphetamine compared with those given placebo and with others given no medication. More recently Maletzky (1974) reported that 14 delinquents treated with d-amphetamine had a significant positive effect when compared with placebo. Moreover, there was a strong relationship between a clinical response to the dexedrine and a past of present history of hyperkinesis. The latter study would suggest that there is a subgroup of antisocial delinquent children who are grown-up hyperkinetic children and who exhibit the same positive response to stimulants that is characteristic of hyperkinetic children.

DISCUSSION

The data reviewed above strongly suggests that there is an association between the ADDH syndrome in childhood and antisocial disorders in later life. The next question raised by this data is: What are the mechanisms of this association? Three possibilities will be considered: (1) The existence of different outcomes (antisocial vs. non-antisocial) for children with the same disorder; (2) The possibility that those hyperactive children who become antisocial adolescents and adults have an etiologically different form of the ADDH syndrome; (3) The possibility that the ADDH syndrome is not a unique syndrome at all but is a variant of conduct disorder.

The ADDH syndrome is a behavioral syndrome undoubtedly having a multi-factorial etiology. Differences have been demonstrated among ADDH children in physical and neurological factors as well as in neurophysiological and biochemical parameters (Cantwell, 1975a). This heterogeneity suggests that the ADDH syndrome may consist of subgroups of children with different etiological disorders presenting with similar phenomenological pictures in childhood. If this is the case, the different outcomes (such as antisocial disorder versus no antisocial disorder) may be due to the fact that children have different conditions right from the start.

In order to answer this question conclusively, one would need to compare grown-up ADDH children who have become antisocial personalities with those who have not on a variety of parameters. Differences should be looked for in physiological, familial, and environmental factors which may explain the differences in outcome. Ultimately, the question of whether the ADDH child who becomes antisocial has a disorder which is etiologically distinct from other non-antisocial ADDH children will be answered only when biological markers are found to separate out distinctive subgroups of children with the same or similar clinical pictures. While we have no such biological markers at present, there are studies suggesting that some ADDH children and some antisocial adults share the same neurophysiological abnormality.

There is a body of evidence suggesting that in some ADDH children there may be lowered central nervous system arousal and that in this subgroup of ADDH children CNS stimulant medications work by raising CNS arousal level and increasing cortical inhibition (Satterfield et al., 1974). There is also a growing body of evidence suggesting that there is a subgroup of individuals with an antisocial personality disorder who have an autonomic arousal picture similar to ADDH children: lower levels of basal resting physiological activation than age-matched normals. Quay (1965) has hypothesized that the habitually antisocial adult is demonstrating an extreme form of stimulation-seeking behavior secondary to an abnormally low level of physiological activation and/or sensory stimulation.

Speculating somewhat, one might suggest that it is this subgroup of ADDH children with low CNS arousal who become antisocial personalities in later life. And it is this subgroup of antisocial personalities and ADDH children who respond positively to stimulant medication. This would suggest that in some children the mechanism of association between hyperkinesis and antisocial behavior is the persistence of some physiological abnormality.

Of course, the development of antisocial behavior could also represent learning that occurred in childhood which persists even though any underlying biological problem may have been outgrown. If the aberrent physiological problem does persist into adulthood, one might expect that those antisocial personalities would respond to stimulant medications in the same way that ADDH children do. While there is no systematic study of this question, one study (Wood et al., 1976) of "hyperkinetic adults" does suggest that they do respond positively to methylphenidate in a very similar fashion to children with the hyperkinetic syndrome.

The family studies of ADDH children present some data suggesting that there are familial and environmental variables which are associated with an antisocial outcome (Weiss, et al., 1971; Minde et al., 1971, 1972). Those children with the most antisocial behavior at follow-up in Mendelson's study were more likely to have fathers who had learning or behavior problems as children and who had been arrested as adults. Weiss et al. (1971) found that the families of the ultimately antisocial children had been rated as significantly more pathological at initial evaluation. Three specific items on their rating scale (poor mother-child relationship, poor mental health of the parents, and punitive child-rearing practices) distinguished the families of the ultimately antisocial children from the rest of the group. It may be that children model themselves after parents with antisocial behavior. Alternatively, these parents may consciously or unconsciously reinforce certain behaviors in the children which lead to the development of antisocial disorder. Moreover, it is known that antisocial behavior in the parents is associated with the presence of family discord, and family discord is the strongest of all familial factors related to the development of antisocial disorder in children (Rutter, 1971).

While the family studies of ADDH children and of adults with antisocial disorder imply a familial relationship between the two conditions and suggest that the ADDH syndrome may be transmitted from generation to generation, they do not say anything about the nature of this transmission, which could be genetic, environmental, or a combination of environmental-genetic interactions. Morrison and Stewart (1973) and Cantwell (1975b) have conducted adoption studies which suggest that the transmission of the syndrome from generation to generation is a genetic one. These studies indirectly also suggest that the association between the ADDH syndrome and antisocial behavior is a genetic one. Other adoption studies and twin studies suggest that at least one form of the ADDH syndrome may be genetically transmitted (Cantwell, 1976).

There are also twin studies and adoption studies which suggest that a genetic factor plays a role in the development and transmission of antisocial disorder. Christiansen (1974) found that monozygotic twins had a significantly higher concordance rate than dizygotic twins for the presence of antisocial disorder (36% versus 12%). Several adoption studies (Hutchings and Mednick, 1975; Crowe, 1972; Schulsinger, 1972) also hint at a genetic factor operating in antisocial disorder. In essence they reveal that the biological children of adults with antisocial criminal behavior are more likely themselves to develop antisocial behavior when adopted early in life by nonrelatives than are well-matched adopted children whose biological parents were not antisocial. It is intriguing to speculate that this genetically transmitted form of antisocial disorder manifests itself as the ADDH syndrome in childhood and full-fledged antisocial personality and/or alcoholism in adulthood.

Thus for both genetic and environmental reasons ADDH children seem to be at risk for the development of antisocial disorder in later life. Moreover, since most ADDH children are not adopted and are raised by their biological parents, they may be both genetically and environmentally at risk for the development of antisocial disorder.

The ADDH syndrome may be related to antisocial behavior through educational retardation. Virtually all of the follow-up studies have shown that educational retardation of a rather marked degree is a common outcome of the ADDH syndrome (Cantwell, 1975a). It is also well known that there is a strong association between educational retardation (particularly reading disability) and antisocial behavior in childhood (Rutter et al., 1970). Rutter's epidemiologic studies on the Isle of Wight show that one-third of the children with an antisocial conduct disorder have a significant reading disability. One-third of the children with significant reading disability also had an antisocial conduct disorder. When those children with a pure reading disability, *i.e.*, free of antisocial disorder, were compared with those with pure antisocial disorder and those with a combination of antisocial disorder and reading disability, it was found that the pure reading disability group and the group with antisocial disorder plus reading disability were characterized by such symptoms as hyperactivity and short attention span, while the pure antisocial group was not. This suggests a link between symptoms such as hyperactivity and short attention span, which are characteristic of the ADDH syndrome, and the development of antisocial behavior. Rutter suggests that the child is unable to succeed in an academic setting because of short attention span, distractibility, and overactivity, begins to rebel against the values of the society in which he cannot find success, and thus develops an antisocial conduct disorder.

While the ADDH syndrome has come to be generally accepted as a psychiatric disorder with rather broad applications in the United States, in Britain, the diagnosis is much rarer and in fact is made more commonly in children with mental retardation or some form of organic brain disorder such as epilepsy. Rutter and his colleagues in a recent study (Sanberg, et al., 1978) have pointed out the fact that there is a very strong relationship on many variables between the ADDH syndrome and conduct disorder. These include the fact that it is much more common in males, that they are both associated with complications of pregnancy and perinatal problems; that minor physical anomalies tend to be present in both conditions, that learning disorders are common to both ADDH and conduct disorder children as are attention deficits, and that the family history studies suggest that similar disorders occur in parents of children with ADDH syndrome and conduct disorders. Thus Rutter questions whether the ADDH syndrome differs in any meaningful way from the usual form of conduct disorders or whether it is simply a variant. They studied a group of psychiatric clinic attenders using the Conners Parent and Teacher Rating Scales, observational measure of hyperactivity, measure of impulsivity, a neurological examination for soft signs, and examination for minor physical anomalies as well as history of pregnancy and perinatal complications. Using the Conners scales alone to identify "hyperactive" children differentiated little between high and low scorers on the Conners scales. Children clinically diagnosed as hyperkinetic, however, differed from those simply called hyperactive by high scores on the Conners scale. There were 7 children with a clinical diagnosis of hyperkinetic syndrome and 22 with an uncomplicated conduct disorder diagnosis. The hyperactivity rating of both teachers and parents of both groups were similar, but the observational score was much higher in those with the hyperkinetic syndrome. They also differed in the matching familiar figures test, the reaction time, the score on the neurological examination, and in early onset of the disorder in the hyperkinetic group. Even children who were overactive in all situations—parents' ratings, teachers' ratings, and observational methods—were different from their peers who were matched for age, IQ, and diagnosis, with respect to neurological anomalies, erratic responses on the Kagan matching families figures test, and on the early onset of hyperactivity. However, they had a variety of clinical diagnoses, not necessarily the hyperkinetic syndrome alone. Rutter and his colleagues came to the conclusion that overactivity as a symptom was situation specific. It did correlate highly with a diagnosis of conduct disorder, but there were only low and statistically insignificant correlations between different measures of hyperactivity.

When psychiatrically deviant children with and without hyperactivity were compared on a variety of factors, including perinatal history, neurological examination, presence of congenital anomalies, cognitive functioning and psychosocial circumstances, there were few differences between the hyperactive and non-hyperactive psychiatrically disordered group. A further conclusion was that the broader application of the hyperactive child syndrome, at least as diagnosed by rating scale measures, did not obtain support in this study. But there was a smaller group of children who were clinically diagnosed as hyperkinetic who may have a distinct and valid syndrome.

This study needs validation with larger numbers, and there are some methodological problems with it. However, it may be that there is a relatively rare distinct form of the ADDH syndrome which is more associated with CNS dysfunction, and a "broader" form diagnosed more commonly in the United States (which would be considered to be a conduct disorder in Britain). Both of these may be related to the later development of antisocial disorder, or only the latter may be, or there may be no difference between the two. This is certainly a fruitful area for future research.

In summary, the data reviewed above from a variety of clinical, follow-up, family, laboratory, and treatment studies all indicate: (1) There is a relationship between the presence of the ADDH syndrome in childhood and the likelihood of the development of an antisocial disorder later in life. (2) While the mechanism of this association is unknown at present, possibilities include: the persistence of a physiological abnormality; genetic, familial, and environmental factors; educational failure; and the possibility that the ADDH syndrome is simply a variant of conduct disorder. (3) Definitive studies of a complementary nature have not yet been done, *i.e.*, how many unselected delinquent children and antisocial personalities are in fact grown up ADDH children? The studies of Lewis and Balla (1976) provide an invaluable start in this area, but much more work needs to be done.

It may be that early intervention with children manifesting hyperkinesis may preclude subsequent development of an antisocial behavior disorder, which is much more difficult to treat (Cantwell, 1974).

ACKNOWLEDGMENTS

Preparation of this article was supported in part by Grant NIMH 17039-0452; Maternal and Child Health Grant No. 927; SRS 59-P-45192; Easter Seal Research Foundation; and Child Psychiatry Training Grant MC 08467.

Reprints may be requested from Dr. Cantwell at Department of Psychiatry, C8-867 Neuropsychiatric Institute, University of California, 760 Westwood Plaza, Los Angeles, CA 90024.

REFERENCES

Barkley, R. A. (1978). A review of stimulant drug research with hyperactive children. *J. Child Psychol. Psychiat.*, 18 (in press).

Borland, B. L., and Heckman, H. K. (1976). Hyperactive boys and their brothers. *Arch. Gen. Psychiat.*, 33:669–675.

Cantwell, D. P. (1972). Psychiatric illness in families of hyperactive children. *Arch. Gen. Psychiat.*, 27:414–417.

Cantwell, D. P. (1974). Early intervention with hyperactive children. *J. Oper. Psychiat.*, 5:56–67.

Cantwell, D. P. (1975a). *The Hyperactive Child*. New York: Spectrum Publications.

Cantwell, D. P. (1975b). Genetic studies of hyperactive children. In: *Genetic Research in Psychiatry*, R. R. Fieve, D. Rosenthal, and H. Brill (eds.) Baltimore: Johns Hopkins University Press, pp. 273–280.

Cantwell, D. P. (1976). Genetic factors in the hyperkinetic syndrome. *This Journal*, 15:214–223.

Christiansen, K. O. (1974). Seriousness of criminality and concordance among Danish twins. In: *Crime, Criminality and Public Policy*, R. Hood (ed.). London: Heinemann, pp. 63–77.

Cloninger, C. R., and Guze, S. B. (1970). Psychiatric illness and female criminality. *Am. J. Psychiat.*, 127:303–311.

Cloninger, C. R., and Guze, S. B. (1973). Psychiatric illness in the families of female criminals. *Brit. J. Psychiat.*, 122:697–703.

Crowe, R.. R. (1972). The adopted offspring of women criminal offenders. *Arch. Gen. Psychiat.*, 27:600–603.

Eisenberg, L., Lachman, R., Molling, P., Lockner, A., Mizelle, J., and Conners, C. (1963). A psychopharmacologic experiment in a training school for delinquent boys. *Am. J. Orthopsychiat.*, 33:431–447.

Feighner, J. P., Robins, E., Guze, S. B., Woodruff, R. A., Winokur, G., and Munoz, R. (1972). Diagnostic criteria for use in psychiatric research *Arch. Gen. Psychiat.*, 26:57–63.

Forrest, A. D. (1967). The differentation of hysterical personality from hysterical psychopathy. *Brit. J. Med. Psychol.*, 40:65–78.

Hill, D. (1947). Amphetamine in psychopathic states. *Brit. J. Addict.*, 44:50–54.

Hussey, H., Metoyer, M., and Townsend, M. (1974). 8-10 year follow-up of 84 children treated for behavioral disorders in rural Vermont, *Acta Paedopsychiat.*, 10:230–235.

Hutchings, B., and Mednick, S. A. (1975). Registered criminality in the adoptive and biological parents of registered male criminal adoptees. In: *Genetic Research in Psychiatry*, R. R. Fieve, D. Rosenthal, and H. Brill (eds.). Baltimore: Johns Hopkins University Press, pp. 105–116.

Jones, H., Macfarlane, J., and Eichorn, D. (1960). A progress report of growth studies at the University of California. Vita Humana, 3:17–31.

Kohlberg, L., Lacrosse, J., and Ricks, D. (1972). Predictability of adult mental health from childhood behavior. In: *Manual of Child Psychopathology*, B. Wolman (ed.). New York: McGraw-Hill, pp. 1217–1284.

Lewis, D. O., and Balla, D. A. (1976). *Delinquency and Psychopathology*. New York: Grune & Stratton.

Maletzky, B. M. (1974). d-amphetamine and delinquency. *Dis. Nerv. Syst.*, 35:543–547.

McCord, W., and McCord, J. (1960). *Origins of Alcoholism*. Stanford, Calif.: Stanford University Press.

Mendelson, W., Johnson, N., and Stewart, M. A. (1971). Hyperactive children as teenagers. *J. Nerv. Ment. Dis.*, 153:273–279.

Menkes, M., Rowe, J., and Menkes, J. (1967). A twenty-five year follow-up study on the hyperkinetic child with minimal brain dysfunction. *Pediatrics*, 39:393–399.

Minde, K., Lewin, D., Weiss, G., Lavigueur, H., Douglas, V., and Sykes, E. (1971). The hyperactive child in elementary school. *Except. Child.*, 38:215–221.

Minde, K., Weiss, G., and Mendelson, M. (1972). A five-year follow-up study of 91 hyperactive school children. *Journal*, 11:595–610.

Morrison, J. R., and Stewart, M. A. (1971). A family study of the hyperactive child syndrome. *Biol. Psychiat.*, 3:189–195.

Morrison, J. R., and Stewart, M. A. (1973). The psychiatric status of the legal families of adopted hyperactive children. *Arch. Gen. Psychiat.*, 28:888–891.

Quay, H. C. (1965). Psychopathic personality as pathological stimulation seeking. *Am. J. Psychiat.*, 122:180–183.

Quitkin, F., and Klein, D. (1969). Two behavioral syndromes in young adults related to possible minimal brain dysfunction. *J. Psychiat. Res.,*, 7:131–142.

Robins, L. N. (1966). *Deviant Children Grown Up*. Baltimore: Williams & Wilkins.

Rutter, M. (1971). Parent-child separation. *J. Child Psychol. Psychiat.*, 12:233–260.

Rutter, M., Tizard, J., and Whitmore, K. (1970). *Education, Health and Behaviour*. New York: Wiley.

Satterfield, J. H., Cantwell, D. P., and Satterfield, B. T. (1974). The pathophysiology of the hyperkinetic syndrome. *Arch. Gen. Psychiat.*, 31:839–844.

Schulsinger, F. (1972). Psychopathy, heredity, and environment. *Int. J. Ment. Hlth*, 1:190–206.

Shelley, E., and Riester, A. (1972). Syndrome of minimal brain damage in young adults. *Dis. Nerv. Syst.*, 33:335–338.

Weiss, G., Minde, K. Werry, J. S., Douglas, V. I., and Nemeth, E. (1971). Studies on the hyperactive child, VIII. *Arch. Gen. Psychiat.*, 24:409–414.

West, D. J., and Farrington, D. P. (1974). *Who Becomes Delinquent?* London: Heinemann.

Wood, D. R., Reimherr, F. W., Wender, P. H., Bliss, E. L., and Johnson, G. E. (1976). Diagnosis and treatment of minimal brain dysfunction in adults. *Arch. Gen. Psychiat.*, 33:1453–1460.

ADDITIONAL REFERENCES

Morrison, J. R. Adult psychiatric patients with childhood hyperactivity: diagnosis, *Amer. J. Psychiat.*, (in press).

Sandberg, S. T., Rutter, M., and Taylor, E., (1978). Hyperkinetic disorder in psychiatric clinic attenders, *Develop. Med. Child Neurol.*, 20:279–299.

Stewart, Mark A., deBlois, C. Susan, Singer, Sandra. Presented at annual meeting of Research Society on Alcoholism, May 1, 1978.

CHAPTER FOUR

Delinquency and Seizure Disorders: Psychomotor Epileptic Symptomatology and Violence

DOROTHY OTNOW LEWIS, SHELLEY S. SHANOK,
JONATHAN H. PINCUS, GILBERT H. GLASER

Epileptic conditions vary markedly in their outward manifestations and in their electroencephalographic patterns. As Ervin (1975) stated so well, "No doubt there exist as many definitions of epilepsy as there are patients" (p. 1138). Although certain kinds of seizures are accompanied by loss of consciousness, falling, and tonic and clonic muscular movements, others are characterized by much subtler, easily overlooked behavioral symptoms and signs.

Physiological changes in the central nervous system consisting of paroxysmal depolarization of neurons—that is, repetitive discharges of aggregates of neurons—are hypothesized to occur during seizures. These kinds of changes, however, are not always evident on ordinary surface electroencephalograms, even when a seizure is in progress, much less between seizure episodes. Abnormal electrical discharges can occur within the deeper structures of the brain, affect behavior, and yet leave ostensibly undisturbed the surface of the brain. Confusing the situation further is the fact that 10-15% of the nonepileptic population have abnormal electroencephalograms. Because of the episodic nature of seizure disorders, their complex subtle manifestations, and the unreliability of the electroencephalogram as a tool for ascertaining the presence or absence of a seizure disorder, neurologists will often disagree about the diagnosis of epilepsy.

Psychomotor seizures are perhaps the most difficult kinds of epileptic disorders to diagnose. By definition, psychomotor seizures or temporal lobe seizures are seizures produced by discharges usually originating in some part of the limbic system, but occasionally arising in other parts of the brain (*e.g.*, subcortical, diencephalic, or upper brain stem) and spreading to the temporal lobes. There are, however, no pathognomonic electroencephalographic configurations that would make the diagnosis of psychomotor seizures absolutely certain. Moreover, as Glaser and Dixon (1956) have pointed out, the EEGs of children suffering from psychomotor epilepsy often contain diffuse abnormalities, in contrast to the EEGs of adult psychomotor epileptics, whose encephalograms are more likely to contain discrete temporal lobe foci of abnormal discharge. According to Glaser and Dixon, in juvenile psychomotor epileptics "focal temporal spikes are relatively infrequent (10%) and are elicited in only a slightly higher incidence in sleep" (p. 647).

Because of the notoriously unreliable nature of electroencephalographic findings in childhood psychomotor epilepsy, the diagnosis of psychomotor epilepsy must rest heavily on clinical findings. The two most characteristic manifestations of the disorder, subjective experiences and behavioral changes (including automatisms), are difficult for the examiner to assess. For example, among the subjective experiences frequently reported are forced, repetitive, disturbing thoughts; sudden feelings of anxiety; and sudden mood changes such as the feeling of overwhelming anger. Certain behavioral changes, such as lip smacking, are easily recognized as inappropriate behaviors. However, some individuals, during seizures, perform complicated acts that cannot always be distinguished from ordinary volitional behavior.

Although some authors have called attention to an association of psychomotor epilepsy and violence (Glaser and Dixon, 1956; Ounsted, 1969; Serafetinides, 1965; Treffert, 1964; Lewis and Balla, 1976), others have questioned this relationship (Gunn and Bonn, 1971; Gunn and Fenton, 1971; Rodin, 1973; Stevens, 1966; Wilson and Harris, 1966). Furthermore, even in the case of a patient with well-documented psychomotor epilepsy, it is often difficult to determine whether a particular violent act is a manifestation of the disorder or simply an expression of ordinary human anger.

Complicating the diagnostic problem further is the fact that environmental and emotional factors affect seizure activity. It is, therefore, possible for an emotionally taxing situation to give rise to an epileptic attack, which is manifested by a piece of aggressive behavior that appears to be totally volitional. Where a piece of psychologically induced and potentially controllable behavior ends and a nonvolitional seizure state begins is often impossible to determine. Such situations pose especially difficult tasks for judges and juries wrestling with issues of responsibility.

DIAGNOSTIC EVALUATION

The diagnosis of psychomotor epileptic symptomatology can be extremely time-consuming. Usually the clinician evaluating a delinquent child does not have the opportunity to observe the behavior of which his patient is accused. The clinician must therefore rely on what he or she is told or is able to elicit. To repeat, this takes time. In these kinds of cases, one cannot necessarily rely on the patient to volunteer relevant information since the child usually does not have any idea that particular subjective experiences may be manifestations of epileptic symptomatology. The child must, therefore, be asked about sudden feelings of anxiety, anger or sadness, about visceral sensations, about autonomic changes. He must be asked about visual distortions, about inappropriate familiarity or unfamiliarity with situations (*déjà vu, jamais vu*), about unusual tastes or smells. Auditory misperceptions, distortions, or simply the fluctuating ability to hear what someone is saying must be determined. Visual distortions may include not only macropsia or micropsia, but also may be manifested by an object's seeming to change shape or by the words on a page seeming to disappear, then reappear. Because of the detailed nature of such an interview, the possibility of suggesting to the child symptoms he may never have experienced is always a danger and thus a further diagnostic problem to be overcome.

Although the patient, child or adult, should be asked whether or not he has ever been told he did something for which he had no memory, the individual's response may not always be accurate. For example, a youngster, placed in a secure unit for aggressive delinquents, became angry and threw rocks at another child. When this boy was asked whether he ever did things for which he had no memory, he denied that this kind of event ever occurred. Given this response, he was asked, "Why did you throw the rocks at Johnny yesterday?" To this he responded, "What rocks?" On the other hand, delinquent children, particularly those accused of violent acts, have obvious conscious and unconscious reasons for forgetting their behaviors.

All of the above issues illustrate the need for the clinician, whenever possible, to take a history from a family member or from any other available individual familiar with the child's behavior, as well as from the child himself. For example, periodic lapses of attention and alterations of behavior are often more likely to be recognized by others than by the child himself.

It is, of course, difficult to distinguish behavior influenced by psychomotor symptoms from episodic aberrant behaviors caused by psychodynamic factors, psychoses, drugs, or other kinds of psychobiological phenomena. Seven questions regarding the patient's history are especially helpful in ascertaining the likelihood that an individual may suffer from psychomotor epilepsy:

1. Does the person describe any of the subjective experiences we have previously outlined as being typical of psychomotor attacks?

2. Has the patient been observed performing any of the characteristic behaviors previously discussed, including automatisms?

3. Was the individual seemingly confused during the episode in question?

4. Was his memory absent or distorted for the event?

5. Following the apparent psychomotor epileptic event, did the patient feel extremely tired, wish to lie down, actually sleep, complain of headaches, or complain of not feeling well?

6. Did the patient at other times experience lapses or behavior patterns similar to the episode that brought him to the attention of the clinician?

7. Is there a family history of epilepsy? (Such a history is often positive in individuals with psychomotor seizures.) This fact may add to one's conviction in the diagnosis.

PSYCHOMOTOR SEIZURES VS. PSYCHOMOTOR EPILEPTIC SYMPTOMATOLOGY

In our own studies we have avoided the usually irresolvable debate whether or not a given child suffered from a seizure disorder by concentrating exclusively on symptomatology. Our initial work in this area (Lewis, 1976; Lewis and Balla, 1976) consisted of a retrospective study of the psychiatric, psychological, and medical records of delinquent children referred to a court clinic for diagnosis and considered to have manifested psychomotor symptomatology. Children were considered to have demonstrated psychomotor epileptic symptomatology if they evidenced four or more of the following signs and symptoms: auras of anxiety or fear; visceral symptoms; alterations of consciousness (*e.g.,* absence of fully conscious contact with reality); automatic behaviors; auditory, visual, tactile, olfactory, or gustatory hallucinations; frequent visual distortions; frequent episodes of *déjà vu*; and complex, sometimes aggressive behaviors observed by others for which the child had little or no memory.

Of the 285 children referred to the court clinic during the course of the study period, 18 (6%) demonstrated or gave histories consistent with a finding of psychomotor epileptic symptomatology. This prevalence was many times that of all forms of epilepsy in the general population, which has been estimated to be between 0.3 and 0.4% of the population. Psychomotor epilepsy is thought by some to be far less common than grand mal epilepsy (Ervin, 1975; Glaser, 1967; Gold, 1974). The finding, therefore, that 6% of the referred delinquent children had psychomotor epileptic symptoms was noteworthy.

The commonest symptom, one characteristic of the entire group, was episodic alteration of fully conscious contact with reality. These episodes lasted from several seconds to several hours, and were often observed during interviewing and testing. In some cases, children experienced "blackouts," often manifested by staring episodes or falling episodes. In three cases, loss of fully conscious contact with reality was manifested by episodes of wandering aimlessly, oblivious to surroundings. Another example of a lapse of fully conscious contact with reality was evident in the case of a girl who was periodically unable to comprehend what was being said to her. After losing full awareness of her surroundings, she would retrospectively misinterpret what had been said to her and believe that she had been verbally threatened or chastised. Several other children evidenced periodic fluctuations in their ability to comprehend and respond appropriately to their environments. At times they could cope with extremely complex tasks; at other times they were unable to understand or solve the simplest of problems.

It was difficult to assess the timing of altered states of awareness and the relationship of these states to particular behaviors. When attempting to understand the nature of certain violent behaviors, it was hard to determine whether a particular violent act occurred prior to a seizure episode, or whether the violent act was itself the manifestation of a seizure. In many instances the most that could be said with conviction was that a given child did suffer from episodic psychomotor epileptic symptomatology and that the child's behavior following a violent act (*e.g.,* wandering aimlessly, feeling extremely fatigued, having a clouded memory for the event) was consistent with the possibility that the violent act had been performed at the time of an abnormal electrical discharge in the brain.

Other common symptoms noted in the charts of 50% of these 18 children were auditory and visual hallucinatory phenomena and/or auditory and visual distortions. Also common to the group were frequent severe headaches, dizziness, and nausea.

Half of the sample of 18 children was memory-impaired for particular behaviors. It is, as mentioned, difficult to assess the existence of memory impairment, much less its causes, in a group of individuals accused of behaviors they would often prefer to forget. We always had to ask ourselves how many of the memory problems were psychodynamically mediated and how many could be accounted for electrophysiologically. Ultimately, the assessment of memory impairment for events was a clinical judgment we had to make. We tended to believe children who frankly reported especially violent or unacceptable behaviors but, nevertheless, seemed to have impaired memory for their less seriously antisocial acts.

The so-called classical automatisms of psychomotor seizures occurred rarely in our clinic sample. Only four children performed automatisms. Two had recurrent episodes of involuntary lip movements, and two had episodes of more complex automatic behaviors, such as polishing and repolishing a table. Only four of the subjects in this sample complained of frequent episodes of déjà vu.

Fourteen of the 18 children had received waking electroencephalograms. We found that 11 of these were characterized as abnormal or possibly abnormal. The commonest abnormality reported was diffuse slowing; however, in three cases temporal lobe foci of abnormality were reported.

From a psychiatric standpoint, the most striking symptomatology associated with the psychomotor symptoms was paranoid ideation and behaviors. Sixteen of the 18 children with psychomotor symptoms evidenced paranoid delusions.

It required considerable experience to ascertain, as far as possible, the difference between appropriate wariness in an interview situation and pathological suspiciousness. Paranoid symptoms were considered to exist only if children had frequently mistakenly believed they were about to be attacked and could give several examples of this kind of experience. Paranoid symptoms were also considered present if a child described the constant need to carry weapons such as guns and metal pipes for protection in the absence of any identifiable dangers. These delusions ranged from feeling whispered about and picked on or persecuted by friends, teachers, and police to feeling convinced one was being stalked by a murderer. Several children reported feeling "I have to get them before they get me." Four children picked up heavy objects and flung them at others.

BEHAVIORS

Of the 18 symptomatic children, 16 had histories of early school behavior problems and severe learning disabilities. They were reported to fight with other children and to have great difficulty sitting still and concentrating. Were it not for these children's additional psychomotor epileptic symptomatology such as lapses of fully conscious contact with reality, memory impairment, dizziness, and nausea, they might easily have been classified simply as children with minimal brain dysfunction and/or the hyperkinetic syndrome. In fact, our findings suggest the need to study further the frequent overlap in symptoms between these two poorly understood disorders, psychomotor epilepsy and minimal brain dysfunction.

TYPES OF DELINQUENT OFFENSES

At the time of this study, offenses were classified on a 3-point scale in terms of severity. Minor offenses such as truancy and runaway behaviors were classified 1; offenses against property, such as theft or vandalism, 2; and offenses against person, such as assault or murder, 3. Of note, of the 18 children, 8 (44%) had committed offenses against person.

At the time of the study, only about 10% of juvenile court-referred children had committed offenses against persons. Thus, the psychomotor epileptic group appeared to be a more assaultive group than the other court-referred delinquents. Furthermore, six of the 18 children who were charged only with property offenses had attacked individuals at home and at school but managed to have the official charges reduced. In all, 14 of the 18 children with psychomotor symptoms had assaulted others physically. Thus, in our sample of juvenile court-referred delinquent children, psychomotor epileptic symptomatology was often associated with aggression.

PSYCHOMOTOR SYMPTOMATOLOGY IN VIOLENT
INCARCERATED MALE DELINQUENTS

Our study of juvenile court clinic-referred children was a retrospective study of records. Furthermore, it was confined to the study of nonincarcerated court-involved children. Because of the retrospective nature of the study, certain clinical data, such as the results of neurological assessments, were unavailable. Retrospective studies must rely on data already collected and therefore cannot determine the quality or extent of information necessary to answer a given set of questions. Information amassed by juvenile courts for purposes of judicial disposition, while unbiased by the predilections of clinical investigators, is usually clinically incomplete and inadequate for purposes of certain kinds of psychobiological research. In spite of these kinds of limitations, our early study of delinquency and psychomotor epileptic symptomatology suggested the possible association of psychomotor epileptic symptomatology and especially aggressive juvenile delinquent acts. Clearly a systematic study of the neuropsychiatric status of delinquent children, more specifically a study of the possible relationship of psychomotor epileptic symptomatology and violent delinquency, was justified. We therefore embarked on a clinical study.

CLINICAL RESEARCH TEAM

In this study the investigators consisted of a child psychiatrist, a neurologist with special training in child neurology, and a research data analyst with special training in epidemiology and public health. In most cases data from recent psychological and educational testing were also available or such testing could be arranged.

SETTING

Because of our interest in serious juvenile offenders, the setting chosen was the only correctional school serving the entire state of Connecticut. Within this school, a secure unit had recently been constructed to house especially violent juveniles. The major portion of the school consisted of open cottages in a campus setting where the majority of the children were housed. The school thus contained a population of more and less violent children, facilitating a comparison of groups within the school itself. At the time of the study, it was illegal to incarcerate "status" offenders (*e.g.*, mere runaways and truants) with convicted delinquents. Therefore, with very few exceptions all children at the school had committed one or more offenses which for an adult would have also been considered to be against the law.

SAMPLES

The boys in this study consisted of 97 adjudicated delinquents who had spent some time at the correctional school during the 18-month duration of the project and who had been evaluated by the clinical team. The average stay at the school was approximately five months.

ASSESSMENT OF DEGREES OF VIOLENCE

Because of our interest in questions regarding violence and neurological symptoms, particularly psychomotor epileptic symptoms, we needed to devise a way of measuring degrees of aggressiveness. We quickly discovered the difficulties in agreeing on whether or not a child was or was not violent per se. All-or-none categorization simply did not fit the available data.

We therefore devised the following scale of violence and method of evaluation to be used to assess and categorize degrees of violence. After all data had been collected on the 97 boys in the study, the data on each child relating to official offenses and unofficial aggressive behaviors were collected and recorded separately from clinical and social data. The two clinicians and a research data analyst were then required to rate each child on a scale of violence from 1 (least violent) through 4 (most violent), using only information on behaviors and offenses. Raters were asked to use the following broad criteria for group placement:

A child was to be rated 1 if there was no evidence of his having committed any offense against person or having committed arson. Fist fights with peers were not considered violent unless severe injury had been inflicted. There were 8 boys in this group.

Children were rated 2 if there was some indication in their behaviors of what seemed to be a potential for violence (*e.g.*, isolated episodes of fire setting, isolated episodes of threatening with unloaded weapons). There were 11 boys in this group.

Children were rated 3 if they had actually committed serious offenses against persons (*e.g.*, murder, rape, multiple episodes of arson, armed robbery, assault). All in this group had committed more than one offense. There were 55 boys in this group.

Category 4 was reserved for the classification of children who had committed extraordinarily brutal acts. For example, within this group was a boy who stomped on his victim's face and a boy who raped and beat one woman and raped and stabbed another. There were 23 boys in this group.

Categories were fairly distinct from each other and hence there was a strong tendency for raters to agree on categories. There was never a greater-than-one-category discrepancy between raters. When a disagreement existed, the child was categorized according to the opinion of two of three raters.

For purposes of this study, children rated 1 and 2 were together categorized "less violent;" those rated 3 or 4, "more violent."

NEUROPSYCHIATRIC EVALUATIONS

The psychiatric and neurological evaluations conducted have already been described elsewhere (Lewis, 1976; Lewis and Balla, 1976; Lewis et al., 1979).

Whenever possible a sleep electroencephalogram was performed. Results of previous EEGs were also obtained whenever possible. Of note, certain issues were deliberately assessed by both the psychiatrist and the neurologist. That is, both attempted to obtain as detailed a medical history as possible, including a history of headaches, dizziness, nausea, loss of consciousness, and actual grand mal seizures. The standard mental status evaluation was covered by both clinicians. In addition, both assessed the presence or absence of paranoid ideation and/or hallucinatory experiences of a visual, auditory, tactile, olfactory, or gustatory nature.

We tried to be as objective as clinical assessments allow in our assessment of the existence of such subjective phenomena as the existence of paranoid ideation. Ordinary adaptive wariness, particularly during interviews, was not considered paranoid. Paranoid symptomatology was felt to exist only if children had mistakenly believed someone were about to hurt them and they could provide several examples of this, or if they constantly felt the need to carry weapons such as metal pipes or guns for their own protection in the absence of any identifiable dangers and in communities and situations in which this was not the practice of their peers (e.g., a boy who kept a gun in his dresser drawer, stayed in his room most of the day, and took the gun with him for protection when he occasionally ventured into a well-populated downtown shopping area).

The recognition of psychotic symptomatology depended on one or more of the following criteria: clear evidence of disordered illogical thought processes combined with grossly inappropriate affect, auditory and/or visual hallucinations of a nature disconcerting to the child, and unequivocal evidence of delusions. A history of patently bizarre behavior was never taken as the sole basis for our judgment. We were aware of the class and cultural factors that contribute to what may erroneously be interpreted as psychotic symptoms, and a determined effort was made to refrain from reporting questionable cases in which apparently unusual behavior or magical thinking might have been within a normal cultural pattern. Auditory or visual hallucinations or paranoid delusions were considered to be significant if children reported such experiences and acted in response to them or were clearly troubled by them. For instance, many children reported hearing their mothers calling their names. This was not considered abnormal unless it was associated with panic, an attempt to leave the room in which the voice was heard, or search for the source of the voice, such as looking under a table or couch, or out in the hallway.

PSYCHOMOTOR EPILEPTIC SYMPTOMS AND SIGNS

In this clinical study, the following signs and symptoms were considered indicative of possible psychomotor symptomatology: observed staring episodes or other manifestations of periodic loss of fully conscious contact with reality; loss of memory for particular acts or behaviors (violent or nonviolent), followed by confusion, sleep, or fatigue; episodes of inability to understand spoken words or conversations despite awareness that people were speaking; frequent dizzy spells, falling episodes, or blackouts unrelated to alcohol, illness, or hypotension; spontaneous unprovoked episodes of extreme emotion such as anxiety, fear, or rage; multiple episodes of *déjà vu*; olfactory or gustatory hallucinations; episodes of macropsia, micropsia, or other kinds of metamorphopsias; and automatic behaviors and/or forced thinking. Electroencephalographic abnormalities characterized by paroxysmal discharges, spiking, focal abnormalities, asymmetry, and readings of diffuse abnormalities "consistent with a seizure disorder" were also considered signs of a possible indication of a psychomotor epileptiform disorder. We emphasize that our study focused on quality of individual signs and symptoms and numbers of such symptoms, thus avoiding the debate of whether or not a given child had "temporal lobe epilepsy" per se.

FINDINGS

Over 78% of the boys studied had at least one sign or symptom characteristic of psychomotor epilepsy. Thus a single symptom could hardly be considered strong evidence of a probable psychomotor epileptic disorder (unless, of course, it was an EEG abnormality in the temporal area). Even then, however, children with the sign temporal lobe EEG abnormalities (of which there were only 3) invariably had other psychomotor epileptic symptoms as well.

In our previous study of the clinical records of juvenile court clinic-referred delinquents, we used the criterion of 4 or more symptoms or signs as the indicator of strong evidence of psychomotor epileptic symptomatology. We therefore, in this clinical study, decided to use the criterion of 4 or more such symptoms as indicating strongly that a psychomotor epileptic disorder existed. Of the 97 boys studied, 25 (25.8%) had 4 or more psychomotor epileptic symptoms.

PSYCHOMOTOR EPILEPTIC SYMPTOMS AND SIGNS AND DEGREE OF VIOLENCE

We wondered whether the number of psychomotor symptoms correlated with degree of violence as measured by our scale of 1 through 4. We found that a significant correlation between numbers of psychomotor signs and symptoms and degree of violence existed ($r = .384$, $p < .001$).

Among the individual psychomotor epileptic factors assessed, the symptom most highly correlated with degree of violence was impaired or distorted memory for behaviors performed ($r = .367$, $p < .001$). This kind of memory impairment was characteristic of both aggressive and nonaggressive acts. That is, memory impairment often existed for behaviors for which there would be no conscious or unconscious motivation to forget. It seemed, therefore, that the symptom of memory impairment for certain acts was not a manifestation of deliberate subterfuge but was, indeed, evidence of periodic altered activity in the brain, precluding recollection of events occurring during such episodes.

Furthermore, the symptom of memory deficits and distortions was correlated with electroencephalographic abnormalities ($r = .222$, $p < .05$), inability to stop fighting once started ($r = .283$, $p < .05$), and automatisms ($r = .274$, $p < .05$).

MULTIPLE REGRESSION ANALYSIS

In an effort to determine which combination of signs and symptoms best distinguished the 25 children with 4 or more psychomotor epileptic indicators from the other 72 youngsters, a multiple regression analysis was conducted using group membership (4 or more symptoms vs. others) as the dependent variable. Predictor variables were: abnormal electroencephalogram, olfactory or gustatory hallucinations, dizziness or blackouts, recurrent *déjà vu*, periodic inability to hear or comprehend, impaired or distorted memory for events of actions, lapses of fully conscious contact with reality, visual distortions, inablility to stop fighting, sudden episodes of altered feelings, dreamlike states, aggressive episodes followed by sleep or fatigue, and automatisms.

It was found that four variables—impaired or distorted memory for events, visual distortions, recurrent *déjà vu*, and lapses of fully conscious contact with reality—produced an R of 0.708 and accounted for 50.1% of the variance. Impaired memory accounted for 18.7% of the variance; visual distortions, 13.0% of the variance; *déjà vu*, 11.4% of the variance; and lapses of fully conscious contact with reality, 7.1% of the variance.

ELECTROENCEPHALOGRAPHIC FINDINGS

It is noteworthy that electroencephalographic abnormalities were far less significant than the clinical variables outlined, accounting for only 1.9% of the total variance.

Of the 97 children evaluated, electroencephalographic data were obtained or available on 74 children. Of this group, which included children with and without psychomotor epileptic symptoms, 25.68% had abnormal electroencephalograms. Of the 25 children with 4 or more psychomotor symptoms, 43.48% had abnormal electroencephalograms according to the criteria described above. In only 3 cases, however, were actual temporal spikes present.

CORRELATION OF PSYCHOMOTOR EPILEPTIC SYMPTOMATOLOGY WITH OTHER INDICATORS OF PSYCHIATRIC AND COGNITIVE FUNCTION

We wondered whether children manifesting psychomotor epileptic symptomatology also manifested signs and symptoms characteristic of other kinds of psychiatric, neurological, or cognitive problems. Did correlations exist between psychomotor symptomatology and psychiatric factors such as depression, loose or rambling associations, visual hallucinations, auditory hallucinations, or paranoid ideation? Did psychomotor symptomatology correlate with neurological symptoms and signs such as choreiform movements, inability to skip, discrepancy in palm strikes or finger taps, head circumference abnormalities, or Babinski signs? Did psychomotor symptomatology correlate in any way with full scale or subtest performance on the Wechsler Intelligence Scale for Children or with specific learning disabilities?

We found a significant correlation between psychomotor epileptic symptoms and auditory hallucinations ($r = .419$, $p < .001$), loose or rambling associations ($r = .402$, $p < .01$), paranoid ideation ($r = .315$, $p < .01$), visual hallucinations ($r = .242$, $p < .05$), and tactile hallucinations ($r = .225$, $p < .05$).

On the other hand, it did not correlate with any of the above mentioned neurological signs except for a correlation with choreiform movements ($r = .273$, $p < .05$). There was absolutely no significant correlation between psychomotor symptoms and performance on any aspects of the WISC, nor was there a significant correlation with learning disabilities.

CONCLUSION

Our studies of delinquent children referred to a juvenile court clinic and our studies of incarcerated delinquent boys suggest that psychomotor epileptic symptomatology is far more prevalent in the juvenile delinquent population than in the general population. The fact that approximately 6% of the court group demonstrated 4 or more psychomotor signs or symptoms, whereas approximately 25.8% of the 97 incarcerated children studied had 4 or more signs or symptoms, suggests that severity of delinquency may be associated with psychomotor symptomatology. Furthermore, looking exclusively at the incarcerated sample, the greater the number of psychomotor symptoms, the greater was the degree of violence.

That memory impairment or distortion for particular behaviors was most closely correlated with violence could not be dismissed merely as evidence that a child was either blocking or lying. Evidence for this assertion lies in the association of memory impairment with a variety of other psychomotor symptoms and in the fact that there was memory impairment for nonviolent as well as violent behaviors.

Although electroencephalographic abnormalities were significantly more prevalent in children who also manifested evidence of other psychomotor epileptic symptoms, it was, nevertheless, characteristic of a minority of delinquent children with other strong evidence of psychomotor symptoms. Furthermore, abnormal temporal lobe foci were extremely rare in this group. Only 3 of 19 children with abnormal EEGs had temporal lobe foci. Therefore, while the presence of an abnormal temporal lobe focus of discharge may be considered diagnostic, its absence is inconclusive. Most delinquent children with psychomotor symptoms have normal electroencephalograms.

Given the variety of different kinds of signs and symptoms of psychomotor epileptic disorders, as well as the numerous combinations of signs and symptoms, diagnosis is difficult. This is particularly so for violent delinquents whose veracity is always suspect and whose conscious and unconscious motivations to experience particular symptoms are obvious. A danger exists that the clinician may dismiss certain kinds of epileptic symptomatology such as memory impairment as blocking or as conscious prevarication. Interviews with relatives, staff members, and others familiar with the child's history and/or involved in the child's day-to-day care are therefore useful in providing additional information and corroborating information supplied by the child.

The diagnosis of psychomotor epileptic symptomatology and its contribution to a particular act is, obviously, a painstaking, time-consuming task. In addition to careful observation and interviewing, sometimes a trial of antiepileptic medication is helpful. A measurable, positive behavioral response may confirm the diagnosis. A negative response is, of course, inconclusive. Sometimes adequate dosages of Dilantin alone (as measured by blood concentration) yield remarkably favorable results. Where Dilantin is ineffective, often a change in medication will prove effective. For example, one periodically violent and disoriented child became even more disruptive and uncomfortable when medicated with Dilantin. Subsequent treatment with Tegretol, however, totally relieved the child's epileptic symptoms and the child reported a period of feeling better than he had in months. (Unfortunately, medication was discontinued when the child returned home on a visit, and symptoms recurred.)

In several instances, effective symptomatic control was achieved only with a combination of medications. When, however, the suspicion is strong that psychomotor symptoms exist and affect behavior, it is well worth spending the weeks and months necessary to discern whether or not a given regimen will relieve symptoms. (In one case of a child with psychomotor symptoms and an attentional disorder, a combination of Dilantin, phenobarbital, and Ritalin was required in order for the child to function appropriately and effectively.)

Another major finding of our studies was the strong correlation of psychomotor symptoms and psychotic symptoms such as paranoia, loose associations, and hallucinations. It has long been recognized that psychomotor epileptics may be confused diagnostically with schizophrenics (Hill, 1957; Small et al., 1964; Treffert, 1964; Tucker et al., 1965).

When both kinds of symptoms occur simultaneously, it is usually impossible to determine whether one is dealing with epilepsy, schizophrenia, or both. Faced with this kind of situation, our practice has usually been to begin by treating one type of symptom at a time, usually the epileptic symptomatology, on the chance that anticonvulsant medication will affect both kinds of symptoms. Often a combination of antiepileptic and antipsychotic medication is required. In our limited experience, we have not found that phenothiazine medication in moderate dosages increases epileptic activity. On occasion, when definite epileptic and psychotic symptoms coexist, we have been surprised to find that antipsychotic medication alone has been more beneficial than antiepileptic medication alone or in conjunction with antipsychotic medication.

Finally, many violent delinquent children suffer both from symptoms characteristic of psychomotor epilepsy and from psychotic symptoms characteristic of what we presently tend to term schizophrenia. Moreover, antiepileptic and antipsychotic medication separately or together often have favorable behavioral effects. These two findings have heuristic implications for the future understanding and treatment of psychomotor epileptic and psychotic symptomatology.

REFERENCES

Ervin, F. (1975). Organic brain syndrome associated with epilepsy. In: *Comprehensive Textbook of Psychiatry*, Vol. II, 2nd Ed., A. M. Freedman et. al. (eds.). Baltimore: Williams & Wilkins, pp. 1138–1157.

Glaser, G. H. (1967). Limbic epilepsy in childhood. *J. Nerv. Ment. Dis.*, 144:391–397.

Glaser, G. H., and Dixon, M. S. (1956). Psychomotor seizures in childhood: a clinical study. *Neurology* (Minneapolis), 6:646–655.

Gold, A. P. (1974). Psychomotor epilepsy in childhood. *Pediatrics*, 53:540–542.

Gunn, J., and Bonn, J. (1971). Criminality and violence in epileptic prisoners. *Brit. J. Psychiat.*, 118:337–343.

Gunn, J., and Fenton, G. (1971). Epilepsy, automatisms and crime. *Lancet*, I:1173–1176.

Hill, D. (1957). Electroencephalogram in schizophrenia. In: *Schizophrenia: Somatic Aspects*, D. Richter (ed.). London: Pergamon Press, 1957, pp. WHAT PAGE.

Lewis, D. O. (1976). Delinquency, psychomotor epileptic symptomatology, and paranoid symptomatology: a triad. *Am. J. Psychiat.*, 133:1395–1398.

Lewis, D. O., and Balla, D. A. (1976). *Delinquency and Psychopathology*. New York: Grune & Stratton.

Lewis, D. O., Shanok, S. S., Pincus, J. H., and Glaser, G. (1979). Violent juvenile delinquents: psychiatric, neurological, psychological and abuse factors. *J. Am. Acad. Child Psychiat.*, 18:307–319.

Ounsted, C. (1969). Aggression and epilepsy rage in children with temporal lobe epilepsy. *J. Psychol. Res.*, 13:237–242.

Rodin, E. A. (1973). Psychomotor epilepsy and aggressive behavior. *Arch. Gen. Psychiat.*, 28:210–213.

Serafetenides, E. A. (1965). Aggressiveness in temporal lobe epileptics and its relation to cerebral dysfunction and environmental factors. *Epilepsia*, 6:33–42.

Small, J. G., Small, I. F., and Surphils, W. R. P. (1964). Temporal EEG abnormalities in acute schizophrenia. *Am. J. Psychiat.*, 121:262–264.

Stevens, J. R. (1966). Psychiatric implications of psychomotor epilepsy. *Arch. Gen. Psychiat.*, 14:461–471.

Treffert, D. A. (1964). The psychiatric patient with an EEG temporal lobe focus. *Am. J. Psychiat.*, 120:765–771.

Tucker, G. J., Dedre, T., Harrow, M., and Glaser, G. H. (1965). Behavior and symptoms of psychiatric patients in the electroencephalogram. *Arch. Gen. Psychiat.*, 12:278–286.

Wilson, W. P., and Harris, B. S. H. III (1966). Psychiatric problems in children with frontal central and temporal lobe epilepsy. *South. Med. J.*, 59:49–53.

CHAPTER FIVE

Delinquency and Reading Disabilities

DOROTHY OTNOW LEWIS, SHELLEY S. SHANOK,
DAVID A. BALLA, BARBARA BARD

Reading disabilities abound in the delinquent population. This is one of the few facts about delinquents for which there is consensus in the literature. The research to date indicates that the majority of juvenile delinquents are at least two years and perhaps as much as five to seven years below grade level expectancy in reading achievement. Margolin (1955) noted that 76% of the children in a court clinic population were at least two years behind in reading, and within this group, over half were reading at least five years below expectation. Critchley (1968) found that approximately 51% of his research sample of delinquents were three or more years retarded in reading achievement, with "many" subjects six to seven years below expected achievement. Tarnapol (1970) reported that in his study of high-school and post-high-school age delinquents, 58-64% read below the sixth grade level. Rutter and his colleagues (1970) found that one quarter of children with reading retardation showed antisocial behavior, and, conversely, that fully a third of children with so-called conduct disorders were reading disabled. Figures for the general population they studied indicated that only 4% suffered from reading retardation. Furthermore, they reported that aggressive anti-social children who had not come in conflict with the law had a prevalence of reading disabilities similar to that of court identified delinquents.

Additional references to the high prevalence of severe reading problems in the juvenile offender population include Mauser's citation (1974) of Ahlstrom's and Havinghurst's findings in a 1971 study. The latter authors reported that the average delinquent, after seven years in school, read two to four years below his expected level. Even greater deficits were noted by Poremba (1975), who reported that in 1974 the average delinquent was 13 years old, had an IQ of 95, and was three to five years below grade level placement in his academic subjects. Reading deficits were of greatest severity, followed by lagging skills in spelling and mathematics. Furthermore, Slavin (1977), in his discussion of information-processing deficits in delinquent children, referred to a 1976 study conducted by the Virginia State Department of Education in which they found that in the delinquent population, "one half of all students read two or three years below acceptable reading levels. One third read three or more grades below acceptable levels."

THEORIES OF CAUSALITY

Perceptual Problems

Although there is a concensus regarding the high prevalence of reading disorders in the delinquent population, there is little agreement regarding its causes. In the past 15 years much attention has focused on the possible relevance of perceptual problems to learning disabilities in the delinquent population. According to perceptual theory, specific neural pathways must function adequately in order for learning to progress successfully. Intact auditory, visual, and tactile-kinesthetic pathways are considered prerequisites for optimal learning. The high prevalence of learning disabilities in the delinquent population and the presumed association of learning disabilities and perceptual problems have led to several studies of the prevalence of perceptual problems in the delinquent population.

Tarnapol (1970) studied a delinquent population from a minority ghetto. Only 33% of the delinquent population executed normal Bender-Gestalt tests compared to 85% of the non-delinquent population. Further testing determined that visual-motor coordination or visual-motor integration deficits, rather than poor visual acuity, accounted for impaired performance.

Fitzhugh (1973) compared the performance of court-referred juveniles to emotionally disturbed non-court referrals on the Halstead-Reitan tests and the Wechsler Intelligence Scale for Children (WISC). The delinquents demonstrated inferior neuro-perceptual abilities on several of the Halstead-Reitan subtests, including Speech Perception,

Tactual Performance Location, and Finger Tapping of the Right Hand. In addition, they performed less well than the comparison group on the WISC subtests of Information, Comprehension, Arithmetic, Vocabulary, Picture Completion, and Block Design.

Similarly, Berman and Siegel (1976) compared the scores of 45 delinquents to 45 non-delinquents matched for age, race, sex, and socioeconomic status on the Halstead-Reitan battery and the Wechsler Adult-Intelligence Scale (WAIS). Delinquents performed less well than their non-delinquent counterparts on all subtests of the Halstead-Reitan and the WAIS.

Slavin (1977), an optometrist working in the Thirteenth District Juvenile and Domestic Relations Court Project, Richmond, Virginia, 1975, reviewed the findings of a five-professional multi-disciplinary team evaluating delinquent subjects. In the optometric evaluation, 85% of the delinquents demonstrated at least one major near-point visual-perceptual problem. On the auditory battery, 90% of the subjects evidenced at least one auditory-processing deficit. Of special note, the average short-term auditory memory of the subjects was 50% less than chronological age expectancy.

Whether or not there is an etiological relationship between perceptual problems and learning disabilities, particularly reading disability, is equivocal. For example, Robinson and Schwartz (1973) in a follow up study of 41 children ages 5 and 6 years with documented disorders of visual perception and/or visuo-motor coordination, found that three years later this group had no greater prevalence of reading problems than a matched sample of children who were not perceptually impaired at ages 5 and 6 years. On the other hand, Bax and Whitmore (1973) found neuro-developmental difficulties at the time of school entry to be positively associated with subsequent reading and behavioral disorders. Studies of reading disabilities in children with cerebral palsy (Rutter et al., 1970; Seidel et al., 1975) and in children of especially low birth weight (Rutter and Yule, 1973), also tend to support the theory that neurodevelopmental problems affect reading. The exact nature of the central nervous system dysfunction [e.g., deficits in cross-modal intersensory integration (Birch and Belmont, 1964), problems in sequencing (Bakker, 1967, 1972; Doehring, 1968), and right-left confusion (Rutter et al., 1970)] has not been clearly delineated. There are, in fact, investigators today, such as Rutter, who are skeptical about the importance of perceptual problems in the genesis of severe reading problems (Rutter and Yule, 1977).

Attentional Disorders

There is much evidence to suggest that attentional problems, (those syndromes previously labeled hyperkinesis or minimal brain dysfunction) are strongly associated with both reading disorders and delinquency. Feshbach et al. (1973) found that teachers' behavior ratings of children during their first school year were predictive of the children's reading skills one year later, a study which highlighted the close association of early behavioral and reading problems. Similarly, Rutter and Yule (1973) reported that children with restlessness, poor concentration, and impulsiveness were especially likely to have problems learning to read. De Hirsch and his colleagues (1966) reported hyperactive, distractable, impulsive, disinhibited behavior to be associated with reading disabilities. Similar findings have also been reported by Kagan (1965), and Malmquist (1956).

Weiss and co-workers (1971) reported that in a five year follow-up of 64 hyperactive children, 10 had court referrals as teenagers. The authors felt, however, that family pathology rather than hyperactivity, distractability, I.Q., or socioeconomic status was the best predictor of delinquent behavior in their subjects. Similarly, Mendelson, Johnson, and Stewart (1971), conducted a follow-up study of 83 hyperactive children as teenagers. Contrary to the prevailing expectation, only one-half of these hyperactive youngsters were markedly improved in adolescence. Furthermore, "eighteen had long histories of lying, stealing, fighting, and destructiveness, and seemed liable to be sociopaths as adults" (p.275). Of special note, 59% of the subjects had some contact with the police and 18% had made juvenile court appearances.

Three additional related studies which indicate a persistence of hyperactive symptomatology and accompanying adjustment problems into adolescence are those of Borland and Heckman (1976), Virkkunen and Nuutila (1976), and Ackerman, Dykman, and Peters (1977). Borland and Heckman, in a comparative follow-up of hyperactive children and their normal siblings in adulthood, noted the hyperactive children to achieve lower socioeconomic status and to have a higher incidence of psychiatric problems than their brothers. Furthermore, hyperactive symptoms were persistent past puberty. Virkkunen and Nuutila studied 224 male adolescents with specific reading retardation; hyperactivity syndrome, rather than the severity of reading retardation in itself, was found to be the significant factor in the "propensity" for 12.1% of these boys to commit antisocial acts compared to 1.5% of the general adolescent population they studied. Finally, Ackerman, Dykman, and Peters reported that of 62 hyperactive learning disabled subjects followed up into adolescence, almost one half were exhibiting school, home, or community disruptive behavior compared with only one of their "normoactive" comparison subjects.

Epilepsy and Reading Disability

Extensive data regarding the prevalence of seizure disorders in the juvenile offender population are not presently available. There are, however, some data which suggest a disproportionately high prevalence of epileptiform symptomatology including attentional lapses and lapses of fully conscious contact with reality in the delinquent population. These symptoms are especially common among incarcerated delinquents (Lewis et al., in press). This group has also been reported to suffer from severe reading retardation as well as a variety of other neuropsychiatric symptoms and signs. Schain (1977) has reported evidence of undiagnosed seizure disorders interfering with attention and the acquisition of reading skills. These data are consistent with the earlier report by Ingram and his colleagues (1970) of a higher prevalence of electroencephalographic abnormalities in reading disabled children than in the general population.

To whatever extent untreated seizure activity interferes with attention and reading, the attentional problem seems to be quite different from that of hyperkinetic youngsters (and is, probably, a rarer cause of reading difficulties). Epileptic activity causes actual lapses of awareness, whereas the attentional deficits usually associated with reading disability are thought to be related more to impulsiveness and difficulty concentrating. We might add, however, that these two kinds of problems, lapses of attention and poor concentration, can coexist and thereby complicate diagnosis and treatment.

Psychiatric Factors

In the past, when investigators have considered the relationship between psychopathology and reading difficulties, they have focused on issues of neurotic conflict. That is, primarily psychodynamic theories have been formulated to explain reading problems. For example, Margolin and colleagues (1955) believed that children from lower socioeconomic sectors of society vented their hostility to school by resisting reading instruction and thereby developing into poor or non-readers. Children from the middle and upper classes who read poorly were said to be expressing hostility toward parents. Others have blamed reading problems on poor teaching in which children were punished for academic failure and so rejected educational tasks (Pearson, 1952). Peer pressure against academic achievement has also been cited to explain some learning failures (Rutter, 1974). Bettelheim (1960) proposed that reading retardation often sprang from severe emotional problems related to anxiety and guilt. Others have hypothesized that reading may be inhibited because it is associated in a child's mind with sexual "looking" (Jarvis, 1958; Walters, 1961). These psychogenic theories of reading disabilities are extremely speculative and many have come to be considered outmoded. In fact, neurotic symptoms in dyslexic children now tend to be viewed as a secondary reaction to the learning disability and not a causative factor (Critchley, 1970).

The issue of psychosis and reading disability has been largely ignored or limited to generalizations regarding overall underachievement and the onset of severe depression or clearcut schizophrenia in adolescence (Rutter and Yule, 1977; Offord and Cross, 1969; Robins, 1966). In our own study of the neuropsychiatric status and reading grade level of 59 incarcerated delinquents (Lewis et al., 1980), we were surprised to find severe reading retardation to be significantly associated with such psychotic symptoms as paranoid ideation, loose-rambling-illogical thought processes, and visual hallucinations. On the other hand, there were no significant neurological differences found between incarcerated delinquents with IQ's 80 and above reading five years or more below expected grade level and those with I.Q.'s 80 and above reading less than five years below grade level. There was a tendency for the poorer readers to have a greater prevalence of abnormal EEG's, inability to skip, and choreiform movements, but these differences never reached conventional levels of significance. Poor readers did have special difficulty subtracting serial 7's in their heads and recalling four digits backward. Of special note, degree of violence and a history of having been abused were correlated with severity of reading impairment.

To summarize the findings of this study, the cognitive-psychiatric deficits associated with severe reading disability were characterized by difficulty in organizing thoughts coherently, impaired short-term memory, violent behaviors, and having experienced physical abuse. Although temporal factors could not be determined (*i.e.*, which came first, violence or reading problems, or whether they were simultaneous), our findings strongly suggested that in many instances seriously antisocial behavior was not simply a reaction to the frustrations generated by the inability to read. Rather, in the cases we studied, we would have to suspect that the same kinds of cognitive-psychiatric deficits that affected reading also affected general adaptation and the ability to control impulses and conform behavior to the expectations of society.

One way we conceptualized the combination of psychiatric and behavioral correlates of severe reading disability in our study population was to recognize the similarities between the overall functioning of our delinquent group and the functioning of children at a preoperational stage of development as described by Piaget. For example, the "loose, rambling, illogical" thought processes of the delinquent youngsters could be seen as manifestations of the egocentric language and autistic logic characteristic of young children. According to Piaget, children prior to approximately eight years of age may successively adopt different, mutually contradictory opinions. Their explanations for behavior and events lack coherent order or a logical sense of causality. Thus an ostensibly psychotic symptom, "loose, rambling, illogical" speech, can also be understood as a manifestation of an extreme delay in cognitive maturation.

Consonant with the conceptualization of cognitive delay in our delinquent population is our finding that their short-term memory, as measured by the ability to recall four digits backward, was also impaired. The ability to recall four or more digits in reverse order depends in part on an individual's ability to envision a sequence of numbers and, in effect, read them backward. According to Piaget, the child under age seven has great difficulty sustaining the mental image of an object he has just seen and reproducing it from memory. It is plausible that the very same maturational lag that makes it difficult for some children to sustain a mental image, and to recall digits in reverse, makes it hard for such children to keep in mind the beginning words of a sentence while their eyes and attention move toward the completion of the sentence. Thus words may be strung together and their meaning lost.

Given the parallels between some characteristics of the Piagetian preoperational stage of development and the psychiatric and cognitive functioning of our reading-disabled delinquents, it is tempting to consider the possibility that in some instances the very behaviors of delinquent children leading to incarceration are reflections of an immaturity resulting in poor impulse control and an inability to appreciate the point of view of the victim of an aggressive act. Piaget describes a normal egocentrism of young children that prevents them from viewing objects or people from perspectives other than their own. In fact, egocentrism, illogical thought processes, and the inability to retain and duplicate mental images, phenomena typical of reading-disabled delinquents, are all characteristic of the preoperational stage of cognitive development. If a child cannot organize his thoughts, remember the immediate past, or put himself in another's place, not only might he have especially serious reading difficulties, but he might also be unable to imagine or appreciate the consequences of his actions, much less control them.

It would seem, from our own studies and from a review of the literature, that the reading disabilities so frequently documented in the delinquent population have many different causes. Perceptual problems, attentional disorders, psychotic symptomatology, epilepsy, maturational delays, motivational problems, and social deprivation are but a few of the biopsychosocial phenomena associated with both behavioral problems and reading disability in the delinquent population. Given the many neuropsychiatric signs and symptoms associated with reading disability among delinquents, we must conclude that reading disability does not cause delinquency, nor does delinquency lead to reading disability. Both together are often indications of pervasive adaptational difficulties reflecting a variety of different etiologies.

REFERENCES

Ackerman, P., Dykman, R., and Peters, J. (1977). Learning disabled boys as adolescents: cognitive factors and achievements. *J. Child Psychiat.*, 47: 577–595.

Bakker, D. J. (1967). Temporal order, meaningfulness and reading ability *Percept. Motor Skills*, 24: 1027–1030.

Bakker, D. J. (1972). *Temporal Order in Disturbed Reading*. Rotterdam: University Press.

Bax, M., and Whitmore, K. (1973). Neuro-developmental screening in the school-entrant medical examination. *Lancet*, ii: 368–370.

Berman, A., and Siegel, A. (1976). A neuropsychological approach to the etiology, prevention and treatment of juvenile delinquency. In: *Child Personality and Psychopathy: Current Topics*, Vol. III, A. Davis (ed.). NY: Wiley, pp. 259–295.

Bettelheim, B. (1960). Emotional blocks to learning. *Parent's Magazine*, 35:52.

Birch, H. G., and Belmont, L. (1964). Auditory-visual integration in normal and retarded readers. *Am. J. Orthopsychiat.*, 34:852–861.

Borland, B., and Heckman, H. (1976). Hyperactive boys and their brothers; a 25-year follow-up study. *Am. Gen. Psychiat.*, 33:669–675.

Critchley, E. M. R. (1968). Reading retardation, dyslexia, and delinquency. *Brit. J. Psychiat.*, 115:1537–1547.

Critchley, E. M. R. (1970). *The Dyslexic Child*, 2nd Ed. Springfield, Ill.: C. C. Thomas.

De Hirsch, K., Jansky, J. J., and Langford, W. S. (1966). *Predicting Reading Failure*. NY: Harper.

Doehring, D. G. (1968). *Patterns of Impairment in Specific Reading Disability: A Neuropsychological Investigation*. Bloomington: Indiana University Press.

Feshbach, S., Adelman, H., and Fuller, W. W. (1973). Early identification of children with high risk of reading failure. As cited in *Child Psychiatry: Modern Approaches*, M. Rutter and L. Hershov (eds.). London: Blackwell, p. 560.

Fitzhugh, K. B. (1973). Some neuropsychological features of delinquent subjects. *Percept. Motor Skill*, 36:494.

Ingram, T. T. S., Mason, A. W., and Blackburn, I. (1970). A retroactive study of 82 children with reading disability. *Develop. Med. Child Neurol.*, 12:271–281.

Jarvis, V. (1958). Clinical observation on the visual problem in reading disabilities. *Psychoanal. Study Child*, 13:451–470.

Kagan, J. (1965). Reflection: impulsivity and reading ability in primary grade children. *Child Dev.*, 36:609–628.

Lewis, D. O., Shanok, S. S., Balla, D. S., and Bard, B. (1980). Psychiatric correlates of severe reading disabilities in an incarcerated delinquent population. *J. Am. Acad. Child Psychiat.*, 19:611–622.

Lewis, D. O., Pincus, J. H., Shanok, S. S., Glaser, G. H. (in press). Psychomotor epilepsy and violence in an incarcerated adolescent population. *Am. J. Psychiat.*

Malmquist, E. (1958). *Factor Related to Reading Disabilities in the First Grade of Elementary School*. Stockholm: Almquist.

Margolin, J., Roman, M., and Harari, C. (1955). Reading disability in the delinquent child: a microcosm of psychosocial pathology. *Am. J. Orthopsychiat.*, 25:31–Mauser, A. (1974). Learning disabilities and delinquent youth. *Acad. Therapy*, 9:389–402.

Mendelson, W., Johnson, N., and Stewart, M. (1971). Hyperactive children as teenagers: a follow-up study. *J. Nerv. Ment. Dis.*, 153:273–279.

Offord, D. R., and Cross, L. A. (1969). Behavioral antecendents of adult schizophrenia: a review. *Arch. Gen. Psychiat.*, 21:267–283.

Pearson, G. H. I. (1952). A survey of learning difficulties in children. *Psychoanal. Study Child*, 7:322–386.

Poremba, C. (1975). Learning disabilities, youth and dlinquency: programs for intervention. In: *Progress in Learning Disabilities*, Vol. III, H. R. Myklebust (ed.). N.Y.: Grune & Stratton, pp. 123–149.

Robins, L. (1966). *Deviant Children Grown Up*. Baltimore: Williams and Wilkins.

Robinson, M. W., and Schwartz, L. B. (1973). Visuo-motor skills and reading ability: a longitudinal study. *Dev. Med. Child Neurol.*, 15:281–286.

Rutter, M. (1974). Emotional disorder and educational underachievement. *Arch. Dis. Child.*, 49:249–256.

Rutter, M., Tizard, J., and Whitmore, K. (eds.) (1970). *Education, Health and Behavior*. London: Longmans.

Rutter, M., and Yule, W. (1973). Specific reading retardation. In: *The First Review of Special Education*, L. Mern and D. Sabatino (eds.). Philadelphia: Buttonwood Farms.

Rutter, M., and Yule, W. (1977). Reading difficulties. In: *Child Psychiatry: Modern Approaches*, M. Rutter and L. Hershov (eds.). London: Blackwell Scientific Publications.

Schain, R. (1977). *Neurology of Childhood Learning Disorders*, 2nd Ed. Baltimore: Williams and Wilkins.

Seidel, V. P., Chadwick, O., and Rutter, M. (1975). Psychological disorders in crippled children: a comparative study of children with and without brain damage. *Dev. Med. Child Neurol.*, 17:563–573.

Slavin, S. H. (1977). Information processing deficits in delinquents. In: *Ecology–Biochemical Approaches to the Treatment of Delinquents and Criminals*, L. J. Hippchen (ed.). N.Y.: Van Nostrand Reinhold Comp., pp. 75–102.

Tarnapol, L. (1970). Delinquency and minimal brain dysfunction. *J. Learn. Dis.*, 3:200–207.

Virkkunen, N., and Nuutila, A. (1976). Specific reading retardation, hyperactive child syndrome and juvenile delinquency. *Acta Psychiatrica Scanda.*, 54:25–28.

Walters, R. H., Van Loan, M., and Croft, I. (1961). A study of reading disabilities. *J. Consult. Psychol.*, 25:277–283.

Weiss, G., Minde, K., Werry, J., Douglas, V., and Nemeth, E. (1974). Studies on the hyperactive child: five year follow-up. *Arch. Gen. Psychiat.*, 24:409–414.

CHAPTER SIX

The Neuropsychiatric Status of Violent Male Juvenile Delinquents

DOROTHY OTNOW LEWIS, SHELLEY S. SHANOK,
JONATHAN H. PINCUS

Debate flourishes in the neurological and psychiatric literature between those who assert that neurological dysfunction is an insignificant factor in serious antisocial behavior and those who claim, with equal conviction, that there is an association between neurological impairment and violence. The fact that violence in animals may be a symptom of disturbance in brain function has long been established. For example, decorticate cats have been shown to respond with rage to a variety of stimuli that would not elicit such responses in normal animals (Bard, 1928). Electrical stimulation of different parts of the limbic system can elicit violent behaviors in cats and monkeys (Mark and Ervin, 1970), just as destruction of these regions or stimulation of other regions of the limbic system will inhibit this induced rage. Similarly, bilateral amygdalectomy will usually make ferocious animals permanently placid (Klüver and Bucy, 1939) (although occasionally the reverse will occur).

The study of human aggression and neurological dysfunction poses far more difficult questions to answer. Although some investigators have conducted experiments involving stimulation and ablation of parts of the brain (Mark and Ervin, 1970; Penfield and Boldery, 1973), ethical considerations prohibit most human experimentation in this field. Because experimental stimulation or destruction of areas of the human brain, except under extraordinary circumstances, is not permissible, the assessment of neurological impairment in humans is necessarily an extremely inexact science. It often depends on the study of naturally occurring phenomena such as the behavior of individuals with lesions that have occurred in particular areas of the brain or the study of individuals who have experienced trauma to the head. The nature, location, and extent of such trauma often cannot be determined with great accuracy. It is also difficult to determine whether aberrant behaviors preexisted the CNS trauma and also whether behavioral changes are psychodynamically rather than neurologically engendered.

Complicating further the study of neurological impairment and aggression is the difficulty establishing criteria for measuring the nature and degree of violence in humans. Acts do not speak for themselves. The youngster who feels constantly endangered by imaginary enemies and carries dangerous weapons for self-defense may be more violent than the child who accidentally injures another while playing with his father's rifle. Suffice it to say that the measurement of central nervous system dysfunction and the evaluation of dangerous behaviors are both frequently based on subjective clinical impressions and even on moral judgments of the examiner.

CENTRAL NERVOUS SYSTEM DAMAGE AND THE PERINATAL PERIOD

Special interest has focused on the very earliest weeks and months of life. Rutter (1970) and his colleagues have stressed the crucial factor of the timing of medical insult to the growing fetus and young child, saying, "In general, immature organs are more susceptible to injury than are mature ones; furthermore, organs are most susceptible to damage at the time of their most rapid growth" (p. 14). They go on to assert, "Accordingly the effects of infections or other trauma should be most marked during the infancy period" (p. 14).

Pasamanick and associates (1956) found a relationship to exist between a variety of different prenatal disturbances and subsequent behavior disorders in children. Similarly, Cravioto and Delicardi (1970) called attention to the effect of early malnutrition on subsequent childhood and adult maladaptation. Fraser and Wilks (1959), in a clinical study of 100 children known to have suffered neonatal anoxia, found little evidence of hard neurological abnormalities but found a high prevalence of minor personality disorders and perceptual-motor problems manifesting themselves by age five-seven years.

Some investigators have focused primarily on the intrauterine, prenatal period of development. Brandon (1975) found a relationship to exist between psychological stress on the pregnant mother and subsequent maladjustment of the child. Stott (1957, 1962) too found a relationship to exist between anxiety in the mother during pregnancy and subsequent maladjustment in the child. A difficulty of course in this line of reasoning lies in the fact that maternal anxiety or other emotional disorder prior to a child's birth is likely to persist into the infant's childhood and make it extremely difficult to ascertain the prenatal and postnatal effects of a mother's emotional state.

More recently, Stott (1976) has turned his attention to a variety of physical disorders affecting mothers while the child is in utero and the possible relationship of these events to the subsequent adjustment of children. He has even called attention to the possible relationship of ostensibly minor viral and gastrointestinal disorders in the mother during pregnancy and subsequent maladaptation of the child.

In contrast to the above findings, the Gluecks (1950) did not find birth injury to be significantly more prevalent in the histories of delinquents than in those of nondelinquents. The McCords (1959) too found no relationship between perinatal difficulties and subsequent delinquency.

Our own studies of the medical histories of delinquents suggested a relationship between perinatal difficulties and especially violent delinquents. In our initial comparison of a random sample of children known to the juvenile court and a matched sample of nondelinquents from the same area we found no significant difference in perinatal difficulties between the two groups (Lewis and Shanok, 1977). Our subsequent study of the medical histories of incarcerated delinquents compared with nonincarcerated delinquents indicated that seriously delinquent children did have a higher prevalence of perinatal problems, and that extremely violent delinquents were even more likely to have suffered from perinatal complications (Lewis et al., 1979). Thus perinatal problems did not seem to be an important medical factor in the histories of ordinary delinquent children (*e.g.*, shoplifters, runaways), but were, rather, characteristic of those children who posed the greatest physical danger to society.

POSTNATAL NEUROLOGICAL DISORDERS AND DELINQUENT BEHAVIORS

There is a growing body of literature suggesting an association between central nervous system trauma and negative behavioral changes. Terzian and dalle Ore (1955) reported inhibition affecting a variety of behaviors following bilateral temporal lobectomy in humans. Epstein (1960) suggested that certain brain lesions created organismic excitability affecting behavior. Rowbotham and his colleagues (1954) reported that, of a sample of 82 children who had received head injuries prior to age 12 years, 27 were found on follow-up to have experienced a change in temperament after the accident. Among the symptoms noted in this group were poor ability to concentrate, bad temper, and enuresis, symptoms often reported to be characteristic of delinquent children. Bochner (1957) too reported a post-traumatic unevenness of temperament in children who sustained head injury. The McCords (1959), who found no association between perinatal difficulties and delinquency, did report that "boys who had definite neurological handicaps (brain damage, epilepsy, and so forth) had a statistically greater tendency to turn to crime" (p. 66). Dillon and Leopold (1961), in a clinical study of 50 children who had experienced head trauma ranging from simple concussion to concussion with contusion and skull fracture, found that in 47 cases personality changes were the most outstanding post-concussion symptoms. Dillon and Leopold observed that initially abnormal electroencephalograms tended, over time, to revert to normal, while the psychological sequelae persisted. In 31 of these children, behavioral changes included aggressiveness, regression and withdrawal, and antisocial behaviors. They asserted, "Frequently what appear to be primarily psychological disturbances are ameliorated by the simple expedient of placing the child on appropriate doses of anticonvulsive drugs" (p. 92).

Rutter (1970), in his study of the medical status of children on the Isle of Wight, found that children with known central nervous system disorders had a much greater prevalence of psychiatric disorder than did their non-neuroepileptic peers (34.3% for children with neurological disorders compared with 6.3% of children free from such central nervous system handicaps). Of special interest to this study was the finding that the most common psychiatric disorders in both groups were neurotic or antisocial. Eilenberg (1961), comparing the medical status of Remand Home boys with the medical status of the general population as reported in London County Council figures, found a "high percentage of minor physical disease" in the delinquent group, including auditory and visual problems. Gibbens (1963), in his study of 200 Borstal Boys in England, found a major disease or defect to exist in 18% of these children, and a minor physical disorder in 22% of this population. Gibbens went on to note that while obviously serious head injury such as encephalitis or skull fracture had occurred in only 1-2% of delinquents, many other delinquents had histories of having sustained what seemed at the time of accident to be minor injuries. Unwilling to dismiss these apparently trivial injuries, Gibbens speculated, "the effects of these minor head injuries and of special handicaps are very difficult to assess" (p. 1087).

Scott (1975), in a review of medical factors affecting delinquency, stated, "These and similar studies strongly suggest that brain damage rarely has a directly causative relationship to crime, though it may frequently release disordered behavior, which is motivated by the same background factors as operate in other, undamaged persons" (p. 289). Although reluctant to conclude that clinicians might be overlooking subtle evidence of central nervous system damage in the deliquents, the impressive body of evidence Scott amassed forces the critical reader to suspect that many clinicians may indeed be overlooking neurological vulnerabilities in many delinquent children which, when coupled with adverse social and intrafamilial conditions, make such children more susceptible than their neurologically intact peers to antisocial influences around them.

Our own clinical and epidemiological studies of delinquent children (Lewis and Shanok, 1977, 1979) strongly suggest an association between head and face trauma, child abuse, and delinquency. We are careful to speak of "associations" rather than causality. The sociofamilial conditions from which most delinquents come are characterized by so many other kinds of negative stimuli, including parental violence, abuse, and neglect, that it would be intellectually naive to place inordinate emphasis on head trauma, which may prove, over time, to be but a concomitant of social deprivation rather than a major cause of maladaptation. Furthermore, as Fabian (1956) has highlighted, it is hard to distinguish between the neurological sequelae of head injury and the psychological reaction to having experienced injury to so vital a part of the child's anatomy as his head.

Because of the extreme difficulty in documenting the cause-effect relationships in humans, a number of investigators have hedged their bets. Harris (1956) reported that only 13% of his subjects experienced psychological changes following head injury but then considered the possibility that cases had been overlooked because of the difficulty of communication with child subjects. Dencker (1960) reported relatively minor psychological differences between monozygotic twins, one of whom had experienced trauma to the central nervous system. The traumatized twins were significantly more likely than their intact twins to suffer cognitive deficits following injury, but these differences were not considered to be of practical importance in terms of social functioning.

A theme that pervades the literature on neurological disorders and behavioral aberrations is the recognition that although gross abnormalities such as paralysis and other clearcut neurological signs are infrequent in the delinquent population, many delinquent children have experienced head trauma, perinatal difficulties, and learning disabilities, and have suffered from hyperkinesis (Cantwell, 1978). This amalgam of CNS factors suggests that the contribution of central nervous system dysfunction to antisocial behavior may be to create vulnerabilities to antisocial acts and to violence in certain socially deprived children who otherwise would be able to adapt more appropriately to adverse family and environmental circumstances.

Counter to the above studies suggesting an association between neuropathology and serious behavior problems are the studies of the Gluecks (1950), Harrington and Letemendia (1958), Grunberg and Pond (1942), and Craft (1965). These investigators found that children's disordered behaviors, even their seriously aggressive behaviors, seemed to be related more to their social backgrounds and disordered home situations than to neurological impairment secondary to trauma. We must add that an equally contradictory literature regarding the relationship of epilepsy to violence exists. This subgroup of neurologically impaired delinquents was the focus of a previous chapter.

Given the contradictory findings cited, we recognize a need at least to assess the neuropsychiatric status of antisocial delinquent children. We were not convinced by Scott's conclusion that "The nagging doubt of the clinician that he is missing large numbers of 'formes frustes' of brain damaged delinquent children is very unlikely to be true by the evidence to date" (p. 289). We therefore embarked on the clinical study of the neuropsychiatric status of delinquents.

A CLINICAL NEUROPSYCHIATRIC STUDY OF INCARCERATED JUVENILE DELINQUENTS

Our interest was primarily in serious offenders, those whose violent behaviors had led to incarceration. We therefore chose as our setting the only correctional school serving the entire state of Connecticut. The correctional school setting allowed us to evaluate some of the most seriously delinquent children throughout the entire state. Furthermore, as previously mentioned, within the correctional school, a secure unit had recently been constructed to house especially violent juveniles. Thus the possibility existed of comparing more and less violent children at the school itself.

As previously described in the chapter devoted to epilepsy, the study samples consisted of 97 boys, all of whom were incarcerated at the correctional school at some time during the 18-month duration of the project and were evaluated by the clinical team.

Psychiatric Assessment

Children in the study were evaluated by a child psychiatrist and a neurologist. The psychiatric evaluation has already been described (Lewis, 1976; Lewis and Balla, 1976). Suffice it to say that multiple psychiatric interviews were often required, and most children were seen at length on several different occasions and under a variety of circumstances. Criteria for the presence or absence of particular psychiatric symptomatology have already been described in the previous chapter on "Delinquency and Seizure Disorders."

Neurological Assessment

Standard neurological measurements were carried out. These included measurement of head circumference, evaluation of cranial nerves, motor, sensory, and reflex functions. Tests of coordination included quantification of the number of alternating palm strikes the child could perform during pronation-supination movements in 10 seconds and the number of finger taps the child could perform with his index finger in 10 seconds with each hand. The presence of choreiform movements was determined by asking the child to extend his arms and fingers in front of him and above his head for five seconds each. All were asked to skip after the examiner demonstrated the requested pattern of movement.

Mental status examination in the course of the neurological evaluation included orientation for time and place. The ability to remember up to six numbers forward and four numbers backward was tested. Calculation skills were tested by four serial subtractions of seven, starting with 100.

Certain issues were covered both by the neurologist and the psychiatrist. Both attempted to obtain as detailed a medical history as possible. Both tried to ascertain whether or not the child had been a victim of abuse or had witnessed extreme violence. A child was considered to have been abused by his parents or guardians if he had been punched; beaten with a stick, board, pipe, or belt buckle; or beaten with a belt or switch other than on the buttocks. He was also considered to have been abused if he had been deliberately cut, burned, or thrown across a room.

A child was considered not to have been abused if he was only struck with an open hand, beaten with the leather part of a belt, or beaten with a switch on the buttocks only.

Whenever possible, a sleep electroencephalogram was performed. Results of previous electroencephalograms were also obtained whenever possible.

Evidence of major neurological abnormality was defined as a documented history of grand mal epilepsy, an abnormal electroencephalogram, positive Babinski sign, or head circumference that was plus or minus two standard deviations from the mean for the child's age. Evidence of minor neurological abnormality was defined as inability to skip, choreiform movements, abnormal reflexes, abnormalities in coordination, and mixed dominance of hands and feet.

In this study subjects were considered to have psychomotor epileptic symptomatology if at least two of the following were present: observed staring episodes with loss of fully conscious contact with reality; loss of memory for violent or nonviolent acts, followed by fatigue; episodes of inability to understand conversations despite an attempt to do so; dizzy spells followed by fatigue or headache; episodes of unprovoked extreme anxiety; olfactory or gustatory hallucinations; many recurrent episodes of *déjà vu*; macropsia or micropsia; forced thinking; and automatic repetitive behavior.

In most cases the results of recent intellectual testing were available or testing was performed during the course of the neuropsychiatric evaluation. For this purpose, the Wechsler Intelligence Scale for Children (or, when indicated, for adults) was the measure used.

Issues of Bias

Possible bias was introduced in the study because in most cases the investigators knew whether or not a subject was considered violent by virtue of the fact that most violent subjects were seen in the secure unit, while most of the less violent subjects lived in open settings and were seen at the school infirmary. Ethically it would have been impossible to have nonviolent children randomly placed in a securely locked unit. Thus it is possible that the preconceived notions of the examiners influenced the quality of the data collected. An attempt to minimize the effects of possible examiner bias is described in the following section.

The Assessment of Violence

We tried to correct for possible bias by devising a uniform scale for rating degrees of violence. After all data pertaining to behaviors had been collected from court, school, and clinical reports, three of the investigators independently rated each child on a scale of violence from 1 (least violent) to 4 (most violent), using only data regarding behaviors and offenses excerpted separately from records and reports. Raters did not have available psychiatric, psychological, or neurological data. Raters attempted to use the broad criteria for group placement described previously in the chapter on "Delinquency and Seizure Disorders." To summarize, there were 8 children rated 1; 11 children rated 2; 55 children rated 3; and 23 children rated 4.

COMPARISON OF TOTALLY NONVIOLENT SUBJECTS WITH VIOLENT SUBJECTS

Of the 97 children evaluated, only 8 were considered by all raters to be totally nonviolent. When the psychiatric, neurological, and psychoeducational status of these children was compared with all of the other violent subjects (*i.e.*, groups 2, 3 and 4), more of the violent children had paranoid symptomatology documented in their charts (75.5% vs. 0%, $X_y^2 = 15.386$, p < .001); more were loose, rambling, and illogical (57.1% vs. 0%, $X_y^2 = 7.000$, p = .009); and more were unable to remember four digits backward (55.2% vs. 12.5%, $X_y^2 = 3.556$, p = .060). None of the nonviolent children had experienced auditory hallucinations, compared with 40.8% of the violent boys; none had experienced visual hallucinations, compared with 28.2% of the violent boys; and none had experienced olfactory or gustatory hallucinations, compared with 12.9% of the violent group, although differences in these symptoms did not reach conventional levels of significance.

The nonviolent group was also more neurologically intact than the violent group. For example, not one of the nonviolent sample had major neurological signs or symptoms, compared with 41.6% of the violent group. Of the violent group, 58.7% had choreiform movements, compared with 14.3% of the nonviolent group; and 38% of the violent group were unable to skip, compared with 14.3% of the nonviolent group. Because of the very small number of subjects in the nonviolent group, however, these neurological differences did not reach conventional levels of significance. Statistically significant differences between the nonviolent group and the rest of the sample were found in the proportion of children with a greater than 10% discrepancy between right and left palm strikes (14.3% nonviolent vs. 60.8% violent, $X_y^2 = 3.904$, p = .049). Intellectually there were no significant differences between the groups in terms of overall IQ as measured by the WISC or on verbal or performance scores, although there was a tendency for the violent group to score lower on the verbal area (91.500 nonviolent vs. 83.158 violent, t = 1.726, p = .088).

Statistically significant differences in the two groups were found between the proportion of totally nonviolent and violent children with psychomotor epileptic symptomatology. These differences were discussed in the chapter on "Delinquency and Seizure Disorders."

COMPARISON OF MORE AND LESS VIOLENT DELINQUENTS

We were surprised to discover how few of the children evaluated at the school could be characterized as totally nonviolent. Although this discovery reflected rather well on the juvenile justice system of Connecticut, because relatively few nonviolent children were incarcerated, it made the study of the neuropsychiatric status of violent and nonviolent delinquents extremely difficult. We would like to have been able to compare a larger sample of totally nonviolent delinquents with our more aggressive group. They were simply unavailable at the correctional school.

At the time of the study, access to a large sample of totally nonviolent nonincarcerated delinquents known only to the juvenile court system was not possible. In addition to the obvious funding and staffing problems posed by such a study, it would have been extremely hard to convince juvenile justice authorities, much less the children and families themselves coming to court for minor offenses, to participate in detailed, extended neurological, psychiatric, and psychological evaluations. Furthermore, were we fortunate enough to obtain the cooperation of the juvenile court and the participation of court-involved children, it would have been difficult to ascertain whether those children and families referred by the court and willing to undergo such extensive evaluations were composed of children about whom there was special concern regarding neurological or psychiatric problems.

We found at the time that we had to content ourselves with the data provided from evaluations of students at the correctional school. Fortunately this kind of data could still furnish additional information regarding the possible association of violence and neuropsychiatric status. For example, a study comparing the more and less violent children in our sample of 97 delinquent boys could lend further insight into differences between groups of delinquent children. In order to investigate this question, the 97 subjects were divided into two groups, those children rated 1 or 2 constituting the Less Violent group, and those rated 3 or 4 constituting the More Violent group.

Psychiatric Findings

A summary of the psychiatric findings comparing groups 1 and 2 with groups 3 and 4 is presented in Table 1.

TABLE 1

A Comparison of the Number and Percentage of More Violent and Less Violent Delinquent Boys with Specific Psychiatric Symptomatology

	More Violent		Less Violent			
	#	%*	#	%*	X_y^2	p Value
Depressive symptoms	23	65.7	11	84.6	0.852	.356
Visual hallucinations	18	30.0	2	11.1	1.695	.193
Auditory hallucinations	28	43.3	3	17.6	2.704	.101
Olfactory or gustatory hallucinations	11	15.1	0	0	2.126	.145
Tactile hallucinations	6	8.2	0	0	0.659	.417
Paranoid symptomatology	54	81.8	3	16.7	24.618	<.001
Loose, rambling, illogical	28	59.6	4	23.5	5.126	.024
Inability to subtract serial 7's	41	69.5	6	33.3	6.138	.014
Inability to remember 6 digits forward	14	26.9	13	18.8	0.109	>.5
Inability to remember 4 digits backward	31	60.8	2	13.3	8.627	.004

*Percentages are based upon the actual number of subjects on whom information was available for each category.

The most striking difference psychiatrically between the two groups was the finding that a significantly greater proportion of very violent children demonstrated or gave clear histories of paranoid symptomatology. Furthermore, they were significantly more likely than their less aggressive peers to be loose, rambling, and illogical in their thought processes during interviewing. We found that although there was a definite tendency for more of the more violent children to have experienced hallucinations, particularly auditory hallucinations, differences between the two groups in this regard did not reach conventional levels of significance. In the formal mental status evaluations, the more violent children had extreme difficulty remembering even four digits backward, and the majority were unable to subtract serial 7's, even when given the opportunity to practice the task. On the other hand, when given the opportunity to practice the task of remembering digits backward, occasionally their performance improved. That is, when the examiner suggested that they wait a few seconds, picture the number in their minds, then repeat it backward, the task became easier for some of the children, suggesting that in some instances their failures were the result of impulsivity (*i.e.,* the need to respond instantly) rather than a reflection of poor short-term memory or inability to conceptualize the problem.

TABLE 2
Specific Neurological Signs: Comparison of More Violent and Less Violent Boys

Specific Signs	More Violent	Less Violent	X_y^2 Test	p Value
One or more major neurological signs	31 (46.3%)*	1 (6.7%)	$X_y^2 = 6.499$	.011
Abnormal EEG	19 (29.7%)	0 (0%)	$X_y^2 = 2.590$	.18
Positive Babinski	11 (15.9%)	1 (5.6%)	$X_y^2 = 0.569$	>.5
One or more minor neurological signs	71 (98.6%)	12 (66.7%)	$X_y^2 = 16.275$	.001
Inability to skip	26 (43.3%)	2 (11.1%)	$X_y^2 = 4.926$	.027
Choreiform movements	40 (60.6%)	5 (31.1%)	$X_y^2 = 3.375$	.067
Psychomotor symptomatology	46 (71.9%)	6 (37.5%)	$X_y^2 = 5.223$	.023
Greater than 10% discrepancy between right and left palm strike	40 (61.5%)	6 (37.5%)	$X_y^2 = 2.123$	.145
Greater than 10% discrepancy between right and left finger taps	26 (44.8%)	7 (50.0%)	$X_y^2 = 0.002$	>.5

*Percentages are based upon the actual number of children for whom data were available for each category.

Depressive symptoms were prevalent in both groups. That they were recognized more frequently in the less violent group may be a reflection of the fact that the less violent group was generally more articulate and hence able to describe moods and somatic symptoms more easily than their more psychiatrically disturbed violent peers.

Neurological Findings

Neurological differences between the very violent and less violent samples of delinquents are summarized in Table 2.

Almost the entire sample of more violent children (98.6%) had one or more minor signs of neurological impairment, which was significantly different from the less violent sample, 66.7% of whom evidenced minor neurological abnormalities.

The presence of major signs of neurological abnormality significantly distinguished the two groups. Of note, almost 30% of the very violent children had grossly abnormal electroencephalograms, usually of a paroxysmal or focal nature, and/or a history of grand mal epilepsy, compared with none of the less violent sample.

TABLE 3

A Comparison of Psychoeducational Test Results of More Violent and Less Violent Delinquent Children

	More Violent	Less Violent	t Test	p Value
Average full scale IQ WISC	86.459	93.000	1.943	.056
WISC verbal score	82.597	88.812	1.978	.052
WISC performance score	92.875	98.875	1.507	.136
Comprehension subtest	7.615	8.800	1.413	.163
Arithmetic subtest	6.981	9.909	3.902	<.001
Similarities subtest	8.115	8.000	0.115	>.500
Vocabulary subtest	6.321	7.400	1.395	.169
Picture completion subtest	10.623	10.545	0.034	>.500
Picture arrangement	9.922	10.750	0.915	.364
Block design	8.250	9.818	1.478	.145
Object assembly	9.694	10.364	0.580	>.500
Coding	7.604	8.583	0.934	.354
Reading grade discrepancy	4.4	2.3	2.148	.037
Math grade discrepancy	3.4	2.2	1.602	.115

Psychological Test Results

Differences in performance on psychological testing between the two groups are summarized in Table 3.

Intelligence, as measured on the WISC, indicated a tendency for the less violent children to function somewhat better intellectually, but overall differences between the two groups were not striking. The more violent group did less well on the verbal section of the WISC, the greatest difference between groups occurring on the arithmetic subtest. Both groups scored relatively well on the Picture Completion and Picture Arrangement subtests, and both groups received their poorest scores on the vocabulary subtest.

History of Abuse

Another set of factors that strongly distinguished the more violent from the less violent children related to a history of abuse by parents or parent substitutes. Differences are summarized in Table 4.

TABLE 4

Comparison of the Number and Percentage of More Violent and Less Violent Delinquents with a History of Abuse

	More Violent		Less Violent			
	#	%*	#	%*	X_y^2	p Value
Abused by mother	21	43.8	2	14.3	2.869	.091
Abused by father	29	54.7	5	29.4	2.364	.125
Abused by others	23	45.1	2	14.3	3.200	.074
Ever abused	52	75.4	6	33.3	9.535	.003
Witness to extreme violence	44	78.6	3	20.0	15.615	<.001

*Percentages are based upon the actual numbers of subjects on whom information was available for each category.

The more violent children had been physically abused by mothers, fathers, step-parents, other relatives, and "friends" of the family. The degree of abuse to which they were subjected was often extraordinary. One parent broke her son's legs with a broom; another broke a son's fingers and his sister's arm; another chained and burned his son; and yet another threw his son downstairs, injuring his head, following which the boy developed epilepsy.

The two samples also differed significantly in their exposure to violence. The fact that 78.6% of the more violent children were known to have witnessed extreme violence directed at others, mostly in their homes, compared with 20.0% of the less violent children tells only part of the story. The degree of violence witnessed by these children went beyond mere fist fights. Several children witnessed their fathers, step-fathers, or mothers' boyfriends slash their mothers with knives. They saw their siblings tortured with cigarette butts, chained to beds, and thrown into walls. They saw their relatives—male and female—arm themselves with guns, knives, and other sharp instruments and, at times, use these weapons against each other. Some children ran away from home at the approach of certain relatives, while many children reported defending their mothers with pipes and sticks while their mothers were being attacked. We wondered whether degree of violence as rated 1-4 correlated in any way with having been abused. A correlation coefficient of $r = .373$, $p < .001$ was found, indicating that a child's degree of violence was associated with his having been abused.

Of note, the family constellation of the more and less violent delinquents (*e.g.*, broken homes, mother in home, father in home) was similar in both groups. It was, rather, the violent quality of family interactions that distinguished the two groups from each other.

Combinations of Factors Associated with Violent Delinquency

In an effort to determine which combination of factors best distinguished the more violent from the less violent delinquents, a multiple regression analysis was conducted, using group membership (more violent vs. less violent) as the dependent variable. Predictor variables were: major neurological signs, minor neurological signs, paranoid symptomatology, visual hallucinations, auditory hallucinations, olfactory/gustatory hallucinations, depressive symptoms, memory for four numbers backward, verbal IQ, performance IQ, having been abused, reading grade discrepancy, and math grade discrepancy. It was found that two variables, paranoid symptomatology and minor neurological signs, produced an R of 0.633 and accounted for 40% of the total variance. Paranoid symptoms accounted for 29.3% of the total variance, and minor neurological signs accounted for the other 10.7% of the variance.

DISCUSSION

The literature pertaining to perinatal and childhood central nervous system trauma suggests that the sequelae of such injuries are often characterized more by behavioral changes than by obvious neurological dysfunction. The vast repertoire of human behaviors and the multitude of factors capable of modifying behaviors make it extremely difficult to ascertain a cause-effect relationship between central nervous system injury and subsequent behavioral changes. One can almost invariably find a possible psychodynamic explanation for a behavioral change that follows a physical trauma. In human investigation, one cannot isolate the organism and vary individual factors impinging on it, then measure the organism's response to the environmental change. Moreover, in humans as well as in animals, the very act of isolation has been demonstrated to affect the central nervous system functioning of the organism (Spitz and Wolff, 1946; Provence and Lipton, 1962; Harlow and Harlow, 1971), and even to modify its chemistry (Sahakian, 1975; Sahakian, this book; Alpert et al., 1978).

When a growing child is physically traumatized it is virtually impossible to distinguish with certainty which subsequent behavioral changes are attributable to central nervous system alterations, which to the child's psychological reaction to having experienced injury to a major organ system, which to the ways in which the child's environment (e.g., his parents, siblings, friends, teachers) has altered its ways of responding to the child, and which to an interaction of all of these factors. Given this variety of possible explanations for behavioral changes, the responsible investigator is often limited to tentative hypotheses based both on the discovery of associations between events and behaviors, and, most important, on careful clinical observations. It would impede the increasing understanding of human behavior were one to discount clinical observation because of its necessarily subjective nature.

Our own data strongly suggest that extremely violent juvenile offenders differ neurologically and psychiatrically from their less violent peers. Our violent subjects were more likely to manifest signs and symptoms of paranoid ideations and of major and minor neurological dysfunction. They were also more likely to have suffered severe physical and psychological abuse at the hands of parental figures. Given these findings, it is reasonable to hypothesize that the interactions of neurologically mediated impulsivity, inordinate suspiciousness, and psychodynamically engendered conscious or unconscious rage would predispose a child to retaliate quickly and violently to real or imagined threats.

The violent youngsters we evaluated rarely perceived themselves as provocateurs. Rather, they interpreted most interpersonal encounters as potential threats against which they had to protect themselves.

Further clinical evidence of the possible contribution of neurological vulnerability to their violent behaviors was the observation that, once started, the violent children often seemed totally unable to curtail their violence. Many children could remember well certain aspects of their violent behaviors, but at times were either totally unable to recall an act of which they were accused, or they recalled it in a semi-coherent, distorted manner. It often seemed unlikely that a child's memory lapse was a reflection of deliberate lying or of the operation of a variety of defense mechanisms since often the child was extremely confused and described acts which were far worse than those he had performed.

For example, one youngster told one of the clinicians that he was incarcerated because of attempted murder. He said that he had tried to strangle a woman. In actuality, neither the official charge nor the actual piece of behavior for which the child was placed in custody involved attempted murder or strangling. Furthermore, the fearfulness with which this particular boy described what he thought were the charges against him precluded the likelihood that the imagined charges were manifestations of adolescent bravado. Another youngster who was overtly proud of his dangerous exploits claimed to recall clearly all of his violent behaviors. When, however, he was asked why, on a previous day, he had thrown heavy rocks at the head of a schoolmate, he looked blank, puzzled, and asked, "What rocks?" This boy had been given up at birth by his mother, was diagnosed in infancy as brain-damaged at a university developmental diagnostic service, and since that time had been considered ineligible for adoption. He also was observed to have episodes of assaultiveness when his eyes would roll backward and he would seem out of contact with secure unit staff. His electroencephalogram, however, was normal. He, like several of his peers on the unit, insisted that he could recall perfectly all of his behaviors, violent and otherwise, in spite of the fact that witnesses to the events in question gave entirely different descriptions of what had occurred.

Another factor that we believe also contributed to these children's violent behaviors was their extreme verbal deficiencies. Although they tended to be of average intelligence, their scores on the verbal section of the WISC and on tests of reading ability were markedly lower than were the scores of the less violent group. Whether or not these verbal deficiencies were culturally, neurologically, or psychologically engendered, or whether they resulted from a combination of all these factors, these children had extreme difficulty putting their thoughts and feelings into words. The thought—or better, the impulse—became the action without any mediation through reasoning or discussion. At times it was as though the magical thinking of childhood, the cognitive stage in which a thought is said to seem tantamount to an action, had been reversed. With many violent youngsters, the impulsive, dangerous act seemed to precede the thought and then require some post-event rationale to explain the behavior.

SUMMARY AND IMPLICATIONS

Especially violent juvenile delinquents were found to have paranoid symptoms; loose, rambling, illogical thought processes; and a multiplicity of major and minor neurological abnormalities. The most striking social factors distinguishing the more violent from the less violent group were not related to family constellation but rather were factors related to abuse. Violent delinquents, in contrast to less violent delinquents, had been severely abused and had witnessed extreme violence in their homes.

The identification of the neuropsychiatric and emotional problems of these children was a subtle and time-consuming process. Because of the need for lengthy, often expensive diagnosis and treatment, violent juveniles are usually dismissed merely as incorrigible sociopaths and simply incarcerated. Our findings suggest that enlightened psychological, educational, and medical programs can and should be devised to meet the needs of these multiply damaged children.

We would also suggest that programs to diminish violence which focus primarily on socioeconomic and psychological factors are likely to be unsuccessful if they ignore the medical problems (*e.g.*, psychotic symptoms, neurological impairment) that contribute so strongly to the expression of violence. The role of specific medications as part of the treatment of violent adolescents (*e.g.*, anticonvulsants, stimulants, antipsychotics, antidepressants) is an important area that has yet to be explored. We have been especially gratified by the short-term results we have achieved when we have had the opportunity to implement multi-faceted programs for some of the violent children incarcerated in the secure unit.

Some of the extremely violent children placed in the secure unit seemed to be able to relate more appropriately and less aggressively with peers and adults simply by virtue of having been placed in a small 12-bed unit with a structured program and considerable individual attention. Many of these children, however, in spite of the relatively nonthreatening, somewhat supportive milieu, were, nevertheless, unable to form positive relationships with children or staff, take advantage of a small individualized classroom program, and refrain from extremely aggressive behaviors.

Unfortunately, because our neuropsychiatric staff was not considered by the administration to be an integral part of the correctional school medical team, it was often difficult to implement what we considered to be appropriate treatment programs for all of the children we evaluated. We were, however, in a small number of cases, permitted to design comprehensive medical and educational programs.

We found, for example, that when we were permitted to design a regimen for an epileptic, learning-disabled, extremely paranoid youngster, which included antiepileptic and antipsychotic medication, supportive psychotherapy, and special education projects, this child was able to participate in the life of the unit and eventually to gain acceptance in a therapeutic group living program outside the correctional school. Another psychotic, brain-damaged youngster, who had raped and brutally beaten his victim, was continuously assaultive to staff and boys, terrorizing the entire unit. This boy roamed the corridors of the unit, staying close to the walls to protect himself. He seemed to provoke altercations with staff in order to invite scuffles and justify his own acts of aggression. Over time, we were able to gain the trust of this boy enough to discuss his apparent anxiety and discomfort. He usually insisted that interviews be conducted in his room, where he could cover himself with his bedspread and thus hide his expression. When we finally suggested the possibility that a particular medication might help him feel more comfortable and less frightened, he considered the possibility from beneath the safety of his bedspread. After several minutes his right hand emerged from beneath the spread and a therapeutic alliance was clinched with a handshake.

Because this boy's most prominent symptom was his paranoia, antipsychotic medication was instituted extremely slowly. We feared that any side effects or discomfort would destroy our carefully nurtured alliance with the boy. Within two to three weeks our patient was noticeably less assaultive and had begun to participate in the program on the unit. Only then was he willing to submit to psychological and educational testing, which revealed extremely serious learning disabilities. Approximately two weeks after medication had been started, the boy voluntarily sought out our learning disabilities specialist and asked, rather sheepishly, "Would you teach me to read?" Neither our psychotherapeutic efforts, nor the use of medication, nor the provision of special educational training alone would have affected this child's behavior. It was our clinical impression that the multifaceted approach to diagnosis and treatment enabled this extremely dangerous boy to function appropriately. We should add that in the several cases in which the clinical team was permitted to intervene therapeutically using a multifaceted approach, children's violent behaviors diminished and they were able to take advantage of whatever the program had to offer.

It would be misleading to suggest that any of the violent children treated had been cured. Their disorders were longstanding, some of their disabilities chronic, and it was clear that only intensive, ongoing medical, psychological, and educational programs could be expected to diminish the aggressive behaviors for which the children had been incarcerated. Nevertheless, the response of these violent youngsters to appropriate, rational, individualized interventions convinced us that we were working with a population of eminently treatable, responsive youngsters.

REFERENCES

Alpert, J.E., Cohen, E.J., Shaywitz, B.A., Piccirillo, M. and Shaywitz, S.E. (1978). Animal models & childhood behavioral disturbances. *J. Am. Acad. Child. Psychi.*, 12:239–251.

Bard, P. (1928). A diencephalic mechanism for the expression of rage with special reference to the sympathetic nervous system. *Am. J. Physiol.*, 84:490–515.

Bochner, A.K. (1957). Psychiatric evaluation of post-traumatic syndrome of head injury, in Western Reserve University, Law-Medicine Center: Head: Law-Medicine Problem, Cleveland: Multi-State Copy Company.

Brandon, S. (1975). M.D. Thesis, University of Durham as cited in Scott, P.D.: *Contemporary Psychiatry: Selected Reviews from the British Journal of Hospital Medicine.* Edited by Silverstone, T. and Barraclough, B. Ashford; Kent: Headley Brothers Ltd., pp. 287–295.

Cantwell, D.P. (1978). Hyperactivity and antisocial behavior. *J. Am. Acad. Child. Psychi.*, 17:252–262.

Craft, M. (1965). *Ten Studies into Psychopathic Personality.* Bristol, England: Wright.

Cravioto, J. and Delicardie, E.R., (1970). Mental performance in school age children: findings after recovery from early severe malnutrition. *Am. J. Dis. Childhood*, 120:404–410.

Dencker, S.J. (1960). Closed-head injuries in twins. *Arch. Gen. Psychi.*, 2:569–575.

Dillon, H. and Leopold, R.L. (1961). Children and the post-concussion syndrome. *J.Am. Med. Assoc.*, 175:110–116.

Eilenberg, M.D. (1961). Remand home boys 1930–1955. *Brit. J. Criminology*, 2:111–131.

Epstein, A.W. (1960). Fetishism: a study of its psychopathology with particular reference to a proposed disorder in brain mechanisms as an etiological factor. *J. Nerv. Ment. Dis.*, 130:107–119.

Fabian, A.A. (1956). Prognosis of head injuries in children. *J. Nerv. Ment. Dis.*, 12:428–431.

Fraser, M.S. and Wilks, J. (1959). The residual effects of neonatal asphyxia. *J. Obstet.Gynaec. Brit. Emp.*, 66:748–752.

Gibbins, T.N.C. (1973). The effects of physical ill-health in adolescent delinquents. *Proc. Roy. Soc. Med.*, 56:1086–1088.

Glueck, O. and Glueck, E. (1950). *Unravelling Juvenile Delinquency.* New York: Commonwealth Fund.

Grunberg, F. and Pond, D.A. (1957). Conduct disorders in epileptic children. *J. Neurol. Neurosurg. Psychiat.*, 20:65–68.

Harlow, H.F. and Harlow, M.K. (1971). Psychopathology in monkeys. In: *Experimental Psychopathology: Recent Research and Theory*, H.D. Kimmel, ed. New York: Academic Press, p. 210.

Harrington, J.A. and Letemendia, F.J.J. (1958). Persistent psychiatric disorders after head injuries in children. *J.Ment.Sci.*, 104:1205–1218.

Harris, P. (1956). Head injuries in childhood. *Arch. Dis. Child.*, 32:488–491.

Klüver, H. and Bucy, P.C. (1939). Preliminary analysis of functions of the temporal lobes in monkeys. *Arch. Neurol. Psychiat.*, 42:979–1000.

Lewis, D.O. (1976). Delinquency, psychomotor epilepsy symptoms and paranoid ideation: a triad. *Amer. J. Psychiat.*, 133:1395–1398.

Lewis, D.O. and Balla, D.A. (1976). *Delinquency and Psychopathology*. New York: Grune and Stratton.

Lewis, D.O. and Shanok, S.S. (1977). Medical histories of delinquents and non-delinquents. *Amer. J. Psychiat.* 134:1020–1025.

Lewis, D.O. and Shanok, S.S. (1979). A comparison of the medical histories of incarcerated delinquent children and a matched sample of nondelinquent children. *Child Psychiat. & Human Development*, 9:210–214.

Lewis, D.O., Shanok, S.S. and Balla, D.A. (1979). Perinatal difficulties, head and face trauma and child abuse in the medical histories of serious youthful offenders. *Amer. J. Psychiat.*, 136:419–423.

Lipton, R.C. and Provence, S.A. (1962). *Infants in Institutions: A Comparison of Their Development with Family-Reared Infants during the First Year of Life*. New York: International Universities Press.

McCord, W. and McCord, J. (1959). *Origins of Crime: A New Evaluation of the Cambridge-Somerville Youth Study*. New York: Columbia University Press.

Mark, V.H. and Ervin, F.R. (1970). *Violence and the Brain*. New York: Harper and Row.

Pasamanick, B., Rodger, M.E. and Lilienfield, A.M. (1956). Pregnancy experience and the development of behavior disorders in children. *Amer. J. Psychiat.*, 112:613–618.

Penfield, W. and Boldery, E. (1937). Somatic motor and sensory representation in the cerebral cortex of man as studied by electrical stimulation. *Brain*, 60:389–443.

Rowbotham, G.F., MacIver, I.N., Dickson, J. and Bousfield, M.E. (1954). Analysis of 1,400 cases of acute injury to head. *Brit. Med. J.*, 1:726–730.

Rutter, M., Graham, D. and Yule, W. (1970). *A Neuropsychiatric Study in Childhood*. Philadelphia: J.B. Lippincott Company.

Sahakian, B.J. (This book). The neurochemical basis of hyperactivity and aggression induced by social deprivation: the use of animal models to help elucidate some human behaviors.

Sahakian, B., Robbins, T., Morgan, M. and Iversen, S. (1975). The effects of psychomotor stimulants on stereotyping and locomotor activity in socially deprived and control rats. *Brain Research*, 84:195–205.

Scott, P.D. (1975). Medical aspects of delinquency, in *Contemporary Psychiatry: Selected Reviews from the British Journal of Hospital Medicine*, Edited by Silverstone, T. and Barraclough, B. Ashford, Kent: Headley Brothers Ltd., pp. 287–295.

Spitz, R. and Wolff, A.M. (1946). Hospitalism: an inquiry into the psychiatric conditions in early childhood. *Psychoanal. Stud. Child.*, 1:53–74.

Stott, D.H. (1957). Physical and mental handicaps following a disturbed pregnancy. *Lancet*, 272-II:1006–1012.

Stott, D.H. (1962). Evidence for a congenital factor in maladjustment and delinquency. *Amer. J. Psychiat.*, 118:781–794.

Stott, D.H. and Latchford, S.A. (1976). Prenatal antecedents of child healthy development and behavior: An epidemiological report of incidence and association. *J. Am. Acad. Child. Psychi.*, 15:161–191.

Terzian, H. and dalle Ore, G. (1955). Syndrome of Klüver and Bucy reproduced in man by bilateral removal of the temporal lobes. *Neurology* (Minneap.), 5:373–380.

CHAPTER SEVEN

Juvenile Male Sexual Assaulters: Psychiatric, Neurological, Psychoeducational, and Abuse Factors

DOROTHY OTNOW LEWIS, SHELLEY S. SHANOK,
JONATHAN H. PINCUS

It is commonly assumed that sexual assaulters are a distinct group from other violent individuals. This assumption has in some instances led to the development of treatment programs specifically designed for sexual offenders (Money et al., 1976; Rose, 1976; Bartholomew, 1976). Whether or not youthful sexual assaulters are actually different in any particular identifiable characteristics from other violent juveniles remains unclear.

The literature on juvenile sexual assaulters is sparse. The little that has been written on the subject is curiously reassuring. For example, Doshay (1943) reported in his study of over 1,000 New York males that "male sex delinquents very seldom return to the court" (p. V). He went on to assert, "Male juvenile sex delinquency is self-curing, provided the latent forces of shame and guilt inherent in the moral-cultural patterns are properly stimulated into action" (p. 168).

Markey (1950) was equally optimistic. In his study of 50 adolescent sex offenders (25 boys and 25 girls), he concluded, "A grave outlook from the standpoint of future criminal sexuality was not offered in any of the cases, but the personality picture was nevertheless frequently discouraging" (p. 731). Atcheson and Williams (1954) found that there was a lower recidivist rate among male juvenile sex offenders than among other types of juvenile delinquents. They stated, "It is extremely unlikely that the male juvenile sex offender will reappear on a second sex charge, at least up to the age of 16" (p. 369).

Most recently, the report of the Vera institute (Strasberg, 1978) emphasized the fact that sexual assault and murder by juveniles constituted a small fraction of offenses committed by children, the implication being that sexual assault by juveniles was a relatively insignificant problem to society.

Perhaps the sanguine tone of the literature on sexual assault by juveniles reflects our reluctance to recognize the existence of serious psychopathology in children manifested by extremely violent sexual behaviors. Perhaps the dearth of research on this subject results in part from the common belief that all children are polymorphously perverse and that most will outgrow ostensibly aberrant sexual behaviors and achieve mature sexual identities.

Even when juvenile sex offenders are recognized as psychiatrically impaired, diagnoses tend to be vague and impressionistic. Thus Markey (1950) diagnosed unresolved neurotic problems and poor "personality stability" (p. 730) in the adolescent sex offenders he studied. He speculated that "adolescents who are apprehended in sexual acts, which might in themselves be without great significance, may be unconsciously exposing evidence of a need for help" (p. 731). This would seem to be a fairly safe hunch!

Atcheson and Williams (1954) reported psychiatric disorders to be six times as prevalent in the male sex offenders they studied as in their comparison sample. Unfortunately, the nature of their psychopathology was left ill-defined. And Waggoner and Boyd (1941) described their sample of sexually aberrant juveniles as suffering from "defects in personality structure [which] appeared to be closely associated with, and a reflection of, unwholesome familial relationships" (p. 290). They concluded, "The home, church, school, and community had failed to exert a practical and healthy influence in preventing the development of the problem" (another safe speculation!). They blamed a turbulent home life for creating tensions and insecurities for which sexual deviance was an outlet. Other parents were taken to task by Waggoner and Boyd (1941) for establishing excessive degrees of intimacy with their children, thereby precluding normal sexual development. The parents of sexually aberrant juveniles were accused of failing to provide their children with adequate information about sex. Consequently, children were left ignorant "of sexuality in its spiritual and biological aspects, or any wholesome ideas regarding marriage and the love life of the individual" (p. 291). Groth and Burgess (1977), in their study of adult rapists, found their subjects to be suffering from a variety of different psychiatric disorders ranging from personality disorders to psychoses. They concluded that "the act of rape in this group represents a symptom of developmental defect: a failure to achieve an adequate sense of self-identity and self-worth, the consequences of which become especially acute in adolescence" (p. 405). It would seem that most of the psychiatric literature pertaining to adolescent sexual offenders focuses on psychodynamic issues to the relative exclusion of possible neurological and other kinds of psychiatric factors contributing to sexually aberrant behaviors. It is likely that, in addition to a wish to cast a benign eye on youthful sex violence, there exists the fact that many studies of youthful sex offenders include in their samples a diverse group of offenders ranging from masturbators and exhibitionists to rapists, hence the tendency to deemphasize issues of violence and severe psychopathology.

Sociological explanations for adolescent sexual aggression have been in keeping with the psychodynamic tradition. For example, Parsons (1947), an extremely influential investigator and theoretician, hypothesized that adolescent aggressive sexuality represented a repudiation of their feminine identification by socioeconomically deprived males from matriarchal households. Toby (1966) hypothesized that boys raised in matriarchal homes, lacking a father with whom to identify, would develop a compulsive masculinity. Other investigators (Clark, 1965; Liebow, 1967; Wolfgang and Ferracuti, 1967; Rosen, 1969; Silverman and Dinitz, 1974) formulated similar explanations for sexual aggressivity in lower socioeconomic class minority males.

Noteworthy in both the psychiatric and the sociological literature is the tendency to seek predominantly psychodynamic explanations for sexually aggressive behaviors by juveniles to the exclusion of other kinds of factors.

The literature pertaining to adult sexual assaulters, while not abundant, is more diverse in nature than is that regarding juveniles. First, there is little agreement regarding the issue of dangerousness. The Cambridge University Study (Gibbens, 1977) reported that only 9% of convicted rapists had previous convictions for sexual assault. Similarly, Amir (1971), in his study of forcible rape, highlighted the finding that of those sexual assaulters with previous criminal records, only 9% had a previous arrest for rape. Running somewhat counter to the "thrust" of these studies was Gibbens's (1977) report that 39% of convicted sexual assaulters had previous convictions for personal violence, although the previous violence was not necessarily of a sexual nature. Equally alarming was his finding that 66% of sexually assaultive adult males committed violent offenses against person subsequent to their convictions for rape.

Researchers focusing on adult sexual assault have tended to distinguish between nonviolent sexual deviants and sexual assaulters. Hence Gibbens (1977), Ellis and Brancale (1956), Karpman (1954), and Christiansen (1965) all reported that sexually assaultive males tended to commit more nonsexual antisocial acts than did other kinds of sexual offenders (*e.g.*, paedophiles, exhibitionists). It may be that these investigators had better access to behavioral data than did those studying juvenile sexual aberrations because of the greater confidentiality accorded infractions of the law by juveniles.

There is little agreement regarding the psychiatric status of adult sexual assaulters. A favorite topic of debate is whether sexual assault is an expression of aggressive drives (Groth and Burgess, 1977) ("We find rape to be more a hostile than a sexual act" [pp. 401-402]), or whether its motivating force is primarily sexual and secondarily aggressive (Guttmacher and Weihofen, 1952; Gebhard et al., 1965; Cohen et al., 1971). The explanation for sexual assault, while probably academic to the victim (*i.e.*, to the victim, "a rape is a rape is a rape"), may have implications for treatment and prevention.

Research on adult sexual assaulters has included the study of biological as well as psychological factors. Hormonal studies (Blumer and Migeon, 1975; Sachar, 1976; Money et al., 1976); studies of sex chromatin abnormalities (Casey et al., 1966); and studies of limbic system dysfunction have broadened and enriched our understanding of sexually deviant behavior.

A major reason for the dearth of information regarding sexual assaulters is probably the fact that so few have been studied at all. According to Groth and Burgess (1977), rapists have rarely come to the attention of psychiatrists because they rarely seek help for their deviance. They tend rather to act out their impulses. When apprehended, they are usually processed through the correctional system and either never see a psychiatrist or receive a perfunctory examination by a prison psychiatrist. His interest may be more in behavioral management than in the understanding of underlying biopsychosocial factors contributing to sexual assault. Groth and Burgess (1977) call attention to the failure of most mental health professionals to acquire the magnitude of clinical experience that would enable them to gain understanding of the neuropsychiatric vulnerabilities that contribute to sexually assaultive behaviors. This deficit in clinical experience applies as much, if not more, to child psychiatrists as it does to psychiatrists who treat adults.

The legal and medical professions may also be reluctant to consider issues of psychopathology when their discovery might be used to exonerate an individual who had performed an especially heinous act.

The dearth of information pertaining to adolescent sex offenders, and our own unexpected opportunity to evaluate a relatively large number of such children, encouraged us to examine our clinical findings systematically. The following section of this chapter, therefore, will report the neuropsychiatric and psychoeducational findings that emerged from the detailed assessment of a sample of 17 incarcerated sexually assaultive males, boys evaluated in the course of a larger study of violent incarcerated males.

METHOD

Definition of Sexual Assault

Sexual assault, like delinquency, is a legal term that covers a multitude of sins as well as a multitude of more and less deviant behaviors. For purposes of this study, we used the legal designation. That is, sexual assault was defined as having been found guilty of the act of sexual assault by a juvenile court, sentenced to a correctional school, and placed by judges or school administrators in secure custody because of the nature of the acts committed. Examples of sexual assault are rape, attempted rape, forcible sodomy, and sexually assaultive acts such as grabbing at women's breasts or knocking them down, then fondling them against their will. Acts such as exposure of genitalia, sexual activity by mutual consent, or fondling in the nature of sexual experimentation among adolescents were not included as sexual assault. We excluded from this sample one boy who physically assaulted and tried to choke a woman on the street for no apparent motive but whose behavior was not ostensibly sexual.

Samples

We studied three groups of adolescents:

1. Our sample of sexual assaulters consisted of all male juveniles who had committed sexual assault, were incarcerated in the only correctional school in Connecticut, and were referred to a special project for violent juvenile offenders over a given 18-month period (N = 17).

2. Our first comparison sample consisted of all boys referred to the same project over the same period of time who had committed violent

offenses against others (*e.g.*, murder, arson, armed robbery), but none of whom had ever committed a sexual offense (N = 61).

3. Our second comparison sample was of less violent boys. This sample consisted of all boys admitted to the correctional school during the 18-month period of the study about whom there was no indication of seriously violent behaviors (*e.g.*, serious injury of a person) from the correctional school records or from clinical interviews. As far as could be determined, none had ever committed a sexual assault of any kind (N = 19).

The average age of the children in each group was 15 years. There were no significant differences in the ages of the children in the three groups at the time of assessment.

Diagnostic Evaluation

Children in the study were examined by a child psychiatrist and a neurologist. The nature of the psychiatric and neurological evaluations has already been reported (Lewis and Balla 1976; Lewis 1976; this book, chapter 6).

Psychological tests, including the WISC, Bender-Gestalt, and Rorschach tests, were performed by a developmental child psychologist except in cases in which extensive recent psychological testing had been performed or in cases when the child was transferred elsewhere prior to testing. When two different test results were available, the most recent and complete was used for purposes of this study. Educational assessments were performed by a learning disabilities specialist.

Previous placements in psychiatric residential facilities, the age at which a child was first known to the courts, and the age of other antisocial acts were ascertained from school records and interviews with children and their parents.

FINDINGS

Timing and Nature of Deviant Sexual Acts

The nature and timing of sexual offenses, as well as the nature and timing of other antisocial and aberrant behaviors, are reported in Table 1. As can be seen, most of the juvenile sexual assaulters had been behaving in deviant ways since early childhood. Eight boys had actually been involved in sexual offenses prior to their current offense, and assaultive behaviors of one kind or another throughout childhood were characteristic of almost the entire sample of sex offenders.

The average age of the first official juvenile offense was 11.9 years, whereas the average age at which the child's most current offense for which he was incarcerated occurred was 14.6 years. Most noteworthy

TABLE 1

Case #	Age 1st documented aberrant behavior	Nature of aberrant behaviors prior to Juv. Ct. referral	Age 1st known to Juv. Ct.	Non-sexual delinquent offenses	Nature and age of sexual offenses
1	6 years	Cursed teachers. Hit children & staff. Eventually placed on homebound instruction.	12 yr 2 mo	2 assaults; 2 robberies; 2 attempted assaults.	Age 12 yr 8 mo grabbed woman's breasts & buttocks; hit her with bicycle chain.
2	4 years	Burnt own bed. Injured siblings. Fought w/ teachers.	12 yr 9 mo	Burglary, larceny, threatening w/knives.	Sexual assault of old woman at ?13 yrs. At 14 yrs sexually assaulted young boy & forced anal intercourse.
3	Before 10 years	Stomped child at school. Placed on homebound age 10.	9 yr 10 mo	Burglary & larceny.	Age 12½ yrs, indecent exposure. Age 13½ 2 counts of sexually assaulting girls at school. Age 15 stabbed, kicked, beat woman.
4	6 years	Beat up a child at age 6. Stealing since age 7.	12 years	Beat male with pipe. 3 episodes fire-setting. Carried 2 knives with 10" blades.	Age 15 attempted to hang young boy when he refused fellatio. Beat up women on several occasions.

TABLE 1 (Continued)

Case #	Age 1st documented aberrant behavior	Nature of aberrant behaviors prior to Juv. Ct. referral	Age 1st known to Juv. Ct.	Non-sexual delinquent offenses	Nature and age of sexual offenses
5	8 years	Frequently sent to principal's office since 3rd grade for fighting.	9 years	Beyond control of parents. Larceny, burglary, robbery.	Age 15 sexually assaulted & ?raped 8-yr-old girl in school bathroom.
6	2 years	After lengthy hospitalization for burn, wouldn't speak. Age 9 sexually assaulted 7-yr-old girl.	11 yr 6 mo	Reckless endangerment.	Sexual contact ?11½ yrs. Exposure. 14½ yrs 2 sexual assaults on women; threatened one with knife.
7	6 years	Fought w/teachers. Threatened mother & sisters w/violence. Wore female panties.	12 yr 7 mo	Burglary, larceny, criminal attempt at robbery.	Age 15 raped a girl.
8	5 years	Age 5 stabbed girl in kindergarten. Multiple firesetting episodes & fights. Psych. hosp. 8–12½ yrs.	13 yr 5 mo	—	3 counts of sexual assault in which he grabbed at women's breasts, all after discharge from hospital.
9	2 years	Age 2 choked pet bird. Age 5 threw puppy out window. Broke brother's arm. Many school fights.	14 yr 1 mo	Assault, theft, smashed up relative's car with crowbar.	Raped & beat 16-yr-old girl at almost 16. Subsequently escaped raped 2 women & stabbed one of them.

TABLE 1 (Continued)

Case #	Age 1st documented aberrant behavior	Nature of aberrant behaviors prior to Juv. Ct. referral	Age 1st known to Juv. Ct.	Non-sexual delinquent offenses	Nature and age of sexual offenses
10	5 years	School fights since age 5. Hit teachers & children. Carried large knife to school.	8 yr 6 mo	Theft, robbery, shoplifting, arson, truancy, carrying dangerous weapon, trespass.	Age 15 raped 9-yr-old girl at knifepoint. Forced her brothers to perform sexual acts on her while he watched.
11	8 years	Obsessed w/sexually attacking women. Grabbed at teacher's breasts.	13 years	Breaking & entering.	Age 13 fondled 5-yr-old girl; put tongue in her mouth. Age 13½ yrs attempted to rape girl bit her breast; beat her up.
12	6 years	Truancy. Fights with peers & siblings. Carried knives & chaco sticks.	13 yr 3 mo	35 arrests, including larceny, assault, run-away, pushed down women & took purses, breaking & entering.	Age 15 participated in gang rape of a girl.
13	6 years	Serious school problems. Attacked children w/bats, knives, etc. Fought w/ adults. Threatened to set fire to home & to kill mother.	12 years	Burglary, weapons charges.	Age 12 sexual assault charge, ?nature. Age 13 smacked around a girl, then stood guard while friend raped her.

TABLE 1 (Continued)

Case #	Age 1st documented aberrant behavior	Nature of aberrant behaviors prior to Juv. Ct. referral	Age 1st known to Juv. Ct.	Non-sexual delinquent offenses	Nature and age of sexual offenses
14	?	History unavailable. Age 12 suddenly felt need to hit strange boy w/board.	12 yr 4 mo	Total 16 offenses, including larceny, threatening, burglary.	Age 13 sexual assault charge. Age 14½ raped & brutally beat girl.
15	6 years	School fights since earliest years. Hit boy w/bottle. Carried knife, razor, gun.	8 yr 10 mo	Breaking & entering, theft.	Age 15½ grabbed at breasts of woman in church.
16	10 years	Failed everything at school, disruptive, disrespectful. Sent to psychiatrist for "overactivity."	13 yr 6 mo	Burglary, mugging, car theft, robbery, pursesnatching, 2 assault charges.	Age 15 assaulted woman over age 60. Convicted of "sexual contact."
17	?	Fights w/peers & adults. Threatened to kill a boy while under influence of alcohol.	10 yr 4 mo	Larceny, burglary, conspiracy to commit robbery, criminal mischief.	Age almost 16 yrs sexually molested 4-yr-old girl.

was the finding that the average age at which seriously antisocial behavior was noted, either in records or by parents, was 6 years of age, and some children's behaviors were notably deviant as early as 2 years of age.

Comparison of Sexual Assaulters and Other Violent Delinquents

Sexual offenders were slightly younger than other violent delinquents when first known to court (139.00 mo. vs. 147.48 mo., t = 1.341, p = .184). As can be seen in Table 2, when we compared the 17 juveniles who had committed sexual assault with the 61 violent delinquents who had not been sexually assaultive, we found that the two samples were remarkably similar neurologically, psychiatrically, and intellectually.

We found that, in spite of their similar symptomatology, sexual offenders averaged fewer psychiatric residential placements than did the other violent delinquents (0.375 vs. 0.930, t = 1.877, p = .065). They also tended to have fewer placements out of the home in general than did the other violent delinquents (1.25 vs. 2.196, t = 1.613, p = .112).

Comparison of Sexual Assaulters and Less Violent Delinquent Children

Sexual offenders committed their first delinquent acts significantly earlier than did their less violent nonsexually assaultive peers (139.0 mo. vs. 159.9 mo., t = 2.633, p = .013). Psychiatric, neurological, and intellectual differences between the sexual offenders and the less violent sample are presented in Table 3. Most striking were the differences in paranoid symptomatology between the two groups and differences in thought processes. All sex offenders manifested minor signs of neurological abnormality, contrasting significantly with 64.7% of the less violent subjects.

The scores of the sexual offenders on the WISC were significantly lower than the scores of the less violent group. Their verbal scores were especially depressed. Of special note, however, was the finding that sex offenders had unusually high scores on the picture completion subtest of the WISC, averaging a scaled score of 12.059. This was, in fact, the only subtest on which they scored higher than the less violent sample (i.e., 12.059 vs. 10.600). A matched t-test, comparing the average score of the sexual offenders on picture completion with their average scores on all the other subtests of the WISC, indicated that they scored significantly higher on picture completion than on other subjects (t = 2.838, p = .013). On the other hand, the average score on picture completion of the less violent sample compared with their average score on all other subjects of the WISC was not significantly higher.

TABLE 2
Comparison of Psychiatric, Neurological, and Intellectual Characteristics of Juvenile Sexual Assaulters and Other Violent Juveniles

Specific Problem	Sex Assaulters	Violent	Test	p Value
Depressive symptoms	6 (75.0%*)	17 (63.0%)	Fisher's exact	= .429
Auditory hallucinations	7 (46.7%)	21 (41.2%)	X_v^2 = .007	>.5
Visual hallucinations	1 (6.7%)	17 (37.0%)	X_v^2 = 3.639	.057
Olfactory/gustatory hallucinations	3 (18.8%)	8 (13.8%)	X_v^2 = .009	>.5
Paranoid symptoms	11 (73.3%)	43 (82.7%)	X_v^2 = .191	>.5
Loose, rambling, illogical	7 (70.0%)	22 (57.9%)	X_v^2 = .111	>.5
Inability to subtract serial 7's	11 (84.6%)	31 (66.0%)	X_v^2 = .917	.338
Poor memory for 6 digits forward	5 (45.5%)	10 (23.8%)	X_v^2 = 1.087	.297
Poor memory for 4 digits backward	9 (81.8%)	23 (56.1%)	X_v^2 = 1.459	.227
One or more major neurological signs	5 (29.4%)	26 (51.0%)	X_v^2 = 1.601	.206
Abnormal EEG or grand mal seizures	4 (23.5%)	15 (31.3%)	X_v^2 = .085	>.5
One or more minor neurological signs	17 (100%)	55 (98.2%)	X_v^2 = .405	>.5
Average full scale IQ	83.235	87.328	t = 1.213	.229
Average verbal score	79.647	83.357	t = 1.194	.237
Average performance score	90.353	93.643	t = .807	.423
Average reading grade discrepancy	5.59	3.95	t = 1.859	.070
Average math grade discrepancy	3.93	3.17	t = 1.057	.297

*Percentages are based upon the actual numbers of subjects on whom information was available for each category.

TABLE 3
Comparison of Psychiatric, Neurological, and Intellectual Characteristics of Juvenile Sexual Assaulters and Less Violent Offenders

Specific Problem	Sex Assaulters	Less Violent	Test	p Value
Depressive symptoms	6 (75.0%*)	11 (84.6%)	Fisher's exact =	.499
Auditory hallucinations	7 (46.7%)	3 (18.8%)	Fisher's exact =	.101
Visual hallucinations	1 (6.7%)	2 (11.8%)	Fisher's exact =	.549
Olfactory/gustatory hallucinations	3 (18.8%)	0 (0%)	Fisher's exact =	.086
Paranoid symptoms	11 (73.3%)	3 (17.6%)	$X_y^2 = 7.906$	.005
Loose, rambling, illogical train of thought	7 (70.0%)	3 (18.8%)	Fisher's exact =	.014
Inability to subtract serial 7's	11 (84.6%)	5 (29.4%)	$X_y^2 = 6.938$	.009
Poor memory for 6 digits forward	5 (45.5%)	2 (13.3%)	Fisher's exact =	.085
Poor memory for 4 digits backward	9 (81.8%)	1 (7.1%)	Fisher's exact =	.001
One or more major neurological signs	5 (29.4%)	1 (7.1%)	Fisher's exact =	.135
Abnormal EEG or grand grand mal seizures	4 (23.5%)	0 (0%)	Fisher's exact =	.160
One or more minor neurological signs	17 (100%)	11 (64.7%)	Fisher's exact =	.010
Average full scale IQ	83.2	93.7	t = 2.566	.016
Average verbal score	79.647	89.733	t = 2.715	.011
Average performance score	90.3	99.3	t = 1.819	.079
Average reading grade discrepancy	5.59	2.35	t = 3.394	.003
Average math grade discrepancy	3.93	2.20	t = 2.059	.053

*Percentages are based upon the actual numbers of subjects on whom information was available for each category.

Abuse Factors

Table 4 presents the contrast among the sexual offenders, the violent nonsexual offenders, and the less violent sample in terms of having experienced abuse or having witnessed extreme violence. Both sexual offenders and violent nonsexual offenders were far more likely to have been the victims of abuse than their less violent peers. Abuse was inflicted by mothers, fathers, and by other individuals associated with the family (mothers' boyfriends, uncles, etc.). Furthermore, most violent offenders, sexual and otherwise, had witnessed extreme violence. The experience of having seen a father slash a mother, or a mother attack a father, was not uncommon in both violent populations.

TABLE 4
Number and Percent of Sexual Assaulters, Violent Nonsexual Assaulters, and Less Violent Offenders with a History of Abuse

Abuse	Sexual Assaulters		Violent Nonsexual Assaulters		Less Violent	
	#	%*	#	%*	#	%*
By mother	6	46.2	15	42.9	2	14.3
By father	7	58.3	23	54.8	4	25.0
By others	6	42.9	17	45.9	2	14.3
Ever abused	13	76.5	40	75.5	5	29.4
Witness to extreme violence	11	78.6	33	78.6	3	20.0

*Percentages are based upon the actual numbers of subjects on whom information was available for each category.

DISCUSSION AND IMPLICATIONS

Sexual offenses by juveniles are not as rare or as benign as the current literature—or paucity of literature—would suggest. Children who are eventually known to court for sexual assault are often known to court much earlier for a variety of different antisocial behaviors. As was seen in Table 1, their previous histories often contained other kinds of violent behaviors, including attacks on children and women that were not overtly sexual in nature. Such reassuring statements as "male juvenile sex delinquency is self-curing" (Atcheson and Williams, 1954, p. 168); "male sex delinquents very seldom return to the court"

(Atcheson and Williams, 1954, p. v); and "a grave outlook from the standpoint of future criminal sexuality is not offered" (Markey, 1950, p. 731) are called into question because of the longstanding, recurrent, seriously violent behaviors of our sample of juvenile sex offenders. That our findings are at variance with the literature cited may be explained, at least in part, by the fact that ours was a study of incarcerated children, whereas other studies of childhood sexual deviance have tended to focus on sexually delinquent children in general and therefore presumably have included a greater proportion of less violent children. Nevertheless, the fact that 21.8% of the violent incarcerated juveniles studied had committed sexual offenses before age 16 suggests that this group of children is larger than has previously been appreciated and constitutes a greater societal threat than we would like to believe.

The assumption that sexually assaultive juveniles differ neuropsychiatrically from other violent juveniles was contradicted by our data. The sexually assaultive children we evaluated were, like their violent, nonsexually assaultive peers, found to suffer from similar kinds of identifiable psychiatric and neurological disorders. Hallucinations, paranoid ideation, and major and minor neurological impairment were similarly prevalent in sexually assaultive juveniles and other violent juveniles. Noteworthy, the clinical observation of paranoid ideation in the sexually assaultive group was consistent with particular aspects of their performance on psychological testing. Sexually assaultive boys attained markedly high scores on picture completion in contrast to scores on other subtests, which may well have been a manifestation of their hypervigilance. In addition to psychiatric and neurological problems, the sexual offenders suffered from severe learning disabilities that were out of proportion to their essentially low normal intellectual capacities.

A puzzling finding was that juvenile sexual assaulters, in spite of their severe psychiatric symptomatology, were less likely than other violent delinquents to have received residential psychiatric treatment. This finding may reflect a failure of clinicians and court personnel to appreciate the severity of these children's psychopathology. Another plausible explanation for the difference in prevalence of residential treatment may be a reluctance of residential institutions to accept sexually deviant youngsters. Hence, intensive psychiatric treatment may be less accessible to sexually assaultive youngsters than to youngsters with other manifestations of psychopathology. This finding is consistent with the hypothesis of Groth and Burgess regarding adult sexual assaulters.

A promising clinical finding of this study was that the kinds of psychiatric, neurological, and educational problems diagnosed seemed amenable to treatment. Our data indicated that the therapeutic needs of juvenile sexual assaulters were similar to those of other violent juvenile offenders. Therefore, treatment programs designed for violent juveniles in general can be expected also to meet the needs of sexually assaultive juveniles.

The usefulness of antipsychotic, antidepressant, antiepileptic, and stimulant medications in this population, as adjuncts to a comprehensive treatment program, is yet to be explored in controlled, well-designed studies. Our clinical experience suggests, however, that psychological counseling and educational assistance alone are unlikely to be effective in modifying the behavior of those sexually and non-sexually aggressive children whose behaviors reflect, at least in part, psychotic symptomatology, epileptic disorders, minimal brain dysfunction, attentional disorders, or other medical problems.

Of theoretical interest is the fact that juvenile sexual assaulters have also committed extraordinarily violent nonsexual acts. This finding calls into question the psychoanalytic distinction traditionally made between the sexual and aggressive drives. The importance of the hypothalamus and limbic system as a whole in appetitive and/or instinctual behaviors has been well documented. That sexually assaultive juveniles and nonsexually assaultive violent juveniles have similar kinds of neurological dysfunction, including olfactory and gustatory hallucinations, lends credence to the hypothesis that violence of any kind and sexual violence per se may reflect similar underlying neuropsychiatric vulnerabilities.

REFERENCES

Amir, M. (1971). *Patterns in Forcible Rape*. Chicago: University of Chicago Press.

Atcheson, J. D., and Williams, D. C. (1954). A study of juvenile sex offenders. *Am. J. Psychiat.*, 111:366–370.

Bartholomew, A. A. (1976). A long-acting phenothiazine as a possible agent to control deviant sexual behavior. *Am. J. Psychiat.*, 124:917–Blumer, M. D., and Migeon, C. (1975). Hormone and hormonal agents in the treatment of aggression. *J. Nerv. Ment. Dis.*, 160:127–136.

Casey, M.D., Segall, L.J., Street, D.R., and Blank, C.E. (1966). Sex chromosome abnormalities in two state hospitals for patients requiring special security. *Nature*, 209:641–642.

Christiansen, K. O., Elers-Nielsen, M., LeMaire, L., and Sturup, G. K. (1965). Recidivism among sexual offenders. In: *Scandinavian Studies in Criminology*, Christiansen, K.O. (ed.). London: Tavistock, pp. 55–85.

Clark, K. (1965). *Dark Ghetto: Dilemmas of Social Power*. New York: Harper & Row.

Cohen, M., Garofalo, R., Boucher, R., and Seghorn, T. (1971). The psychology of rapists. *Semin. Psychiat.*, 3: 307–327.

Doshay, L. J. (1943). *The Boy Sex Offender and His Later Career*. New York: Grune & Stratton.

Ellis, A., and Brancale, R. (1956). *The Psychology of Sex Offenders*. Springfield, Ill.: Charles C. Thomas.

Gebhard, P. (1965). *Sex Offenders*. New York: Harper & Row.

Gibbens, T. N. C., Way, C., and Soothill, K. L. (1977). Behavioural types of rape. *Brit. J. Psychiat.*, 130:32–42.

Groth, A. N., and Burgess, A. W. (1977). Rape: a sexual deviation. *Am. J. Orthopsychiat.*, 47:400–406.

Guttmacher, M., and Weihofen, H. (1952). *Psychiatry and the Law*. New York: Norton.

Karpman, B. (1954). *The Sexual Offender and His Offenses*. London: The Julian Press.

Lewis, D. O. (1976). Diagnostic evaluation of the juvenile offender. *J. Child Psychiat. Human Developm.*, 6:198–213.

Lewis, D. O., and Balla, D. A. (1976). *Delinquency and Psychopathology*. New York: Grune and Stratton.

Liebow, E. (1967). *Tally's Corner: A Study of Negro Street Corner Men*. Boston: Little Brown.

Markey, O. B. (1950). A study of aggressive sex misbehavior in adolescents brought to juvenile court. *Am. J. Orthopsychiat.*, 20:719–731.

Money, J., Wiedeking, C., Walker, P. A., et al. (1976). Combined antiandrogenic and counseling programs for treatment of 46XY and 47XYY sex offenders. In: *Hormones, Behavior and Psychopathology*, E. J. Sachar (ed.). New York: Raven Press, pp. 105–120.

Parsons, T. (1947). Certain primary sources and patterns of aggression in the social structure of the Western world. *Psychiatry*, 10:167–181.

Rose, R. M. (1976). Antiandrogen therapy of sex offenders. In: *Hormones, Behavior and Psychopathology*, E. J. Sachar (ed.). New York: Raven Press, pp. 121-124.

Rosen, L. (1969). Matriarchy and lower class Negro male delinquency. *Social Problems*, 17:175–189.

Sachar, E. J., ed. (1976). *Hormones, Behavior and Psychopathology*. New York: Raven Press.

Silverman, I. J., and Dinitz, S. (1974). Compulsive masculinity and delinquency: an empirical investigation. *Criminology*, 11:498–515.

Strasberg, P. A. (1978). *Violent Delinquents*. New York: Monarch.

Toby, J. (1966). Violence and the masculine ideal: some qualitative data. *Ann. Am. Soc. Pol. Soc. Sci.*, 364:19–27.

Waggoner, R. W., and Boyd, D. A. (1941). Juvenile aberrant sexual behavior. *Am. J. Orthopsychiat.*, 11:275–292.

Wolfgang, M. E., and Ferracuti, F. (1967). *The Subculture of Violence: Toward an Integrated Theory of Criminology*. London: Associated Book Publishers.

Part II

Some Physiologic Factors

CHAPTER EIGHT

Neurochemical and Behavioral Organization: Disorders of Attention, Activity, and Aggression

JONATHAN E. ALPERT, DONALD J. COHEN,
BENNETT A. SHAYWITZ, MARK PICCIRILLO

Integrity of the central nervous system is essential to effective orchestration of the endocrine, autonomic, sensorimotor, cognitive, and affective elements involved in the maintenance of physiological homeostasis and the elaboration of behavior responsive to environmental demands. Considerable advances within recent years have made possible the characterization, measurement, and manipulation of an increasingly large number of neurochemicals believed to play critical roles in central nervous system function. Of particular interest are the neurotransmitters and neuromodulators, together called neuroregulators, responsible for chemical communication between neurons (Table 1). Although present understanding of the ways in which these compounds act and interact in neuronal systems to influence behavior is at an early stage, evidence suggests that alterations in the activity or metabolism of at least some of these substances may sometimes have an important part in the pathogenesis of deviant human development. Biochemical disturbances involving the biogenic amines dopamine, norepinephrine, and serotonin have been implicated in several psychiatric and neurological disorders with varying degrees of empirical support. Notable among these are Parkinson's disease, depressive conditions, and schizophrenia (Hornykiewicz, 1973; Maas, 1975; Meltzer and Stahl, 1976). Study and speculation has also extended to developmental disorders such as childhood autism and minimal brain dysfunction (Cohen and Young, 1977; Shaywitz et al., 1980) and to other neurochemicals including the amino acid and peptide neuro-regulators as well as histamine and acetylcholine (Lipton et al., 1978; Usdin et al., 1977). The motivation behind work in this area is rooted in the belief that a fuller understanding of the molecular mechanisms of brain processes may help clarify some of the ways in which social, psychological, and biological dynamics collaborate to produce behavioral pathology and may contribute to a comprehensive view of the field against which disordered behavior unfolds.

TABLE 1
A Partial List of Putative Neurotransmitters and Neuromodulators, Collectively Neuroregulators, in the Central Nervous System.*

Acetylcholine	Peptides
Biogenic Amines	Thyrotrophic-Releasing Hormone
Catecholamines	Lutenizing Hormone-Releasing Hormone
Dopamine	Somatostatin
Norepinephrine	Enkephalins and Beta-Endorphin (Opioids)
Epinephrine	Angiotensin II
Serotonin	Oxytocin and Vasopressin
Histamine	Substance P
	Neurotensin
Amino Acids	Gastrin
Glutamic Acid	Vasoactive Intestinal Peptide
Aspartic Acid	Cholecystokinin
Cysteic Acid	Adrenocorticotropic Hormone (ACTH)
Homocysteic Acid	Steriods
Gamma-Aminobutyric	Corticosteroids
acid (GABA)	Estrogens
Glycine	Androgens
Taurine	
Beta-Alanine	Thyroid Hormones
Guanidinoacetic Acid	Prostaglandins

*Many of these endogenous substances are localized in other parts of the body, in addition to brain, including the peripheral nervous system, gastrointestinal tract, endocrine organs and blood platelets. All affect neuronal activity in the central nervous system. The most well-studied with regard to behavior and disease are acetylcholine and the biogenic amines.

The first section of this chapter introduces general principles concerning neurotransmission in the central nervous system. Remaining sections discuss two areas of current study which are of potential relevance to behavioral deviance in childhood and adolescence.

CHEMICAL NEUROTRANSMISSION

Encompassing brain and spinal cord, the central nervous system (CNS) is comprised of *nerve cells* or *neurons* and a variety of supportive cells called collectively the *neuroglia*. It is bathed in circulating *cerebrospinal fluid* (CSF) and receives essential substances through blood capillaries whose specialized permeability characteristics largely account for the selectively restrictive *blood-brain barrier.*

The primary activities of the central nervous system are reception, communication, and control for which neurons constitute the principal functional units. The morphological features of the neuron include the *cell body* (perikaryon), the metabolic center of the cell from which typically project multiple elongated processes called the *dendrites*, specialized in receiving external stimuli or signals from a great many neurons, and a single process, the *axon*, specialized in conducting nerve impulses to other cells. The functional interrelationships between neurons, upon which CNS activity depends, occur at the *synapse*, a distinctive region of intercellular contact. As classically described, the synapse represents a junction between an enlarged *bouton* or *varicosity* along the terminal end of a presynaptic axon and the membrane of a dendritic process of a postsynaptic cell (Figure 1). In addition to these axodendritic synapses, however, synapses between an axon and a cell body (axosomatic) and, more rarely, between two axons (axoaxonic) or between two dendrites (dendrodendritic) are also known to exist. In the peripheral nervous system, synapses occur between presynaptic neurons and postsynaptic effector cells such as muscle or gland cells as well. In a small proportion of synapses (electrical synapses) transmission between neurons involves electrical coupling. The great majority of synapses are exclusively chemical, however, and involve release by the presynaptic cell of a chemical neurotransmitter which diffuses across the synapse and conveys its message by altering the state of the postsynaptic cell.

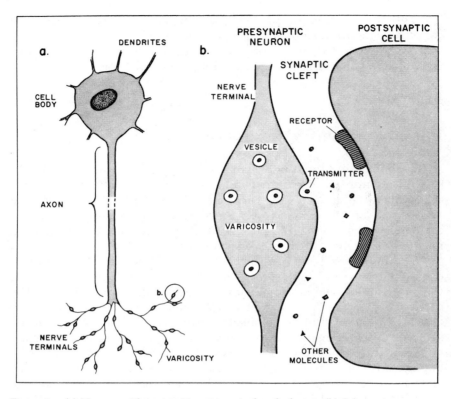

Figure 1.   (a) Neuron with varicosities at terminal end of axon; (b) Schematic representation of presynaptic axon varicosity, synaptic cleft, and postsynaptic cell. Modified from Axelrod (1974).

An overview of the currently accepted model of CNS neuro-transmission will be useful; extensive presentations are available elsewhere (Cooper et al., 1978; Siegel et al., 1976). As Table 1 indicates, there are many potential neuroregulator substances which have been identified in the central nervous system: candidate *neurotransmitters*, which are believed to be directly involved in interneuronal communication at the synapse, and *neuromodulators*, which are nontransmitter neurochemicals thought to amplify or dampen neuronal activity according to mechanisms as yet uncharted (Barchas et al., 1978; Lipton et al., 1978). The life cycle of the putative transmitter dopamine is relatively well understood and can serve to exemplify principles of general importance in neurotransmitter activity. Figure 2 depicts, schematically, a dopaminergic synapse and the steps involved in neurotransmission.

(1). *Precursor Uptake*: Prior to the synthesis of a neurotransmitter by the neuron which will secrete it, essential raw materials are taken up from the circulation. Thus the amino acid precursor of the catecholamines, tyrosine, to which the blood-brain barrier is permeable, is actively transported from bloodstream to brain where it is incorporated by neurons that synthesize and release catecholamines. Tyrosine is derived directly from the diet or through metabolism of dietary phenylalanine to tyrosine which occurs primarily in the liver. (2). *Transmitter Synthesis*: Once inside the neuron, a precursor is transformed into its specific neurotransmitter product by a series of biosynthetic steps catalyzed by enzymes which are themselves synthesized in the cell body of the neuron and then transported to the site of transmitter synthesis, idealized in this diagram as a synthesis pool. In dopaminergic neurons, tyrosine is converted to DOPA (dihydroxyphenylalanine) in the critical rate-limiting step of catecholamine synthesis, catalyzed by the enzyme tyrosine hydroxylase in the presence of iron, oxygen, and an activating cofactor, tetrahydropteridine. DOPA, in turn, is enzymatically converted to dopamine by the activity of DOPA

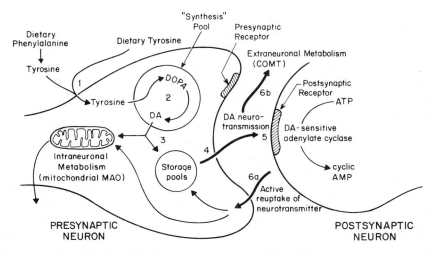

Figure 2.   Idealized model of a dopaminergic synapse. (1) Precursor uptake; (2) Transmitter synthesis; (3) Storage (or inactivation); (4) Release; (5) Receptor interaction and postsynaptic cascade; (6) Transmitter inactivation (intraneuronal or extraneuronal). Modified from Barchas et al., (1978).

decarboxylase and its cofactor, pyridoxal phosphate (vitamin B₆). In dopaminergic neurons, dopamine (DA) is the final transmitter product and is either stored or degraded if not needed subsequent to synthesis. In noradrenergic neurons, however, norepinephrine is synthesized from stored dopamine in a reaction catalyzed by dopamine-beta-hydroxylase (DBH). In cells which secrete it, epinephrine is synthesized from norepinephrine in a further reaction. (3). *Storage*: a distinctive morphological feature of chemical synapses is the presence of small vesicles or granules in presynaptic terminals which provide for the storage and eventual release of the neurotransmitter following synthesis. In some cases, there may be more than one kind of synaptic vesicle differentiated by physical characteristics and the readiness with which their contents are released. (4). *Release*: When a neuron is excited by external stimuli or another neuron, an *action potential* is triggered at a region known as the *axon hillock* and thereupon propagates throughout the cell by successive changes in membrane permeability to electrolytes, sodium and potassium, which maintain a wave of depolarization culminating in transmitter release. The mechanism linking nerve impulses to release (stimulus-secretion coupling) is not well established but is known to depend upon an influx of calcium that occurs at the nerve terminal upon arrival of an action potential and is thought, by some, to require actin and myosin. Transmitter release in catecholaminergic and other neurons appears to involve exocytosis, a process by which vesicles fuse with the cell membrane and liberate their contents in the synaptic cleft. (5). *Receptor Interaction*: Once released, the transmitter molecules are free to diffuse across the synapse and bind to *receptor* macromolecular complexes which are selectively responsive to them and which are embedded in the membrane of the postsynaptic cell. Often there may be two or more subclasses of receptor specific to a single neurotransmitter. In at least some neurotransmitter systems, including those involving the catecholamines, receptor binding is thought to result in activation of a particular adenylate cyclase, an enzyme which, in turn, catalyzes the synthesis of cyclic AMP (adenosine 3′,5′ monophosphate), a so-called *second messenger* whose function is to initiate a cascade of reactions translating receptor stimulation into intracellular physiological responses in the postsynaptic neuron. The instantaneous status of the postsynaptic cell—in particular whether it is excited (*depolarized*) or inhibited (*hyperpolarized*)—depends upon simultaneous input often from thousands of neurons, each impinging on postsynaptic receptors at separate synaptic sites along the neuron. In addition to receptors on the postsynaptic cell, presynaptic receptors have also been described for a number of transmitter systems. These *autoreceptors*, as they are sometimes called, furnish one of the mechanisms for *feedback inhibition* whereby a neurotransmitter can modulate subsequent firing and release by the neuron which secreted it and thereby regulate neuronal activity at the presynaptic level. (6). *Transmitter Inactivation*: The termination of neurotransmitter activity following release and receptor stimulation depends upon rapid and efficient removal of transmitter molecules from the synaptic cleft. The predominant means of inactivation in most transmitter systems, including dopaminergic systems, appears to involve (a) *active reuptake* of the neurotransmitter by a membrane transport mechanism in the pre-synaptic cell. Once returned, the neurotransmitter may either be stored again for later use or catabolized by an intraneuronal degradative enzyme. In neurons which synthesize and release catecholamines or serotonin, this enzyme is monoamine oxidase (MAO), localized to the outer membranes of mitochondria within the cell. Metabolic products of degradation are released and may be measured for clincial purposes in the cerebrospinal fluid. An alternate route of inactivation, thought to be far less important for most neurotransmitters with the exception of acetylcholine which relies on it exclusively, is (b) *extraneuronal metabolism* whereby a transmitter is enzymatically catabolized in the region of the synapse, obviating reuptake. For catecholamines, the principal extraneuronal degradative enzyme is catechol-O-methyl transferase (COMT). Acetylcholine inactivation is accomplished by enzymes known as the cholinesterases.

Of great current interest are the biological mechanisms which regulate the sequence of events just described. While one method of feedback control depends upon stimulation of presynaptic autoreceptors by released transmitter molecules, as noted above, another relies upon the inhibitory influence of excess transmitter molecules still within the cell acting on the biosynthetic enzymes critical to their formation. Long and short-term changes in neuronal firing may also affect neurotransmitter synthesis through changes in the concentrations and physical characteristics of these key enzymes. In some transmitter systems, the rate of synthesis is closely associated with the availability of precursors and cofactors. Regulation at any number of steps in the life cycle of neurotransmission is now thought to involve, as well, the contribution of neuromodulators—neuroactive, nontransmitter substances released from neurons, neuroglia, specialized secretory cells in the vicinity of neurons, or distant endocrine organs—about whose site and mode of action much remains to be learned.

Perturbations in neurochemical function may potentially arise from a variety of causes. Most obvious, perhaps, are genetically determined alterations in the availability or structure of precursors, cofactors, and enzymes involved in transmitter synthesis and catabolism, in mechanisms of cellular transport, storage, and release, in receptor macromolecules and their link to postsynaptic events, or in regulatory processes and their effective coupling to neurotransmission. Neurochemical dysfunction, however, does not necessarily imply an inherited defect nor a static condition. Drugs, toxins, diet, hormonal changes, stress, trauma, and other factors in the ongoing life of an organism exert a powerful impact on neurochemical processes, a point returned to on numerous occasions below. Recently the basis of the peripheral nervous system disease myasthenia gravis has been discovered in an autoimmune disorder involving proliferation of antibodies in affected individuals that bind to and block a particular subclass of acetylcholine receptors as though they were antigenic substrate from a foreign body, thereby drastically reducing the number of receptors with which acetycholine can interact (Drachman, 1978). This suggests yet another means by which neurochemical processes may be impaired.

The following sections consider disturbances in neurochemical transmission as they are expressed in behavioral pathology. The first examines the effects of disruption of a single transmitter system on a multiplicity of behaviors: dopaminergic dysfunction in an animal model of behaviors related to those observed in minimal brain dysfunction and other developmental disorders. The second discusses the impact of perturbations in a multiplicity of neurochemical systems on a single family of behaviors: neurochemical aspects of aggression. Together these sections exemplify some of the tools with which neurochemical factors affecting behavior may be explored and some of the insights these explorations furnish.

MINIMAL BRAIN DYSFUNCTION: A NEUROCHEMICAL INVESTIGATION

Minimal brain dysfunction (MBD), also known as minimal cerebral dysfunction, the hyperkinetic syndrome, or attentional deficit disorder, is a common problem affecting an estimated 5–10% of the school-age population. The characteristic behavioral phenotype includes hyperactivity, impulsivity, distractability, short attention span, irritability, and a variety of cognitive, motor, and perceptual disturbances (Cantwell, 1975a; Wender, 1971). While hyperactivity appears to abate by adolescence, problems of social adjustment, emotional stability, and school performance may often persist. Follow-up studies of children with MBD as well as retrospective studies of the early histories of adults manifesting antisocial behavior suggest a relationship between the childhood syndrome and later deviance and delinquency (Cantwell, 1978).

The search for neurochemical abnormalities in MBD is motivated by a number of observations:

Heredity

Evidence of a genetic predisposition in MBD has been obtained utilizing several diverse but complementary research stratagems including family, twin, and adoption studies as well as studies of full and half siblings in foster homes (Cantwell, 1972, 1975b; Morrison and Stewart, 1971, 1973; Safer, 1973; Willerman, 1973). Demonstration of an hereditary pattern for MBD, as for any clinical syndrome, emphasizes the importance of biological factors in its etiology.

Neurological signs

The frequent presence of soft neurological signs in MBD, including problems in motor control and central processing, highlights immaturity or dysfunction of the nervous system in particular as a significant biological factor. Among the deficits often noted are mild involuntary movements and impairments in motor coordination and in stereognosis, the ability to recognize the form of an object by means of touch (Pincus and Tucker, 1974; Touwen and Kalberboer, 1973).

Animal studies

Animal studies in which behaviors potentially relevant to MBD have been produced have involved a variety of manipulations including lead intoxication, anoxia, hyperthyroidism, intracerebral viral infection, drug administration, undernutrition, and neuroanatomical lesions (e.g., Ahlenius et al., 1977; Campbell and Randall, 1975; Culver and Norton, 1976; Lycke and Roos, 1975; Michaelson et al., 1977; Rastogi and Singhal, 1976; Sechzer et al., 1976; Silbergeld and Goldberg, 1975). Though quite disparate in their approach, these treatments frequently entail measurable impact on neurotransmitter systems, notably CNS catecholamines, serotonin, acetylcholine and GABA, indicating a possible common neurochemical basis for their similar behavioral effects (Dodge et al., 1975; Goldberg and Silbergeld, 1977; Leahy et al., 1978; Shaywitz et al., 1978a). Recently, an endogenous animal model has been proposed involving hybrid dogs whose natural behavioral characteristics and pharmacological responses resemble aspects of the hyperkinetic syndrome. Biochemically these dogs are distinguished by lower levels of brain catecholamines when compared with controls (Bareggi et al., 1979). Especially noteworthy with regard to attentional dysfunction in particular are lesion studies of the dorsal noradrenergic bundle, a fiber tract which emanates from the locus coeruleus in the brain stem, the major cluster of noradrenergic neurons in the CNS, and which terminates in numerous forebrain structures including cortex and hippocampus (Mason and Iversen, 1979). Following destruction of the dorsal bundle, adult rats exhibit a consistent pattern of behavioral disruption. They are slow to extinguish a previously rewarded response when reinforcement is no longer forthcoming and also resist resuming previously punished responses after punishment is discontinued (phenomena now termed the *dorsal bundle extinction effect*). These rats are also more readily distracted than control animals whose catecholamine systems are intact. Careful work has served to cast doubt upon the importance to these deficits of such proposed mechanisms as general hyperactivity, impaired response inhibition, abnormal reaction to frustration, and altered motivational status. The most powerful explanation of the observations to date is framed in attentional terms. A considerable body of evidence suggests that the dorsal bundle in rats is involved in the filtering of irrelevant stimuli and that animals in whom these fibers are damaged suffer an impairment in their capacity to focus upon stimuli which are salient to the task at hand while excluding those which are less relevant. In support of this theory, lesioned rats show performance superior to that of controls in learning paradigms in which the inability to ignore extraneous stimuli is an advantage. Whether these investigations will culminate in the demonstration of a precise link between catecholamine dysfunction and attentional impairment in man remains to be seen. Surely they represent an intriguing advance in that direction.

Response to Stimulants

The principal actions of amphetamine and methylphenidate are thought to involve enhancement of catecholamine transmission through the facilitation of transmitter release and the inhibition of reuptake (Moore, 1978). Initially reported in 1937 and repeatedly confirmed since, these stimulants are an effective treatment for approximately three-quarters of the childhood population diagnosed as having MBD. In these children restless activity and impulsive behavior are significantly diminished and social conduct and attention span are markedly improved (Barkley, 1977). Often children respond more positively to one stimulant than to the other for reasons which are not yet known (Arnold et al., 1978). Also, behaviors appear to be differentially affected by different drug doses; methylphenidate dose-response curves for social behavior and learning performance demonstrate that an optimal dose for enhancement of one may be ineffective or even deleterious with respect to the other (Sprague and Sleator, 1977). Recognition that later behavioral disorders may be associated with childhood MBD has prompted clinical investigations in which amphetamine or methyl-phenidate has been administered to irritable, impulsive, and antisocial adolescents and adults who have a history of childhood hyperkinesis. Although further systematic study is required, reports document an impressive therapeutic response which includes reduction in emotional lability and aggressive misconduct (Allen et al., 1975; Maletzky, 1974; Richmond et al., 1978; Wood et al., 1976). Sociopathic and other atypical behavior in such individuals might, plausibly, arise in response to childhood deficits undermining peer and family relations, academic and athletic achievement, and the development of healthy autonomy and self-esteem. Nevertheless, the continued and immediate responsiveness of such behaviors to CNS stimulants raises the possibility that, in addition to reflecting psychological derivatives from childhood, they reflect endurance of a neurochemical abnormality into later life. Persisting neurochemical dysfunction may augment the vulnerability of these individuals to an unsupportive, disappointing or hostile environ-ment and increase the likelihood that deviant behavior will emerge. The amelioration of cardinal symptoms of MBD in childhood and, perhaps, in later life by agonists of catecholamine transmission is hardly proof that catecholaminergic underactivity is the primary defect in this disorder. First, enhanced catecholaminergic transmission might have a beneficial effect by masking or compensating for aberrations in other systems, neurochemical or otherwise, which are themselves unaffected by these drugs. Also, ancillary to their facilitory effects on the catecholamine systems in the brain, amphetamines may also provoke changes in serotonin and acetylcholine activity as well (Moore, 1978). Although, under normal circumstances, these effects are considered relatively inconsequential, in individuals in whom pathological proces-ses are operating, they may take on greater significance. Finally, aspects of the so-called *paradoxical* response of children with MBD to stimulant medication may not be peculiar to such children but may be observed in the general population at certain stages of maturation, reflecting normal developmental patterns rather than CNS pathology (Rapoport et al., 1978). Nonetheless, the susceptibility of MBD to treatment by drugs which amplify catecholamine activity at the synapse is consistent with a neurochemical hypothesis of the disorder and indicates that further investigation along these lines is necessary and worthwhile.

Post-encephalitic disorders

Behavioral disturbances resembling those observed in MBD such as restlessness, moodiness, and disobedience have been described many times since the pandemic of von Economo's encephalitis early in this century in childhood survivors of this disease (Hohman, 1922; Greenbaum and Lurie, 1948). In adults, the same viral form of encephalitis is among the several causative factors of Parkinsonism, associated with degeneration of the dopaminergic nigrostriatal pathways in the brain and profound reductions of brain dopamine in affected regions (Hornykiewicz, 1973). That encephalitis can leave in its aftermath atypical behavior in children similar to that seen in MBD and that it is known, at least in adults, to produce specific damage to dopamine systems is suggestive of the possibility that modifications in central dopaminergic function, occurring in early life, could result in the symptom constellation commonly diagnosed as MBD.

Cerebrospinal fluid metabolites

Analysis of the metabolites of CNS neurochemicals in samples of cerebrospinal fluid (CSF), clinically obtained through lumbar puncture, offers indirect access to brain chemical activity in childhood disorders (Cohen et al., 1980; Shaywitz et al., 1980). Prior administration of probenecid, which blocks the active transport of biogenic amine metabolites out of the CSF and thereby effects an elevation in their concentration, is thought to increase the sensitivity of the procedure to changes in amine turnover in the brain otherwise difficult to detect. When this technique was employed to study homovanillic acid (HVA) and 5-hydroxyindoleacetic acid (5-HIAA), the principal metabolites of dopamine and serotonin respectively, lower concentrations of HVA were found in children with MBD when compared with controls, suggesting reduced dopaminergic activity in the small group of children assessed (Shaywitz et al., 1977a). In a similar study, however, in which probenecid was not administered, HVA concentrations for children with MBD did not differ significantly from those of controls (Shetty and Chase, 1976). These equivocal results invite further pursuit to distinguish fact from artifact and determine whether this discrepancy is due to diff nces in methodology or in the composition of subject populations.

Several lines of research and clinical observation, then, provide the rationale for the study of neurochemical mechanisms in MBD. Demonstration of a genetic predisposition to the disorder indicates that constitutional factors play a role in its etiology. The presence of mild neurological symptoms in children with MBD, together with relevant animal studies involving direct or indirect CNS alteration, point especially to dysfunction or delayed maturation of the central nervous system as a fundamental factor. The responsiveness of MBD to treatment with pharmacological agents which facilitate catecholamine transmission isolates problems in chemical neuroregulation as being of potential importance. And, finally, the observation of post-encephalitic behavioral disorders which share several characteristic symptoms with MBD and in which dopamine transmission may be impaired, and a possible reduction of homovanillic acid in the cerebrospinal fluid of children with MBD, suggest that dopaminergic dysfunction, in particular, may be worthy of closer attention.

An Animal Model

As a first approach to an understanding of how catecholamine alterations might affect a developing organism we have studied the behavior of rats selectively depleted of brain dopamine shortly after birth. Animal research can make limited but meaningful contributions to the study of brain-behavior relations in childhood and adolescence, an area in which ethical and practical considerations impose formidable constraints on human experimentation. Animal populations allow investigators substantial control over variables of interest and permit access to tissue and body-fluid samples which are normally unavailable from human subjects. Early life experiences can be manipulated with considerable precision and the entire course of maturation from prenatal life through adulthood may be examined in a short time frame amenable to detailed investigation. Animal studies make possible the exploitation of the most sophisticated available pharmacological techniques; they help elucidate sensitive periods in the biological and behavioral development of young organisms; and they can provide a broad range of behaviors on which to test the effects of candidate therapeutic agents and procedures (Kornetsky, 1977; McKinney, 1974; and Plaut, 1975). While utmost care must be involved in the extrapolation from infrahuman data to human behavior and disease, the blanket rejection of such studies in the name of caution is an indiscriminate abandonment of a valuable research tool. In this regard, Freedman (1977) remarks:

> We can conceive of the processing of information being systematically skewed throughout a child's development by but a slight change or disregulation in a neuroregulatory system; this could lead to subsequent neural adaptations that eventually would make a particular clinical manifestation highly probable in the young adult. We are not now at that point. Yet if our knowledge of genetics was built from such banal witnesses as garden peas and *E. coli*, we will pay careful attention to simple systems that are analyzable and learn what they provide in the way of fundamental knowledge of control mechanisms.

Given thoughtful interpretation, animal studies may help isolate neurochemical aspects of the complex causal network which underlies vulnerability to deviant development and may suggest possible avenues of human research in the laboratory and in clinical settings.

Animal models of human developmental disorders are most useful when they satisfy basic criteria of evaluation: (1) The syndrome produced in animal subjects obviously must display important phenotypic similarities to the cardinal features of the human syndrome under investigation; (2) the pathogenesis of the syndrome in the animal model must bear a clear relationship to what is believed or postulated to be the pathogenesis of the disorder in children; (3) the syndrome in the animal model must be produced in the developing animal and, ideally, follow a developmental course similar to that found in the human counterpart; and (4) the response of the animal syndrome to therapeutic intervention must parallel the response seen clinically in the childhood disorder (Shaywitz et al., 1978a). In our animal studies we have used a rather unique pharmacological agent, 6-hydroxydopamine, to explore the impact of CNS dopamine dysfunction in neonatal rat pups and have developed a methodology by which the above criteria can be tested.

6-Hydroxydopamine

6-hydroxydopamine (6-OHDA), a structural analogue of the catecholamines, has provided an innovative means by which to examine their function (Breese, 1975). When introduced directly into the brain through intracisternal injection, 6-OHDA is actively incorporated into catecholaminergic terminals by the neuronal membrane pump responsible for catecholamine reuptake. Once inside the neuron, 6-OHDA spontaneously oxidizes creating products which prove toxic to the cell. The result is neuronal degeneration more selective, with respect to neurochemically homogeneous pathways in the CNS, than could be produced by electrolytic or surgical lesion techniques. Moreover, if the incorporation of 6-OHDA by noradrenergic terminals is blocked by pretreatment with desmethylimipramine (DMI), a potent temporary inhibitor of noradrenergic reuptake, 6-OHDA is preferentially seques- tered by dopaminergic terminals. In developing rats, this procedure leads to marked, rapid, and permanent reduction of brain dopamine content while leaving norepinephrine concentrations virtually intact (Shaywitz et al., 1976a; Smith et al., 1973). A valuable method is thus provided by which to examine the role of dopaminergic pathways in the brain in a variety of physiological, behavioral, and pharmacological responses during development.

We have studied rats, treated with 6-OHDA and DMI at 5 days of age, in relation to motor activity, habituation, learning performance, susceptibility to chemical therapy, social behavior, and mother-infant interaction. The effects of selective CNS dopamine depletion on these dimensions are discussed below.

Activity

During the first month of postnatal life, the normal rat pup, when tested in isolation, manifests a distinct pattern of activity change, termed the ontogeny of behavioral arousal, which is thought to be a general developmental phenomenon for many mammalian species. The new- born rat pup initially shows little spontaneous activity. Beginning before the second week of life, however, and continuing throughout the next 10 days, the pup's total activity (ambulation, climbing, rearing, eating, drinking, scratching, sniffing, grooming) increases dramatically, peak- ing at several times its previous amount. By the fourth week postpartum, total activity has declined and is stabilized at a level only moderately higher than that prior to the rapid increase. The ontogenetic sequence described for the rat, involving a transient increase in activity in early life which subsides with maturity, may reflect the changing neuronal organization of the young animal, in particular, the pattern of development of catecholaminergic, cholinergic, and serotonergic path- ways in the central nervous system (Campbell et al., 1969; Campbell and Mabry, 1973; Fibiger et al., 1970; Mabry and Campbell, 1974; Moorcroft, 1971).

Neonatal rat pups depleted of brain dopamine through 6-OHDA and DMI treatment manifest a similar developmental trend. However, they attain to increased activity levels earlier and to a significantly greater degree than do littermate controls (Figure 3). When tested at 15,

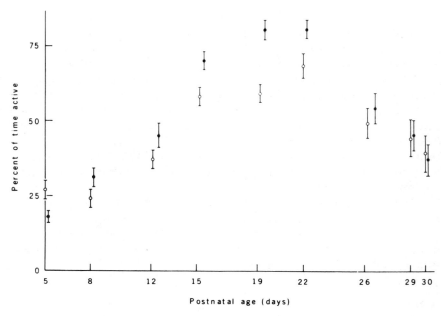

Figure 3.   Mean total activity in control rat pups (open circles) and rat pups treated with 6-OHDA + DMI (closed circles) during the first month of postnatal life. Bars represent ± standard error of the mean (Shaywitz et al., 1976b).

19, and 22 days of age, activity is markedly elevated for treated rats when compared with controls. By day 26 postpartum, total activity of treated rats is decreasing and subsequent activity levels of treated and control animals are indistinquishable (Shaywitz et al., 1976b). The pattern of activity change dopamine-depleted rat pups display is, therefore, an exaggeration of the normal ontogeny of behavioral arousal and bears some resemblance to the pattern of hyperactivity in MBD which also often abates with maturity. Studies in which newborn rats have been depleted of both dopamine and norepinephrine, through 6-OHDA treatment without DMI, have found either normal activity levels (Eastgate et al., 1978) or mild elevations in activity which were often insignificant (Sorenson et al., 1976; Stoof et al., 1978). These findings underscore the importance of selective depletion of dopamine to the significant hyperactivity we have observed. They also support the hypothesis that simultaneous disruption of two related transmitter systems may sometimes have less dramatic behavioral consequences than disruption of either one alone, presumably by preserving a critical balance of interaction between them (Antelman and Caggiula, 1977).

Also critical is the developmental context in which CNS alteration occurs. Abundant evidence suggests that, far from increased activity, general disruption of dopaminergic transmission in adult rats eventuates in hypokinesia (Iversen, 1977; Smith et al., 1973). Small, partial lesions, however, which incompletely damage one of several clusters of brain dopamine neurons (the so-called A-10 group) can produce a hyperkinetic state in the mature animal (Koob et al., 1981) as can localized destruction of dopamine axon terminals in the medial prefrontal cortex (Carter and Pycock, 1980).

The ontogeny of behavioral arousal refers to the predictable sequence of activity change demonstrated by the normal young rat when isolated and observed in unfamiliar surroundings. When rats are tested, however, in the presence of siblings, an anesthetized adult male or female rat, or in an environment resembling the home cage, the distinctive activity pattern fails to emerge (Campbell and Raskin, 1978; Randall and Campbell, 1976). The transient hyperactivity of normal, isolated rat pups and, perhaps, the intensified hyperactivity of dopamine-depleted rat pups, may therefore be related to underdeveloped or impaired capacity to habituate to novel surroundings in early life, a suggestion we have examined more closely.

Habituation

Habituation is generally defined as the response decrement, following repeated or continuous stimulation, which is independent of peripheral factors such as effector fatigue or sensory adaptation (Horn and Hinde, 1970). Providing a mechanism by which to navigate between environmental constancy and change, it enables organisms to attend to the new and salient demands of their surroundings. Animal investigations, involving study of exploratory behavior, locomotion, general activity, and the startle response, have discerned definite developmental trends in the ability to habituate to novel situations (Bronstein et al., 1974; Feigley et al., 1972; Martinek and Lat, 1968; Shaywitz et al., 1979; and Williams et al., 1975). Not surprisingly, habituation does not appear to be a unitary phenomenon and is apparently subserved by more than one neuroregulatory system. Significant disruption in the habituation of a variety of behaviors, such as the startle response, orienting response, and exploratory activity, has followed pharmacological interference with catecholaminergic, cholinergic, and serotonergic transmission in adult rats (Carlton and Advokat, 1973; File, 1975; Hole et al., 1977; Swonger and Rech, 1972; and Williams et al., 1974). In neonatal rats, similar interference is associated with disruption of the normal ontogeny of behavioral arousal, as noted above. The temporal link between early patterns of activity and development of the ability to habituate may be rooted in the maturation of neurochemical systems essential to both.

In our animal studies of dopamine-depleted rats, habituation of total activity was investigated in 30-minute observation periods during the first four weeks of life. Through the first week and one-half, dopamine-depleted and control rat pups both exhibit low levels of activity which are indistinquishable and whose decreases over time do not significantly differ. By 12 days postpartum, dopamine-depleted pups have begun to exhibit greater activity than controls, but their activity declines at a similar rate. At day 15, however, the activity of treated pups is significantly greater than that of controls and the activity decrement is significantly less. While treated pups display a 10% reduction in activity for each 10-minute interval, control pups display almost twice that, 19%, during the same period. At 19 days of age, activity continues to be much higher and to decline more slowly for dopamine-depleted pups than for controls; 3% reduction for treated rats compared with 10% reduction for controls. By day 22, activity is still much higher for dopamine depleted pups but there is no longer a significant lag in activity decline. And, finally, by day 26, differences in activity and in response decrement are no longer apparent (Shaywitz et al., 1977b). Corroborating these findings, a recent study reports that while control animals placed in a novel environment for a half-hour observation period shift from initial locomotion and rearing to grooming and finally to relative immobility, dopamine-depleted rat pups remain in a prolonged phase of restless locomotion (Stoof et al., 1978). Though it is obvious that impaired habituation of activity will lead to an increase in activity levels, it is not certain that the intensified hyperactivity of dopamine-depleted pups is entirely explained in terms of a disability to habituate. We have seen significant hyperactivity at age 22 days, for example, when activity decrements for treated and control pups are comparable. Nevertheless, it is clear that disruption of dopaminergic function has a measurable impact on the ability of the developing rat to regulate its activity and to habituate to unfamiliar surroundings during certain phases of maturation. While the leap from rat to human requires a more ambitious sprint than these studies provide, it is possible that neurochemical dysfunction responsible for habituational difficulties in the young rat may also have a role in problems involving the modulation of activity and attention in human developmental disorders.

Operant Behavior

In addition to intensified hyperactivity and deficiencies in habituation, rat pups selectively depleted of brain dopamine display impaired operant behavior when tested in T-maze and shuttlebox between the third and fourth week of life (Shaywitz et al., 1976a, 1978b; Shaywitz and Pearson, 1978). In contrast to the other deficits so far studied, disrupted learning performance does not subside with development but is still evident when treated rats are assessed at two months postpartum (Smith et al., 1973). Since learning disturbances are significant when hyperactivity is no longer observed, it is probable that these behavioral problems are autonomous phenomena of depletion with no simple causal relationship between them. Though neonatal depletion of both dopamine and norepinephrine also leads to enduring impairment of operant conditioning (Nyakas et al., 1973), preferential depletion of norepinephrine results in some improvements in performance relative to untreated controls (Smith et al., 1973). Thus, while disruption in learning performance is not as dependent upon the specifity of depletion as was hyperactivity, reduction of brain dopamine again appears to be the essential element involved. Interestingly, examination of the brain chemistry of cats selected for particularly poor performance on a more complicated learning task revealed significantly lower dopamine levels than controls (Kitsikis et al., 1972). It is notable that although hyperactivity in rats was producible only through dopamine depletion of the newborn, with depletion of mature rats leading to depressed activity, significant disturbances in operant behavior are seen in rats depleted of brain dopamine whether this alteration takes place in adulthood or during the first days of life (Howard et al., 1974). And, at least in adult rats, these disturbances can occur in the absence of motor incapacity or nutritional deficiencies (Delacour et al., 1977). Provided the critical reduction of CNS dopamine is achieved, such alterations in learning behavior appear to be relatively insensitive to developmental changes and, possibly, independent of other important behavioral abnormalities associated with dopamine depletion. The abatement of hyperactivity during development in dopamine-depleted rats together with the persistence of cognitive impairments into adulthood are again suggestive of clinical patterns often observed in MBD.

Drug Effects

An important aspect of the animal studies under consideration concerns the response of cardinal symptoms associated with dopamine

depletion to treatment with agents that exert their principal pharmacological effects through CNS mechanisms. Administration of
amphetamine in doses ranging from 0.25 to 5.0 mg kg^{-1} typically results
in increased total activity in the normal developing rat pup (Shaywitz et
al., 1976a; Sobrian et al., 1975). In the dopamine-depleted pup,
however, administration of amphetamine results either in no significant
alteration or in marked reductions in activity, particularly in ambulatory
activity, when tested during the first four weeks postpartum (Figure 4)
(Shaywitz et al., 1976a). Amphetamine also reduces the increased
activity seen in older rats following lesions of A-10 dopaminergic
neurons (Stinus et al., 1977).

The pattern of response to methylphenidate appears to be more
sensitive to dose and age. Again, however, dopamine-depleted rat pups
manifest resistance to the locomotor stimulatory effects of the drug,
responding with either no change or with significant reductions in
activity, even on doses and days when controls' activity levels are

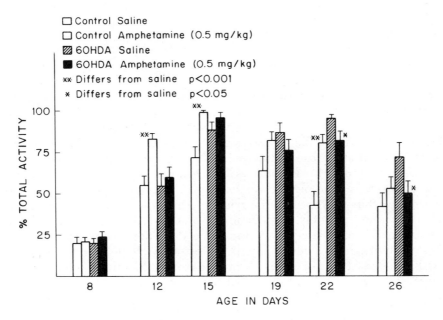

Figure 4.   Effect of acute injection of amphetamine (0.5 mg kg^{-1}) or saline placebo on
activity in rat pups treated at 5 days of age with 6-OHDA + DMI or control solution.
(Shaywitz et al., 1976a).

strongly enhanced (Shaywitz et al., 1978b). Recently, a differential response has been revealed with barbiturates as well. When administered phenobarbital at age 26 days, control pups display significant reductions in activity while dopamine-depleted pups' activity is markedly increased (Shaywitz and Pearson, 1978). These studies indicate that dopamine depletion often results in so-called paradoxical responses of treated animals to stimulant and barbiturate medication. Nevertheless, such responses may also be produced through other kinds of experimental intervention, raising the question of specificity. Thus, neonatal rats depleted of both dopamine and norepinephrine also show either paradoxical or, at least, attenuated responses to amphetamine and methylphenidate (Sorenson et al., 1977; Eastgate et al., 1978); lead-intoxicated mice show activity reduction in response to stimulants and activity enhancement in response to phenobarbital (Silbergeld and Goldberg, 1975); and undernourished mice display decreases in activity after amphetamine (Michaelson et al., 1977). Several hypotheses may be advanced in this regard, all of which deserve further study. Paradoxical responses to certain agents which intervene in central nervous system function may be characteristic of no specific impairment in particular but may be general among animals whose baseline performance is atypical or among immature animals experimentally disturbed during sensitive periods in development. Alternatively, retarded growth which is often associated with catecholamine depletion, lead administration and, of course, undernutrition may be the essential common denominator subserving a paradoxical response through some as yet unspecified mechanism. Or, it may be that all three manipulations entail similar neurochemical correlates responsible for the unusual patterns of drug response observed.

In addition to activity, operant performance of dopamine-depleted rats is also significantly affected by pharmacological treatment in a way in which the behavior of control animals is not. While methylphenidate at doses between 0.25 and 2.0 mg kg^{-1} has no discernable impact on T-maze learning in control rats, the latter dose results in significantly improved performance for rats depleted of dopamine (Shaywitz et al., 1978b). In a similar animal model, reduced dopaminergic transmission is achieved in newborn rats through administration of the dopamine receptor blocker, pimozide, conveyed indirectly to neonates through treatment of their lactating mothers. Here, too, learning deficits noted at four weeks of age are effectively countered when pups receive amphetamine (Ahlenius et al., 1975). Conversely, phenobarbital leads to marked disruption of the already impaired performance of dopamine-depleted rats on T-maze and shuttlebox tasks while having no significant effect on the performance of controls in the dose range studied (Figure 5) (Shaywitz and Pearson, 1978).

While demonstration of activity reduction and learning enhancement in dopamine-depleted pups treated with CNS stimulants strengthens the analogy between the animal model and MBD, the specificity of these responses and the precise mechanism by which they are mediated in rat and human are questions that require continued attention.

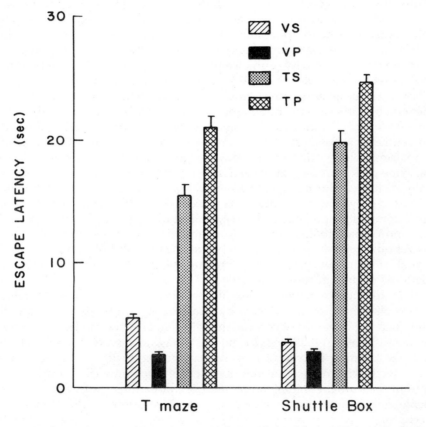

Figure 5.   Escape latency in T-maze at age 20 days and shuttlebox at 28 days. On both tasks, phenobarbital significantly interferes with performance of 6-OHDA + DMI treated rat pups (Treated pups on phenobarbital [TP] compared with treated pups on saline [TS]), $p < 0.001$, while having no effect on performance of controls (Vehicle pups on phenobarbital [VP] compared with vehicle pups on saline [VS]). (Shaywitz and Pearson, 1978).

Social Behavior

Our investigations of dopamine-depleted developing rats take an ethological turn with the study of social behavior and mother-infant interaction. Whether observed in field or in laboratory, rats are, by nature, gregarious. They display definite patterns of social organization and an impressive repertoire of socially meaningful transactions (Barnett, 1975; Grant, 1963; Lore and Flannelly, 1977; MacKintosh et al., 1977). Given the opportunity to interact freely in an unstructured open space, monosexual pairs of rats manifest markedly greater affiliation than would be predicted by chance approaches or by their attraction to inanimate stimulus objects, and exhibit less indication of fear than when alone (Latané et al., 1972). Prolonged absence of social contact results in neurochemical, hormonal, and behavioral alterations and abnormalities in drug response (Brain and Benton, 1979; Lokiec et al., 1978; Sahakian et al., 1975; Thoa et al., 1977; Weinstock et al., 1978). Surgical lesions of the frontal cortex, hippocampus, hypothalamus, amygdala, and septum all result in pecularities in rat social behavior as does pharmacological interference with neurotransmission (e.g. Curzon and Marsden, 1976; Dalhouse, 1976; Ellison et al., 1978; Enloe, 1975; Kolb and Nonneman, 1974). In view of its ethological significance, its reciprocal relationship with modifications in CNS function, as well as the coordinated array of behavioral responses it involves, social interaction provides a rich dimension in which brain-behavior relations may be explored.

We have examined the dyadic behavior of two-month-old male rats, depleted of brain dopamine as neonates. While definitions of adulthood in the rat in terms of CNS maturity vary widely according to the parameters chosen (Himwich, 1975; Norton, 1977), the onset of sexual behavior in laboratory rats occurs after 35 days (Barnett, 1975). In a scientifically casual sense, then, the rats studied may be considered adolescent or young adult, though most human connotations of these terms do not, of course, apply.

In our laboratory setup, involving a one-square-meter open field, both dopamine-depleted and control rats display behaviors—including allo-grooming, huddling, following, threat posturing, and rare attack—that have been carefully described in the literature. Also consistent with research on untreated laboratory rats, both treated and control rats are more active and defecate less when paired than when alone, rough measures of reduced fearfulness in a social setting (Archer, 1973). Our preliminary observations indicate, however, that dopamine-depleted rats do not show as marked and consistent an elevation in activity when paired as is seen in controls. Furthermore, they appear to differ from controls in the amount of time they spend in physical contact with one another. Though of comparable frequency, contacts within pairs of dopamine depleted rats are of shorter duration than those within mixed pairs or within pairs of control rats; periods of sustained contact are much less common for treated pairs than for others (Alpert et al., 1978, unpublished pilot observations). Depression of social contact has also been reported in non-human primates following experimental attenuation of catecholamine activity (Redmond et al., 1971). Whether the difference we have found between controls and treated rats suggests an impairment specific to social affiliation or is simply an instance of a more general problem, such as distractability, remains to be seen. In either case, these observations clearly indicate that dopamine depletion in the newborn period has lasting and definite, if subtle, impact not only on an animal's interactions with its physical environment, as exemplified by learning disturbances, but on transactions with its social surroundings as well.

Mother-Infant Interaction

It is now generally recognized that there exists reciprocal behavioral influence between caretaker and offspring among mammalian species (Bell, 1971; Harper, 1971). Not only does a parent's behavior affect offspring status, but offspring status also determines, in part, the future style of parenting which will be received. In a recent double-blind study, for example, hyperactive children on a placebo elicited more intrusive and critical responses from their mothers than when they were on methylphenidate; when children were medicated mothers were rated by investigators as more positive and less controlling, thus both responding to and augmenting the beneficial effects of the drug (Humphries et al., 1978). The results of dopamine depletion in the newborn rat are far-reaching. They include growth retardation, hyperactivity, habituational disturbances, persistent learning problems, atypical behavioral responses to pharmacological agents, and possible abnormalities in social behavior. In light of the bidirectionality of mother-infant interaction, the possibility arises that rat pups treated with 6-OHDA and DMI at five days of age provoke pathologically altered care because of stimulus cues associated with neonatal CNS disruption. We have therefore studied the maternal behavior of untreated adult rats raising litters of dopamine-depleted or control pups, in order to determine the degree to which the constellation of deficits associated with dopamine depletion may be mediated by inadequate maternal care elicited during the first weeks of pup life.

Rat maternal behavior unfolded with sufficient uniformity in our laboratory facilities to suggest a stable behavioral profile (Figure 6). After a brief period of separation, mothers placed in an unfamiliar enclosure with their young typically explore the area and then proceed to establish initial contact with their pups within the first minute of observation. Thereafter mothers continue to engage in exploratory activity, returning to the pups at short intervals. Within two to three minutes following initial contact, mothers generally begin to retrieve their litter from the center of the enclosure, where the pups had been positioned, to the shelter of a corner. Once initiated, retrieval activity is pursued until all pups are brought to a corner nest over the course of one to two minutes. During one-hour observation periods, mothers invest the majority of the remaining time nursing suckling pups, periodically embarking upon brief reconnaissances and occasionally returning with paper strips with which to construct loosely piled nests. A very similar pattern of mothering has also been observed for mice studied in our laboratory (Cohen, Felig, and Shaywitz, 1979).

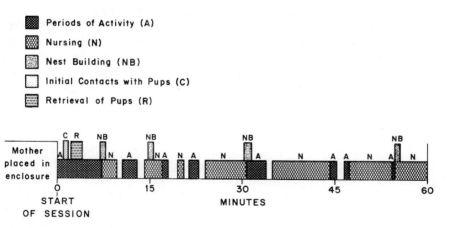

SCHEMATIC DIAGRAM OF TYPICAL SEQUENCE OF MATERNAL BEHAVIOR DURING 60 MINUTE OBSERVATION PERIOD

Periods of Activity (A)

Nursing (N)

Nest Building (NB)

Initial Contacts with Pups (C)

Retrieval of Pups (R)

– Overlap indicates simultaneity of behavior.
– Gaps indicate behaviors which were not systematically assessed (e.g. resting away from the nest).

Figure 6.   Diagrammatic view of the sequence and duration of rat maternal activities during typical 60 minute observation period. (Piccirillo et al., 1979).

We have found that, despite the profound neurological alteration sustained by dopamine-depleted pups, the maternal care they receive is comparable to that received by controls. Mothers of treated pups, like mothers of controls, feed and groom their offspring during the first two weeks of dependency. They build nests, gather stray pups, and manifest protective behaviors at least of the quality of mothers of controls. If anything, mothers of treated pups seem to respond in compensatory fashion to the retarded development of their young by providing them with somewhat more prompt retrieval than is received by control litters. The deficits associated with dopamine depletion which we have examined in a series of studies do not, then, appear to be mediated by maternal neglect or abuse during early development; rather, these disturbances occur in the presence of apparently adequate, if not more attentive, care and are, it seems, direct correlates of abnormal catecholaminergic activity induced by 6-OHDA and DMI treatment (Piccirillo et al., 1979).

With regard to the lesioned pup's response to its mother, recent work has made it clear that mere proximity of the mother can be a crucial factor in modulating activity levels of dopamine depleted offspring (Teicher et al., 1981). When evaluated in isolation or in the presence of an anesthetized sibling, three week old dopamine depleted pups are indeed hyperactive and slow to habituate. In the presence of an anesthetized mother, however, their activity and habituation patterns become indistinguishable from those of control pups. Just as damage to dopamine systems alters social behavior, the social environment exerts considerable reciprocal impact on the functional consequences of dopamine damage. Pharmacological intervention is but one part of the therapeutic endeavor in modifying disordered behavior, even when known neurochemical dysfunction is its cause.

Conclusion

Though far abstracted from immediate clinical concerns, the developmental syndrome produced by neonatal dopamine depletion is a potentially important sort of neurochemical investigation. It begins with a specific etiology, selective experimental destruction of brain dopaminergic pathways in an immature animal, as might, in nature, be associated with a genetic abnormality or trauma during prenatal life, at birth, or during early childhood. Since rats are studied not only during infancy but in later life as well, the syndrome involves not merely dopaminergic deficiency but also long-term, biological concomitants which arise in adaptive response to the original insult. These may include an increase in the biosynthesis and release of dopamine in residual neurons which have escaped destruction; a decrease in presynaptic reuptake; possible collateral growth from intact dopaminergic fibers; increased sensitivity or *supersensitivity* of postsynaptic receptors to stimulation by remaining terminals; and adjustments within other neuroregulatory systems that are functionally interrelated with dopaminergic systems (Zigmond and Stricker, 1974; 1977). Similar compensatory changes may be active in human disorders such as Parkinson's disease, in which prominent symptoms are often undetected, unless unmasked by stress or dopamine receptor blockers which accentuate the deficiency, until nigrostriatal dopamine depletions reach 70 to 90% (Hornykiewicz, 1973). It is therefore not suprising that despite a profound neurochemical change effected in early life, dopamine-depleted rats are substantially functional animals. Treated rats show initial disturbances in ingestive behavior but can feed well enough to sustain life; they are transiently hyperactive and show habituational disturbances which also appear to wane with maturity; they are able to acquire and perform operant behaviors, albeit less successfully than controls; they display social postures and activities associated with normal rat behavior, though they seem to spend less time than controls in actual physical contact with conspecifics; and they respond peculiarly to pharmacological agents, which is a finding of scientific interest but not, probably, of ethological concern. While alteration of neurochemical function in a fully mature animal who has had a normal behavioral and biological history and who has not had the opportunity to adjust to experimental changes during a plastic period in its development might result in drastic, immediate behavioral consequences, such treatment in early life may have more subtle, if pervasive and enduring, developmental effects, suitable for modelling a reasonably mild human disorder such as minimal brain dysfunction. We have seen that dopamine depletion of an infrahuman animal during infancy can lead to behavioral patterns and drug responses which resemble those identified in children diagnosed as having MBD. Far from establishing that childhood MBD and associated problems in later life may sometimes involve a disorder of biogenic amine function, these investigations nevertheless assume their place in a mosaic of research strategies—ranging from examination of receptor molecules and drug kinetics to analysis of transmitter metabolites in cerebrospinal fluid to classroom observation and longitudinal studies—which will ultimately determine the plausibility of such a view.

AGGRESSION: NEUROCHEMICAL ASPECTS

Aggression appears to be more diverse in etiology, character, and responsiveness to therapy than the use of a single term might imply. In pathological form, it is frequently associated with other syndromes including schizophrenia, seizure disorders, organic brain syndromes, hypersexuality, depressive disorders, characterological problems, mental retardation, drug abuse, opiate withdrawal, Tourette's syndrome, minimal brain dysfunction as noted previously, and several metabolic disorders which have effects on the central nervous system including Lesch-Nyhan, Sanfilippo, and Speilmeyer-Vogt syndromes and phenylketonuria (Cohen et al., 1979a; Goldstein, 1974; Itil and Mukhopadhyay, 1978; Kelley and Wyngaarden, 1978; Lion, 1975). Even in aggressive individuals in whom no other major disorder is diagnosed, there may sometimes be detectable impairments in brain function; thus, in a study of adolescent offenders at a residential treatment facility, violent delinquents were distinquishable from those whose offenses were typically non-violent on the basis of cognitive, perceptual and psychomotor performance on a battery of neuropsychological tests (Spellacy, 1977). Soft evidence suggests that patterns of illicit drug preference and use among delinquent youths may be explained, in part, by efforts on their own behalf to control aggressive tendencies with psychopharmacological help (Tinklenberg and Woodrow, 1974). A multiplicity of pharmacological agents have been used with some success in the clinical management of aggressive behavior (Valzelli, 1978). Unfortunately, there are, at present, no generally accepted chemical agents which exert selective anti-aggressive effects and which can be used uniformly for all types of aggression without adversely affecting other areas of function. Futhermore, there is only limited understanding of the brain mechanisms mobilized during treatment in inhibiting the pathological expression of anger, irritability, and destructiveness toward oneself and others. The optimal aim of psychopharmacological intervention in cases of abnormal aggressive behavior is to restore to the individual an ability to modulate aggression without inducing maladaptive passivity or sedation and with minimal imposition upon other dimensions of behavior. The rational achievement of such a goal requires knowledge of the biological parameters involved in the various types of pathological aggression and in their response to centrally active medications. Animal studies of neurochemical factors affecting aggressive behaviors represent a challenging step in this direction.

Several classificatory schemes of animal aggression have been developed. Moyer (1968) has identified seven categories of aggressive behaviors including predatory, intermale, fear-induced, irritable, territorial, maternal, and instrumental, which may be differentiated on the basis of the initiating stimuli, culminating responses, and physiological components involved. A simpler behavioral subdivision is suggested by Miczek and Barry (1976), who distinquish between intraspecies aggression, interspecies aggression, and non-specific aggressive reactions in which attack behavior is directed against some other object. The general distinction drawn by Wasman and Flynn (1962) between affective and predatory aggression has been particularly useful in the parsimonious interpretation of data from neuroanatomical and neurochemical studies of aggressive behaviors. Forms of affective aggression are characterized by intense autonomic arousal, threatening and defensive postures and vocalizations, and, often, frenzied attack. Affective aggression is not always goal-directed and may be intraspecific as well as interspecific. Frequently it involves aversive motivation. Predatory aggression, on the other hand, entails less autonomic activation, stalking rather than display postures, little vocalization, and lethally directed attack on interspecific prey. Often it involves appetitive motivation. Primarily within the last two decades, research strategies involving pharmacological, neurophysiological, and behavioral techniques have been marshalled in efforts to delineate neuroregulatory aspects of animal aggression; the results of these investigations are the subject of several good reviews (Allikmets, 1974; Avis, 1974; Eichelman, 1973; Goldstein, 1974; Pradhan, 1975; Reis, 1974; Sheard, 1977), and have contributed to a gradually emerging picture of significant neurochemical influences on at least some forms of aggressive behavior.

Catecholamines and Aggression

An aggressive defense reaction or *sham rage* can be evoked in cats by stimulation or ablation of specific brain areas. These manipulations elicit savage outbursts of snarling, piloerection, retraction of ears, hissing, clawing, and other components of excitation and attack, and have indicated a role for brain catecholamines in affective aggression. Production of sham rage behavior, through electrical stimulation of the amygdala or lateral hypothalamus or surgical transection of the upper brainstem rostral to the posterior hypothalamus, is associated with a selective fall in brain norepinephrine concentrations which is thought to reflect an increase in neuronal release exceeding the rate of neuronal resynthesis (Fuxe and Gunne, 1966; Gunne and Lewander, 1966; Reis and Fuxe, 1968; Sweet and Reis, 1971). Prolonged induction of rage behavior results in an increase in the activity of tyrosine hydroxylase, the enzyme catalyzing the rate-limiting step in catecholamine synthesis, to meet the biosynthetic demands of enhanced transmitter release (Reis et al., 1970). Although the extent of noradrenergic release appears to be proportional to the intensity of the aggression precipitated by treatment (Reis and Fuxe, 1969), correlation is not necessarily cause. However, even when body movements and reflex changes in cardiovascular function that usually accompany sham rage are prevented by spinal cord transection, an increase in noradrenergic release is still reported following ablation; whereas, when catecholamine transmission is attenuated by temporary depletion of neuronally stored amine with the drug reserpine and blockage of further synthesis with alpha-methylparatyrosine (AMPT), which temporarily inhibits tyrosine hydroxylase, sham rage behavior is suppressed (Reis, 1972). Changes in brain catecholamine activity during stimulation or ablation are, thus, more likely a causal factor than a result of aggressive excitation.

Another approach to the study of affective aggressive behaviors involves the delivery of aversive stimulation, such as periodic, low-intensity electric footshock, to paired animals (Ulrich and Symannek, 1969). Research on shock-elicited aggression, as on sham rage, has also indicated catecholaminergic involvement. Paired rats, in whom fighting has been shock-induced, present in the aftermath an increased turnover of brain norepinephrine which is reported to correlate with the number of attack behaviors observed during shock (Stolk et al., 1974). Repeated foot-shock is also associated with dopaminergic activation (Fadda et al., 1978), though no attempt to correlate the degree of change with aggressive behavior during pairing has yet been reported. Administration of rubidium, which causes an increase in noradrenergic turnover, also causes an increase in shock-elicited aggression in treated rats (Stolk et al., 1971). So too, an increase in fighting is observed following rapid-eye-movement (REM) sleep deprivation (Morden et al., 1968; Eichelman and Thoa, 1973) which appears to increase noradrenergic turnover as well (Schildkraut and Hartmann, 1972). When rats are stressed by repeated daily immobilization periods over the course of four weeks, there is a measurable elevation in hypothalamic tyrosine hydroxylase which persists after peripheral indications of stress have disappeared, which is thought to reflect increased central catecholamine activity, and which is also associated with an increase in shock-elicited aggression (Lamprecht et al., 1972). Tricyclic antidepressants, which inhibit noradrenergic reuptake, and monoamine oxidase inhibitors (MAOIs), which retard catecholamine catabolism, both therefore increase the availability of catecholamines and both have been shown to augment shock-elicited aggression (Eichelman and Barchas, 1975); these drug effects, however, are probably more complex in view of earlier work indicating suppression of fighting at certain doses (Crowley, 1972; Tedeschi et al., 1969). Occasional pro-aggressive effects of the tricyclic antidepressants have also been noted in man (Gottschalk et al., 1965; Rambling, 1978).

Research on affective aggression arising in association with morphine withdrawal has provided another avenue of evidence of catecholaminergic involvement in aggressive behaviors (Gianutsos and Lal, 1978); these investigations may assume increasing significance as study continues concerning the naturally-occurring or endogenous opioid peptides, their behavioral influence, and their interaction with other brain neuroregulatory systems. The acute administration of morphine at doses which are non-debilitating suppresses aggressive behaviors evoked by a variety of experimental manipulations. That it blocks shock-elicited aggression in monkeys (Emley et al., 1970) may be due to analgesic effects. But morphine also reduces aggression associated with prolonged isolation in mice (DaVanzo et al., 1966), with brain lesions in rats (Bernard et al., 1974), and with high doses of drugs which potentiate catecholamine activity such as amphetamines, the catecholamine intermediate precursor, dopa, and the dopamine receptor stimulant, apomorphine (Gianutsos and Lal, 1976; Lal et al., 1972; Yen et al., 1970). In contrast to the anti-aggressive effects of acute injection of morphine, however, withdrawal from chronic morphine administration results in considerable spontaneous violence, shock-elicited aggression, and general difficulty in handling (Davis and Khalsa, 1971; Gianutsos et al., 1975; Stollerman et al., 1975) which may parallel the anxiety and irritability seen clinically following the initiation of opiate abstinence in man (Jaffe, 1975). These observations accord with the notion that, biologically and behaviorally, the development of opiate tolerance and dependence represents mobilization of homeostatic mechanisms which tend to compensate for opiate-induced changes, while withdrawal involves the exaggerated expression of these opposing, adaptive responses which, during abstinence, are no longer opposed nor adaptive; withdrawal symptoms subsequently wane as a new equilibrium takes root (Way and Glasgow, 1978). Studies on withdrawal phenomena suggest that intense catecholaminergic activation may be one of the rebound effects which underlie the aggression observed upon termination of chronic morphine intake. Aggravation of withdrawal aggression is produced by amphetamine, dopa, and apomorphine at doses much lower than those required to elicit aggression in rats which have never had morphine; conversely, the neuroleptic haloperidol, an agent which blocks catecholamine receptors, is effective is suppressing withdrawal aggression, as is the inhibition of catecholamine synthesis with AMPT (Gianutsos and Lal, 1978; Puri and Lal, 1973). Behavioral studies such as these have contributed to the formulation of trial therapies in the medical management of drug withdrawal. Gold et al. (1978) have obtained preliminary but promising results in the treatment of human opiate withdrawal with the imidazol derivative clonidine, which at low doses is a potent inhibitor of noradrenergic activity through preferential stimulation of presynaptic autoreceptors, the so-called alpha$_2$ adrenergic receptors, which diminishes transmission (Aghajanian, 1978; Svensson et al., 1975). It is likely that, in addition to norepinephrine and dopamine, rebound effects encompassing other neuroregulators including serotonin and acetylcholine are also involved in withdrawal symptomatology (Way and Glasgow, 1978) and may also have a role in aggression during abstinence. Though of undoubted relevance to problems of drug abuse, study of the perturbations associated with chronic opiate use and withdrawal will be most fruitful if it finds, along the way, clues that concern neurochemical mechanisms of general importance operating in pathological behavior.

Corroborative evidence for enhanced catecholamine activity in some forms of affective aggression has also come from investigations of isolation-induced aggression and spontaneous fighting. Evidence indicates that during prolonged isolation noradrenergic activity in rats declines in response to the absence of social stimulation; this, in turn, may result in compensatory supersensitivity of postsynaptic receptors which augments transmission above normal levels when stimulation returns (Thoa, et al., 1977; Weinstock et al., 1978). In at least some species, these changes may provide the basis of post-isolation aggression. Consistent with this suggestion, small amounts of clonidine, as well as inhibitors of dopamine-beta-hydroxylase (DBH) which block the synthesis of norepinephrine from dopamine, produce significant reduction in aggression observed after long-term isolation in mice (Lassen, 1978; Ross and Ogren, 1976). On the other hand, facilitation of spontaneous aggression in mice has been produced with much higher, and perhaps toxic, doses of clonidine (Morpurgo, 1968; Ozawa et al., 1975); at higher doses, the drug is thought to exert primarily stimulatory effects on noradrenergic transmission through interaction with postsynaptic alpha$_1$ adrenergic receptors (Svensson et al., 1975). Similarly, a dietary regimen supplemented with additional tyrosine, the catecholamine precursor two and three biosynthetic steps removed from dopamine and norepinephrine, respectively, increased the incidence and promptness of attacks by treated mice upon strange mice introduced into their cages (Thurmond et al., 1977); however, since catecholamine synthesis appears to be less sensitive to fluctuations in tyrosine availability than, for example, are acetylcholine and serotonin to fluctuations in their respective dietary precursors, choline and tryptophan, (Wurtman et al., 1977), this finding must be interpreted with particular caution. Another tentative line of work involves study of inbred strains of mice which present developmental differences in catecholamine content and activity. A genetically homogeneous mouse strain, ICR, in which males become significantly more aggressive over time, shows a marked increase in brain dopamine levels and turnover with age compared with a modest elevation with age in these parameters in another inbred strain, C57BL6J, in which relatively stable and benign social behavior is observed throughout development (Everett, 1977). Increased dopaminergic activity, however, is not accompanied by increased aggression in ICR female mice, indicating that the association is merely circumstantial or that hormonal variables are a critical mitigating factor. Only recently has examination been directed to neurochemical changes occurring in the human brain in later life. Potentially important maturational alterations have been discovered in neurotransmitter and enzyme concentrations and activity in various brain regions (Domino, Dren, and Giardina, 1978). Studies of cerebro-spinal fluid monoamine metabolites and dopamine and serotonin have revealed a major developmental change in HVA but relative stability in CSF concentrations of 5-HIAA over the course of development. Compared to adult psychiatric patients, neuropsychiatrically disturbed children have much higher levels of CSF HVA (Leckman, et al., 1980), Cohen, et al., 1980). This may represent developmental changes in dopamine receptor sensitivity, reduction in neurotransmitter turnover, or the maturation of other systems affecting neuromodulation. Future investigations of CSF metabolites and peripheral metabolites offer the promise of revealing correlations between cognitive development, the regulation of mood and motor activity, and CNS maturation.

Although it would appear from the foregoing that enhanced activity of central noradrenergic and/or dopaminergic systems are involved in affective aggression in ways which suggest a causal link, the picture is complicated in an interesting way by research concerning brain catecholamine depletion. Contrary to what might be expected, mice and rats in whom both noradrenergic and dopaminergic or only noradrener-gic terminals in the central nervous system are permanently destroyed by 6-hydroxydopamine or its analogue 6-hydroxydopa, respectively, develop marked irritability following treatment, and display increased instances of shock-elicited aggression when tested (Coscina et al., 1973; Nakamura and Thoenen, 1972; Pöschlová et al., 1975; Thoa et al., 1972; Thoa et al., 1972b). Several plausible hypotheses may be proposed; none have yet been established satisfactorily. The brain regions in which enhanced catecholamine transmission is associated with enhanced affective aggressive behaviors may represent a small percentage of the total catecholamine receptor sites in the central nervous system, while other sites may be associated with either no effect or antagonistic effects on these behaviors. The behavioral outcome of depletion may, therefore, reflect disruption of conceivably preponderant catecholaminergic pathways that have inhibitory effects on aggressive behaviors, producing aggression through net disinhibition. The notion that catecholaminergic influence over aggressive behaviors may be heterogeneous, differing depending on specific pathway and termination sites, may also explain why diffuse intraventricular administration of norepinephrine has failed to achieve consistent impact on aggressive behaviors (Reis, 1974) and why studies involving amphetamines and other catecholamine facilitating agents in affective aggression are often similarly inconclusive (Kulkarni and Plotnikoff, 1978; Miczek and O'Donnell, 1978). So too, it may account for the fact that, when injected intracranially into specific septal regions of the rat brain, certain noradrenergic antagonists, the alpha-adrenergic receptor blockers, induce rather than suppress aggressive behavior (Albert and Richmond, 1977). Another hypothesis deserving further study is the possibility that depletion of brain norepinephrine and dopamine results in a syndrome of hyperreactivity in which aggression is a symptom of a general reduction in the response threshhold to exogenous stimuli rather than a primary manifestation of altered catecholamines (Sorenson and Gordon, 1975). The question remains, however, whether aggression in the rat with augmented catecholamine transmission differs from this in being a central and specific feature of treatment or whether it, too, is an epiphenomenon of a more basic and pervasive behavioral state. If the latter is true, an additional issue is whether the basic behavioral conditions that underlie the aggression produced are the same in catecholamine depletion as in catecholamine augmentation. Of possible relevance in this regard are primate studies (Redmond, 1977; Redmond et al., 1976) in which stimulation of the locus coeruleus, the brain area richest in cell bodies of noradrenergic neurons, results in manifestations of general anxiety and alarm. These states might reasonably be expected to increase the probability of aggressive behavior under circumstances, common to experimental models, in which flight from perceived threat is impossible. Conversely, electrolytic lesions of the locus coeruleus, effecting a selective depletion of norepinephrine in the CNS, increase aggression as well as general activity but decrease threat-associated behaviors and time spent in physical contact. Quite hypothetically, then, potentiation of certain catecholamine systems may produce aggression through behavioral anxiety and alarm, while destruction of these systems may produce aggression through hyperreactivity, impulsivity, and lack of a sense of imminent danger. Finally, it may well be significant that the enhanced aggressiveness of depleted animals does not develop until several days after treatment (Thoa et al., 1972b) and that temporary, reversible depletion of both catecholamines (DA and NE) with alpha-methylparatyrosine (AMPT) or of norepinephrine (NE) alone with a dopamine-beta-hydroxylase (DBH) inhibitor produces no increase in shock-elicited aggression (McLain et al., 1974; Thoa et al., 1972a). Chronic neurochemical dysfunction, as previously discussed in regard to neonatal dopamine depletion, provokes long-term changes, probably including receptor supersensitivity and augmented transmitter activity in residual terminals which escape destruction. The behavioral consequences of permanent depletion therefore reflect a more intricate biological state of affairs, involving compensatory transformations, than would be suggested by the simple reduction in brain neurotransmitter levels that is revealed in postmortem assay. That animals sustaining the destruction of a considerable proportion of catecholamine neurons appear to resemble, in their aggressive propensity, animals in whom catecholamine activity is increased, more than they resemble animals in whom catecholamine transmission is transiently attenuated, is not necessarily an inconsistency but rather a potentially revealing source of knowledge about the behavioral offspring of CNS damage and manipulation.

Behavioral models which have been developed to examine brain mechanisms in predatory aggression include the mouse-, frog-, chick-, and turtle-killing behavior of rats (Bandler and Moyer, 1970) and the quiet biting attack of cats (Chi and Flynn, 1971). Neurochemical exploration of predatory aggression has largely centered around rat muricide and feline attack, leaving in unfortunate abeyance the question of generalization to other predators and prey. Findings suggest a possible inhibitory contribution by one or more central catecholaminergic, and particularly noradrenergic, systems, but the data thus far are by no means conclusive; at present it is difficult to ascribe a single, consistent role to these neuroregulators in predatory aggression (Katz, 1978). While tranquilizers are typically ineffective inhibitors, except at doses producing major, general impairment, pharmacological facilitators of catecholamine transmission—amphetamines, MAO inhibitors, and tricyclic antidepressants—are reliable antimuricidal agents, even at doses which are frequently several fold less than that causing behavioral debilitation (Goldberg and Horovitz, 1978; Malick, 1975; Vogel, 1975). These agents appear to block rat frog-killing as well (Barr et al., 1976). The tricyclic antidepressant imipramine, has also blocked predatory attack elicited by hypothalamic stimulation in the cat (Dubinsky and Goldberg, 1971). Although MAOIs and tricyclic antidepressants often entail serotonergic augmentation and anticholinergic action which might, in part, account for their effects, the direct application of norepinephrine or an amphetamine derivative to amygdaloid sites in the rat brain also produces suppression of predatory behaviors (Leaf et al., 1969). Muricide has been effectively blocked by a chronic regimen of electroconvulsive shock (ECS) which is reported to have resulted in a significant increase in brain concentrations of norepinephrine and a statistically insignificant trend toward increased serotonin (Vogel and Haubrich, 1973). However, these elevations also occurred in a small number of ECS treated rats in whom a reduction in predatory aggression was not evident. Studies of similarly uncertain interpretation are described by Salama and Goldberg (1977), who have found elevated concentrations and turnover of norepinephrine in the forebrain of muricidal rats when examined two hours after a killing response. This increase was also detected in rats sacrificed and assayed 24 but not 48 hours after attack. While a transient acceleration in noradrenergic activity may represent the response of forebrain noradrenergic systems that serve to inhibit subsequent aggression of this kind for a finite period of time after a predatory act, the rise may simply be related to the stress or excitation associated with the mouse-killing episode. Blockade of catecholamine systems which might be anticipated to potentiate predatory behavior by diminishing catecholaminergic inhibitory influences, if they exist, has produced inconsistent results. Although the tyrosine hydroxylase inhibitor, AMPT, may increase muricide and exert no significant effect on frog-killing (Leaf et al., 1969; McLain et al., 1974), inhibitory effects on predatory aggression have also been reported (Katz and Thomas, 1975; Salama and Goldberg, 1977). Equivocal results are also associated with destruction of noradrenergic and dopaminergic fibers in the lateral hypothalamus with 6-hydroxydopamine (Jimerson and Reis, 1973); treated rats manifested a reduction in the latency to attack and kill a frog, but also in the probability that such an act would occur. Efforts at interpretation are further confounded by the diverse behavioral impairments authors observed following lateral hypothalamic 6-OHDA administration. Specific alteration of noradrenergic or dopaminergic transmission which leaves the other catecholamine intact may be a more profitable avenue of further study.

Though attractively parsimonious, the notion that catecholaminergic systems are facilitory for affective aggression and inhibitory for predatory aggression clearly requires greater refinement. Not only must the contributions of the various central noradrenergic and dopaminergic systems be disentangled, but a wider range of behaviors and animals, and the role of other neuroregulators, must be carefully examined.

Serotonin and Aggression

Research on the brain indoleamine serotonin (5-hydroxytryptamine or 5-HT) indicates important involvement in the modulation of essential drives and behaviors. One of the ways in which the role of serotonin may be investigated is through temporary, reversible depletion by para-chlorophenylalanine (PCPA), which inhibits tryptophan hydroxylase, a critical enzyme in serotonin biosynthesis, and is therefore analogous in its actions to AMPT, which blocks catecholamine biosynthesis (Sanders-Bush and Massari, 1977). Following PCPA treatment, rats and cats display a wide range of aggressive behaviors, increased sexual activity and aberrant sexual behavior, and disturbances in normal patterns of sleep (Dalhouse, 1976; Ferguson et al., 1970; MacDonnell et al., 1971; Sheard, 1969). Filicidal behavior has been produced through PCPA treatment in maternal rats characteristically protective of their young (Copenhaver et al., 1978). And exacerbation of isolation-induced fighting is observed in serotonin-depleted mice (Hodge and Butcher, 1974). In all cases, subsequent administration of the serotonin precursor, 5-hydroxytryptophan, or intracranial administration of serotonin results in abatement of these behaviors. The cell bodies (perikarya) in the central nervous system from which serotonergic fibers project are largely concentrated in the raphe nuclei of the brain. Raphe lesions, whether electrolytic or produced by a selective serotonergic neurotoxin, 5,7-dihydroxytryptamine, analogous to 6-OHDA, cause marked reduction in CNS serotonin and are associated with enhanced irritability and intraspecific aggression in rats (Kostowski et al., 1975; Paxinos and Atrens, 1977). Conversely, raphe stimulation, which augments serotonin release, has been shown to inhibit affective attack elicited in cats by stimulation of hypothalamic sites (Sheard, 1974). There is also evidence that the brain concentration and turnover of serotonin is higher in tame, domesticated foxes than in relatively wild, aggressive age-matched controls (Popova et al., 1976), though the causal relationship, if one exists, remains to be clarified.

The effects of PCPA treatment on shock-elicited aggression have been variable. While in several studies, no difference has been observed between PCPA-treated and control rats (Conner et al., 1970; Eichelman and Thoa, 1973; McLain et al., 1974), in others, treated rats have been found to be more aggressive (Ellison and Bresler, 1974; Sheard, 1977). The discrepancy may be due to methodological issues such as the length of the interval between periodic shocks (Sheard, 1977), the intensity of the shock delivered, the natural docility of the subjects used, and the extensiveness of serotonin depletion produced. Moreover, an important limitation of PCPA is its ability to effect a mild reduction in brain catecholamines as well as a much greater depletion of serotonin (Peters et al., 1972); hence, treatment may have a combination of inhibitory and facilitory consequences, if, in fact, catecholaminergic activity promotes affective aggression in response to shock while serotonergic activity tends to suppress it. Para-choloramphetamine (PCA), another agent that depletes brain serotonin, is more selective and enduring in its impact than PCPA and involves a transient period of serotonin release, followed by prolonged serotonin reduction (Sanders-Bush and Massari, 1977). Compatible with this sequence of biochemical events and the hypothesis that serotonin exerts an inhibitory influence over affective aggression is the biphasic response described by Sheard and Davis (1976); PCA treated rats present a short-term reduction in shock-elicited aggression followed by a long-term increase. At low doses, the indoleamine hallucinogen d-lysergic acid diethylamide (LSD) inhibits the firing rate of presynaptic serotonergic neurons in the raphe nuclei and decreases serotonin release (Gallager and Aghajanian, 1975); whereas at higher doses it mimics serotonin at postsynaptic receptors (Haigler and Aghajanian, 1974). When administered in small amounts, LSD potentiates shock-elicited aggression in rats; whereas at higher doses, the increased aggression associated with low doses is no longer observed (Sheard et al., 1977). More directly, when delivered to amygdaloid sites through brain cannulae, methysergide, a serotonin antagonist, produces a significant elevation in shock-elicited aggression, whereas serotonin produces a significant decrease (Rodgers, 1977). Considerable increases in shock-elicited aggression have also followed permanent and directed serotonin-depleting lesions, whether electrolytic (Jacobs and Cohen, 1976) or pharmacologic using the neurotoxin 5,7-dihydroxytryptamine (Hole et al., 1977).

In addition to its facilitory impact on the kinds of affective aggression assessed, disruption of serotonergic transmission is reliably associated with greater predatory aggression as well; it remains to be seen whether these effects should be regarded as distinct. Induction of, or a significant rise in, muricidal behavior in the rat or rat-killing in the cat has been observed after PCPA treatment (DiChiara et al., 1971; Ferguson et al., 1970; MacDonnell et al., 1971; McLain et al., 1974; Miczek et al., 1975; Paxinos et al., 1977; Sheard, 1969); after PCA (Sheard 1976); after pharmacological destruction of serotonergic systems with 5,7-dihydroxytryptamine, or the similar agent 5,6-dihydroxytryptamine, (Breese et al., 1974; Breese and Cooper, 1975; Hole et al., 1977; Marks et al., 1977; Paxinos and Atrens, 1977); and after electrolytic serotonin depleting lesions of the raphe nuclei (Grant et al., 1973; Vergnes et al., 1973; Vergnes et al., 1974). In one study, electrolytically produced raphe lesions heralded an increase in affective aggression but none in muricide (Kostowski et al., 1975). However, a small but significant elevation in brain norepinephrine was found upon assay and may have mitigated against the expression of predatory behavior. In contrast to serotonin depletion, augmentation of serotonin activity, either through administration of the serotonin precursor 5-hydroxytryptamine (5-HTP), or stimulation of the raphe nuclei, coincides with a reduction in predatory aggression (Kulkarni, 1968; Sheard, 1974).

Given the diversity of research methods which have been applied, the data are remarkably consistent in their support of a general inhibitory role for serotonin in affective and predatory aggression. Nevertheless, although aggressive behavior is far more probable in the animal in whom serotonergic function has been diminished, there were animal subjects in virtually all studies whose aggressiveness was evidently unaffected by treatment. Certainly, many biological and behavioral variables are involved in the regulation of aggression. Among these is the reciprocal interplay between different neurochemical systems which are functionally interrelated. Lycke et al. (1969) have studied mice infected with herpes simplex virus (HSV) encephalitis which leads to increased dopaminergic and serotonergic synthesis in affected animals. Untreated HSV mice manifest behavioral excitation but little aggression. When serotonin is depleted with a PCPA analogue, however, HSV produced intense fighting and irritability. Similarly, in previously normal animals, the combined regimen of serotonin depletion and dopa administration results in aggressive behavior which is markedly more pronounced than that associated with either treatment individually (Benkert et al., 1973; Lycke et al., 1969; Ozawa et al., 1975). These studies indicate that a predisposition to affective aggressive behavior is bolstered when reduced serotonergic transmission is coupled to greater catecholaminergic transmission, presumably strengthening the preponderance of facilitory over inhibitory influences. The obvious corollary is that increased serotonergic activity together with decreased catecholaminergic activity might have the opposite effect, namely a reinforcement of inhibition. In agreement with these hypotheses are the findings of Lagerspetz et al. (1968), who have examined the 13th and 14th generations of two strains of mice selectively bred for a tendency toward aggressive or non-aggressive behavior. The aggressive strain was found to have brain stem norepinephrine concentrations 11% higher than that of non-aggressive controls, while forebrain serotonin concentrations were 19% lower. Likewise, Bernard and Paolino (1974) have reported that the taming effect of castration on male rats, ensuing over a several-week period, parallels the development of reduced brain catecholamine/serotonin ratios in castrated animals when compared with controls, perhaps a mediating factor between hormonal alteration and behavioral change. Examination of the major CNS metabolites of serotonin, norepinephrine and dopamine— 5-HIAA, MHPG, and HVA respectively—in the cerebrospinal fluid of young adult male patients hospitalized with personality disorders has provided preliminary evidence that catecholamine/serotonin ratios may be important in the predisposition to abnormal aggressive behavior not only in infrahuman animals but in man as well (Brown et al., 1979). Within the group studied, aggression scores based upon the history of aggressive behavior of each individual showed a significant negative correlation with 5-HIAA levels and a significant positive correlation with MHPG and with the ratio of MHPG to 5-HIAA. A history of suicide attempts was also related to transmitter metabolites in this manner. That low 5-HIAA and high MHPG values in CSF are associated with a tendency toward aggression in man must be cautiously regarded as a tentative rather than established conclusion. However, its plausability is strengthened by the animal studies described above. Also of note are the reasonably selective anti-aggressive effects of lithium which have been demonstrated in several animal models of aggression and, more crucially, in aggressive behavior in human populations including prison inmates and psychiatric patients (Sheard, 1978). Among the putative biochemical effects lithium exerts on the central nervous system are a decrease in the availability of norepinephrine to postsynaptic receptors and a short-term increase in serotonin synthesis possibly followed by subsequent reequilibration (Gerbino et al., 1978). In view of the foregoing, these neurochemical modifications may be relevant to the efficacy of lithium in the treatment of pathological aggression.

Acetylcholine and Aggression

Although a role for brain acetylcholine in aggressive behavior was indicated as early as 1963 (Allikmets, 1974), the want, until recently, of feasible, sensitive assay techniques for the measurement and localization of CNS acetylcholine (Cooper et al., 1978) together with the absence of cholinergic selective neurotoxins analogous to 6-hydroxydopamine and 5,7-dihydroxytryptamine have limited the range of methodologies available for study in this area. Research has relied heavily upon pharmacological agents such as the anticholinergics, which block either of the two known subclasses of acetylcholine receptor (muscarinic or nicotinic) and therefore reduce transmission; the anticholinesterases which do the converse by inhibiting or inactivating cholinesterases, the enzymes responsible for acetylcholine degradation, and thereby increasing the functional availability of acetylcholine at the synapse; and the cholinomimetics, which mimic acetylcholine at receptor sites and therefore also potentiate transmission. Direct application of acetylcholine to brain sites has had extensive use as well.

Numerous investigators have elicited affective aggressive behavior in rat and cat by cholinergic stimulation at a variety of brain regions including amygdala, septum, hippocampus, hypothalamus, and mesencephalon, using acetylcholine, the cholinomimetic carbachol, or the anticholinesterase physostigmine; behaviors observed include vocal and postural displays of threat, rage, irritability, autonomic arousal, and intraspecific attack (Allikmets, 1974; Baxter, 1967; Dickinson and Levitt, 1977; Grossman, 1963; Hernandez-Peon et al., 1963; Hull et al., 1967; Igic et al., 1970; Myers, 1964). Although cholinergic stimulation of certain brain regions leads to behavioral suppression (Allikmets, 1974), the results of systemic administration of cholinergic compounds, which ensures wide distribution in the brain, indicate that diffuse stimulation of cholinergic systems exerts an overall facilitory influence on affective aggression. The systemic injection of the cholinomimetic arecoline, during which effects on the peripheral nervous system are simultaneously controlled for, produces rage and affective attack in cats (Katz, 1976). Similarly, systemic pre-treatment with the anticholinesterase physostigmine fosters the affective aggressive behavior elicited by hypothalamic stimulation in cats; while pre-treatment with anticholinergics which block primarily muscarinic acetylcholine receptors results in inhibition of aggression. Anticholinergics which block only nicotinic receptors, however, are ineffective as inhibitors of aggression, suggesting the possible primacy of muscarinic systems in these behaviors (Allikmets, 1974).

Few studies have investigated potential cholinergic involvement in affective aggression elicited by foot-shock. The muscarinic anticholinergic scopolamine, appears to decrease shock-elicited fighting, whereas a scopolamine derivative which acts principally on the peripheral rather than central nervous system is ineffective (Powell et al., 1973). Muscarinic blockade in the basolateral amygdala is also followed by significant reduction in shock-elicited aggression, whereas increased fighting follows cholinergic stimulation with physostigmine; in both cases, pain sensitivity threshholds were tested and no change was observed with treatment (Rodgers and Brown, 1976). These findings, though they warrant replication, lend further support to a facilitory role for central cholinergic systems in affective aggression.

Much attention has been directed to cholinergic mechanisms in predatory aggression. Cholinergic stimulation of lateral hypothalamic sites with acetylcholine, acetylcholinesterases, or cholinomimetics, has augmented stereotyped frog-killing and muricidal behavior in killer rats (Bandler, 1970) and has induced muricide in natural non-killers (Dickinson and Levitt, 1977; Smith et al., 1970). Application of the anticholinesterase amitone to septal and amygdaloid regions has also produced rat muricide (Igic et al., 1970). Repeated systemic injections of the muscarinic cholinomimetic, pilocarpine, have been effective, as well, in eliciting rat muricide in previous non-killers (Gay et al., 1976; McCarthy, 1966; Vogel and Leaf, 1972; Wnek and Leaf, 1973). Similarly, predatory attack in cats has been observed after systemic treatment with the muscarinic cholinomimetics, oxotremorine and arecoline (Berntson and Leibowitz, 1973; Katz, 1976). Central muscarinic blockers, on the other hand, reduce predatory aggression, both when aggression is spontaneous or induced by hypothalamic, septal, amygdaloid, or systemic drug regimens, and when it is elicited in cats by electrical brain stimulation (Katz and Thomas, 1975) and in rats by prolonged isolation (Yoshimura and Ueki, 1977) or lesioning of the olfactory bulbs (Malick, 1976). Consistent with these data, although not well established, evidence of increased concentrations of acetylcholine and its biosynthetic enzyme, choline acetyltransferase, has been found in certain brain regions in muricidal rats, possibly reflecting greater cholinergic activation in these animals (Ebel et al., 1973; Yoshimura and Ueki, 1977). It is worth noting that, although some investigators have observed well-defined and patterned predatory attack following cholinergic stimulation (e.g. Bandler, 1970; Berntson and Leibowitz, 1973), others report a combination of inter- and intraspecific aggression as well as affective aggressive displays (e.g. Dickinson and Levitt, 1977; Katz, 1976; Wnek and Leaf, 1973). Thus while enhanced cholinergic transmission is persuasively associated with increases in both affective and predatory aggressive behaviors, it is not yet clear whether or not these effects arise independently and whether each is behaviorally uncontaminated by the other.

Finally, aggression elicited or enhanced by cholinergic stimulation is sensitive to the activity of other neuroregulatory systems, underscoring, again, the importance of neurochemical interplay in the balance between inhibitory and facilitory influences. Rat muricide induced by pilocarpine treatment is suppressed substantially by amphetamine (Gay et al., 1976; Vogel and Leaf, 1972) presumably through a catecholamine-mediated inhibition of predatory behavior. The serotonin precursor tryptophan also reduces aggression of cholinergic origin, while the serotonergic antagonist methysergide aggravates these behaviors (Allikmets, 1974). The potency of many antidepressants in the inhibition of predatory aggression may well be due to a synergistic coalition of the pro-catecholaminergic, pro-serotonergic, and anti-cholinergic effects they often entail.

Additional Avenues of Study

Clearly, no single neuroregulatory system monopolizes control over an animal's proclivity to aggressive behaviors or the intensity of those behaviors when they occur. It is now evident that aggressive behaviors are affected in a significant way by alterations in any one of several systems and by interactions between them. Augmentation of CNS acetylcholine transmission is often followed by considerable increases in both affective and predatory aggression, while attenuation of transmission is associated with reduction in these activities. The converse pattern holds for serotonergic involvement in aggression. Enhanced catecholamine transmission may exert a facilitory impact on affective aggression, while inhibiting predatory aggression; though several anomalous findings deserve pursuit and may indicate that catecholaminergic effects are heterogenous or quite indirect. There is no reason to suspect that these, the most well studied CNS neuroregulators to date, exhaust the list of neurochemicals relevant to aggression in higher animals. A small number of studies suggest that changes in aggressive behavior may also coincide with alterations in the central neuronal activity of glutamic acid (Brody et al., 1969), gamma-aminobutyric acid (GABA) (Earley and Leonard, 1977), and histamine (Avis, 1974). The endogenous opioid peptides may also have a role in the modulation of aggression in view of their putative involvement in pain response, mood, and social attachment (Herman and Panksepp, 1978; Verebey et al., 1978). Study is being devoted to neurochemical changes at the postsynaptic level as well. Preliminary evidence indicates a correlation between aggressiveness and brain concentrations of cyclic AMP, the so-called second messenger which translates and amplifies receptor stimulation into postsynaptic events (Eichelman et al., 1976; Orenberg et al., 1975). Neurochemicals less fully explored or as yet undiscovered may also participate in the mediation of aggressive behavior.

That aggressive behaviors come under the influence of multiple neurochemical systems is not surprising since these behaviors involve complex, coordinated responses and are expressed as one aspect of a larger constellation of behaviors and psychophysiological states. Because pathological aggression associated with hypersexuality, for example, may have a different basis than that associated with a depressive condition or with chronic general over-arousal, it is imperative to define the context in which aggression arises to a greater extent than has often been the case, in order to arrive at a comprehensive biological and behavioral profile. Physiological parameters in animals whose aggressive behavior has been modified through neurochemical intervention deserve study. These include endocrine status, heart rate, blood pressure, and sleep and ingestive functions. The topography of social transactions among these animals also merits description, not only with regard to aggressive encounters but also parent-offspring interactions, sexual activity, pro-social or cooperative behaviors, and other forms of social contact. Additional behaviors of relevance are response to frustration, reactivity to aversive and non-aversive stimuli, motor activity, learning and habituation, as well as fearfulness, arousal, and depression, central variables whose assessment in animal models is problematic but not necessarily impossible. Long-term developmental phenomena attending modifications in neurochemical functioning which affect aggressive behaviors have been left virtually unexamined. Investigation of the ontogeny of aggression throughout life following neurochemical alteration in an immature animal can furnish a critical view of the impact of a neurochemical dysfunction meshing with normal and compensatory developmental changes as it does in nature if not always in short-term laboratory studies.

The combination of greater depth and greater breadth in the neurochemical study of aggressive behavior will, of course, provide the basis for more accurate conclusions and the possibility of meaningful extrapolation. More broadly, however, the behavioral neurochemical perspective is but one among a number of important vantage points from which aggressive behavior may be examined. These include other biomedical disciplines as well as ethology, anthropology, sociology, and psychology, each with distinctive insights and methods of inquiry which can shed light on the issues under consideration and which can discern issues previously unrecognized. Apart from its alliance with contributions from fields such as these, a neurochemical understanding of aggression is essentially incomplete.

Human Investigation

Advances in biological psychiatry have permitted studies of major neurotransmitter enzymes, substrates, and metabolites in various human disorders (Cohen and Young, 1977). As with studies of the attention-deficit syndromes described earlier, the extrapolation from animal to human investigations, and the other way, must be extremely cautious in relation to disorders involving inhibition and the regulation of aggression.

As an example of possible cross-referencing between animal and clinical research, the syndrome of chronic multiple tics of Gilles de la Tourette may be especially interesting. Tourette's syndrome (TS) is a neuropsychiatric disorder that emerges between ages 3 and 14 years and may persist throughout life (Shapiro et al., 1978). It is characterized by a spectrum of disturbances in behavioral regulation: motor tics (twitching, jerking movements), phonic symptoms (echolalia, palilalia, coprolalia), compulsive or stereotypic actions (hopping, snapping, touching), and impairment in concentration, attention, and academic learning. Personality difficulties may reflect the underlying neurophysiological disorder or follow upon the embarrassment and social difficulties of the disorder. Phenomenologically, the dysfunction in TS may be understood as a pervasive disturbance involving mechanisms of inhibition. Motor impulses, thoughts, and wishes, sometimes of an aggressive or sexual nature, which usually remain subliminal, inhibited, or otherwise muted in normal individuals become expressed in the action and consciousness of TS patients. The aggressive impulses may be expressed in actions against the patient's own body (biting, pinching, scratching), or against others, usually in the form of verbal outbursts of temper, but sometimes in physical action.

A dopaminergic basis for TS has been postulated on several grounds. There is some similarity between the stereotypic behavior in TS and the stereotypy produced in animals treated with dopamine agonists; for example, rats given high doses of amphetamine may lick, rear, sniff, gnaw, bob their heads restlessly, and engage in numerous other types of repetitive, non-goal-directed activity. Second, medications which inhibit amphetamine-induced stereotypy and dopaminergic overactivity in animals may be therapeutically very helpful in TS. Over 40% of patients with TS respond benefically to haloperidol, a potent inhibitor of dopaminergic activity. Finally, medications which augment catecholaminergic activity, such as amphetamine, exacerbate the symptoms of TS patients. Noradrenergic mechanisms may also play a role in TS, since some patients who are unresponsive or poorly responsive to haloperidol have had remarkable therapeutic improvement with clonidine, the central inhibitor of noradrenergic activity discussed previously (Cohen et al., 1979b).

Studies of CSF acid monoamine metabolites have led to new findings about the pathophysiology of TS. TS patients appear to have reductions in both the major metabolite of dopamine (HVA) and serotonin (5-HIAA). Several alternative hypotheses have been suggested for these results. If dopamine receptor supersensitivity is related to the clinical and pharmacological evidence of dopaminergic overactivity, the reduced CSF HVA might then represent the result of neuronal feedback inhibition of presynaptic dopamine activity. A similar inhibitory feedback may result in the reduction of the serotonin metabolite. However, it is also possible that the reduced CSF 5-HIAA reflects inadequate mobilization of serotonergic mechanisms. Clearly, considerably more research will be required to analyze the various pathways that might lead to similar CSF findings. It is of interest, however, that reduced CSF 5-HIAA has been associated with other disorders involving the regulation of mood and behavioral inhibition. There is a subgroup of depressed adults with lowered levels of CSF 5-HIAA (as reviewed by Garver and Davis, 1979) and a subgroup of autistic children with more severe symptomatology with relatively lower CSF 5-HIAA (Cohen et al., 1979a). As cited earlier, preliminary reports have suggested that in some adults, aggressive behavior may also be associated with reduced CSF 5-HIAA (Brown, et al., 1979).

The clarity of the symptomatology in TS and the response of the disorder to pharmacological intervention, as well as the preliminary findings of altered neurotransmitter metabolites in CSF, make TS a useful model for correlating brain mechanisms with complex mechanisms of behavioral regulation. The neurochemical model that has emerged from the animal studies may be held up against the clinical and biological findings, with each domain of research offering new suggestions and alternative explanations that may enrich the other. The possibility of studying similar neurochemical systems in various species of animals and in various human disorders offers a bridge between otherwise quite distinctive areas of investigation.

Conclusion

Although most of the studies considered in this chapter have involved infrahuman animal subjects, restricting the kinds of inferences that can be made, several themes have emerged which undoubtedly bear on neurochemical dysfunction and human behavior. (1) The synapse is the functional focal point of communication between neurons, the predominant language of which is neurochemical. Synaptic transmission involves a series of steps including precursor uptake, transmitter synthesis, storage, release, receptor interaction, reuptake, and catabolism. Alterations in neurotransmission may be introduced at any point in this sequence of events, as well as in the coupling of receptor stimulation to postsynaptic response or in the multiple control mechanisms by which these processes are regulated. (2) Although neurochemical functioning is under partial genetic control, it retains considerable plasticity throughout life. It is susceptible to modification by drugs, toxins, viruses, structural brain damage, early insults such as hypoxia and undernutrition, and even autoimmune reactions. It is responsive to stress, social experience, and hormonal variables, and undergoes changes during development and aging. When these alterations have a significant impact on central nervous system activity, they are reflected in changes in physiological status, overt behavior, mood, and cognition, which, in turn, may exert a reciprocal influence on subsequent neurochemical processes. CNS neurochemistry is thus a nexus upon which heredity, experience, and behavior converge. (3) In neurochemical dysfunction, homeostatic mechanisms that act to oppose disruption are of central importance. Seeking to restore equilibrium, they marshall such various means as compensations in receptor sensitivity, in the rate of transmitter synthesis, and in the rapidity of transmitter inactivation. One possible neurochemical conception of vulnerability or predisposition to a behavioral disorder that may, therefore, be proposed involves the notion of a defect in neurotransmission which is subclinical by virtue of the adaptive adjustments which have been made in response to it. Only when stretched beyond the limits of homeostatic capacity by changes due, for example, to stress and maturational processes affecting the impaired system, does the defect assume clinical significance, unmasked by the failure of compensatory mechanisms to counterbalance the additional load. (4) Although the goal in neurochemical research is often to identify the individual contributions of neuroregulatory systems, recognition is increasingly being given to the extensive interplay between systems in influencing behavior. Another hypothetical model of vulnerability, therefore, might direct attention to a neuroregulatory system whose own activities are intact but have become engaged in offsetting a defect in a companion system. In so doing it may become locked into an extreme level of functioning, sacrificing, in the name of compensation, the resiliency it once had with respect to environmental change. In this case, not the defect itself but the biological response it provokes in another system is the potential proximal cause of pathology. Especially inappropriate behavior may become noticeable when acute external contingencies call for behaviors which rely on greater responsiveness from the overextended system than it is capable of attaining; or, on other other hand, if the original disruption in function is removed, as in the case of opiate withdrawal, and the adaptive response, having lost its *raison d'etre*, is no longer subserving an equilibrium but rather is the new source of imbalance. Alternatively, a primary defect in neurotransmission may, by itself, be virtually inconsequential, requiring but minimal homeostatic effort to prevent behavioral manifestations. However, subsequently acquired dysfunction in an interrelated system might become a precipitating cause for the expression of behavioral disturbance by further disrupting a CNS control network in which they are jointly involved. (5) A selective perturbation in a neurotransmitter system, as in dopamine depletion, may have ramifications in a great diversity of ostensibly unrelated behaviors, producing a constellation of deficits rather than a single, specific disturbance. Symptomatology which is evidently diffuse does not, therefore, rule out a highly specific etiology. Conversely, what is often regarded as a single behavioral entity, such as affective aggression, may be rooted in disruption in any one of several neurotransmitter systems which enter at various levels of behavioral organization; some primarily affect the modulation of mood or motivational states, others, sensorimotor competence or cognitive functions. (6) Finally, the factors which influence behavior are no less complex nor variegated than the behaviors they influence. Neurochemical factors take their place as one among many variables which must be consulted in formulating explanations about behavior.

Fruitful advance in the understanding of neurochemistry and behavioral disorders in childhood, adolescence, and beyond requires imaginative transitions. The scientific focus must range from molecular events at the synapse to cellular and multicellular activity to fragments of animal behavior isolated for refined analysis to aspects of human behavior, phenomenology, and disease and to influential psycho-social dynamics with which neurochemical dysfunction is enmeshed throughout development. Through the close collaboration of researchers and clinicians in a community of interrelated fields, speculation is gradually giving way to an established body of knowledge.

ACKNOWLEDGMENTS

We thank Ms. Margrethe Cone for editorial assistance. These studies were supported in part by the NIMH Mental Health Clinical Research Center grant #1 P50 MH30929, Children's Clinical Research Center grant RR00125, NIH grant HD 03008, the Hood Foundation, the Nutrition Foundation, Mr. Leonard Berger, The Ford Foundation, and The Solomon R. & Rebecca D. Baker Foundation, Inc.

For reprints: Donald J. Cohen, M.D., Child Study Center, 333 Cedar Street, New Haven, Connecticut 06510.

REFERENCES

Aghajanian, G. K. (1978). Tolerance of locus coeruleus neurones to morphine and suppressiion of withdrawal response by clonidine. *Nature*, 276(5684):186–188.

Ahlenius, S., Engel, J., Hard, E., Larsson, K., Lundborg, P., and Sinnerstedt, P. (1977). Open field behavior and gross motor development in offspring of nursing rat mothers given penfluridol. *Pharmacol. Biochem. Behav.*, 6:343–347.

Ahlenius, S., Engel, J., and Lundborg, P., (1975). Antagonism by d-Amphetamine of learning deficits in rats induced by exposure to antipsychotic drugs during early postnatal life. *Naunyn-Schmiedeberg's Arch. Pharmacol.*, 288:185–193.

Albert, D. J., and Richmond, S. E. (1977). Reactivity and aggression in the rat: Induction by α-adrenergic blocking agents injected ventral to anterior septum but not into lateral septum. *J. Comp. Physiol. Psychol.*, 91:886-896.

Allen, R. P., Safer, D., and Covi, L. (1975). Effects of psychostimulants on aggression. *J. Nerv. Ment. Dis.*, 160:138–145.

Allikmets, L. H. (1974), Cholinergic mechanisms in aggressive behavior. *Med. Biol.*, 52:19-30.

Antelman, S. M., and Caggiula, A. R. (1977). Norepinephrine-dopamine interactions and behavior. *Science*, 195:646–653.

Archer, J. (1973), Tests for emotionality in rats and mice: A review. *Animal Behav.*, 21:205–235.

Arnold, L. E., Christopher, J., Huestis, R., and Smeltzer, D. J. (1978). Methylphenidate vs. dextroamphetamine vs. caffeine in minimal brain dysfunction. *Arch. Gen. Psychiat.*, 35: 463–473.

Avis, H. H. (1974). The neuropharmacology of aggression: A critical review. *Psychol. Bull.*, 81:47–63.

Axelrod, J. (1974). Neurotransmitters. *Sci. Am.*, 230(6): 59–67.

Bandler, R. J. (1970). Cholinergic synapses in the lateral hypothalamus for the control of predatory aggression in the rat. *Brain Res.*, 20:409–424.

Bandler, R. J., and Moyer, K. E. (1970). Animals spontaneously attacked by rats. *Commun. Behav. Biol.*, 5:177–182.

Barchas, J. D., Akil, H., Elliot, G. R., Holman, R. B., and Watson, S. J. (1978). Behavioral neurochemistry: Neuroregulators and behavioral states. *Science*, 200:964–973.

Barkley, R. A. (1977). A review of stimulant drug research with hyperactive children. *J. Child Psychol. Psychiat.*, 18:137–165.

Barnett, S. A. (1975). *The Rat: A Study in Behavior.* Chicago: University of Chicago Press.

Barr, G. A., Moyer, K. E., and Gibbons, J. L. (1976). Effects of imipramine, d-amphetamine and tripelennamine on mouse and frog killing by the rat. *Physiol. Behav.*, 16:267–269.

Bareggi, S. R., Becker, R. E., Ginsburg, B. E., and Genovese, E. (1979). Neurochemical investigation of an endogenous model of the "hyperkinetic syndrome" in a hybrid dog. *Life Sci.*, 24:481–488.

Baxter, B. L. (1967). Comparison of the behavioral effects of electrical or chemical stimulation applied at the same brain loci. *Exp. Neurol.*, 19:412–432.

Bell, R. Q. (1971). Stimulus control of parent or caretaker behavior by offspring. *Dev. Psychol.*, 4:63–72.

Benkert, O., Renz, A., and Matussek, N. (1973). Dopamine, noradrenaline and 5-hydroxytryptamine in relation to motor activity, fighting, and mounting behaviour, *Neuropharm.*, 12:187–193.

Bernard, B. K. and Paolino, R. M. (1974). Time-dependent changes in brain biogenic amine dynamics following castration in male rats. *J. Neurochem.*, 22:951–956.

Bernard, P., Welch, J., Emberley, J., and Fielding, S. (1974). The behavioral effects of morphine in rats with septal and hypothalamic lesions. In *Drug Addiction*, Vol. 3, J. M. Singh and H. Lal, (eds.). Miami: Symposia Specialists, pp. 297–307.

Berntson, G. G., and Leibowitz, S. F. (1973). Biting attack in cats: Evidence for central muscarinic mediation. *Brain Res.*, 51:366–370.

Brain, P. and Benton, D. (1979). The interpretation of physiological correlates of differential housing in laboratory rats. *Life Sci.*, 24:99–116.

Breese, G. R. (1975). Chemical and immunochemical lesions by specific neurotoxic substances and antisera. In: *Handbook of Psychopharmacology*, Vol. 1, L. L. Iversen, S. D. Iversen, and S. H. Snyder, (eds.). New York: Plenum Publishing, pp. 137–189.

Breese, G. R., and Cooper, B. R. (1975). Behavioral and biochemical interactions of 5,7-dihydroxytryptamine with various drugs when administered intracisternally to adult and developing rats. *Brain Res.*, 98:517–527.

Breese, G. R., Cooper, B. R., Grant, L. D., and Smith, R. D. (1974). Biochemical and behavioral alterations following 5,6-dihydroxytryptamine administration into brain. *Neuropharm.*, 13:177–187.

Brody, J. F., DeFeudis, P. A., and DeFeudis, F. V. (1969). Effects of microinjections of L-glutamate into the hypothalamus on attack and fight behaviour in cats. *Nature*, 224:1330.

Bronstein, P. M., Neiman, H., Wolkoff, F. D., and Levine, M. J. (1974). The development of habituation in the rat. *Animal Learn. and Behav.*, 2:92–96.

Brown, G. L., Ballanger, J. C., Minichiello, M. D., and Goodwin, F. K. (1979). Human aggression and its relationship to cerebrospinal fluid 5-hydroxy-indoleacetic acid, 3-methoxy-4-hydroxy-phenyl-glycol, and homovanillic acid. In: *Psychopharmacology of Aggression*, M. Sandler, (ed.). New York: Raven, pp. 131–148.

Campbell, B. A., Lytle, L. D., and Fibiger, H. C. (1969). Ontogeny of adrenergic arousal and cholinergic inhibitory mechanisms in the rat. *Science*, 166:637–638.

Campbell, B. A., and Mabry, P. D. (1973). The role of catecholamines in behavioral arousal during ontogenesis. *Psychopharmacol.* 31:253–264.

Campbell, B. A. and Randall, P. K. (1975). Paradoxical effects of amphetamine on behavioral arousal in neonatal and adult rats. In: *Aberrant Development in Infancy*, N. R. Ellis, (ed.): Hillsdale, N. Y.: Earlbaum Association, pp. 105–112.

Campbell, B. A., and Raskin, L. A. (1978). Ontogeny of behavioral arousal: The role of environmental stimuli. *JCPP*, 92:176–184.

Cantwell, D. P. (1972). Psychiatric illness in the families of hyperactive children. *Arch. Gen. Psychiat.*, 27:414–417.

Cantwell, D. P. (ed.) (1975a). *The Hyperactive Child*. New York: Spectrum.

Cantwell, D. P. (1975b). Genetic studies of hyperactive children. Psychiatric illness in biological and adopting parents. In: *Genetic Research in Psychiatry*, R. R. Fieve, D. Rosenthal, and H. Brill (eds.). Baltimore: Johns Hopkins University Press, pp. 273–280.

Cantwell, D. P. (1978). Hyperactivity and antisocial behavior. *J. Am. Acad. Child Psychiat.*, 17:252–262.

Carlton, P. L., and Advokat, C. (1973). Attenuated habituation due to parachlorophenylalanine. *Pharmacol. Biochem. Behav.*, 1:657–663.

Carter, C. J., and Pycock, C. J. (1980). Behavioural and biochemical effects of dopamine and noradrenaline depletion within the medial prefrontal cortex of the rat. *Brain Res.*, 192:163–176.

Chi, C. C., and Flynn, J. P. (1971). Neuroanatomical projections related to biting attack elicited from hypothalamus in cats. *Brain Res.*, 35:49–66.

Cohen, D. J., Shaywitz, B. A., Caparulo, B., Young, J. G., and Bowers, M. B., Jr. (1978). Chronic, multiple tics of Gilles de la Tourette's disease. *Arch. Gen. Psychiat.*, 35:245–250.

Cohen, D. J., Shaywitz, B. A., Young, J. G., and Bowers, M. B., Jr. (1980). Cerebrospinal fluid monoamine metabolites in neuropsychiatric disorders of childhood. In: *Neurobiology of Cerebrospinal Fluid*, J. Wood, (ed.). New York: Plenum Press, pp. 665–683.

Cohen, D. J., Shaywitz, B. A., Young, J. G., Carbonari, C. M., Nathanson, J. A., Lieberman, D., Bowers, M. B., Jr., and Maas, J. W. (1979a). Central biogenic amine metabolism in children with the syndrome of chronic multiple tics of Gilles de la Tourette. *J. Am. Acad. Child Psychiat.*, 18:320–341.

Cohen, D. J. and Young, J. G. (1977). Neurochemistry and child psychiatry. *J. Am. Acad. Child Psychiat.*, 16:353–411.

Cohen, D. J., Young, J. G., Nathanson, J. A., and Shaywitz, B. A. (1979b). Clonidine in Tourette's syndrome. *Lancet*, September 15, 1979:551–553.

Cohen, M., Felig, E., and Shaywitz, D. (1979). Mothering behavior of mice: Genetic and pharmacological effects. In preparation.

Conner, R. L., Stolk, J. M., Barchas, J. D., Dement, W. C., and Levine, S. (1970). Effects of PCPA on shock-induced fighting behaviour in rats. *Physiol. Behav.*, 5:1221–1224.

Cooper, J. R., Bloom, F. E., and Roth, R. H. (1978). *The Biochemical Basis of Neuropharmacology*. New York: Oxford University Press.

Copenhaver, J. H., Schalock, R. L., and Carver, M. J. (1978). Para-chloro-D,L-phenylalanine induced filicidal behavior in the female rat. *Pharmacol. Biochem. Behav.*, 8:263–270.

Coscina, D. V., Seggie, J., Godse, D. D., and Stancer, H. C. (1973). Induction of rage in rats by central injection of 6-hydroxydopamine. *Pharmacol. Biochem. Behav.*, 1:1–6.

Crowley, T. J. (1972). Dose-dependent facilitation or suppression of rat fighting by methamphetamine, phenobarbital, or imipramine. *Psychopharmacol.* 27:213–222.

Culver, B. and Norton, S. (1976). Juvenile hyperactivity in rats after acute exposure to carbon monoxide. *Exp. Neurol.*, 50:80-98.

Curzon, C. and Marsden, C. A. (1976). Effects of p-chlorophenyl-alanine and α-methyltryptophan on rat social behavior. *Brit. J. Pharmacol.*, 58:455P-456P.

Dalhouse, A. D. (1976). Social cohesiveness, hypersexuality and irritability induced by p-CPA in the rat. *Physiol. Behav.*, 17:679–686.

DaVanzo, J. P., Daugherty, M., Ruckart, R., and Kang, L. (1966). Pharmacological and biochemical studies in isolation-induced fighting mice. *Psychopharmacol.*, 9:210–219.

Davis, W. M., and Khalsa, J. H. (1971). Increased shock-induced aggression during morphine withdrawal. *Life Sci.*, 10 (Part 1): 1321–1327.

Delacour, J., Echavarria, M. T., Senault, B., and Houcine, O. (1977). Specifity of avoidance deficits produced by 6-hydroxy-dopamine lesions of the nigrostriatal system of the rat. *JCPP*, 91:875–885.

DiChiara, G., Camba, R., and Spano, P. F. (1971). Evidence for inhibition by brain serotonin of mouse-killing behaviour in rats. *Nature*, 233:272–273.

Dickinson, W. A. and Levitt, R. A. (1977). Carbachol-elicited mouse-killing in the rat: Animals attacked and wound location. *Physiol. Psychol.*, 5:239–242.

Dodge, P. R., Prensky, A. L., and Feigen, R. D. (1975). *Nutrition and the Developing Nervous System*. St. Louis: C. V. Mosby.

Domino, E. F., Dren, A. T., and Giardina, W. J. (1978). Biochemical and neurotransmitter changes in the aging brain. In: *Psychopharmacology: A Generation of Progress*, M. A. Lipton, A. DiMascio, and K. F. Killam, (eds.): New York: Raven Press, pp. 1507–1515.

Drachman, D. B. (1978). Myasthenia gravis. *N. Eng. J. Med.*, 298:136–142.

Dubinsky, B., and Goldberg, M. E. (1971). The effect of imipramine and selected drugs on attack elicited by hypothalamic stimulation in the cat. *Neuropharmacol.*, 10:537–545.

Earley, C. J., and Leonard, B. E. (1977). The effect of testosterone and cyproterone acetate on the concentration of γ-amino-butyric acid in brain areas of aggressive and non-aggressive mice. *Pharmacol. Biochem. Behav.*, 6:409–413.

Eastgate, S. M., Wright, J. J., and Werry, J. S. (1978). Behavioural effects of methylphenidate in 6-hydroxydopamine-treated neonatal rats. *Psychopharmacol.*, 58:157–159.

Ebel, A., Mack, G., Stefanovic, V., and Mandel, P. (1973). Activity of choline acetyltransferase and acetylcholinesterase in the amygdala of spontaneous mouse-killer rats and in rats after olfactory lobe removal. *Brain Res.*, 57:248–251.

Eichelman, B. (1973). The catecholamines and aggressive behavior, *Neurosci. Res.*, 5:109–129.

Eichelman, B., and Barchas, J. D. (1975). Facilitated shock-induced aggression following antidepressive medication in the rat. *Pharmacol. Biochem. Behav.*, 3:601–604.

Eichelman, B., Orenberg, E., Seagraves, E., and Barchas, J. (1976). Influence of social setting on the induction of brain cyclic AMP in response to electric shock in the rat. *Nature*, 263:433–434.

Eichelman, B., and Thoa, N. B. (1973). The aggressive monoamines. *Biol. Psychiat.*, 6:143–164.

Ellison, G. D., and Bresler, D. E. (1974). Tests of emotional behaviour in rats following depletion of norepinephrine, of serotonin, or of both. *Psychopharmacol.*, 34:275–288.

Ellison, G. D, Eison, M. S., and Huberman, H. S. (1978). Stages of constant amphetamine intoxication: Delayed appearance of abnormal social behaviors in rat colonies. *Psychopharmacol.*, 56: 293–299.

Emley, G. S., Hutchinson, R. R., and Brannan, I. B. (1970). Aggression: Effects of acute and chronic morphine. *Mich. Ment. Health Res. Bull.*, 4:23–26.

Enloe, L. J. (1975). Extralimbic mediation of emotionality and social cohesiveness effects. *Physiol. Behav.*, 15:271–276.

Everett, G. M. (1977). Changes in brain dopamine levels and aggressive behavior with aging in 2 mouse strains. *Experientia*, 33:645–646.

Fadda, F., Argiolas, A., Melis, M. R., Tissari, A. H., Onali, P. L., and Gessa, G. L. (1978). Stress-induced increase in 3,4-dihydroxyphenylacetic acid (DOPAC) levels in the cerebral cortex and in n. accumbens: Reversal by diazepam. *Life Sci.*, 23:2219–2224.

Feigley, D. A., Parsons, P. J., Hamilton, L. W., and Spear, N. E. (1972). Development of habituation to novel environments in the rat. *JCPP*, 79:443–452.

Ferguson, J., Henriksen, S., Cohen, H., Mitchell, G., Barchas, J., Dement, W. (1970). "Hypersexuality" and behavioral changes in cats caused by administration of p-cholorophenylalanine. *Science*, 168:499–501.

Fibiger, H. C., Lytle, L. D., and Campbell, B. A. (1970). Cholinergic modulation of adrenergic arousal in the developing rat. *JCPP*, 72:384–389.

File, S. E. (1975). Effects of parachlorophenylalanine and amphetamine on habituation of orienting. *Pharmacol. Biochem. Behav.*, 3:979–983.

Freedman, D. X. (1977). Concluding remarks. In: *Neuroregulators and Psychiatric Disorders*, E. Usdin, D. A. Hamburg, and J. D. Barchas (eds.). New York: Oxford University Press, pp. 596–598.

Fuxe, K., and Gunne, L. M. (1966). Depletion of the amine stores in brain catecholamine terminals in amygdaloid stimulation. *Acta Physiol. Scand.*, 62:493–494.

Gallager, D. W., and Aghajanian, G. K. (1975). Effects of chlorimipramine and lysergic acid diethylamide on efflux of precursor-formed ^{3}H-serotonin: Correlations with serotonergic impulse flow. *J. Pharmacol. Exp. Ther.*, 193:785–795.

Garver, D. L., and Davis, J. M. (1979). Mini review. Biogenic amine hypotheses of affective disorders. *Life Sci.*, 24: 383–394.

Gay, P. E., Sherwood, O. C., and Leaf, R. C. (1976). Interactions of amygdala lesions with effects of pilocarpine and d-amphetamine on mouse killing, feeding, and drinking in rats. *JCPP*, 90:630–642.

Gerbino, L., Oleshansky, M., and Gershon, S. (1978). Clinical use and mode of action of lithium. In: *Psychopharmacology: A Generation of Progress*, M. A. Lipton, A. DiMascio, and K. F. Killam, (eds.): New York: Raven Press, pp. 1261–1275.

Gianutsos, G., Drawbaugh, R. B., Hynes, M. D., and Lal, H. (1975). The morphine withdrawal syndrome in the rat. In: *Methods in Narcotic Research*, S. Ehrenpreis, and A. Neidle, (eds.). New York: Dekker, pp. 293–309.

Gianutsos, G., and Lal, H. (1976). Blockade of apomorphine-induced aggression by morphine or neuroleptics: Differential alteration by antimuscarinics and naloxone. *Pharmacol. Biochem. Behav.*, 4:639–642.

Gianatsos, G., and Lal, H. (1978). Narcotic analgesics and aggression. *Modern Problems in Pharmacopsychiat.*, 13:114–138.

Gold, M. S., Redmond, D. E., Jr., and Kleber, H. D. (1978). Clonidine blocks acute opiate-withdrawal symptoms. *Lancet*, ii, 599–602.

Goldberg, A. M., and Silbergeld, E. K. (1977). Animal models of hyperactivity. In: *Animal Models in Psychiatry and Neurology*, I. Hanin, and E. Usdin, (eds.). New York: Pergamon Press, pp. 371–384.

Goldberg, M. E., and Horovitz, Z. P. (1978). Antidepressants and aggressive behavior. *Modern Problems in Pharmacopsychiat.*, 13:29–52.

Goldstein, M. (1974). Brain research and violent behavior. *Arch. Neurol.*, 30:1–35.

Gottschalk, L. A., Gleser, G. C., Wylie, H. W., and Kaplan, W. W. (1965). Effects of imipramine on anxiety and hostility levels. *Psychopharmacol.*, 7:303–310.

Grant, E. C. (1963). An analysis of the social behaviour of the male laboratory rat. *Behaviour*, 21:260–281.

Grant, L. D., Coscina, D. V., Grossman, S. P., and Freedman, D. X. (1973). Muricide after serotonin depleting lesions of midbrain raphé nuclei. *Pharmacol. Biochem. Behav.*, 1:77–80.

Greenbaum, J. V. and Lurie, L. A. (1948). Encephalitis as a causative factor in behavior disorders of children. *JAMA.*, 136:923–930.

Grossman, S. P. (1963), Chemically induced epileptiform seizures in the cat. *Science*, 142:409–411.

Gunne, L. M. and Lewander, T. (1966). Monoamines in brain and adrenal glands of cat after electrically induced defense reaction. *Acta Physiol. Scand.*, 67:405–410.

Haigler, H. J., and Aghajanian, G. K. (1974). Lysergic acid diethylamide and serotonin, a comparison of effects on serotonergic neurons and neurons receiving a serotonergic input. *J. Pharmacol. Exp. Ther.*, 188:688–699.

Harper, L. V. (1971). The young as a source of stimuli controlling caretaker behavior. *Dev. Psychol.*, 4:73–88.

Herman, B. H., and Panksepp, J. (1978). Effects of morphine and naloxone on separation distress and approach attachment: Evidence for opiate mediation of social affect. *Pharmacol. Biochem. Behav.*, 9:213–220.

Hernandez-Peon, R., Chavez-Ibarra, G., Morgane, P. J., and Timo-Iaria, C. (1963). Limbic cholinergic pathways involved in sleep and emotional behavior. *Exp. Neurol.*, 8:93–111.

Himwich, W. A. (1975). Forging a link between basic and clinical research: Developing brain. *Biol. Psychiat.*, 10:125–139.

Hodge, G. K., and Butcher, L. L. (1974). 5-Hydroxytryptamine correlates of isolation-induced aggression in mice. *Eur. J. Pharmacol.*, 28:326–337.

Hohman, L. B. (1922). Post-encephalitic behavior disorders in children. *Johns Hopkins Hospital Bull.*, 38:372–375.

Hole, K., Espolin, J., and Berge, O. G. (1977). 5,7-Dihydroxytryptamine lesions of the ascending 5-hydroxytryptamine pathways: Habituation, motor activity and agonistic behavior. *Pharmacol. Biochem. Behav.*, 7:205–210.

Horn, G., and Hinde, R. A. (eds.) (1970). *Behavioral Habituation*. Cambridge: Cambridge University Press.

Hornykiewicz, O. (1973). Parkinson's disease: From brain homogenate to treatment. *Federation Proceedings*, 32:183–190.

Howard, J. L., Grant, L. D., and Breese, G. R. (1974). Effects of intracisternal 6-hydroxydopamine treatment on acquisition and performance of rats in a double T-maze. *JCPP*, 86:995–1007.

Hull, C. D., Buchwald, N. A., and Ling, G. (1967). Effects of direct cholinergic stimulation of forebrain structures. *Brain Res.*, 6:22–35.

Humphries, T., Kinsbourne, M., and Swanson, J. (1978). Stimulant effects on cooperation and social interaction between hyperactive children and their mothers. *J. Child Psychol. Psychiat.*, 19:13–22.

Igic, R., Stern, P., and Basagic, E. (1970). Changes in emotional behaviour after application of cholinesterase inhibitor in the septal and amygdala region. *Neuropharmacol.*, 9:73–75.

Itil, T. M. and Mukhopadhyay, S. (1978). Pharmacological management of human violence. *Modern Problems in Pharmacopsychiat.*, 13:139–158.

Iversen, S. D. (1977). Brain dopamine systems and behavior. In: *Handbook of Psychopharmacology*, Vol. 8, L. L. Iversen, S. D. Iversen, and S. H. Snyder, (eds.). New York: Plenum Press, pp. 333–384.

Jacobs, B. L., and Cohen, A. (1976). Differential behavioral effects of lesions of the median or dorsal raphe nuclei in rats: Open field and pain-elicited aggression. *JCPP*, 90: 102–108.

Jaffe, J. H. (1975). Drug addiction and drug abuse. In: *The Pharmacological Basis of Therapeutics*, L. S. Goodman, and A. Gilman, (eds.). New York: MacMillan, pp. 284–324.

Jimerson, D., and Reis, D. J. (1973). Effects of intrahypothalamic 6-hydroxydopamine on predatory aggression in rat. *Brain Res.*, 61:141–153.

Katz, R. J. (1976). Effects of the cholinomimetic drug arecoline upon aggression: Intra- vs. inter-specific allocation of attack. *Aggressive Behav.*, 2:205–212.

Katz, R. J. (1978). Catecholamines in predatory behavior: A review and critique. *Aggressive Behav.*, 4:153–172.

Katz, R. J., and Thomas, E. (1975). Effects of scopolamine and α-methyl-paratyrosine upon predatory attack in cats. *Psychopharmacol.*, 42:153–157.

Kelley, W. N., and Wyngaarden, J. B. (1978). The lesch-nyhan syndrome. In: *The Metabolic Basis of Inherited Disease*, J. B. Stanbury, J. B. Wyngaarden, and D. S. Fredrickson (eds.), New York: McGraw-Hill, pp. 1011–1036.

Kitsikis, A., Roberge, A. G., and Frenette, G. (1972). Effect of L-dopa on delayed response and visual discrimination in cats and its relation to brain chemistry. *Exp. Brain Res.*, 15:305–317.

Kolb, B., and Nonneman, A. J. (1974). Frontolimbic lesions and social behavior in the rat. *Physiol. and Behav.*, 13:637–643.

Koob, G. F., Stinus, L., and LeMoal, M. (1981). Hyperactivity and hypoactivity produced by lesions to the mesolimbic dopamine system. *Brain Res.* (in press).

Kornetsky, C. (1977). Animal models: Promises and problems. In: *Animal Models in Psychiatry and Neurology*, I. Hanin, and E. Usdin (eds.). New York: Pergamon Press, pp. 1–7.

Kostowski, W., Cztonkowski, A., Markowska, L., and Markiewicz, L. (1975). Intraspecific aggressiveness after lesions of midbrain raphe nuclei in rats. *Pharmacology*, 13:81–85.

Kulkarni, A. S. (1968). Muricidal block produced by 5-hydroxy-tryptophan and various drugs. *Life Sci.*, 7:125–128.

Kulkarni, A. S., and Plotnikoff, N. P. (1978). Effects of central stimulants on aggressive behavior. *Modern Problems in Pharmacopsychiat.*, 13:69–81.

Lagerspetz, K. Y. H., Tirri, R., and Lagerspetz, K. M. J. (1968). Neurochemical and endocrinological studies of mice selectively bred for aggressiveness. *Scand. J. Psychol.*, 9:157–160.

Lal, H., O'Brien, J., Pitterman, A., Gianutsos, G., and Reddy, C. (1972). Aggression after amphetamines and dihydroxyphenylalanine. *Fed. Proc. Fed. Am. Soc. Exp. Biol.*, 13:529.

Lamprecht, F., Eichelman, B., Thoa, N. B., Williams, R. B., and Kopin, I. J. (1972). Rat fighting behavior: Serum dopamine-beta-hydroxylase and hypothalamic tyrosine hydroxylase. *Science*, 177:1214–1215.

Lassen, J. B. (1978). Piperoxane reduces the effects of clonidine on aggression in mice and on noradrenaline dependent hypermotility in rats. *Eur. J. Pharmacol.*, 47:45–49.

Latané, B., Joy, V., Meltzer, J., Lubell, B., and Cappell, H. (1972). Stimulus determinants of social attraction in rats. *JCPP*, 79:13–21.

Leaf, R. C., Lerner, L., and Horovitz, Z. P. (1969). The role of the amygdala in the pharmacological and endocrinological manipulation of aggression. In: *Aggressive Behaviour*, S. Garattini and E. B. Sigg (eds.). New York: John Wiley & Sons, pp. 120–131.

Leahy, J. P., Stern, W. C., Resnick, O., and Morgane, P. J. (1978). A neuropharmacological analysis of central nervous system catecholamine systems in developmental protein malnutrition. *Dev. Psychobiol.*, 11:361–370.

Leckman, J. F., Cohen, D. J., Shaywitz, B. A., Caparulo, B. K., Heninger, G. R., and Bowers, M. B., Jr. (1980). CSF monoamine metabolites in child and adult psychiatric patients: A developmental perspective. *Arch.Gen. Psychiat.*, 37:677–681.

Lion, J. R. (1975). Conceptual issues in the use of drugs for the treatment of aggression in man. *J. Nerv. Ment. Dis.*, 160:76–82.

Lipton, A. DiMascio, and K. F. Killam (eds.). New York: Raven Press, pp.1535–1555. *Generation of Progress*. New York: Raven Press.

Lokiec, F., Rapin, J. R., Jacquot, C., and Cohen Y., (1978). A comparison of the kinetics of d- and l-amphetamine in the brain of isolated and aggregated rats. *Psychopharmacol.* 58:73–77.

Lore, R. and Flannelly, K. (1977). Rat societies. *Sci. Amer.*, 236(5):106–116.

Lycke, E., Modigh, K., and Roos, B. E. (1969). Aggression in mice associated with changes in the monoamine metabolism of the brain. *Experientia*, 25:951–953.

Lycke, E., and Roos, B. F. (1975). Virus infections in infant mice causing persistent impairment of turnover of brain catecholamines. *J. Neurol. Sci.*, 26:49–60.

Maas, J. W. (1975). Biogenic amines and depression. *Arch. Gen. Psychiat.*, 32:1357–1361.

Mabry, P. D., and Campbell, B. A. (1974). Ontogeny of serotonergic inhibition of behavioral arousal in the rat. *JCPP*, 86:193–201.

MacDonnell, M. F., Fessock, L., and Brown, S. H. (1971). Aggression and associated neural events in cats: Effects of p-chlorophenylalanine compared with alcohol. *Quart. J. Stud. Alc.*, 32:748–763.

MacKintosh, J. H., Chance, M. R. A., and Silverman, A. P. (1977). The contribution of ethological techniques to the study of drug effects. In: *Handbook of Psychopharmacology*, Vol. 7, L. L. Iversen, S. D. Iversen, and S. H. Snyder (eds.). New York: Plenum Publishing, pp. 3–35.

McCarthy, D. (1966). Mouse-killing in rats treated with pilocarpine. *Fed. Proc.*, 25:385.

McKinney, W. T. (1974). Animal models in psychiatry. *Perspectives in Biol. and Med.*, (Summer):529–541.

McLain, W. C., III, Cole, B. T., Schrieber, R., and Powell, D. A. (1974). Central catechol- and indolamine systems and aggression. *Pharmacol. Biochem. Behav.*, 2:123–126.

Maletzky, B. M. (1974), d-amphetamine and delinquency: Hyperkinesis persisting? *Dis. Nerv. Sys.*, 35:543–547.

Malick, J. B. (1975). Differential effects of d- and l-amphetamine on mouse-killing behavior in rats. *Pharmacol. Biochem. Behav.*, 3:697–699.

Malick, J. B (1976). Pharmacological antagonism of mouse-killing behavior in the olfactory bulb lesion-induced killer rat. *Aggressive Behav.*, 2:123–130.

Marks, P. C., O'Brien, M., and Paxinos, G. (1977). 5,7-DHT-induced muricide: Inhibition as a result of preoperative exposure of rats to mice. *Brain Res.*, 135:383–388.

Martinek, Z., and Lat, J. (1968). Ontogenetic differences in spontaneous reactions of dogs to a new environment. *Psychiological Bohemoslovaca*, 17:545–552.

Mason, S. T., and Iversen, S. D. (1979). Theories of the dorsal bundle extinction effect. *Brain Research Reviews*, 1:107–137.

Meltzer, H. Y., and Stahl, S. M. (1976). The dopamine hypothesis of schizophrenia: A review. *Schizophrenia Bull.*, 2:19–76.

Michaelson, I. A., Bornschein, R. L., Loch, R. K., and Rafales, L. S. (1977). Minimal brain dysfunction hyperkinesis: Significance of nutritional status in animal models of hyperactivity. In: *Animal Models in Psychiatry and Neurology*, I. Hanin and E. Usdin (eds.). New York: Pergamon Press, pp. 37–49.

Miczek, K. A., Altman, J. L., Appel, J. B., and Boggan W. O. (1975). Para-chlorophenylalanine, serotonin and killing behavior. *Pharmacol. Biochem. Behav.*, 3:355–361.

Miczek, K. A., and Barry, H. (1976). Pharmacology of sex and aggression. In: *Behavioral Pharmacology*, S. D. Glick and J. Goldfarb (eds.). St. Louis: C. V. Mosby, pp. 176–257.

Miczek, K. A., and O'Donnell, J. M. (1978). Intruder-evoked aggression in isolated and nonisolated mice: Effects of psychomotor stimulants and L-dopa. *Psychopharmacol.*, 57:47–55.

Moorcroft, W. H. (1971). Ontogeny of behavioral inhibition by forebrain structures in the rat. *Brain Res.*, 35:513–525.

Moore, K. E. (1978). Amphetamines: Biochemical and behavioral actions in animals. In: *Handbook of Psychopharmacology*, Vol. 11, L. L. Iversen, S. D. Iversen, and S. H. Snyder (eds.). New York: Plenum Publishing, pp. 41–98.

Morden, B., Conner, R., Mitchell, G., Dement, W., and Levine, S. (1968). Effects of rapid eye movement (REM) sleep deprivation on shock-induced fighting. *Physiol. Behav.*, 3:425–432.

Morpurgo, C. (1968). Aggressive behavior induced by large doses of 2-(2,6-dichlorophenylamino)-2-imidazoline hydrochloride (ST 155) in mice. *Eur. J. Pharmacol.*, 3:374–377.

Morrison, J., and Stewart, M. (1971). A family study of hyperactive child syndrome. *Biol. Psychiat.*, 3:189–195.

Morrison, J., and Stewart, M. (1973). The psychiatric status of the legal families of adopted hyperactive children. *Arch. Gen. Psychiat.*, 28:888–891.

Moyer, K. E. (1968). Kinds of aggression and their physiological basis. *Commun. Behav. Biol.* 2A:65–87.

Myers, R. D. (1964). Emotional and autonomic responses following hypothalamic chemical stimulation. *Canad. J. Psychol.*, 18:6–14.

Nakamura, K., and Thoenen, H. (1972). Increased irritability: A permanent behavior change induced in the rat by intraventricular administration of 6-hydroxydopamine. *Psychopharmacol.*, 24:359–372.

Norton, S. (1977). Significance of sex and age differences. In: *Animal Models in Psychiatry and Neurology*, I. Hanin and E. Usdin (eds.). New York: Pergamon Press, pp. 7–25.

Nyakas, C., van Delft, A. M. L., Kaplanski, J., and Smelik, P. G. (1973). Exploratory activity and conditioned avoidance acquisition after early postnatal 6-hydroxydopamine administration. *J. Neural Transmission*, 34:253–266.

Orenberg, E. K., Renson, J., Elliot, G. R., Barchas, J. D., and Kessler, S. (1975). Genetic determination of aggressive behavior and brain cyclic AMP. *Psychopharmacol. Commun.*, 1:99–107.

Ozawa, H., Miyauchi, T., and Sugawara, K. (1975). Potentiating effect of lithium chloride on aggressive behaviour induced in mice by nialamide plus L-dopa and by clonidine. *Eur. J. Pharmacol.*, 34:169–179.

Paxinos, G., and Atrens, D. M. (1977). 5,7-Dihydroxytryptamine lesions: Effects on body weight, irritability, and muricide. *Aggressive Behav.*, 3:107–118.

Paxinos, G., Burt, J., Atrens, D. M., and Jackson, D. M. (1977). 5-Hydroxytryptamine depletion with para-chlorophenylalanine: Effects on eating, drinking, irritability, muricide, and copulation. *Pharmacol. Biochem. Behav.*, 6:439–447.

Peters, D. A. V., Filczewski, M., and Mazurkiewicz-Kwilecki, I. M. (1972). Effects of p-chlorophenylalanine upon catecholamine synthesis in rat brain, heart and adrenals. *Biochem. Pharmac.*, 21:2282–2284.

Piccirillo, M., Cohen, D. J., Shaywitz, B. A., Alpert, J. E., and Marinelli, D. (1979). Maternal care received by rat pups treated with 6-hydroxydopamine. *Physiol. Behav.*, 22:69–75, 1979.

Pincus, J. H., and Tucker, G. T. (1974). *Behavioral Neurology.* New York: Oxford University Press.

Plaut, S. M. (1975). Animal models in developmental research. *Pediat. Clin. North Am.*, 22:619–631.

Popova, N. K., Voitenko, N. N., and Trut, L. N. (1976). Changes in the content of serotonin and 5-hydroxyindoleacetic acid in the brain in the selection of silver foxes according to behavior. *Neurosci. Behav. Physiol.*, 7:72–74.

Pöschlová, N., Masek, K., and Kršiak, M. (1975). The effect of 6-hydroxydopamine and 5,6-dihydroxytryptamine on social behaviour in mice. *Activ. Nerv. Sup. (Praha)*, 17:245–255.

Powell, D. A., Milligan, W. L. and Walters, K. (1973). The effects of muscarinic cholinergic blockade upon shock-elicited aggression. *Pharmacol. Biochem. Behav.*, 1:389–394.

Pradhan, S. N. (1975). Aggression and central neurotransmitters. *International Review of Neurobiology*, 18:213–262.

Puri, S. K. and Lal, H. (1973). Effect of dopaminergic stimulation or blockade on morphine withdrawal aggression. *Psychopharmacol.* 32:113–118.

Rambling, D. (1978). Aggression: A paradoxical response to tricyclic antidepressants. *Am. J. Psychiatr.*, 135:117–118.

Randall, P. K. and Campbell, B. A. (1976). Ontogeny of behavioral arousal in rats. Effect of maternal and sibling presence. *JCPP*, 90:453–459.

Rapaport, J., Buchsbaum, M. S., Zahn, T. P., Weingartner, H., Ludlow, C., and Mikkelsen, E. J. (1978). Dextroamphetamine: Cognitive and behavioral effects in normal prepubertal boys. *Science*, 199:560–563.

Rastogi, R. B. and Singhal, R. L. (1976). Influence of neonatal and adult hyperthyroidism on behavior and biosynthetic capacity for norepinephrine, dopamine and 5-hydroxytryptamine in rat brain. *J. Pharm. Exp. Ther.*, 198:609–618.

Redmond, D. E., Jr. (1977). Alterations in the function of the nucleus locus coeruleus: A possible model for studies of anxiety. In: *Animal Models in Psychiatry and Neurology*, I. Hanin and E. Usdin (eds.). New York: Pergamon Press, pp. 293–304.

Redmond, D. E., Jr., Huang, Y. H., Snyder, D. R., Mass, J. W., and Baulu, J. (1976). Behavioral changes following lesions of the locus coeruleus in *macaca arctoides*. *Neurosci. Abs.*, 1:472.

Redmond, D. E., Jr., Maas, J. W., Kling, A., Graham, C. W., and Dekirmenjian, H. (1971). Social behavior of monkeys selectively depleted of monoamines. *Science*, 174:428–431.

Reis, D. J. (1972). The relationship between brain norepinephrine and aggressive behavior. *Res. Publ. Assoc. Res. Nerv. Ment. Dis.*, 50:266–297.

Reis, D. J. (1974). Central neurotransmitters in aggression. *Res. Publ. Nerv. Ment. Dis.*, 52:119–148.

Reis, D. J., and Fuxe, K. (1968). Depletion of noradrenaline in brainstem neurons during sham rage behaviour produced by acute brainstem transection in cat. *Brain Res.*, 7:448–451.

Reis, D. J., and Fuxe, K. (1969). Brain norepinephrine: Evidence that neuronal release is essential for sham rage behavior following brainstem transection in cat. *Proc. Natl. Acad. Sci.*, 64:108–112.

Reis, D. J., Moorhead, D. T., II, Rifkin, M., Joh, T., and Goldstein, M. (1970). Changes in enzymes synthesizing catecholamines resulting from hypothalamic stimulation producing attack behavior in cat. *Trans. Am. Neurol. Assn.*, 95:104–107.

Richmond, J. S., Young, J. R., and Groves, J. E. (1978). Violent dyscontrol responsive to d-amphetamine. *Am. J. Psychiat.*, 135:365–366.

Rodgers, R. J. (1977). The medial amygdala: Serotonergic inhibition of shock-induced aggression and pain sensitivty in rats. *Aggressive Behav.*, 3:277–288.

Rodgers, R. J., and Brown, K. (1976). Amygdaloid function in the central cholinergic mediation of shock-induced aggression in the rat. *Aggressive Behav.*, 2:131–152.

Ross, S. B., and Ogren, S. O. (1976). Anti-aggressive action of dopamine-β-hydroxylase inhibitors in mice. *J. Pharm. Pharmol.*, 28:590–592.

Safer, D. J. (1973). A familial factor in minimal brain dysfunction. *Behav. Genet.*, 3:175–186.

Sahakian, B. J., Robbins, T. W., Morgan, M. J., and Iversen, S. D. (1975). The effects of psychomotor stimulants on stereotypy and locomotor activity in socially-deprived and control rats. *Brain Res.*, 84:195–205.

Salama, A. I., and Goldberg, M. E. (1977). Biogenic amine metabolism in the aggressive mouse-killing rat. In: *Animal Models in Psychiatry and Neurology*, I. Hanin and E. Usdin (eds.). New York: Pergamon Press, pp. 259–267.

Sanders-Bush, E., and Massari, V. J. (1977). Actions of drugs that deplete serotonin. *Fed. Proc.*, 2149–2153.

Schildkraut, J. J., and Hartmann, E. (1972). Turnover and metabolism of norepinephrine in rat brain after 72 hours on a d-deprivation island. *Psychopharmacol.*, 27:17–27.

Sechzer, J. A., Kessler, P. G., Folstein, S. F., Geiger, E. H., and Meehan, S. M. (1976). An animal model for the minimal brain dysfunction syndrome. In: *Mental Health in Children*, D. V. Sankar. Westbury, N.Y.: PJD Publications, 2:411–428.

Shapiro, A. K., Shapiro, E., Brunn, R. D., and Sweet, R. D. (1978). *Gilles de la Tourette Syndrome*. New York: Raven Press.

Shaywitz, B. A., Cohen, D. J., and Bowers, M. B., Jr. (1977a). CSF monoamine metabolites in children with minimal brain dysfunction: evidence for alteration of brain dopamine. *J. Pediat.*, 90:67–71.

Shaywitz, B. A., Cohen, D. J., and Bowers, M. B., Jr. (1980). Cerebrospinal fluid monoamine metabolites in neurological disorders of childhood. In: *Neurobiology of Cerebrospinal Fluid*, J. Wood (ed.). New York: Plenum, pp. 219–236.

Shaywitz, B. A., Gordon, J. W., Klopper, J. H., and Zelterman, D. A. (1977b). The effect of 6-hydroxydopamine on habituation of activity in the developing rat pup. *Pharmac. Biochem. Behav.*, 6:391–396.

Shaywitz, B. A., Gordon, J. W., Klopper, J. H., Zelterman, D. A., and Irvine, J. (1979). Ontogenesis of spontaneous activity and habituation of activity in the rat pup. *Dev. Psychobiol.*, 12:359.

Shaywitz, B. A., Klopper, J. H., and Gordon, J. W. (1978b). Methylphenidate in 6-hydroxydopamine-treated developing rat pups. *Arch. Neurol.*, 35:463–469.

Shaywitz, B. A., Klopper, J. H., Yager, R. D., and Gordon, J. W. (1976a). Paradoxical response to amphetamine in developing rats treated with 6-hydroxydopamine. *Nature*, 261:153–155.

Shaywitz, B. A. and Pearson, D. A. (1978). Effects of phenobarbital on activity and learning in 6-hydroxydopamine treated rat pups. *Pharmac. Biochem. Behav.*, 9:173–179.

Shaywitz, B. A., Yager, R. D., and Klopper, J. H. (1976b). Selective brain dopamine depletion in developing rats. *Science*, 191:305–308.

Shaywitz, S. E., Cohen, D. J., and Shaywitz, B. A. (1978a). The biochemical basis of minimal brain dysfunction. *J. Pediat.*, 92:179–187.

Sheard, M. H. (1969). The effect of p-chlorophenylalanine on behavior in rats: relation to brain serotonin and 5-hydroxyindoleacetic acid. *Brain Res.*, 15:524–528.

Sheard, M. H. (1974). Hypothalamically elicited attack behavior in cats: effects of raphe stimulation. *J. Psychiat. Res.*, 10:151.

Sheard, M. H. (1976). The effect of para-chloroamphetamine (PCA) on behavior. *Psychopharmacol. Bull.*, 12:59–61.

Sheard, M. H. (1977). Animal models of aggressive behavior. In: *Animal Models in Psychiatry and Neurology*, I. Hanin and E. Usdin (eds.). New York: Pergamon, pp. 247–257.

Sheard, M. H. (1978). The effect of lithium and other ions on aggressive behavior. *Modern Problems in Pharmacopsychiat.*, 13:53–68.

Sheard, M. H., Astrachan, D. I., and Davis, M. (1977). The effect of D-lysergic acid diethylamide (LSD) upon shock-elicited fighting in rats. *Life Sci.*, 20:427–430.

Sheard, M. H. and Davis, M. (1976). p-Chloroamphetamine: short and long term effects upon shock-elicited aggression. *Eur. J. Pharmacol.*, 40:295–302.

Shetty, T., and Chase, T. N. (1976). Central monoamines and hyperkinesis of childhood. *Neurology*, 26:1000–1002.

Siegel, G. J., Albers, R. W., Katzman, R., and Agranoff, B. W., eds. (1976). *Basic Neurochemistry*. Boston: Little, Brown and Company.

Silbergeld, E. K., and Goldberg, A. M. (1975). Pharmacological and neurochemical investigations of lead-induced hyperactivity. *Neuropharmacology*, 14:431–444.

Smith, D. E., King, M. B., and Hoebel, B. G. (1970). Lateral hypothalamic control of killing: evidence for a cholinoceptive mechanism. *Science*, 167:900–901.

Smith, R. D., Cooper, B. R., and Breese, G. R. (1973). Growth and behavioral changes in developing rats treated intracisternally with 6-hydroxydopamine: evidence for involvement of brain dopamine. *J. Pharmacol. Exp. Ther.*, 185:609–619.

Sobrian, S. K., Weltman, M., and Pappas, B. A. (1975). Neonatal locomotor and long-term behavioral effects of d-amphetamine in the rat. *Dev. Psychobiol.*, 8:241–250.

Sorenson, C. A., and Gordon, M. (1975). Effects of 6-hydroxydopamine on shock-elicited aggression, emotionality and maternal behavior in female rats. *Pharmacol. Biochem. Behav.*, 3:331–335.

Sorenson, C. A., Vayer, J. S., and Goldberg, C. S. (1977). Amphetamine reduction of motor activity in rats after neonatal administration of 6-hydroxydopamine. *Biol. Psychiat.*, 12:133–137.

Spellacy, F. (1977). Neuropsychological differences between violent and nonviolent adolescents. *J. Clin. Psychol.*, 33:966–969.

Sprague, R. L., and Sleator, E. K. (1977). Methylphenidate in hyperkinetic children: differences in dose effects on learning and social behavior. *Science*, 198:1274–1276.

Stinus, L., Gaffori, O., Simon, H., and LeMoal, M. (1977). Small doses of apomorphine and chronic administration of d-amphetamine reduce locomotor hyperactivity produced by radiofrequency lesions of dopaminergic A10 neurons area. *Biol. Psychiat.*, 12:719–732.

Stolk, J. M., Conner, R. L., and Barchas, J. D. (1971). Rubidium-induced increase in shock-elicited aggression in rats. *Psycopharmacol.*, 22:250–260.

Stolk, J. M., Conner, R. L., Levine, S., and Barchas, J. D. (1974). Brain norepinephrine metabolism and shock-induced fighting behavior in rats: differential effects of shock and fighting on the neurochemical response to a common foot-shock stimulus. *J. Pharm. Exp. Ther.*, 190:193–209.

Stollerman, I. P., Johnson, C. A., Bunker, P., and Jarvik, M. E. (1975). Weight loss and shock-elicited aggression as indices of morphine abstinence in rats. *Psychopharmacol.*, 45:157–161.

Stoof, J. C., Dijkstra, H., and Hillegers, J. P. M. (1978). Changes in the behavioral response to a novel environment following lesioning of the central dopaminergic system in rat pups. *Psycopharmacol.*, 57:163–166.

Svensson, T. H., Bunney, B. S., and Aghajanian, G. K. (1975). Inhibition of both noradrenergic and serotonergic neurons in brain by the α-adrenergic agonist clonidine. *Brain Res.*, 92:291–306.

Sweet, R. D., and Reis, D. J. (1971). Collection of [3H] norepinephrine in ventriculocisternal perfusate during hypothalamic stimulation in cat. *Brain Res.*, 33:584–588.

Swonger, A. K., and Rech, R. H. (1972). Serotonergic and cholinergic involvement in habituation of activity and spontaneous alternation of rats in a Y-maze. *JCPP*, 81:509–522.

Tedeschi, D. H., Fowler, P. J., Miller, R. B., and Macko, E. (1969). Pharmacological analysis of foot shock-induced fighting behavior. In: *Aggressive Behaviour*, S. Garattini and E. B. Sigg (eds.). New York: Wiley, pp. 245–252.

Teicher, M. H., Shaywitz, B. A., Kootz, H. L., and Cohen, D. J. (1981). Differential effects of maternal and sibling presence on hyperactivity of 6-hydroxydopamine-treated developing rats. *J. Comp. Physiol. Psychol.*, 95:134–135.

Thoa, N. B., Eichelman, B., and Ng, L. K. (1972a). Shock-induced aggression: effects of 6-hydroxydopamine and other pharmacological agents. *Brain Res.*, 43:467–475.

Thoa, N. B., Eichelman, B., Richardson, J. S., and Jacobwitz, D. (1972b). 6-hydroxydopa depletion of brain norepinephrine and the facilitation of aggressive behavior. *Science*, 178:75–77.

Thoa, B., Tizabi, Y., and Jacobowitz, D. M. (1977). The effect of isolation on catecholamine concentration and turnover in discrete areas of the rat brain. *Brain Res.*, 131:259–269.

Thurmond, J. B., Lasley, S. M., Conkin, A. L., and Brown, J. W. (1977). Effects of dietary tyrosine, phenylalanine, and tryptophan on aggression in mice. *Pharmacol. Biochem. Behav.*, 6:475–478.

Tinklenberg, J. R., and Woodrow, K. M. (1974). Drug use among youthful assaultive and sexual offenders. *Res. Publ. Assoc. Res. Nerv. Ment. Dis.*, 52:209–224.

Touwen, B. C. L., and Kalberboer, A. F. (1973). Neurological and behavioral assessment of children with minimal brain dysfunction. In: *Minimal Cerebral Dysfunction in Children*, S. Walzer and P. H. Wolff, (eds.). New York: Grune & Stratton.

Ulrich, R., and Symannek, B. (1969). Pain as a stimulus for aggression. In: *Aggressive Behaviour*, S. Garattini and E. B. Sigg (eds.). New York: Wiley, pp. 59–69.

Usdin, E., Hamburg, D. A., and Barchas, J. E., eds. (1977). *Neuroregulators and Psychiatric Disorders*. New York: Oxford University Press.

Valzelli, L., ed. (1978). Psychopharmacology of aggression. *Modern Problems in Pharmacopsychiat.*, 13:1–180.

Verebey, K., Volavka, J., and Clouet, D. (1978). Endorphins in psychiatry. *Arch. Gen. Psychiat.*, 35:877–888.

Vergnes, M., Boehrer, A., and Karli, P. (1974). Interspecific aggressiveness and reactivity in mouse-killing and nonkilling rats: Compared effects of olfactory bulb removal and raphe lesions. *Aggressive Behav.*, 1:1–16.

Vergnes, M., Mack, G., and Kempf, E. (1973). Behavioural and biochemical effects of lesions of the raphe on rat-mouse interspecific aggressive behaviour. *Brain Res.*, 57:67–74.

Vogel, J. R. (1975). Antidepressants and mouse-killing (muricide) behavior. In: *Antidepressants; Industrial Pharmacology*, S. Fielding and H. Lal (eds.). Mt. Kisco, New York: Futura, 2:99–112.

Vogel, J. R., and Haubrich, D. R. (1973). Chronic administration of electroconvulsive shock effects on mouse-killing activity and brain monoamines in rats. *Physiol. Behav.*, 11:725–728.

Vogel, J. R., and Leaf, R. C. (1972). Initiation of mouse killing in non-killer rats by repeated pilocarpine treatment. *Physiol. Behav.*, 8:421–424.

Wasman, M., and Flynn, J. P. (1962). Directed attack elicited from hypothalamus. *Arch. Neurol.*, 6:220–227.

Way, E. L., and Glasgow, C. (1978). Recent developments in morphine analgesia: tolerance and dependence. In: *Psychopharmacology: A Generation of Progress*, M. A. Lipton, A. DiMascio, and K. F. Killam (eds.). New York: Raven Press, pp. 1535–1555.

Weinstock, M., Speiser, Z., and Ashkenazi, R. (1978). Changes in brain catecholamine turnover and receptor sensitivity induced by social deprivation in rats. *Psycopharmacol.*, 56:205–209.

Wender, P. H. (1971). *Minimal Brain Dysfunction in Children*. New York: Wiley.

Willerman, L. (1973). Activity level and hyperactivity in twins. *Child Dev.*, 44:288–293.

Williams, J. M., Hamilton, L. W., and Carlton, P. L. (1974). Pharmacological and anatomical dissociation of 2 types of habituation. *JCPP*, 87:724–732.

Williams, J. M., Hamilton, L. W., and Carlton, P. L. (1975). Ontogenetic dissociation of two classes of habituation. *JCPP*, 89:733–737.

Wnek, D. J., and Leaf, R. C. (1973). Effects of cholinergic drugs on prey-killing by rodents. *Physiol. Behav.*, 10:1107–1113.

Wood, D. R., Reimherr, F. W., Wender, P. H., Bliss, E. L., and Johnson, G. E. (1976). Diagnosis and treatment of minimal brain dysfunction in adults. *Arch. Gen. Psychiat.*, 33:1453–1460.

Wurtman, R. J., Cohen, E. L., and Fernstrom, J. D. (1977). Control of brain neurotransmitter synthesis by precursor availability and food consumption. In: *Neuroregulators and Psychiatric Disorders*, E. Usdin, D. A. Hamburg, and J. D. Barchas (eds.). New York: Oxford University Press, pp. 103–121.

Yen, H. C. Y., Katz, M. H., and Krop, S. (1970). Effects of various drugs on 3, 4-hydroxyphenylalanine (DL-dopa)-induced excitation (aggressive behavior) in mice. *Toxic Appl. Pharmac.*, 17:597–604.

Yoshimura, H., and Ueki, S. (1977). Biochemical correlates in mouse-killing behavior of the rat: Prolonged isolation and brain cholinergic function. *Pharmacol. Biochem. Behav.*, 6:193–196.

Zigmond, M. J., and Stricker, E. M. (1977). Behavioral and neurochemical effects of central catecholamine depletion: a possible model for "subclinical" brain damage. In: *Animal Models in Psychiatry and Neurology*, I. Hanin and E. Usdin (eds.). New York: Pergamon, pp. 415–429.

Zigmond, M. J., and Stricker, E. M. (1974). Ingestive behavior following damage to central dopamine neurons: implications for homeostasis and recovery of function. In: *Neuropsychopharmacology of Monoamines and their Regulatory Enzymes*, E. Usdin (ed.). New York: Raven Press, pp. 385–402.

CHAPTER NINE

The Neurochemical Basis of Hyperactivity and Aggression Induced by Social Deprivation

B. J. SAHAKIAN

The potential for the treatment of some of the major psychiatric disorders through an understanding of their biochemistry has changed the study of biological factors in delinquency from a morally questionable labeling process to search for effective treatments. (Lewis, 1978).

GENERAL INTRODUCTION

This chapter is concerned with the correlation of aggressive behavior with neurochemical changes in the brain induced by social deprivation. It reviews the complex behavioral syndrome which results from deficient social interaction and discusses the possible underlying mechanisms responsible for controlling this syndrome. Certain of the human clinical data which elucidate the brain mechanisms involved in the mediation of aggressive behavior will be discussed. However, for the most part, data obtained using experimental animals, such as the rat, will be examined, for the obvious reason that it is unethical to do many of the kinds of studies necessary to investigate the brain mechanisms involved in the control of aggression using humans as subjects. The advantages of using animal models in investigating the underlying mechanisms involved in various human disorders and in determining the most effective treatment for these disorders will also be discussed.

RATIONALE FOR THE USE OF ANIMAL MODELS TO INVESTIGATE AGGRESSION

In the development of an animal model, one applies treatments to animals which make them mimic in various ways the behavior of human subjects with a particular behavioral syndrome. A well-developed animal model of a human disorder must have the three following features: a common etiology, strong behavioral similarities, and a common treatment.

There are several benefits to using animal models. Firstly, experimental animals are available in large quantities for research purposes, and they can be manipulated in diverse ways that would be considered unethical were one using humans as subjects. Secondly, these models permit a thorough experimental analysis of a simplified system. For example, in experimenting with animals, the experimenter can be in control of the animal's environment and its past history. Therefore he can alter one variable and investigate the effect of this manipulation while holding the other variables constant. Rarely in the "real world" is one able to exert such complete control. Thirdly, it is preferable to screen potential therapeutic agents on an animal model before proceeding to use these agents in clinical trials.

There are two major disadvantages of animal models: the danger of oversimplification and the difficulty in extrapolating from one species to another. However, if one is aware that these problems exist and bears them in mind, then animal models can be used to great advantage.

TOWARD UNDERSTANDING AGGRESSIVE BEHAVIOR

"Aggression" is not a unitary concept, but rather a description of a category of behavior, including verbal behavior. The different types of aggression can be classified either according to differences in the topography of the behavior shown or according to differences in brain mechanisms. For example, Flynn and others (Roberts and Kiess, 1964; Wasman and Flynn, 1962) have pointed out that a predatory attack shown by a cat looks quite different from a display of "affective" aggression. In the predatory attack, there is relatively little emotional display—the cat is quiet and slinks along close to the floor; while in affective aggression the cat hisses and growls, arches its back, fluffs its tail, and lays its ears back close to its head. There is some evidence which indicates that the brain areas involved in predatory aggression in the cat are not the same as those involved in other types of aggression (Egger and Flynn, 1963; Moyer, 1968; Wasman and Flynn, 1962).

As well as differences in the topography of behavior, there are also differences in the antecedent conditions. In certain instances, the cause and type of aggression are clearly related, as is the case with maternal aggression or defense of the young; while in other instances the relationship is not so obvious, as is the case with sex-related aggression.

What causes one individual to act in an aggressive fashion under a particular set of circumstances, while another individual will not, is not well understood. Ideally, in the study of behavior and brain control of behavior we will eventually understand the various causes of aggression and how to treat aggressive persons so that they can function harmoniously in society. We are beginning to develop a pharmacological therapy for aggressive disorders based on various experimental animal and clinical studies. Carlson (1977) has pointed out that pharmacological treatment is far preferable to that of irreversible damage to the brain, an alternative treatment for aggressive persons.

THE BEHAVIORAL SYNDROME INDUCED BY SOCIAL DEPRIVATION

For several years now, I and my colleagues have been concerned with a syndrome of behavior which is produced by social deprivation. The rearing of an experimental animal, such as a rat or dog, in social deprivation will induce a number of abnormal behaviors in the animal later in life (Melzack, 1968; Morgan, 1973; Sahakian et al., 1975). In rats, characteristics of this syndrome include increased aggressive behavior and hyperactivity or increased locomotor activity (Karli, 1956; Sahakian et al., 1975; Valzelli and Garattini, 1972). Children reared in social impoverishment—any situation where the child is without a good caretaker, for example an inferior institution, a broken home with no loving caretaker, or an abusive home situation—show a behavioral syndrome similar to that seen in socially deprived experimental animals (Bender, 1947; Cantwell, 1978; Goldfarb, 1955; Gore, 1976; Pillai, 1976). This syndrome of behavior seems to be a combination of the "Socialized Conduct Disorder" and the "Attention Deficit Disorder with Hyperactivity" as described in the American Psychiatric Association Diagnostic and Statistical Manual of Mental Disorders (Third Edition, 1977). The predisposing factors for the former disorder are "family poverty, deprivation, large family size, absent or alcoholic father, and residence in a delinquency area." The predisposing factors for the latter disorder are less well defined but include "mental retardation, epilepsy, some forms of cerebral palsy, and probably other neurological disorders". It is not uncommon for these two disorders to coexist (APA DSM III) or for the hyperactive child syndrome to precede antisocial delinquent behavior (Cantwell, 1978).

While the importance of the socialization process has been generally acknowledged, few have discussed in depth the syndrome arising from deficient social interaction. Fox (1968) has said that, "The process of socialization tends to reduce aggression because it is through this process that a young animal develops an emotional bond with its parents and peers." Welch (1965) and others have emphasized the importance of factors such as socialization on aggressive behavior. Certainly, it is clear that for the rat, being housed by itself for prolonged periods of time has profound consequences on its behavior, especially its aggressive behavior and its activity level (Sahakian et al., 1975; Valzelli, 1974). Therefore, environmental and social factors play a role in determining the level of aggressive behavior shown by an animal. In addition, it has been shown that genetic and learning factors also affect the degree of aggression that an animal displays (Kahn, 1951; Valzelli, 1974).

Bender (1947) has reported that social-environmental deprivation in man leads to a lack of "impulse control." Children from low socioeconomic groups have also been said to suffer social-environmental isolation (Gore, 1976), indicating that a child can be effectively socially isolated even though others are present. The incidence of hyperactive children in the low socioeconomic class is greater than in the middle-high socioeconomic groups (Wender, 1972). There are several components of the hyperactive syndrome in children, also referred to as the "hyperkinetic impulse disorder" (Lauter and Denhoff, 1957). In relation to locomotor activity, these children "show involuntary and consistant overactivity which greatly surpasses the normal" (Lauter and Denhoff, 1957).

SOCIAL DEPRIVATION IN ANIMALS

Hyperactivity

The rearing of rats and other species in social isolation produces a syndrome in which hyperactivity is a major component, whether measured in the open field or in photocell cages (Konrad and Melzack, 1975; Morgan, 1973; Sahakian et al., 1975; Syme, 1973; Valzelli, 1973).

Rats reared in social deprivation are initially more active when placed in a novel environment, and also take longer to adapt to that environment as compared with rats reared in social groups (Einon et al., 1975; Sahakian et al., 1975). The behavioral mechanisms underlying the hyperactivity are not known. They may be related to a heightened reactivity to novel stimuli (Konrad and Melzack, 1975; Sahakian et al., 1977) or to an inability to exhibit behavioral inhibition (Morgan et al., 1975), a necessary process for learning (Sahakian, 1976). Einon and Morgan (1976) have found that isolation-reared rats explore their environment less than group-reared animals. In our exploration studies, we found that isolated rats continually interrupted their periods of exploratory behavior with bouts of hyperactivity (Sahakian et al., 1977). This combination of hyperactivity and an inability to complete responses shown by isolation-reared rats resembles the behavior of hyperactive children (Cohen et al., 1971; Douglas, 1972; Sahakian and Robbins, 1977a; Wender, 1972).

What then is the neurochemical basis of this hyperactivity induced by social deprivation? It is unlikely that one neurotransmitter will be the sole determinant of a behavior or a category of behaviors. It is far more probable that one neurotransmitter will be primarily involved in the mediation of a behavior or behaviors, while another or several other neurotransmitters will modulate that or those behaviors. Take for example Parkinson's disease, which is now recognized to be associated with abnormally low levels of dopamine and tyrosine hydroxylase in the caudate nucleus and other regions of the neostriatum (Iversen and Iversen, 1975). Parkinsonian symptoms, which include muscular rigidity, akinesia, and tremor, may result from inadequate activation of dopamine receptors in the caudate nucleus (Hornykiewicz, 1973). The current treatment for Parkinson's disease is L-dopa, an amino acid precursor of dopamine (Iversen and Iversen, 1975). However, before L-dopa therapy existed, anticholinergic drugs were used to alleviate the symptoms of Parkinson's disease. Presumably, anticholinergic treatment was partially effective in that it helped to restore the postulated balance between dopamine and acetylcholine in the striatum (Roth and Bunney, 1976). As DeFeudis and DeFeudis (1977) have pointed out, it would be expected that for the complex disorder Parkinson's disease, and indeed for all complex behavioral phenomena, several neurotransmitters would be involved. Thus it may be the critical balance of or interaction between neurotransmitters which is important, rather than solely one neurotransmitter.

With the importance of neurotransmitter interactions in mind, there is both behavioral and neurochemical evidence suggesting a possible increase in the functional activity of the dopaminergic system as the basis for the hyperactive syndrome induced by social deprivation. For example, amphetamine releases both noradrenaline and dopamine (Carr and Moore, 1969; McKenzie and Szerb, 1968) and blocks the reuptake into the nerve terminal (Glowinski and Baldessarini, 1966; Horn et al., 1974; Von Voigtlander and Moore, 1973). However, the behavioral effects of the drug, the increased motor activity and perseverative behavior, are known to be primarily dependent on central dopaminergic mechanisms (Creese and Iversen, 1972; Kelly et al., 1975). Rats reared in social deprivation were more susceptible to amphetamine as measured by an enhanced behavioral response to the perseverative aspects of the drug as compared with rats reared in social groups (Sahakian et al., 1975). In addition, socially-deprived rats also showed a greater response than group-reared rats to another behavior thought to be dependent on brain dopamine, eating and licking induced by a mild stressor (Antelman et al., 1975; Sahakian and Robbins, 1977b). In a complementary fashion, as would be expected, socially-deprived rats were less susceptible to the effects of neuroleptic drugs, which are dopamine antagonists (Iversen and Iversen, 1975; Kostowski and Czlonkowski, 1973; Sahakian and Robbins, 1977b). More direct neurochemical measurements have also indicated an increase in the functional activity of the dopaminergic system in socially deprived rats. Segal and colleagues (Segal et al., 1973) found evidence for an increase in tyrosine hydroxylase activity in the neostriatum, and Thoa and colleagues (Thoa et al., 1977) have reported increased dopamine turnover in the olfactory tubercle of isolated rats. For a detailed discussion of the role of other neurotransmitters in the hyperactive syndrome induced by social deprivation, see DeFeudis and DeFeudis (1977) or Robbins and Sahakian (in press).

Aggressive Behavior

As previously stated, aggression is a very complex and diverse category of behaviors. For this reason, experimenters have developed a number of different paradigms for measuring aggression. I will not attempt an evaluation of the various methods used to measure aggression, but I would suggest that as with any heterogeneous category, it is advantageous to examine the effects of treatments on several measures rather than on one. One method is to measure the frequency and duration of attacks. Many studies have shown that the delivery of a noxious stimulus, for example an electric shock, will produce, in several species, contact with, and perhaps destruction of other objects in the environment, including other organisms (Miczek and Barry, 1976;

Hutchinson, 1977). Other measures of aggression include biting of the experimenter's hand or competition tests, such as passage through a narrow tube which allows only one animal to pass at a time (Hatch, et al., 1963; Uyeno and White, 1967).

As mentioned earlier, excessive aggression is an effect of isolation or social deprivation on animals. Valzelli (1974) and Welch and Welch (1971) have found that mice kept by themselves show increased aggression, as measured by actual fighting with another mouse introduced into the cage. The fighting is described as "fierce and vicious" (Valzelli, 1974). In rats, the behavior generally observed is mouse-killing, termed "muricide," rather than within-species aggression ("rat to rat aggression").

Beynon, Costello, Robbins, and I (unpublished data) were interested in observing within-species aggression in socially deprived rats and group-housed rats in a relatively natural situation in order to determine whether prolonged social deprivation could increase within-species aggression in the rat. In Valzelli's (1974) review of the area, he found that one of the most important causes driving the animal to aggressive behavior is competition for food. Therefore, in order to elicit high levels of aggression, we used a competitive test situation in which thirsty rats competed for access to a burette containing water. The hypothesis was that socially deprived rats, when placed in a competitive situation which elicits aggression, will show increased aggression as measured by frequency of attack, as compared with rats housed in social groups. Each socially deprived rat was paired as closely as possible with a group-housed rat on the basis of body weight and rate of drinking. The two rats were placed in an apparatus which contained only one water burette, which was enclosed so as to permit access by only one animal at a time. Both rats had received previous training while alone in the apparatus to learn to drink in this situation prior to the "pair tests." Before and after the competitive drinking period, a door was inserted in front of the burette so that no drinking was allowed, and the aggressive behavior of the two rats toward each other was measured. These periods were termed the "pre-competitive" and "post-competitive" periods, respectively. Based on Grant's (1963) description of aggressive behavior in rats, the frequency of the following three measures were taken during these two periods:

1. Forepaws on Shoulder: The rat placed both its forepaws on any part of its opponent's head, shoulders, or back.

2. Vigorous Wrestling: Any rapid sequence of wrestling attack which did not involve biting or characteristic postures, such as "full aggressive posture" and "submissive posture."

3. Tail- or Leg-Biting: The rat bites any part of its opponent's tail or limbs.

As can be seen from Table 1, the socially deprived rats showed significantly more instances of forepaws on the body, vigorous wrestling, and biting as compared with group-housed rats in both the pre- and post-competitive periods.

TABLE 1

Aggressive Behavior in the Pre-Competitive and Post-Competitive Periods
Between Socially Deprived Rats and Rats Housed in Social Groups

Measure of Aggressive Behavior	Pre-Competitive Period (Wilcoxon Test)	Post-Competitive Period (Wilcoxon Test)
Forepaws	T=1.0, p<0.02	T=1.5, p<0.02
Vigorous Wrestling	T=0, p<0.01	T=0, p<0.01
Tail- or leg-bites	(pre- and post-test scores were totaled) T=3, p<0.05	

The results of this study showed that, as predicted, when socially deprived rats are placed in a competitive situation which elicits aggression, they will show significantly more aggressive behavior than rats housed in social groups.

I will now focus on the underlying mechanisms involved in controlling aggression induced by social deprivation. Again, while realizing that many neurotransmitters are involved in the mediation and modulation of aggressive behaviors, I will concentrate on the neurotransmitter for which there is strong evidence for a primary role in controlling at least certain kinds of aggressive behavior, serotonin (5-HT). For example, several investigators have found when comparing a genetically hyperaggressive strain of mouse with a less aggressive mouse strain that the hypergressive strain had lower cerebral concentrations of serotonin (Bourgault et al., 1963) and lower brainstem levels of serotonin (Maas, 1962). To examine the role of other neurotransmitters in aggressive behavior, see DeFeudis and DeFeudis (1977) and Welch and Welch (1971).

In regard to social deprivation, Garattini and colleagues (Garattini et al., 1969; Valzelli, 1974) have reported that an increase in aggressive behavior induced by isolation is correlated with a decrease in turnover rate of brain serotonin. This decrease in brain serotonin turnover rate is a very dramatic and consistent change. Further, it is found only in the aggressive isolated mice and only in the "mouse-killing" rats; in other words, in the percentage of mice or rats that do *not* become aggressive as a result of isolation, this change in serotonin turnover rate is *not* present. Thus, this indicates that the decrease in turnover rate of brain serotonin is correlated specifically with the aggressive behavior induced by isolation, rather than some general effect of isolation (Valzelli, 1974).

This decrease in functional activity of the serotonergic systems which is found in mice and rats made aggressive by social deprivation complements findings showing that decreasing brain serotonin synthesis by pharmacological manipulation produces increased aggression in rats. It has been reported that rats injected with p-chlorophenylalanine (PCPA), an inhibitor of serotonin biosynthesis, were both irritable and highly aggressive when handled (Koe and Weissman, 1966). In addition, Sheard (1969) found that "mouse-killing" rats showed enhanced mouse-killing behavior following PCPA treatment.

If a decrease in functional activity of the brain serotonin system is correlated with aggressive behavior, then it would be predicted that a treatment which acts to restore the functional activity of the system back to its normal level would suppress aggressive behavior. A study by Hodge and Butcher (1974) suggests that this is, in fact, exactly what happens. Hodge and Butcher produced aggressive behavior in mice by rearing them in isolation since weaning, as Valzelli and others had done. They then took baseline rates of aggressive behavior in pairs of aggressive mice, by measuring both the latencies to initiate fights and the number of fights. They then administered D, L-5 hydroxytryptophan (5-HTP) and an agent to minimize potential toxic peripheral effects of the 5-HT precursor to these mice, thereby producing a potentiation of serotonergic function (Iversen and Iversen, 1965). The 5-HTP treated mice showed both an increase in the attack latencies and a decrease in the number of fights, so these rats now delayed their attacks and engaged in far fewer fights. Thus, by using 5-HTP to correct the defect in the functional activity of the serotonin system, one can antagonize the hyperaggressiveness of rats reared in social deprivation.

In addition, it has been reported that 5-hydroxytryptophan and the 5-HT receptor stimulant drug, lysergic acid diethylamide (Anden et al., 1968), reduce aggression in isolated mice and also in "mouse-killing" rats (Di Chiara et al., 1971; Kulkarni, 1968; Uyeno and Benson, 1965). In conclusion, there appears to be a decrease in functional activity of the brain serotonin systems in animals made hyperaggressive by social deprivation. Further, treatments that act to produce an increase in functional activity of the serotonergic system in aggressive animals, thus presumably restoring the system to near normal, can act to reduce aggressive behavior in these animals.

SUGGESTIONS FOR FUTURE RESEARCH: THE DIETARY TREATMENT OF AGGRESSION

Wurtman and Gernstrom have been interested for several years now in the dietary control of brain neurotransmitters. In particular, they have focused on the effects of diet, that is, what you eat, on the synthesis and release of two neurotransmitters, serotonin (5-HT) and acetylcholine (ACh) (Wurtman, 1978; Wurtman and Fernstrom, 1974, 1975; Wurtman and Growdon, 1978). For the purposes of this chapter, we will concentrate on their findings on serotonin. Serotonin is formed, within some brain neurons, from tryptophan, an essential amino acid which the body cannot manufacture by itself. The brain obtains this amino acid from the bloodstream, which obtains it from the diet. The series of studies by Wurtman and Fernstrom demonstrated that brain levels of serotonin are coupled to food consumption. In rat, it was shown that low doses of tryptophan increased the levels of brain serotonin.

Recently, Wurtman, Growdon, and their colleagues have demonstrated a similar relationship between giving choline or lecithin, the dietary form of choline, and corresponding increases in brain choline and acetylcholine levels. This information, which was obtained by studying the brains of rats, was recently applied to a clinical situation, the treatment of the disorder known as tardive dyskinesia. Tardive dyskinesia, a disorder involving the disruption of an antagonistic balance between the two neurotransmitters, acetylcholine and dopamine, in the brain, can be successfully treated by giving patients either choline or lecithin (Wurtman, 1978; Wurtman and Growdon, 1978). Here is one excellent example of the treatment of neurotransmitter abnormality using dietary precursors.

Useful research in the future regarding the suppression of aggressive behavior in aggressive individuals might involve an investigation of dietary trytophan loads or serotonin agonists on aggressive behavior. In this respect, it is interesting to note that diet has already been used to some extent in the treatment of behavioral problems in children, including aggressive behavior and hyperactivity, by Feingold. In a recent discussion that I had with Dr. Benjamin Feingold, he estimated that about 80% of delinquents have histories of behavioral problems and learning disabilities.

CONCLUSION

In conclusion, I would like to suggest that an investigation of the treatment of aggressive disorders by increasing functional activity of the brain serotonin system, through dietary or other means, may prove useful in advancing our knowledge of brain mechanisms involved in the mediation of aggressive behavior and of treatment of aggressive disorders.

Finally, accumulated evidence suggests that deficient social environments can produce a behavioral syndrome marked by hyperactivity and aggressivity. Since prevention is much preferred to treatment, prophylaxis—in the form of healthy structured social interaction—is warranted.

ACKNOWLEDGEMENTS

I am most grateful to Dr. Trevor Robbins for his comments on an earlier version of the manuscript. Ms. Eileen Staples is thanked for typing the manuscript.

REFERENCES

A. P. A. (1977). Diagnostic and Statistical Manual of Mental Disorders, 3rd ed. 4/15/77. Washington, D.C.: American Psychiatric Association.

Anden, N. E., Corrodi, H., Fuxe, K., and Hokfelt, T. (1968). Evidence for a 5-hydroxytryptamine receptor stimulation by lysergic acid diethylamide. *Brit. J. Pharmacol.*, 34:1.

Antelman, S., Szechtman, H., Chin, P., and Fisher, A. (1975). Tail pinch-induced eating, gnawing and licking behavior: Dependence on the nigrostriatal dopamine system. *Brain Res.*, 99:319.

Bender, L. (1947). Psychopathic behavior disorders in children. In: *Handbook of Correctional Psychology*, R. Linder (ed.). New York: Philosophical Library.

Bourgault, P., Karczmar, A., and Scudder, C. (1963). Contrasting behavior, pharmacological, neurophysiological, and biochemical profiles of C57, B 1/6 and SC-1 strains of mice. *Life Sci.*, 8:533.

Cantwell, D. (1978). Hyperactivity and antisocial behavior. *J. Am. Acad. Child Psychiat.*, 17:252.

Carlson, N. R. (1977). *Physiology of Behavior*. Boston: Allyn and Bacon, Inc.

Carr, L., and Moore, K. (1969). Norepinephrine release from brain by d-amphetamine *in vivo*. *Science*, 164:322.

Cohen, N., Douglas, V., and Morgenstern, G. (1971). The effect of methylphenidate on attentive behavior and autonomic activity in hyperactive children. *Psychopharmacol.*, 22: 282.

Creese, I., and Iversen, S. (1972). Amphetamine response in rat after dopamine neurone destruction. *Nature New Biol.*, 238:247.

DeFeudis, F., and DeFeudis, P. (1977). *Elements of the Behavioral Code* New York: Academic.

DiChiara, G., Camba, R., and Spano, P. (1971). Evidence for inhibition by brain serotonin of mouse killing behavior in rats. *Nature*, 233:272.

Douglas, V. (1972). Stop, Look and Listen: The problem of sustained attention and impulse control in hyperactive and normal children. *Canad. J. Behav. Sci./Rev. Canad. Sci. Comp.*, 4:259.

Egger, M., and Flynn, J. (1963). Effect of electrical stimulation of the amygdala on hypothalamically elicited attack behavior in cats. *J. Neurophysiol.*, 26:705.

Einon, D., and Morgan, M. (1976). Habituation of object contact in socially-reared and isolated rats *(Rattus norveqicus) Animal Behav.*, 24:415.

Einon, D., Morgan, M., and Sahakian, B. (1975). The development of intersession habituation and emergence in socially-reared and isolated rats. *Develop. Psychobiol.*, 8:553.

Fox, M. (1968). *Abnormal Behavior in Animals*. London: Saunders, p. 49.

Gerattini, S., Giacolone, E., and Valzelli, L. (1969). Biochemical changes during isolation-induced aggressiveness in mice. In: *Aggressive Behavior*, S. Garattini and E. Sigg (eds.). New York: John Wiley.

Glowinski, J., and Baldessarini, R. (1966). Metabolism of norepinephrine in the central nervous system. *Pharmacol. Rev.*, 18:1201.

Goldfarb, W. (1955). Emotional and intellectual consequences of psychologic deprivation in infancy: A re-evaluation. In: *Psychopathology of Childhood*, P. Hock and J. Zubin (eds.). New York: Grune and Stratton.

Gore, E. (1976). *Child Psychiatry Observed*. Oxford: Pergamon.

Grant, E. (1963). Analysis of social behavior of the male laboratory rat. *Behavior*, 21:260.

Hatch, A. Wiberg, G., Balazs, T. and Grice, H. (1963). Long-term isolation stress in rats. *Science*. 142:507.

Hodge, G., and Butcher, L. (1974). 5-Hydroxytryptamine correlates of isolation-induced aggression in mice. *European J. Pharmacol.*, 28:326.

Horn, A., Cuello, A., and Miller, R. (1974). Dopamine in the mesolimbic system of the rat brain: Endogenous levels and the effects of drugs on the uptake mechanism and stimulation of adenylate cyclase activity. *J. Neurochem.*, 22:265.

Hornykiewicz, O. (1973), Parkinson's disease: From brain homogenate to treatment. *Fed. Proc.*, 32:183.

Hutchinson, R. (1977). By-products of aversive control. In: *Handbook of Operant Behavior*, W. Honig and J. Staddon (eds.). New Jersey: Prentice-Hall.

Iversen, S., and Iversen, L. (1975). *Behavioral Pharmacology*. New York: Oxford University Press.

Kahn, M. (1951). The effect of severe defeat at various age levels on the aggressive behavior of mice. *J. Genetic Psychol.*, 79:117.

Karli, P. (1956). Norway rat's killing response to the white mouse: An experimental study. *Behaviour*, 10:81.

Kelly, P., Seviour, P. and Iversen, S. (1975). Amphetamine and apomorphine responses in the rat following 6—OHDA lesions of the nucleus accumbens septi and corpus striatum. *Brain Res.*, 94:507.

Koe, B., and Weissman, A. (1966). p-Chlorophenylalanine: A specific depletor of brain serotonin. *J. Pharmacol. Exper. Ther.*, 154:499.

Konrad, K., and Melzack, R. (1975). Novelty-enhancement effects associated with early sensory-social isolation. In: *The Developmental Neuropsychology of Sensory Deprivation*. London: Academic.

Kostowski, W., and Czlonkowski, A. (1973). The activity of some neuroleptic drugs and amphetamine in normal and isolated rats. *Pharmacology*, 10:82.

Kulkarni, A. (1968). Muricidal block produced by 5-hydroxytryptophan and various drugs. *Life Sci.*, 7:125.

Lauter, M., and Denhoff, E. (1957). Hyperkinetic behavior syndrome in children. *J. Pediat.*, 50:463.

Lewis, D. O. (1978). Introduction: A historical perspective. *J. Am. Acad. Child Psychiat.*, 17:193.

Maas, J. (1962). Neurochemical differences between two strains of mice. *Science*, 137:621.

McKenzie, G., and Szerb, J. (1968). The effect of dihydroxyphenylalanine, pheniprazine and dextroamphetamine on the *in vivo* release of dopamine from the caudate nucleus. *J. Pharmacol. Exp. Ther.*, 162:302.

Melzack, R. (1968). Early experience: A neuropsychological approach to heredity—environment interactions. In: *Early Experience and Behavior*, G. Newton and S. Levine (eds.). Illinois: Thomas.

Miczek, K., and Barry H. III (1976). Pharmacology of sex and aggression. In: *Behavioral Pharmacology*, S. Glick and J. Goldfarb (eds.). St. Louis: C. V. Mosby Company.

Morgan, M. (1973). Effects of post-weaning environment on learning in the rat. *Animal Behav.*, 21:429.

Morgan, M., Einon, D., and Nicholas, D. (1975). The effects of isolation rearing on behavioural inhibition in the rat. *Q. J. Exp. Psychol.*, 27:615.

Moyer, J. (1968). Kinds of aggression and their physiological basis. *Commun. Behav. Biol.*, 2:65.

Pillai, V. (1976). Talk entitled: Minimal brain dysfunction. The Clinic, Brookside, Cambridge, England.

Robbins, T., and Sahakian, B. (in press). Animal models of mania. In: *Mania: An Evolving Concept*, R. Belmaker and H. van Praag (eds.). New York: Spectrum.

Roberts, W., and Kiess, H. (1964). Motivational properties of hypothalmic aggression in cats. *J. Comp. Physiol. Psychol.*, 58:187.

Roth, R., and Bunney, B. (1976). Interaction of Cholinergic neurons with other chemically defined neuronal systems in the CNS. In: *Biology of Cholinergic Function*. A. Goldberg and I. Hanin (eds.). New York: Raven.

Sahakian, B. (1976). *Effects of Isolation on Unconditioned Behaviour and Response to Drugs in Rats*. Ph.D. Thesis, University of Cambridge.

Sahakian, B., and Robbins, T. (1977a). Are the effects of psychomotor stimulant drugs on hyperactive children really paradoxical? *Medical Hypotheses*, 3:154.

Sahakian, B., and Robbins, T. (1977b). Isolation-rearing enhances tail pinch-induced oral behavior in rats. *Physiol. Behav.*, 18:53.

Sahakian, B., Robbins, T., Beynon, H. and Costello, A. (Unpublished data). The effects of social deprivation on aggressive behaviour and competitive dominance in the rat.

Sahakian, B., Robbins, T., and Iversen, S. (1977). The effects of isolation rearing on exploration in the rat. *Animal Learn. Behav.*, 5:193.

Sahakian, B., Robbins, T., Morgan, M., and Iversen, S. (1975). The effects of psychomotor stimulants on stereotypy and locomotor activity in socially deprived and control rats. *Brain Res.*, 84:195.

Segal, D., Knapp, S., Kuczenski, R., and Mandell, A. (1973). The effects of environmental isolation on behavior and regional rat brain tyrosine hydroxylase and tryptophan hydroxylase activities. *Behav. Biol.*, 8:47.

Sheard, M. (1969). The effect of p-chlorophenylalanine on behavior in rats: Relation to brain serotonin and 5-hydroxyindoleacetic acid. *Brain Res.*, 15:524.

Syme, L. (1973). Social isolation at weaning: Some effects on two measures of activity. *Animal Learn. Behav.*, 1:161.

Thoa, N., Tizabi, Y., and Jacobowitz, D. (1977). The effect of isolation on catecholamine concentration and turnover in discrete areas in rat brain. *Brain Res.*, 131:259.

Uyeno, E., and Benson, W. (1965). Effects of lysergic acid diethylamide on attack behavior of male albino mice. *Psychopharmacol.*, 7:20.

Uyeno, E., and White, M. (1967). Social isolation and dominance behaviour. *J. Comp. Physiol. Psychol.*, 63:157.

Valzelli, L. (1973). The "isolation syndrome" in mice. *Psychopharmacol.*, 31:305.

Valzelli, L. (1974). 5-Hydroxytryptamine in aggressiveness. In: *Advances in Biochemical Psychopharmacology* E. Costa, G. Gessa, and M. Sandler (eds.). New York: Raven.

Valzelli, L., and Garattini, S. (1972). Biochemical and behavioral changes induced by isolation in rats. *Neuropharmacol.*, 11:17.

von Voigtlander, P., and Moore, K. (1973). Involvement of nigro-striatal neurons in the *in vivo* release of dopamine by amphetamine, amantadine and tyramine. *J. Pharmacol. Exp. Ther.*, 181:542.

Wasman, M., and Flynn, J. (1962). Directed attack elicited from hypothalamus. *Arch. Neurol.*, 6:220.

Welch, B. (1965). Psychophysiological response to the mean level of environmental stimulation: A theory of environmental integration. In: *Symposium of Medical Aspects of Stress in the Military Climate*, D. Rioch (ed.). Washington, D.C.: U.S. Government Printing Office.

Welch, A., and Welch, B. (1971). Isolation, Reactivity and aggression: Evidence for an involvement of brain catecholamines and serotonin. In: *The Physiology of Aggression and Defeat*, B. Eleftheriou and J. Scott (eds.). New York: Plenum.

Wender, P. (1972). *Minimal Brain Dysfunction in Children*. New York: John Wiley and Sons.

Wurtman, R. (1978). Food for thought. *The Sciences*, April 6.

Wurtman, R., and Fernstrom, J. (1975). Control of brain monoamine synthesis by diet and plasma amino acids. *Am. J. Clin. Nutrition*, 28:638.

Wurtman, R., and Growdon, J. (1978). Dietary enhancement of CNS neurotransmitters. *Hospital Practice*, March: 71.

CHAPTER TEN

The Learning of Morality: Biosocial Bases

SARNOFF A. MEDNICK

Perhaps it would do no great harm to begin with a discussion of how I define morality. An early publication on this topic is summarized in Table 1. Note that the major thrust of the message is negative, "Thou shalt *not*. . . ." While subsequent moral authorities have added *some* positive acts to elaborate the definition of moral behavior (*e.g.*, "love thy neighbor"), they have also retained the original, basic, inhibitory definitions of moral acts. There are very few who will denounce you if

TABLE 1
The Ten Commandments—Exodus

1.	Thou shalt *not* have other gods before me.
2.	Thou shalt *not* make any graven image.
3.	Thou shalt *not* take the name of the Lord in vain.
4.	Remember the sabbath day.
5.	Honor thy father and thy mother.
6.	Thous shalt *not* kill.
7.	Thou shalt *not* commit adultery.
8.	Thou shalt *not* steal.
9.	Thou shalt *not* bear false witness.
10.	Thou shalt *not* covet thy neighbor's home, wife, maidservant, ox, or ass.

you do not love your neighbor; if you seduce his wife, steal from him and/or kill him (and you are detected), however, you may be certain that your behavior will be classified as immoral. Thus, putting aside (for the moment) highly philosophical, poetic, or artistic musings on morality, we might admit to ourselves that the statements of moral behavior which are critical for everyday activities are essentially negative and inhibitory in character. The fact that someone took the trouble to enumerate these strictures and then carve them onto stone tablets suggests that there must have been a strong need for the insistence on these inhibitions.

People must have evidenced and still do evidence a tendency to exhibit aggressive, adulterous, and avaricious behavior. In self-defense, society has set up moral codes and has struggled to teach its children to inhibit impulses leading to transgression of those codes.

How are these inhibitions taught to children? As far as I can see there are three mechanisms which might help parents teach children civilized behavior: modelling, positive reinforcement, and negative reinforcement. I believe that positive acts such as loving neighbors, helping old ladies across the street, and cleaning the snow and ice from the front walk can be learned by modelling, but for the more inhibitory moral commands, modelling does not seem to be a natural method. It is possible to imagine arranging circumstances in some artificial way, such that modelling *could* teach children not to be adulterous, or aggressive. However, if our civilization had to depend solely on modelling it is conceivable that things might be even more chaotic than they are today. It is also possible to use positive reinforcement to teach inhibition of forbidden behavior; but again, reinforcing a child 24 hours a day while he is *not* stealing seems a rather inefficient method and not very specific. Following the excellent exposition of Gordon Trasler (1972), I would suggest that the avoidance of transgression (*i.e.*, lawful behavior) demanded by the moral commandments is probably in the main learned via contingent negative reinforcements applied by society, family, and peers. I would guess that the critical morality-training forces in childhood are 1) the punishment of asocial responses by family, society, and friends, and 2) the child's individual capacity to *learn* to *inhibit* asocial responses. I wish first to focus my discussion on the determinants of this capacity to learn law abidance. I shall begin by considering whether genetic factors may be relevant to this capacity. My reading of this literature has suggested to me that inherited factors do play some role in the etiology of asocial behavior. I shall describe a theory of how people learn to be law abiding and close with some speculations about a (possibly heritable) autonomic nervous system factor which might relate to the etiology of asocial behavior.

In the following material, when I use the term "criminal" I mean an individual who has been convicted of a violation of the Danish penal code. It is important to note, however, that in no case does this mean that we have utilized a prison population. In almost all of the studies I will discuss, we have attempted to define total birth cohorts, and either to select all individuals that fit our criteria, or to select representative groups of such individuals.

For example, in our study with Herman A. Witkin of the relationship between the XYY chromosome anomaly and its imputed relevance to asocial behavior, we began with a total cohort of all of the 31,436 men born in the municipality of Copenhagen in 1944, 1945, 1946, and 1947. We identified the men who were 184 cm or above in height, visited these men in their homes (N = 4,139), took blood samples, and prepared karyotypes. This process yielded 12 XYY men. There was little behavior on the part of the XYY men that could be construed as being seriously violent. They did evidence significantly more criminality than did the XY men of their age, height, intelligence, and social class (Witkin et al., 1976) From an extensive examination of these XYY subjects and their controls, we can indicate that they evidence remarkably slow alpha, excessive theta (Volavka et al., 1977), very low electrodermal responsiveness, and slow rate of recovery.

TWIN AND ADOPTION STUDIES

But the XYY man is an exceedingly infrequent fellow. Our critical question to the field of genetics is whether more commonly observed criminality and psychopathy is influenced by genetic factors. This is an important question for the researcher because a finding implicating genetic factors would encourage a search for biological factors in asocial behavior. I shall now turn to the twin and adoption studies.

In the first twin-criminality study, the German psychiatrist Lange (1929) found 77% concordance for his MZ twins and 12% concordance for his DZ twins. Lange concluded that "heredity plays a quite preponderant part among the causes of crime." Subsequently, studies of twins (until 1961 there were eight in all) have tended to confirm Lange's results. About 60% concordance has been reported for MZ and about 30% concordance for DZ twins. (See Table 2.)

These eight twin studies suffer from the fact that their sampling was rather haphazard. Many were carried out in Germany or Japan during a politically unfortunate period. They report too high a proportion of MZ twins. Concordant MZ pairs are more likely to be brought to the attention of the investigator. MZ twins prove easier to detect, especially if they end up in the same prison. All these factors tend to inflate MZ

TABLE 2
Twin Studies of Psychopathy and Criminality MZ and Same-Sexed DZ Twins Only

Study	Location	Monozygotic			Dizygotic		
		Total Pairs	Pairs Concordant	% Concordant	Total Pairs	Pairs Concordant	% Concordant
Lange 1929	Bavaria	13	10	77	17	2	12
Legras 1932	Holland	4	4	100	5	1	20
Rosanoff 1934	U.S.A.	37	25	68	28	5	18
Stumpfl 1936	Germany	18	11	61	19	7	37
Kranz 1936	Prussia	32	21	66	43	23	54
Borgström 1939	Finland	4	3	75	5	2	40
Slater 1953 (Psychopathy)	England	2	1	50	10	3	30
Yoshimasu 1961	Japan	28	17	61	18	2	11
Total		138	92	67.2	145	45	31.0

concordance rates in asystematic studies. The recent and continuing study intiated by the late K. O. Christiansen, myself, Gottesman and Hutchings in Copenhagen will overcome these sampling problems. In a pilot study, Christiansen (1974) studied *all* twins born in a well-defined area of Denmark between 1881 and 1910. Of 3,586 such twin pairs he found 799 pairs with at least one of the twins registered for criminality or minor criminality. He used a national, complete criminality register. He reported a pairwise concordance rate of 36% for the MZ twins and 12.5% for the DZ. The MZ concordance is 2.8 times higher than the DZ concordance.

A very recent study by Dalgaard and Kringlen (1976) based on an unselected group of 139 Norwegian twins reports 25.8% MZ concordance and 14.9% DZ concordance. Dalgaard and Kringlen explain the difference as due to the fact that "MZ pairs usually are brought up more similarly than DZ."

In the tradition of Karl O. Christiansen we are now extending his pilot study to all twins born up until 1920, and we will include all of Denmark. This will bring the number of twins up to approximately 13,500 pairs. This number should be sufficient for a more detailed analysis than has been possible before. Despite the limitations of the twin method, these studies do not speak against the existence of some genetic effect in criminality.

THE ADOPTION STUDIES

As mentioned above, the great weakness of the twin method is that in the overwhelming number of cases genetic and environmental factors are not well separated. A design which does a better job in this regard studies individuals adopted at birth. Originally for the study of schizophrenia, a register of all non-familial adoptions in Denmark in the years 1924-1947 was established in Copenhagen at the Psykologisk Institut by a group of American and Danish investigators headed by Kety, Rosenthal, Wender, and Schulsinger (1974). There are 14,537 adoptions recorded including information on the adoptee and his biological and adoptive parents. Thus, the register contains over 70,000 persons.

We will report two investigations completed on this material studying the subpopulation of adoptees born in Copenhagen. From 5,483 *Copenhagen* adoptees, Schulsinger (1972) identified 57 psychopaths from psychiatric registers and police files. He also selected 57 non-psychopath control adoptees matched for sex, age, social class, neighborhood of rearing, and age of transfer to the adoptive family. The numbers are small, but the heaviest weight of psychopathy in the relatives comes in the cell concerning the biological relatives of the psychopathic adoptees. Since the postnatal contact between the adoptee and the relative was in most cases nonexistent or at most minimal, environmental factors probably did not play a very important role in this relationship. The existence of some heritable factor seems the most reasonable interpretation.

Using the same adoptee material, Hutchings and Mednick (1974) conducted a study on the registered criminality of a pilot sample of 1,145 male adoptees born in Copenhagen between 1927 and 1941. Of these 1,145 male adoptees, 185 had been convicted of a violation of the Danish Penal Code. Of these 185 adoptee-criminals we were able to identify 143, for each of whom we were certain of the biological father's identity and where the fathers had been born after 1890 (better police records after 1890). To each of these 143 criminal adoptees we matched a non-criminal adoptive son for age of child and social class of adoptive father. For the criminal and non-criminal groups, the age of parents and age of child at adoption proved to be about the same. The amount of contact between the adoptee and the biological father was, in almost all cases, none at all. Table 3A indicates that the heaviest weight of the registered criminality in the fathers is in the cell of the biological fathers of the criminal adoptees. Again we have evidence that genetic factors play some role in the etiology of registered criminality.

Table 3B presents this information in a different form, analogous to the cross-fostering paradigm. As can be seen in the lower right hand cell, if neither the biological nor the adoptive father is criminal, 10.5% of their sons are criminal. If the biological father is not criminal but the adoptive father is criminal this figure rises to only 11.5%. In the lower left hand corner of Table 3B note that 21.4% of the sons are criminal if the adoptive father is not criminal and the biological father is criminal. Thus the comparison analogous to a cross-fostering comparison seems to favor a partial genetic-etiology assumption. We must caution, however, that simply knowing that the adoptive father has been a criminal does not tell us how criminogenic the adoptee's environment has been. On the other hand, at conception, the genetic influence of the father is already *complete*. Thus as we have arranged the cross-fostering table it is not a fair comparison between environmental and genetic influences. But the genetic effect does seem to exist.

A third adoptee project has been completed by Crowe (1975) in Iowa. This investigation also finds evidence of a relationship between criminality in an adopted child and its biological mother. Crowe further notes an apparent similarity in the types of crimes of the biological mother and the index cases. This suggests some form of specificity of genetic effect. At present we are extending the adoptee-criminality study to encompass all the 14,537 adoptees and their 58,000 (approximately) adoptive and biological parents. From study of these 72,000 (approximately) individuals and Christiansen's 13,500 twin pairs, it should be possible to approach a more precise answer to this question of genetic specificity of type of crime.

TABLE 3
A. Registered Criminality in Biological and Adoptive Relatives of Criminal Adoptees

	Biological Father	Adoptee Father
Criminal Adoptive Sons (N=143)	70	33
Control Adoptive Sons (N=143)	40	14

B. "Cross-Fostering" Analysis: Tabled Values are Percent of Adoptive Sons Who are Registered Criminals

		Is Biological Father Criminal?	
		Yes	No
Is Adoptive Father Criminal?	Yes	$\dfrac{21}{53} = 36.2\%$	$\dfrac{6}{52} = 11.2\%$
	No	$\dfrac{46}{214} = 21\%$	$\dfrac{35}{333} = 10.4\%$

These adoptee studies have a rather strong face validity. This probably is due to their apparent separation of genetic and environmental influences. If anything were to be found which acted to increase the correlation between the genetic and environmental forces this would serve to temper the strength of impact of the findings. As a matter of fact, Hutchings (1972) has pointed out that the adoptive agency in Denmark had a policy of attempting to match the biological and adoptive families for vaguely defined social characteristics. That they partially succeeded is attested to by the significant correlation of the occupational status of the biological and adoptive fathers. ($r = .22$, $p <$ 0.001). If this SES matching were related to the criminality observed in this study then we would expect a relatively large number of adoptees with *both* biological and adoptive fathers criminal. By chance we would expect 55 such cases; we observed 58. In the case of this study, any matching which was attempted did not express itself significantly in a correlation for registration for criminality in the fathers. But other, less direct, possible consequences of this "matching" must be explored.

Another consideration in interpreting the strength of the genetic influence is the fact that the study took place in Denmark. The laboratory experimenter in behavior genetics reduces the variance ascribable to enviornmental influences when he wishes to explore the effects of strain differences. As environmental variance increases, the strain difference effects become more and more masked. While operating in a narrower range than is available to the laboratory researcher, the extent of variability of a natural, human research environment (in our case, Denmark) will also influence the extent to which existent genetic factors will be observed. We would suggest that the amount of variability in Denmark for most crime-related environmental dimensions will be less than that of many other countries. It follows, then, that in practical terms, extrapolation of our Danish findings to other national situations must be conducted with very great caution. We must exercise extreme restraint in extrapolation to a nation like the U.S. with relatively extreme variations in social circumstances.

We must also recall that the adoptive process involves screening of the biological and adoptive parents and the adoptee by the adoption agencies. This screening can produce skewed populations, a possibility which must be checked and taken into account in application of findings to non-adopted populations. The following statement is taken from a 1946 annual report of the largest state adoption organization: "Before a child is cleared for adoption, information is obtained on the child's mother and father; on whether or not there is serious physical or mental illness in the family background; criminal records are obtained for the biological parents; and in many cases school reports are obtained. By means of personal interview with the mother an impression of her is formed."

Another potential problem with the adoption method is that the adoptive family might be informed by the adoption agency of deviance in the biological family. The adoptee's behavior might conceivably be interpreted in accordance with this information, and the adoptee labeled deviant as a result. The probability of the adoptee's manifesting deviance might thus be affected, producing a form of correlation between the biological and adoptive parents which is unwanted in this research design. A social worker was sent to read some of the old adoption journals and formed the impression that serious deviance in the biological parents was more or less routinely reported to the prospective adoptive parents unless they refused the information. What effect might result from such information given to the adoptive parents?

If the biological father's criminal career *began the year after* the birth of the child, this criminality information could not have been transmitted to the adoptive parents. On the other hand, in cases in which the criminality of the biological father started *before* the birth of the adoptee, the information probably was communicated and could perhaps have affected the probability of criminality in the adoptee. Of the 347 criminal biological fathers in the adoptee pilot study, 67% had their first registration for criminality before the birth of the child, and 33% began their criminal career after the birth of the adoptee. For all of the 347 criminal biological fathers the probability of their biological son becoming a criminal is 23%. In the cases where the biological father committed his first offense *before* the birth of the adoptee, 23% of the adoptees became criminal. In the cases where the biological father committed his first offense *after* the birth of the adoptee, 23% of the adoptee became criminal. We can tentatively conclude from this simple analysis that the *possibility* of the adoptive family being informed of the biological father's criminality is not related to an altered likelihood that the adoptive son will become a criminal.

Despite these cautions, it would seem difficult to use the evidence of these twin and adoptee studies to refute a hypothesis involving genetic factors in the etiology of psychiatry and criminality. Accepting the hypothesis for the moment, it seems likely that the operation of this genetic influence could be relatively nonspecific (*e.g.*, general intelligence) or could be via some physiological predisposing factor or factors, or both. I have (Mednick, 1974, 1977) been able to construct a theory that specifies an autonomic variable which seems heritable and which could conceivably play some role in the etiology of asocial behavior.

Hare (1970), Trasler (1972), and others have discussed the possibility that the psychopath and criminal have some defect in avoidance learning which interferes with their ability to learn to inhibit asocial responses. Much of this has been inspired by the 1957 study by Lykken indicating the difficulties psychopaths have in learning to avoid an electric shock. On the whole, these results have found very good empirical support. Hare has suggested that the empirically observed and reobserved autonomic hyporeactivity of the psychopath and criminal may be, partially, the basis of this poor avoidance learning. In order to better understand this, let us consider the avoidance learning situation. In particular, let us follow Trasler (1972), and consider how the law-abiding citizen might learn his admirable self-control.

How do children learn to inhibit aggressive impulses? Frequently when child A is aggressive to child B, child A is punished by a peer or perhaps his mother. After a sufficient quantity or quality of punishment, just the thought of the aggression should be enough to produce a bit of anticipatory fear in child A. If this fear response is large enough, the raised arm will drop and the aggressive response will be successfully inhibited.

Our theory suggests that what happens in this child after he has successfully inhibited such an asocial response is critical for his learning of civilized behavior. Let us consider the situation again in more detail.

1. Child A contemplates aggressive action.
2. Because of previous punishment he suffers fear.
3. He inhibits the aggressive response.

WHAT HAPPENS TO HIS ANTICIPATORY FEAR?

4. It will begin to dissipate, to be reduced. We know that fear-reduction is the most powerful, naturally occurring reinforcement which psychologists have discovered. So the reduction of fear (which immediately follows the inhibition of the aggression) can act as a reinforcement for this *inhibition* and will result in the learning of the inhibition of aggression. The fear-reduction-reinforcement increases the probability that the inhibition of the aggression will occur in the future. After many such experiences, the normal child will learn to inhibit aggressive impulses. Each time such an impulse arises and is inhibited, the inhibition will be strengthened by reinforcement.

What does a child need in order to learn effectively to be civilized (in the context of this approach)?

1. A censuring agent (typically family) *AND*
2. An adequate fear response *AND*
3. The ability to learn the fear response in anticipation of an asocial act *AND*
4. Fast dissipation of fear to quickly reinforce the inhibitory response.

Now we wish to concentrate on point 4. The speed and size of a reinforcement determine its effectiveness. An effective reinforcement is one which is delivered *immediately* after the relevant response. In terms of this discussion, the faster the reduction of fear, the faster the delivery of the reinforcement. The fear response is, to a large extent, controlled by the autonomic nervous system (ANS). We can estimate the activity of the ANS by means of peripheral indicants such as heart rate, blood pressure, and skin conductance. The measure of most relevance will peripherally reflect the rate or speed at which the ANS recovers from periods of imbalance.

If child A has an ANS that characteristically recovers very quickly from fear, then he will receive a quick and large reinforcement and learn inhibition quickly. If he has an ANS that recovers very slowly, he will receive a slow, small reinforcement and learn to inhibit the aggression very slowly, if at all. This orientation would predict that (holding constant critical extra-individual variables such as social status, crime training, poverty level, etc.) those who commit asocial acts will be characterized by slow autonomic recovery. The slower the recovery, the more serious and repetitive the asocial behavior predicted.

TESTS OF THE THEORY

To test this theory we first turned to a longitudinal study of some 13 years duration. We have been following 311 individuals whom we intensively examined, psychophysiologically and otherwise, in 1962. Since that year, a number have had serious disagreements with the law (convictions for violation of the penal code). We checked and noted that in 1962 (some years before their first offense) their electrodermal recovery (EDRec) was considerably slower than that of controls (Loeb and Mednick, 1977). Those who have been recently clinically diagnosed "psychopathic" have remarkably slow recovery.

Siddle, Nicol and Foggitt (1973) examined the electrodermal responsiveness of 67 English borstal inmates, divided into high, medium, and low asociality groups. When Siddle measured skin conductance recovery, speed and rate of recovery varied inversely as a function of asociality. Recovery measured on a single trial was surprisingly effective in differentiating the three groups (Siddle et al., 1977).

Bader-Bartfai and Schalling (1974) reanalysed skin conductance data from a previous investigation of criminals, finding that criminals who tended to be more "delinquent" on a personality measure tended to have slower recovery. Hare (in press) also reports slow recovery for prison inmates. There have been other supportive findings recently reported (Hemming, 1977; Hinton et al., 1977; Eisenberg, 1976; Plovnick, 1976; Waid, 1976). Siddle, in a recent review, states: "The results concerning SCR recovery and antisocial behavior appear to be quite consistent. Subjects who display antisocial behavior (psychopaths, adult criminals, and adolescent delinquents) also display significantly slower SCR recovery than do matched controls" (Siddle, 1977; see also Hare's review in press). When Wadsworth examined pulse rates of all 11-year old boys in the 1946 British birth cohort, those boys who, at age 20, proved to be delinquent, evidenced slow pulse rates, suggesting autonomic *hypo*responsiveness (Wadsworth, 1976). This is a striking finding because of the size and representativeness of the population and the prospective nature of the study.

In view of the relationships which have been reported between psychophysiological variables and asocial behavior and in view of our interest in better understanding the apparent genetic predisposition to asocial behavior, we next turned to a study of the heritability of skin conductance responses. We (Bell et al., 1977) invited pairs of male 12-year old twins into our laboratory. Interestingly enough, only recovery proved to have significant heritability (and only in the left hand). We had hypothesized this result (Mednick and Schulsinger, 1973) when we noted that recovery was the only skin conductance measure which was relatively unaffected by important life variables in a group at high risk for schizophrenia. This pattern of results encourages the speculation that part of the heritability of asocial behavior might be attributed to the heritability of ANS recovery. Thus, slow recovery might be a characteristic a criminal father could pass to a biological son which (given the proper environmental circumstances) could increase

TABLE 4
Skin Conductance Behavior During Orienting Response Testing in Children with Criminal and Noncriminal Fathers

Skin Conductance Function (Right hand)	Mean Score		F	df	p
	Noncriminal Father	Criminal Father			
Basal Level Skin Conductance	2.51	2.33	.09	1,193	n.s.
Amplitude in micromhos	.031	.016	.03	1,193	n.s.
Number of Responses	2.79	1.55	8.51	1,187	.01
Response Onset Latency in seconds	2.11	2.18	.07	1,97	n.s.
Latency to Response Peak in seconds	2.05	2.38	5.32	1,195	.05
Average Half Recovery Time in seconds	3.75	5.43	4.26	1,90	.05
Minimum Half Recovery Time	2.26	4.33	8.80	1,90	.01

NOTE: During Orienting Response testing, the child was presented 14 times with a tone of 1000 cps.

the probability of the child failing to learn adequately to inhibit asocial responses. Thus we would predict that criminal fathers would have children with slow recovery.

Table 4 presents data on the electrodermal behavior of children with criminal and non-criminal fathers. As can be seen, the prediction regarding recovery is not disconfirmed. It is interesting that the pattern of responsiveness of these children closely resembles that which we might anticipate seeing in their criminal fathers. Results of other studies in our laboratory have replicated these findings.

INTERACTION OF FAMILY MILIEU AND ANS FACTORS

The next step which attracted our attention was the study of the interaction of the family censoring factor (mentioned above) with an individual's ANS functioning in determining the probability of his evidencing criminal behavior. The first approach of a group at the Psykologisk Institut, Mednick et al. (1977), to this problem was at best an approximation. For purposes of this study we made the assumption that training for law-abidance was greater in a family with no record of criminality than it would be in a family in which the father (and in some cases the mother also) had been convicted and jailed for a criminal offense. We knew that in families with criminal fathers (in Denmark) the probability of criminality in the sons was increased substantially. In such criminal families we were especially interested in knowing what personal characteristics of the son protect him from criminogenic influences. We also knew that if the father was not a criminal the probability of criminality in the son was considerably reduced. In such a non-criminogenic environment, what personal characteristics of the son might help lead him into crime?

Design of study

We determined to comb a well-defined population to identify those criminal and non-criminal sons who had been reared in a criminal or non-criminal family. We ascertained and registered a population of 1,944 consecutive male deliveries at a large Copenhagen hospital from January 1st, 1936, to September 30th, 1938.

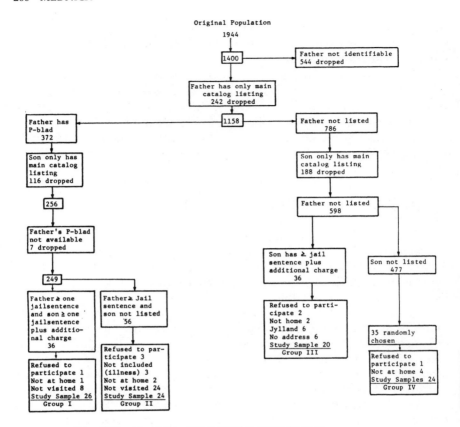

Note: If the mother had a criminal record in Groups III or IV
the family was not included.

Figure 1. Process of subject selection for Copenhagen study (1936–1938).

The flow diagram describing the process of subject selection may be seen in Figure 1. Individuals with minor offenses were dropped from the study.

Contact and selection of subjects

A psychiatrist visited the four groups which resulted from the selection process.

1. Criminal father—Criminal son.
2. Criminal father—Non-criminal son.
3. Non-criminal father—Criminal son.
4. Non-criminal father—Non-criminal son.

Assessment program

The subjects experienced the following test battery:
Psychophysiological assessment.
Psychiatric interview.
Perceptual testing.
Psychological testing.

Results for two key groups

Criminal father—Non-criminal son

The question we raised for this group was "What protected the son from criminality despite the criminogenic milieu?" This group of sons had a mean IQ of 113, significantly higher than the other groups' IQs, which were all about 100. In addition, they evidenced the fastest electrodermal recovery of the four groups. These results may be interpreted as suggesting that these sons, raised in a criminogenic milieu, resist criminality because they are intellectually gifted and perhaps reinforced by their school experiences and have a good ANS aptitude for learning to inhibit antisocial responses.

Non-criminal father—Criminal son

For this group we asked the question: "What personal factors push this individual to criminality despite the non-criminogenic nature of the family?" One factor was outstanding. The son from the non-criminal milieu who becomes criminal evidences the slowest skin conductance recovery of the four groups. In terms of the theory presented above such a finding is not unexpected.

These findings suggest strongly that the psychophysiological researcher would do well to consider the rearing conditions of their psychopathic or criminal subjects since such data may provide some indicant of the environmental push for asocial behavior. It has been our experience that where this environmental push is apparently minimal, the psychophysiological variables most clearly express themselves. Where the environmental push to criminality is great, the physiological and genetic variables explain considerably less variance. Thus the genetic and physiological variables predict most poorly in the lower classes and best in the middle classes (Christiansen, 1968).

MAURITIUS PROJECT

To obtain a meaningful answer to the question of the relevance of these ANS variables for the etiology of asocial behavior, one useful research design would involve testing 100% of a reasonably large population of children, following them and determining the relative probability of asocial behavior among those who are hyporesponsive and have slow recovery. In Mauritius, a group of investigators (Schulsinger et al., 1975) tested the entire population of three-year olds in two well-defined areas (Vacoas and Quatre Bornes). From smallpox vaccination records the 1,800 three-year olds in the two areas were located and invited in for testing. The tests included:

Psychophysiology (heart rate, bilateral skin conductance and skin potential.

EEG (not the entire population).

Birth data (not the entire population).

Cognitive development.

Medical examination.

Laboratory observation ratings.

One interesting question is whether the slowest autonomic recovery children will evidence excessive delinquency in adolescence. But equally important is the question "What other outcomes are observed?" Perhaps there are also some socially useful and valuable outcomes of slow recovery which we cannot foresee. Perhaps the weakness in learning socially conforming modes of behavior is accompanied by some increase in creativity or originality. We must wait ten years for the answers to these questions.

ACKNOWLEDGMENTS

This work was supported by USPHS Grant Nos. 19225, 24872, 25311 (Center for Studies of Crime and Delinquency). We also received support from the Danish Medical Research Council and the World Health Organization.

REFERENCES

Bader-Bartfai, A. and Schalling, D. (1974). Recovery times of skin conductance responses as related to some personality and physiological variables. Psychological Institute, University of Stockholm.

Bell, B., Mednick, S. A., Gottesman, I. I., and Sergeant, J. (1977). Electrodermal parameters in young, normal male twins. In: *Biosocial Bases of Criminal Behavior*, Sarnoff A. Mednick and Karl O. Christiansen (eds.). New York: Gardner Press, Inc.

Borgstrom, C. (1939). Eine Serie von Kriminellen Zwillingen. *Arch. Rass. ges. Biol.*, 33:334–343.

Christiansen, K. O. (1968). Threshold of tolerance in various population groups illustrated by results from the Danish criminologic twin study. In: *The Mentally Abnormal Offender*, A. V. S. de Reuck and R. Porter (eds.). Boston: Little, Brown.

Christiansen, K. O. (1974). The genesis of aggressive criminality. Implications of a study of crime in a Danish twin sample. In: *Determinants and Origins of Aggressive Behavior*, J. Dewit and W. W. Hartrup (eds.). The Hague: Mouton.

Crowe, R. R. (1975). An adoptive study of psychopathy: Preliminary results from arrest records and psychiatric hospital records. In: *Genetic Research in Psychiatry*, Ronald R. Fieve, David Rosenthal, and Henry Brill (eds.). Baltimore: The Johns Hopkins University Press.

Dalgaard, O. S., and Kringlen, E. (1976). A Norwegian twin study of criminality. *Brit. J. Criminol.* 16:213–232.

Eisenberg, J. (1976). Criminality and heart rate: A prospective study. Doctoral Dissertation, New School for Social Research, New York.

Hare, R. D. (1970). *Psychopathy: Theory and Research*, New York: Wiley.

Hare, R. D. (in press). Electrodermal and cardiovascular correlates of psychopathy. In: *Psychopathic Behavior: Approaches to Research*, R. D. Hare and D. Schalling (eds.). London: Wiley.

Hemming, H. (1977). Comparison of electrodermal indices theoretically relevant to anti-social behaviour in a selected prison sample and students. Presented paper, British Psychophysiological Association.

Hinton, J., O'Neill, M., and Webster, S. (1977). Electrodermal indices of psychopathic recidivism and schizophrenia in maximum security patients. Presented paper, British Psychological Society, Exeter.

Hutchings, B. (1972). Environmental and genetic factors in psychopathology and criminality. Thesis, University of London.

Hutchings, B., and Mednick, S. A. (1974). Registered criminality in the adoptive and biological parents of registered male criminal adoptees. In: *Genetics, Environment and Psychopathology*, S. A. Mednick, F. Schulsinger, J. Higgins, and B. Bell (eds.). Amsterdam: North Holland/Elsevier.

Kety, S. A., Rosenthal, D., Wender, P. H., and Schulsinger, F. (1974). The types and prevalence of mental illness in the biological and adoptive families of adopted schizo-phrenics. In: *Genetics, Environment and Psychopathology*, S. A. Mednick, F. Schulsinger, J. Higgins and B. Bell (eds.). Amsterdam: North Holland/Elsevier, 1974.

Kranz, N. (1936). *Lebenschicksale Krimineller Zwillinge*, Berlin: Springer.

Lange, J. (1929). *Verbrechen als Schicksal. Studien an Kriminellen Zwillingen*. Leipzig: Thieme.

LeGras, A. M. (1933). Psychose und Kriminalität bei Zwillingen. *Z. ges. Neurol. Psychiat.*, 144:198–228.

Loeb, J., and Mednick, S. A. (1977). A prospective study of predictors in criminality: 4. School Behavior. In: *Biosocial Bases of Criminal Behavior*, S. A. Mednick and Karl O. Christiansen (eds.). New York: Gardner Press.

Lykken, D. T. (1957). A study of anxiety in the sociopathic personality. *J. Abnorm. Soc. Psychol.*, 55:6–10.

Mednick, S. A. (1974). Electrodermal recovery and psychopathology. In: *Genetics, Environment and Psychopathology*, S. A. Mednick, F. Schulsinger, J. Higgins and B. Bell (eds.). Amsterdam: North Holland/Elsevier.

Mednick, S. A. (1977). A bio-social theory of the learning of law-abiding behavior. In: *Biosocial Bases of Criminal Behavior*, Sarnoff A. Mednick and Karl O. Christiansen (eds.). New York: Gardner Press, Inc.

Mednick, S. A., Kirkegaard-Sørensen, L., Hutchings, B., Knop, J., Rosenberg, R., and Schulsinger, F. (1977). An example of biosocial interaction research: The interplay of socioenvironmental and individual factors in the etiology of criminal behavior. In: *Biosocial Bases of Criminal Behavior*, Sarnoff A. Mednick and Karl O. Christiansen, (eds.). New York: Gardner Press, Inc.

Mednick, S. A., and Schulsinger, F. (1973). Studies of children at high-risk for schizophrnia. In: *Schizophrenia: The First Ten Dean Award Lectures, S. R. Dean (ed.). New York: MSS Information Corporation, pp. 245–293.

Plovnick, N. (1976). Autonomic nervous system functioning as a predisposing influence on personality, psychopathy and schizophrenia. Doctoral Dissertation, New School for Social Research, New York.

Rosanoff, A. J., Handy, L. M., and Plesset, I. R. (1934). Criminality and delinquency in twins. *J. Crim. Law Criminol.*, 24:923–934.

Schulsinger, F. (1974). Psychopathy: Heredity and environment. In: *Genetics, Environment and Psychopathology*, S. A. Mednick, F. Schulsinger, J. Higgins and B. Bell (eds.). Amsterdam: North Holland/Elsevier, 1974.

Schulsinger, F., Mednick, S. A., Venables, P. H., Raman, A. C., and Bell, B. (1975). The early detection and prevention of mental illness: The Mauritius Project. A preliminary report. *Neuropsychobiol.* 1:166–179.

Siddle, D. A. T. (1977). Electrodermal activity and psychopathy. In: *Biosocial Bases of Criminal Behavior*, Karl O. Christiansen and Sarnoff A. Mednick (eds.). New York: Gardner Press, Inc.

Siddle, D. A. T., Mednick, S. A., Nicol, A. R., and Foggitt, R. H. (1977). Skin conductance recovery in antisocial adolescents. In: *Biosocial Bases of Criminal Behavior*, Karl O. Christiansen and Sarnoff A. Mednick (eds.). New York: Gardner Press, Inc.

Siddle, D. A. T., Nicol, A. R., and Foggitt, R. H. (1973). Habituation and overextinction of the GSR component of the orienting response in antisocial adolescents. *Brit. J. Soc. Clin. Psychol.*, 12:303–308.

Slater, E. (1936). The incidence of mental disorder. *Annals of Eugenics*, 6:172.

Stumpfl, F. (1936). *Die Ursprünge des Verbrechens, dargestellt am Lebenslauf von Zwillingen.* Leipzig: Thieme.

Trasler, G. (1972). Criminal behavior. In: *Handbook of Abnormal Psychology*, H. J. Eysenck (ed.). London: Putnam.

Volavka, J., Mednick, S. A., Sergeant, J., and Rasmussen, L. (1977). EEGs of XYY and XXY men found in a large birth cohort. In: *Biosocial Bases of Criminal Behavior*, Sarnoff A. Mednick and Karl O. Christiansen (eds.). New York: Gardner Press, Inc.

Wadsworth, M. E. J. (1976). Delinquency, pulse rates and early emotional deprivation. *Brit. J. Criminol.*, 16:245–256.

Waid, W. M. (1976). Skin conductance response to both signaled and unsignaled noxious stimulation predicts level of socialization. *J. Personality Soc. Psychol.*, 34:923–929.

Witkin, H. A., Mednick, S. A.,,, Schulsinger, F., Bakkestrøm, E., Christiansen, K. O., Goodenough, D. R., Hirschhorn, K., Lundsteen, C., Owen, D. R., Philip, J., Rubin, D. B., and Stocking, M. (1977). Criminality in XYY and XXY men. In: *Biosocial Bases of Criminal Behavior*, Sarnoff A. Mednick and Karl O. Christiansen, (eds.). New York: Gardner Press, Inc., 1977.

Yoshimasu, S. (1961). The criminological significance of the family in the light of the studies of criminal twins. *Acta Criminol. Med. Leg. Jap.* 27:117-141. Cited after *Excerpta Criminologica*, 1962, 2:723–724.

CHAPTER ELEVEN

Psychoendocrine Aspects of Male Delinquency and Aggression

ÅKE MATTSSON

The purpose of this chapter is to present research evidence relating endocrine activity to human aggressiveness and antisocial behavior. The data primarily comes from studies of testosterone production among adolescent and young males. So far, endocrine aspects of female aggression have not been subject to systematic investigation. Delinquency refers to the legal term, which signifies a range of asocial behaviors in youngsters below the statutory age limits.

Many non-scientific, often preposterous, and short-lived attempts have been made to relate criminal and hyperaggressive behavior to biological factors. The early contributions by authors such as Lombroso, who in 1876 reported on "stigmata of degeneration" among many criminals (Lombroso, 1911), and Goddard (1913) who spoke about "bad stock" as the cause of feeblemindedness and other behavioral inferiorities, have made us cautious in reviewing the evidence that certain biological variables are related to aggressive, violent acts (Lewis, 1978).

The study of aggressive behaviors requires a multidimensional etiological approach (Lewis and Balla, 1976; Mattsson et al., 1980). Many factors contribute to the shaping of a delinquent individual. Sociologists and criminologists have emphasized social, psychological, and environmental variables as causative keys to aggressive behavior. Biological scientists understandably are more concerned with genetic and constitutional factors. Some scientists tend to overlook the well-known fact that the genotype reacts with a host of environmental influences following conception, and that the genotype determines the reaction range of the phenotype. A person's constitution is not static and given at birth, but open to many changes as biopsychosocial influences impact upon the phenotype.

BIOPSYCHOSOCIAL MODEL OF AGGRESSIVE BEHAVIOR

An *open systems model* of the various factors that contribute to aggressive, antisocial behavior may be helpful. Such a model shows how antisocial behavior reverberates within the many sub-systems surrounding a delinquent youngster (Figure 1). Well-known family and social contributory factors impinge upon the vulnerable or delinquency-prone child. The child might be prone to antisocial behavior due to a variety of hereditary and congenital factors; perinatal events; temperamental patterns; attachment disorders; physical, mental, and learning disorders; and substance abuse. The psychobiological characteristics of the adolescent stage pose an additional vulnerability for impulsive, violent acts.

Whatever the predisposing vulnerability factors might be in a subject, the antisocial acts result from the operation of the mediating mechanisms of the central nervous system which integrate input stimuli from the external and the internal environment of the subject. Environmental influences equal perceptual experiences or "symbolic events" in the brain and are transduced into neurophysiological arousal. Cognitive defense activities attenuate and determine the magnitude of the psychophysiologic arousal. Via cortical-limbic-hypothalamic pathways, the arousal may activate the three effector systems of the brain: the somatic nervous system, the autonomic nervous system, and the endocrine system (Mason, 1975a).

Through the operation of the CNS mediating mechanisms, aggressive and antisocial behavior may occur. The right side of Figure 1 shows the common expressions of antisocial behavior according to current diagnostic nomenclature and dimensions. The delinquent subject should be assessed along each of these dimensions in order to provide as broad a diagnostic picture as possible which will assist in treatment planning.

The pioneering psychoendocrinologist, John W. Mason, and his co-workers have conducted a series of studies in humans on the relationship between hormonal activity and behavioral states reflecting acute or enduring psychologic influences (Mason, 1975a, 1975b). The documentation of the hormonal output of the endocrine effector systems may illuminate the organization and work of the CNS integrative mechanisms, albeit in a peripheral fashion. Because the endocrine

Figure 1. Open Systems Model of Antisocial Behavior

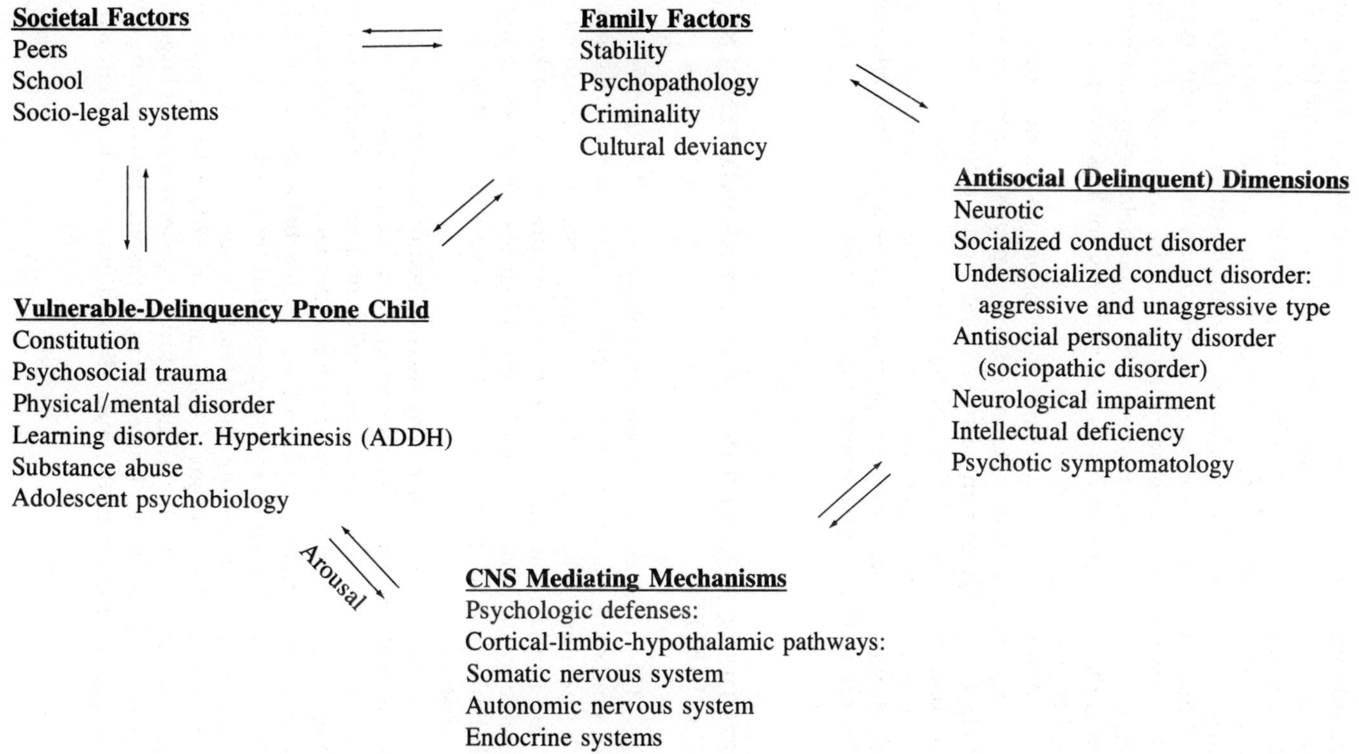

Societal Factors
Peers
School
Socio-legal systems

Family Factors
Stability
Psychopathology
Criminality
Cultural deviancy

Antisocial (Delinquent) Dimensions
Neurotic
Socialized conduct disorder
Undersocialized conduct disorder:
  aggressive and unaggressive type
Antisocial personality disorder
  (sociopathic disorder)
Neurological impairment
Intellectual deficiency
Psychotic symptomatology

Vulnerable-Delinquency Prone Child
Constitution
Psychosocial trauma
Physical/mental disorder
Learning disorder. Hyperkinesis (ADDH)
Substance abuse
Adolescent psychobiology

CNS Mediating Mechanisms
Psychologic defenses:
Cortical-limbic-hypothalamic pathways:
Somatic nervous system
Autonomic nervous system
Endocrine systems

Arousal

glands work in synergisms and antagonisms, it is helpful to assess a spectrum of hormonal activities of a subject at the same time. The aim is to identify hormonal profiles, through blood or urine assessments, that are characteristic for certain behavioral states (*e.g.* normal, stressful, or aggressive-violent) of a subject or group of subjects. The hypothalamic-pituitary axis controls most of the psychoendocrine pathways including the secretion of growth hormone, prolactin, cortisol, the sex hormones, and the thyroid hormones. The hypothalamic-sympathetic-adrenal medullary system serves as the pathway for the secretion of norepinephrine and epinephrine.

Within the open systems model of antisocial, delinquent behavior, emphasizing a multifactorial etiology, psychoendocrine studies may help to identify certain patterns of hormonal activity associated with a propensity for verbal/physical aggressive behaviors. There is no claim of a cause and effect relationship. Such studies are easier to conduct on an adult than on an adolescent population due to the instability of psychological and hormonal assessments of adolescents.

STUDIES OF ENDOCRINE ACTIVITY AS INDEPENDENT VARIABLES

The field of psychoendocrinology usually studies the activity of endocrine glands as dependent variables, while various aspects of the person's behavior and personality serve as independent variables. This contrasts to those situations of nature where marked hormonal influences — normal or pathophysiological — shape or change human behavioral characteristics which thus have been studied as dependent variables.

In the areas of human aggressive behavior some relevant examples of normal and pathological endocrine influences are:

1. The presence of androgens during early fetal life is essential for the normal development of those hypothalamic structures that initiate and control male sexual and aggressive behavior in later life (Rose, 1975). A clinical corollary is represented by genetic females exposed to excess androgen during their fetal life (as seen, for instance, in the adrenogenital syndrome (AGS) and in girls with progestin-induced female hermaphroditism). Longitudinal observations of large samples of such girls, all being treated with cortisone replacement (AGS) and surgical correction of the masculinized genitalia, have shown that they

display an increased level of physical energy expenditure, prefer boys over girls as playmates, and are rated higher on tomboyism when compared to healthy control girls (Ehrhardt, 1975). There is no evidence, however, that these girls as adolescents show an increased frequency of gender identity disorder or homosexual object choice. Boys with AGS, receiving cortisone replacement, show normal physical and psychosexual development with a tendency toward a higher level of physical energy and excellency in sports, compared to normal males (Ehrhardt, 1975).

2. Several studies on lower and higher nonhuman primates have documented the relationship between sexual maturation of male animals, rising testosterone levels, and adult aggressive behavior (Rada et al., 1976a; Rose, 1975). The most recent report by Rose and associates (1978) on hormonal and behavioral variables among groups of male rhesus monkeys documented significant associations between increasing plasma testosterone concentrations in adolescent monkeys and observations of their agonistic, sex, and play behaviors. There is a lack of similar, longitudinal data on human pubertal males, comparing their well-known rapid increase in testosterone levels, as the result of increased LH secretion during sleep (Boyar et al., 1974) to their usual changes in physical energy expenditure and aggressive and sexual behaviors (August et al., 1972; Knorr et al., 1974). Pubertal and adolescent maturation involves complex, still poorly understood biological, cognitive, and psychosocial leaps in a boy's growth and development. Direct or indirect influences of rapidly rising testosterone secretion on his behavior can be hypothesized and should become a subject for further investigation (Mattsson et al., 1980; Olweus et al., 1980; Rose, 1975).

3. Over the years many authors have tried to link the female menstrual cycle and the syndrome of premenstrual tension to an array of minor and major psychiatric events in women, from "aches and pains" and irritability to suicide and crimes of violence; Shah and Roth (1974) give a good historical review. Most of these studies suffer from methodological flaws such as skewed populations and poor control data (Smith, 1975; Weissman and Klerman, 1977). Even some critics, however, have suggested that the fact that epileptic seizures in women tend to be more common during their premenstrual and menstrual phases and are often associated with increased irritability and aggressive outbursts, may imply an estrogen-progesterone imbalance causing ictal phenomena and mood changes via brain neurotransmitters (Smith, 1975).

STUDIES OF AGGRESSIVE BEHAVIORS AS INDEPENDENT VARIABLES

In turning to more truly psychoendocrine studies of normal and of antisocial, at times violent aggressive, behavior in human males, *i.e.* where the hormonal measurements have been dependent variables, we find that most of these have centered on *testosterone production*. The present decade has seen improved techniques for measuring plasma testosterone levels and for assessing various parameters of male aggression. Caution is needed, however, in evaluating the findings on testosterone and behavioral relationships. The recent reports of episodic secretion of gonadotropins and testosterone in normal pubertal boys and mature young men during both waking and sleep periods (Anders, 1978; Boyar et al., 1974) makes it hazardous to draw conclusions about a subject's "mean" testosterone level unless he has provided a series of plasma samples preferably obtained during the same morning hour or at frequent 24-hour intervals (Doering et al, 1975a). Another difficulty in comparing testosterone and behavior studies on men pertains to the variety of psychosocial and psychological instruments used by investigators. Which parameters of male aggression are the most germane ones to measure? Violations of the law, self-assessed assertiveness and hostility, and teacher and peer ratings of aggressive traits are all parameters that have been used.

The first systematic study of male aggression and testosterone levels was reported by Persky et al. in 1971. In a group of healthy young men aged 17-28, they found a positive correlation between self-assessed trait measures of aggression, utilizing the Buss-Durkee Hostility Inventory (BHI) (Buss and Durkee, 1957), and plasma levels of testosterone and also blood production rate of testosterone. Later investigators using a similar technique for the assessment of testosterone production rate or a series of plasma testosterone measurements were not able to replicate Persky's findings of a relation between self-reported aggression and hostility and plasma testosterone levels (Doering et al., 1975b; Kreuz and Rose, 1972; Meyer-Bahlburg et al., 1974; Monti et al., 1977; Rada et al., 1976a). For instance, Meyer-Bahlburg and associates (1974) reported on a comparison of six young men scoring in the lowest range of BDHI-scores and six in the highest range. These men had been selected from a large group of undergraduate students, all given the BDHI. The two extreme groups on hostility scores were retested with the BDHI, along with several other self-assessment personality inventories, while the subjects were infused with labeled testosterone in order to determine their blood production rate. There were no differences between the high and the low trait aggression groups as determined by BDHI and their testosterone production. In a similar vein, Monti and associates (1977) failed to find a correlation between self-rated aggression, using the BDHI, and mean plasma testosterone levels among 101 healthy male volunteers, aged 20-30. Only two blood samples one week apart had been obtained from the subjects.

More recently, several reports on aggressive and violent male offenders and their testosterone concentrations have included behavior observations and ratings of the subjects in addition to using self-administered personality inventories. Four of these studies will be mentioned (their subjects were all incarcerated during the investigations):

(1) Kreuz and Rose (1972) examined 21 young male prisoners over a two-week period, measuring plasma testosterone on six occasions. About one-half of the subjects were rated high on frequency of fighting and verbal aggression, while the others showed little of such behavior. The testosterone levels showed a fair intra-subject stability over time. There was no correlation between mean plasma testosterone levels and the frequency of aggressive behavior in prison or scores related to self-assessed trait hostility (BDHI). However, subjects who had committed more violent crimes, e.g. armed robbery, assault, and murder, during early adolescence had significantly higher levels of testosterone at the time of the study than men without such a history.

(2) In another institution for adult male prisoners, Ehrenkrantz et al. (1974) compared the mean testosterone levels for three groups (12 men in each) of individuals, selected on the basis of the research team's extensive clinical knowledge of them. The first group, selected for their history of chronic, violent, aggressive behavior, as well as the second group, selected for social dominance, showed higher testosterone levels than the third group, consisting of neither aggressive nor dominant prisoners. There was no correlation of individual BDHI-scores and testosterone levels for the 36 subjects.

(3) The report by Rada and associates (1976b) supported the notion that testosterone concentrations tend to correlate with degree of violence. In a study of 52 hospitalized rapists, those men who were judged to have been most physically violent during the commission of the sexual crime had significantly higher testosterone levels than the less violent rapists of their sample and groups of normals and child molesters. There were no correlations between testosterone level and the variables of age, race, length of incarceration, and self-rated hostility (BDHI). Regrettably, only one blood sample was drawn on each subject, which, as mentioned before, weakens conclusions of the study due to

evidence of circadian fluctuations in an individual's testosterone production (Anders, 1978; Doering et al., 1975a).

(4) A recent study on testosterone levels among male delinquents (Mattsson et al., 1980), reported on a group of 40 institutionalized recidivists in Sweden, aged 14 to 19, who were in good general health and of at least normal intelligence. Each subject provided at least three morning samples for testosterone assays. The group mean plasma testosterone level was slightly higher than that of a group of 58 normal male adolescents of the same age.

In controlling for attained pubertal stage, however, assessed according to Tanner (Marshall and Tanner, 1970), we found that the delinquent boys at Tanner stages 3 and 4 had significantly higher testosterone means than the non-delinquent boys at the same stages (no subject was below Tanner stage 3 in pubertal development). Delinquent and normal subjects at Tanner stage 5 had similar testosterone levels. This finding supports the suggestion by Kreuz and Rose (1972) that in *some* boys, predisposed to delinquent behavior due to social factors, rapidly increasing and high levels of testosterone during adolescence may "stimulate increased activity, drive, or assertiveness, and in certain individuals this may be utilized in antisocial, aggressive acts" (p. 330). In comparing the mean testosterone levels of the delinquents to a series of parameters of aggressive behavior, we controlled for the factor of attained pubertal developmental stage. Some of the results were: in regard to degree of violence, the subjects who had committed armed robbery tended to have higher mean testosterone concentration than the "milder" offenders. Age-at-onset of delinquency and number of escapes from institutions showed no correlation with testosterone levels. Ratings by institutional staff and a psychiatrist on a number of aggressive behaviors and psychodiagnostic variables of the boys did not correlate with their testosterone means. On various self-report scales, however, there were positive correlations between testosterone levels and traits of verbal and physical assertiveness, preference for strenuous physical activities, and the personality dimension of extraversion.

There are two additional recent studies on testosterone and aggression in non-delinquent, normal males. The first one (Olweus et al., 1980), conducted in Sweden, included some of the self-report personality inventories utilized in examining the Swedish male delinquents reported on above (Mattsson et al., 1980). Thus, among a group of 58 16-year-old normal adolescent boys, there was a significant positive correlation between plasma testosterone levels and self-reports of physical and verbal aggression, mainly reflecting responsiveness to provocation and threat. Lack of frustration tolerance was also related to testosterone levels.

The second recent study of the relationship between male aggression and plasma testosterone levels used a form of socially accepted aggressive behavior as the independent variable: the behavior of competitive hockey players (Scaramella and Brown, 1978). Two team coaches rated the players on several aspects of their aggressiveness during play. When these independent ratings were compared to the players' testosterone level (only one blood sample was used), there was a significant positive correlation between one aggressiveness item—the response to threat of a player—and testosterone level. The authors suggested that other competitive sports may be used to study testosterone variations in men, using multiple samples controlled for time of day.

In conclusion, most of the reported studies on *male aggression and testosterone* found some positive correlations between aggression parameters and plasma testosterone concentration. No author is suggesting a direct cause and effect relationship between testosterone and aggressiveness. The evidence of a circadian episodic secretion of testosterone has made single sampling techniques obsolete. Most authors also caution about the imperfectness of our current methodology in terms of valid instruments and observations for assessing aggressive behavior— for instance, self-assessment of traits of aggression and hostility seems to lack sensitivity to differences between subjects. In addition, there is no firm agreement on the most meaningful parameters of aggressive, violent behaviors to measure along with plasma testosterone determinations. Several authors have suggested that testosterone levels may reflect an individual's assertiveness and action orientation, his "trait-readiness" to react with an aggressive, maybe violent, response to frustrations (Rada et al., 1976a; Rose, 1975). Some of the data reviewed here support this hypothesis, *e.g.* the evidence of a positive correlation between more violent crimes (often of an "impulsive" nature) and mean plasma testosterone levels (Ehrenkrantz et al., 1974; Kreuz and Rose, 1972; Mattsson et al., 1980; Rada et al., 1976b). This suggests that in some individuals that are "violence prone" due to the interaction of early and marked psychosocial and neuropsychiatric influences, their testosterone levels might reflect a vulnerability for violent, antisocial behavior. In particular, many adolescent males may fall in this category due to their rapidly rising levels of testosterone.

It must be emphasized that the suggested evidence that peaking or above average testosterone levels contribute to instances of violent, deviant behavior, does not imply that it would be appropriate or even efficient to employ *testosterone-suppressive agents in treating violent male offenders*. A few American studies have recently reported on small, carefully selected and followed samples of sex offenders and severely aggressive males who were treated with an androgen-depleting steroid such as medroxyprogesterone acetate (MPA) given in depot form (Blumer and Migeon, 1975; Money et al., 1976). This agent appears to have a suppressing effect both on endogenous testosterone secretion and on cerebral arousal in general. The tentative findings of these studies showed that significant MPA-induced reduction of testosterone levels was associated with diminished frequency and intensity of erotic imagery and practices among the majority of the sex offenders. Some men with a history of severe aggressive behavior, of whom many were of the XYY karyotype, showed a reduction in violent outbursts and antisocial acts. The effects of MPA treatment seemed to cease after the medication was discontinued. The authors stressed the importance of simultaneous psychological therapies given to their patients and that the use of antiandrogenic drugs should only be offered to carefully screened sex offenders and possibly to certain violent, aggressive men unresponsive to other therapeutic methods (Blumer and Migeon, 1975; Money et al., 1976). As we learn more about the interaction between psychosocial factors shaping man's aggressive and sexual behavior and the endocrine correlates and influences in regard to this process, we will be able to evaluate better those situations of human violence where hormonal therapies might serve as an adjuvant to other therapies of social neuropsychiatric nature.

As part of Sheard's ongoing studies of the effect of *lithium* on threatening and violent behavior among incarcerated male delinquents (Sheard et al., 1976; Sheard and Marini, 1978), he and his associates found that lithium treatment for three months was associated with an increase in serum LH with no change in (weekly) serum testosterone levels (Sheard et al, 1977). By making an analogy with lithium's effect on the thyroid—causing a feedback mediated increase in TSH production —the authors suggested that the increase in LH levels may be a feedback-mediated response to an action of lithium on the testis. Its synthesis or release of testosterone might be inhibited by lithium, causing the LH increase. This raises the possibility that the LH-testosterone system might be part of lithium's anti-aggressive effect, which, however, was not associated with changes in testosterone levels in the reported study.

Several *external factors* might affect plasma testosterone levels and are difficult to control for. For instance, heavy drinking and smoking, quite commonly found among criminals, have been shown to suppress testosterone production, at least temporarily (Mendelson and Mello, 1974; Persky et al., 1977). In addition, the effects of long-term incarceration of offenders on their sexual activity and social situation in general might well influence their gonadal functioning and androgen production.

The psychoendocrine research of human aggression and delinquency has, as noted, centered on the male pituitary-gonadal axis. Little is known about the relationship between *aggressive parameters and other hypothalamic-endocrine systems*. In regard to the sympathetic-adrenal medullary system, recent studies have confirmed that epinephrine excretion is a sensitive indicator of behavioral arousal related to a variety of both positive and negative affective states (Frankenhaeuser, 1975). There also is evidence of a positive correlation of epinephrine excretion and cognitive performance in school-age children during test situations (Frankenhaeuser, 1976). Norepinephrine output has not shown the same significant correlations. Investigations along the pituitary-adrenal cortical axis have clearly demonstrated the sensitivity of the human adrenal cortex to states of emotional arousal; marked increases in urinary cortisol excretion usually accompany such states (Mason, 1975c). The mentioned findings primarily reflect endocrine catecholamine and cortisol responses to relatively short periods of arousal situations encompassing a variety of positive and negative affective states. Natural or experimentally induced states of anger and hostility have only been studied from a limited psychoendocrine viewpoint. So far, such states appear related to increased catecholamine and cortisol excretion, similar to any state of emotional arousal, *i.e.* there is no specific hormonal pattern for states of anger and hostility (Frankenhaeuser, 1976). Only a few studies have tried to relate a person's chronic (baseline) catecholamine and cortisol excretion to his habitual coping style or personality traits (Mason, 1975a).

There is a need for longitudinal examinations of endocrine activities that reflect the role of the hypothalamic-pituitary arousal attenuating system, and concomitant, ongoing observations of various expressions of human aggressive behavior. The emphasis should be on a developmental approach to gaining understanding of the relationship between endocrine effector systems and states and traits of aggression, assessed by validated, reliable measures.

DISCUSSION

In regard to another of the CNS effector systems, the autonomic nervous system (ANS), there is growing evidence of a correlation of autonomic activity with the form of aggressive, at times violent, behavior often seen among psychopathic criminals. These correlations have primarily been assessed by heart rate and skin conductance measurements (Hare, 1970; Hare, 1975; Schalling, 1978). Several authors have reported a longer recovery time for electrodermal responses to tone stimuli among criminals and psychopaths and among children with criminal fathers compared to those with non-criminal fathers (Hare and Schalling, 1978; Mednick and Hutchings, 1978). Referring to the observation that psychopaths and criminals have defective avoidance learning (Hare, 1975), Mednick (1978) has suggested a physiological method of examining how children learn to inhibit aggression, a skill that many psychopaths appear to lack. The fear of punishment assists the child in inhibiting an aggressive response. As a result of the inhibition his fear will be reduced or dissipate. Fear reduction is a powerful reinforcement for the inhibition of aggression and seems necessary for assuring that aggressive responses will be controlled at later times. Because the fear response involves arousal of ANS, the activity of which we can measure by skin conductance and heart rate, we may be able to study the speed and the size of fear reduction-reinforcement. "An effective reinforcement is one which is delivered immediately after the relevant response. The faster the reduction of fear, the faster the delivery of the reinforcement" (p. 217). In concluding his thesis, Mednick suggests that an individual whose ANS measurements indicate slow recovery from, for instance, fear arousal, may receive slower and smaller reinforcement and consequently learn to inhibit aggression slowly.

In addition to the findings of long electrodermal recovery time among psychopathic young males, Schalling and associates (1978) have also observed lower skin conductance basal measures and fewer spontaneous conductance fluctuations among such subjects. All those electrodermal findings have been assumed to reflect a habitual low level of cortical arousal (Hare, 1970; Hare and Schalling, 1978). Low CNS arousal appears to be a likely vulnerability factor in the development of certain forms of male aggressive, antisocial behavior. It would be of great interest to conduct simultaneous studies of this vulnerability factor and of plasma testosterone production in adolescent subjects who clinically show evidence of proneness to aggressive, violent behavior. The subjects would be those individuals referred to earlier who have been exposed to a combination of psychosocial and organic traumatization during their childhood (Kreuz and Rose, 1972; Lewis, 1978; Mattsson et al., 1980).

SUMMARY

Psychoendocrine research into human aggression is in an early stage. Such investigations are associated with many methodological problems, such as reliable measurements of hormonal activity, the diurnal variation of plasma testosterone and other hormones, and valid and reliable assessments of aggressive behaviors. The most dramatic form of human aggression—violent behavior—may lend itself to systematic investigation along behavioral-biologic longitudinal lines. Normative, long-term studies on young and adult subjects are sorely needed to provide reference points regarding endocrine activity and human behavior. Despite all the methodological problems, the study of the output of the endocrine effector systems—reflecting the integrative work of the brain—seems promising. Along with studies of ANS-function and of general behavior, psychoendocrine research can help to "map" biological correlates of some aggressive behaviors, including those of a violent, antisocial nature.

REFERENCES

Anders, T. F. (1978). State and rhythmic processes. *J. Am. Acad. Child Psychiat.*, 17:401–420.

August, G. P., Grumbach, M. M., and Kaplan, S. (1972). Hormonal changes in puberty: III. Correlation of plasma testosterone, LH, FSH, testicular size, and bone age with male pubertal development. *J. Clin. Endocrinol. Metab.*, 34:319–326.

Blumer, D., and Migeon, C. (1975). Hormone and hormonal agents in the treatment of aggression. *J. Nerv. Ment. Dis.*, 160:127–137.

Boyar, R. M., Rosenfeld, R. S., Kapen, S., Finkelstein, J. W., Roffwarg, H. P., Weilzman, E. D., and Hellman, L. (1974), Human puberty. Simultaneous augmented secretion of luteinizing hormone and testosterone during sleep. *J. Clin. Invest.*, 54:609–618.

Buss, A. H., and Durkee, A. (1957). An inventory for assessing different kinds of hostility. *J. Consult. Psychol.*, 21:343–349.

Doering, C. H., Brodie, H. K. H., Kraemer, H. C., Moos, R. H., Becker, H. B., and Hamburg, D. A. (1975a). Negative affect and plasma testosterone: a longitudinal human study. *Psychosom. Med.*, 37:484–491.

Doering, C. H., Kraemer, H. C., Brodie, H. K. H., and Hamburg, D. H. (1975b). A cycle of plasma testosterone in the human male. *J. Clin. Endocrin. Metab.*, 40:492–500.

Ehrenkrantz, J., Bliss, E., and Sheard, M. H. (1974). Plasma testosterone: correlation with aggressive behavior and social dominance in man. *Psychosom. Med.*, 36:469–475.

Ehrhardt, A. A. (1975). Prenatal hormonal exposure and psychosexual differentiation. In: *Topics in Psychoendocrinology*, E. J. Sachar, (ed.). New York: Grune & Stratton, pp. 67–82.

Frankenhaeuser, M. (1975). Sympathetic-adrenomedullary activity, behavior, and the psychosocial environment. In: *Research in Psychophysiology*, P. H. Venables and M. J. Christie, (eds.). New York: Wiley, pp. 71–94.

Frankenhaeuser, M. (1976). The role of peripheral catecholamines in adaptation to understimulation and overstimulation. In: *Psychopathology of Human Adaptation*, G. Serban (ed.). New York: Plenum, pp. 173–191.

Goddard, H. H. (1913). *The Kallikak Family. A Study in the Heredity of Feeble Mindedness*. New York: MacMillan.

Hare, R. D. (1970), *Psychopathy. Theory and Research*. New York: Wiley.

Hare, R. D. (1975). Psychopathy. In: *Research in Psychophysiology*, P. H. Venables and M. J. Christie, (eds.). New York: Wiley, pp. 325–348.

Hare, R. D., and Schalling, D. (eds.) (1978). *Psychopathic Behavior: Approaches to Research*. London: Wiley.

Henry, J. P., and Stephens, P. M. (1978). *Stress, Health and the Social Environment*, New York: Springer.

Knorr, D., Bidlingmaier, F., Butenandt, O., Fendel, H., and Ehrt-Wehle, R. (1974). Plasma testosterone in male puberty. *Acta Endocrinologica*, 75:181–194.

Kreuz, L. E., and Rose, R. M. (1972). Assessment of aggressive behavior and plasma testosterone in a young criminal population. *Psychosom. Med.*, 34:321–332.

Lewis, D. O. (1978). Psychobiological vulnerabilities to delinquency. Introduction. A historical perspective. *J. Amer. Acad. Child Psychiat.*, 17:193–196.

Lewis, D. O., and Balla, D. A. (1976). *Delinquency and Psychopathology*. New York: Grune & Stratton.

Lombroso, C. (1911). *Crime, Its Causes, and Remedies*. Translated by H. P. Horton. Boston: Little, Brown.

Marshall, W. A., and Tanner, J. M. (1970). Variations in the patterns of pubertal changes in boys. *Arch. Dis. Child.*, 45:13–23.

Mason, J. W. (1975a). Clinical psychophysiology. Psychoendocrine mechanisms. In: *American Handbook of Psychiatry, Volume IV, Organic Disorders and Psychosomatic Medicine*, M. F. Reiser, (ed.). New York: Basic Books, pp. 553–582.

Mason, J. W. (1975b). Emotion as reflected in patterns of endocrine integration. In: *Emotions–Their Parameters and Measurement*, L. Levi, (ed.). New York: Raven Press, pp. 143–181.

Mason, J. W. (1975c). Psychologic stress and endocrine function. In: *Topics in Psychoendocrinology*, E. J. Sachar, (ed.). New York: Grune & Stratton, pp. 1–18.

Mattsson, Å., Schalling, D., Olweus, D., Löw, H., and Svensson, J. (1980). Plasma testosterone, aggressive behavior, and personality dimensions in young male delinquents. *J. Am. Acad. Child Psychiat.*, 19:476–491.

Mednick, S.A., and Hutchings, B. (1978). Genetic and psychophysiological factors in asocial behavior. *J. Am. Acad. Child Psychiat.*, 17:209–223.

Mendelson, J. H., and Mello, N. K. (1974). Alcohol, aggression, and androgens. *Research Publications Association for Research in Nervous and Mental Disease*, 52:225–247.

Meyer-Bahlburg, H. F. L., Nat, R., Boon, D. A., Sharma, M., and Edwards, J. A. (1974). Aggressiveness and testosterone measures in man. *Psychosom. Med.*, 36:269–274.

Money, J., Wiedeking, C., Walker, P. A., and Gain, D. (1976). Combined antiandrogenic and counselling program for treatment of 46,XY and 47,XYY sex offenders. In: *Hormones, Behavior, and Psychopathology*, E. J. Sachar, (ed.). New York: Raven Press, pp. 105–120.

Monti, P. M., Brown, W. A. and Corriveau, D. P. (1977). Testosterone and components of aggressive and sexual behavior in man. *Am. J. Psychiat.*, 134:692–694.

Olweus, D., Mattsson, Å., Schalling, D., and Löw, H. (1980). Testosterone, aggression, physical and personality dimensions in normal adolescent males. *Psychosom. Med.*, 42:253–269.

Persky, H., O'Brien, C. P., Fine, E., Howard, H. J., Khan, M. A., and Beck, R. W. (1977). The effect of alcohol and smoking on testosterone function and aggression in chronic alcoholics. *Am. J. Psychiat.*, 134:621–625.

Persky, H., Smith, K. D., and Basu, G. K. (1971). Relation of psychologic measures of aggression and hostility to testosterone production in man. *Psychosom. Med.*, 33:265–277.

Rada, R. T., Kellner, R., and Winslow, W. W. (1976a). Plasma testosterone and aggressive behavior. *Psychosomatics*, 17:138–142.

Rada, R. T., Laws, D. R., and Kellner, R. (1976b). Plasma testosterone levels in the rapist. *Psychosom. Med.*, 38:257–268.

Rose, R. M. (1975). Testosterone, aggression, and homosexuality: a review of the literature and implications for future research. In: *Topics in Psychoendocrinology*, E. J. Sachar, (ed.). New York: Grune & Stratton, pp. 83–103.

Rose, R. M., Bernstein, I. S., and Gordon, T. P. (1975). Consequences of social conflict on plasma testosterone levels in rhesus monkeys. *Psychosom. Med.*, 37:50–60.

Rose, R. M., Bernstein, I. S., Gordon, T. P., and Lindsley, J. G. (1978). Changes in testosterone and behavior during adolescence in the male rhesus monkey. *Psychosom. Med.* 40:60–70.

Scaramella, T. J., and Brown, W. A. (1978). Serum testosterone and aggressiveness in hockey players. *Psychosom. Med.*, 40:262–265.

Schalling, D. (1978). Psychopathy-related personality variables and the psychophysiology of socialization. In: *Psychopathic Behavior: Approaches in Research*, R. D. Hare, and D. Schalling, (eds.). London: Wiley, pp. 85–106.

Shah, S. A., and Roth, L. H. (1974). Biological and psychophysiological factors in criminality. In: *Handbook of Criminology*, D. Glasar, (ed.). New York: Rand McNally College Publishing Co., pp. 101–173.

Sheard, M. H., and Marini, J. L. (1978). Treatment of human aggressive behavior: Four case studies of the effect of lithium. *Comp. Psychiat.*, 19:37–45.

Sheard, M. H., Marini, J. L., Bridges, C. I. et al. (1976). The effect of lithium on impulsive aggressive behavior in man. *Am. J. Psychiat.*, 133:1409–1413.

Sheard, M. H., Marini, J. L., and Giddings, S. S. (1977). The effect of lithium on luteinizing hormone and testosterone in man. *Dis. Nerv. Syst.*, 38:765–769.

Smith, S. L. (1975). Mood and the menstrual cycle. In: *Topics in Psychoendocrinology*, E. J. Sachar, (ed.). New York: Grune & Stratton, pp. 19–58.

Weissman, M. M., and Klerman, G. L. (1977). Sex differences and the epidemiology of depression. *Arch. Gen. Psychiat.*, 34:98–111.

CHAPTER TWELVE

Medical Histories of Delinquent Children

SHELLEY S. SHANOK, DOROTHY OTNOW LEWIS

This chapter will explore the relationship between adverse medical histories and juvenile delinquency. We will look at the timing and nature of specific medical events in order to determine if there are any particular ages or types of physical disorders which place a child at increased risk for demonstrating antisocial behaviors. This chapter is based on our own studies of children known to the juvenile justice system in the state of Connecticut (Lewis and Shanok, 1977; Lewis et al., 1979). Our studies included several different samples of children: children known only to the juvenile court, children incarcerated in the state correctional school, and children referred to a project for the diagnosis and treatment of especially violent offenders. We studied children who had committed only minor offenses (*e.g.*, loitering and breach of the peace) and others who had committed very serious offenses (*e.g.*, rape, arson, and murder).

Our research began when we observed clinically that many children seen at a juvenile court clinic told of numerous accidents, injuries, and serious illnesses that they had experienced throughout childhood. It was not uncommon to hear stories of children being hit by cars, falling from second or third stories of houses, or being physically abused by parents. On occasion we were able, by means of child or parent interviews, to pinpoint the onset of poor behavior to a particular accident or serious illness. For example, one girl reported that, prior to an episode of meningitis, she was considered her "mother's angel." Subsequently, she performed numerous destructive acts for which she had no memory, and she was eventually incarcerated in a correctional school. It seemed, clinically, that certain injuries and illnesses had contributed to some children's inability to form appropriate judgments, assess reality, and control behavior. We wondered to what extent most children coming through the juvenile justice system had suffered the kinds of central nervous system damage that might be expected to affect behavior.

THE LITERATURE

There is a debate in the literature between those who assert that the medical histories of delinquents are no worse than those of the general adolescent population and others who insist with equal conviction that they are.

The issues of perinatal insults, childhood CNS trauma, and behavior problems have already been reviewed in the previous chapter on "The Neuropsychiatric Status of Violent Delinquents." Suffice it to say that there is ample evidence suggesting an association between CNS trauma at any developmental stage and subsequent behavioral difficulties.

Nutrition and Maladjusted Behavior

Some investigators have focused their attention on a possible relationship between malnutrition and maladaptive behavior. It is believed that malnutrition during periods of rapid brain development, as in the first few months of life, can affect future adaptation through adulthood. Cravioto and Delicardie (1970), as well as Winick and his colleagues (1975), found malnutrition in infancy to correlate with poor school performance in childhood and maladaptive behavior in adulthood. Other investigators have examined the role of iron deficiency anemia in the development of behavior disorders (Pollitt and Leibel, 1976; Cantwell, 1974; Read, 1975). Cantwell (1974) reported that children who were identified as having had iron deficiency anemia at 6-18 months of age had an increased prevalence of "soft" neurological signs, including short attention span and hyperactivity, compared to children who were not anemic during infancy. Pollitt and Leibel (1976) stressed the need for further research on anemia and behavior. Iron deficiency anemia (Hgb<11.4 gm/ml) affects more than 20% of all age groups of the lower socioeconomic classes in this country, a sector of our nation over-represented in our delinquent and criminal populations.

This subject is discussed in greater detail in the following chapter on "Nutrition, Cognition, and Behavioral Adjustment: In Search of a Connection."

Illnesses in Delinquent Children

The importance of the effects of diseases on the growing child and adolescent is another area of debate. Again, there is little agreement on whether or not significant relationships exist between illnesses in middle childhood and maladaptation during adolescence and adulthood. The Gluecks (1950) were not impressed with the importance of medical histories in the development of delinquency. They focused attention, rather, on body types, and asserted that delinquent children tended to be more muscular and robust than nondelinquent children, a profile not consistent with ill health.

Other investigators have noted a wide variety of medical disorders ranging from the severe (*e.g.*, skull fractures, encephalitis) to the minor (viral infections, acne) that seem to be associated with juvenile delinquency. Burt (1925) reported defective physical conditions to be 1.25 times as common in delinquent children as in nondelinquent children. Eilenberg (1961), comparing the medical status of delinquent boys in London incarcerated in a Remand Home with the medical status of the general population, found "no differences in gross physical disease between delinquents and nondelinquents" (p. 128). He did note that the delinquent boys suffered from "a high percentage of minor physical disease." He considered the possibility that these ostensibly minor disorders might affect delinquent behavior by causing poor communication between the child and his environment and by creating a general state of lowered resistance to physical and psychological stresses. Finally, Eilenberg noted that in a country where medical services are free and available to everyone, a high percentage of minor physical infections among delinquents might reflect chronic parental inadequacy.

Carper (1974) described his experiences as pediatrician for the Massachusetts Department of Youth Services. He reported, in a study based on a review of health records and a one-half hour interview and examination of 390 delinquent boys, that 41% had suffered a fracture of one or more bones and 23% had experienced serious accidents and trauma. Other common disorders were asthma (8.0%), skin conditions (8.0%), and ear, nose, and throat problems (5.4%). However, he was unable to determine the implications of these findings to the development of deviant behaviors since he did not have a nondelinquent comparison group. Carper noted that delinquent children had good memories for significant medical events such as fractures, operations, major accidents, hospitalizations, epilepsy, and allergies. He stressed that many of the boys in detention had a deep concern about the intactness of their bodies and would often show up at sick call several times a week, complaining of minor problems. He believed that medical staff should take all complaints of ill health seriously no matter how trivial the ostensible problem. He also recommended that nurses be trained to encourage the boys to talk about their problems regardless of their nature and that nurses provide sympathetic support and understanding, as well as good medical care.

Gibbens (1963), in his study of 200 Borstal boys in England, ages 17-20, found a major disease or defect in 18% of these adolescents. A minor physical disorder was found in 22% of the boys. He then compared these percentages with those reported for young men called up for National Service. In this latter group, only 4% were reported to have a major disease or defect and 11% to have a minor one. The relatively high prevalence of physical disorder in Borstal boys surprised Gibbens because all Borstal boys had been examined prior to their commitment to correctional settings in order to screen out those with a gross mental or physical ailment.

From the review of the literature regarding the medical status of delinquents, there is disagreement regarding, first, the nature of the medical history of delinquents; second, whether their medical histories differ in any way from nondelinquents; and third, whether an especially poor medical history is merely associated with or has an etiologic relationship to delinquent behaviors.

In light of the above controversy, we wondered:

1. Whether there was a particular disorder or combination of medical disorders associated with childhood antisocial behavior;

2. Whether there were crucial periods of time for medical problems that were associated with a child's becoming delinquent (*i.e.*, was trauma to the central nervous system during infancy more closely associated with deviant behavior than trauma during late childhood?);

3. Whether delinquent children who committed violent offenses (*e.g.*, murder, rape, arson) were more likely to have experienced more numerous and/or serious medical problems than delinquent children who had committed less serious offenses (*e.g.*, burglary, loitering).

We undertook the following studies in an effort to shed light on these questions.

JUVENILE COURT DELINQUENT CHILDREN VS. NONDELINQUENT CHILDREN

Our first study sprang from our work at the New Haven Juvenile Court Clinic. Many of the children referred to the clinic told of severe accidents and illnesses they had experienced throughout their childhoods. We wondered whether delinquent children had, in fact, experienced a greater number of medical problems than nondelinquent children. Two groups of children were chosen to study: (1) a random sample of 109 delinquent children referred to the juvenile court, but not to the court clinic, and (2) a sample of 109 nondelinquent children from the New Haven area, demographically similar to children in our delinquent sample. We decided to select a random sample of delinquent children rather than a sample of court-clinic referred children because of the likelihood that a clinic referred sample would be biased toward physical pathology as well as psychopathology. By utilizing a random sample of delinquent children, our findings would have implications for the entire juvenile court-related delinquent population, rather than a select group of delinquent children.

Demographic Characteristics

Although the juvenile court records did not always allow for accurate socioeconomic class assignment, it was generally recognized by court and clinic staffs that the great majority of delinquents were from the lower socioeconomic classes in the area. Thus the nondelinquent sample was chosen from a population of which 75% would have been classified as coming from classes IV and V of the general population according to the Hollingshead and Redlich scale (1958).

Each of the 109 delinquent children was matched with a comparison child for age, sex, and race. Two-thirds of each sample were white; the other third were black. Two-thirds of each sample were boys; the other third were girls. At the time of the study the average age of both groups was 19 years.

Assessment of Medical Status

The accidents and illnesses reported verbally by many of the delinquent children in our studies were often so numerous and/or severe that it was often difficult to determine the credibility of their histories. Some investigators (Hoekelman et al., 1976), have noted that histories taken from children or their mothers can be valuable clinically;

however they are often unreliable regarding the exact numbers of illnesses and dates of medical events. We needed objective criteria by which to measure the medical status of each child. We therefore decided to review the medical records of our two samples at the major hospital in New Haven in order to obtain a detailed, yet unbiased, medical history.

This hospital was known as a source of primary as well as emergency care for the less affluent in the community. It therefore seemed likely that many of our sample children would use this hospital to meet their health needs. In fact, the hospital in question subsequently developed a primary care service to meet the needs of this population.

Our choice to limit the study to one large general hospital raises the issue of case loss. Data from other public and private medical facilities were unavailable because of issues of confidentiality; however, as far as we could determine, all children selected for study had equal access to other community resources, making it unlikely that one sample made greater use of such clinics than another. Furthermore, children suffering severe accidents or illnesses would most likely come to a hospital facility for treatment. The choice of private medical care was relatively rare in our samples because of financial considerations. Finally, case loss would create underestimates of the actual prevalence of disorders and use of medical facilities in both samples and therefore have a minimal effect on statistical differences.

Medical records were assessed in terms of numbers of visits to the hospital, timing of visits, use made of different hospital services (*e.g.*, emergency room, clinics, wards), and reasons for visits (*e.g.*, accidents, head or face trauma, respiratory illnesses, child abuse, and psychiatric problems of the child and parents).

Findings

The use of hospital facilities, the kinds of disorders treated, and the longitudinal picture of medical contacts are seen in Tables 1 and 2 and in Figures 1 and 2. As shown in Table 1, delinquent children made significantly greater use of all hospital facilities than did their nondelinquent counterparts. Table 2 indicates that although delinquent children were far more likely than nondelinquent children to be seen for accidents (particularly head or face trauma) and to demonstrate psychiatric disturbance, they were no more likely than nondelinquent children to have suffered from perinatal difficulties. This finding was not predicted and will be discussed at greater length when we report the medical histories of especially violent delinquents. The timing of hospital contacts was of particular interest.

TABLE 1

Hospital Use by Delinquent and Nondelinquent Children Through Age 16

Hospital Service Used	Contacts of Delinquent Children			Contacts of Nondelinquent Children			Analysis*	
	Mean	Median	Range	Mean	Median	Range	t	Significance
Emergency Room	4.029	2	0-33	2.398	1	0-29	2.987	p = .004
Clinic	5.733	2	0-68	3.096	0	0-43	2.411	p = .017
Ward	0.476	0	0-9	0.223	0	0-3	2.295	p = .023
Total	10.286	5	0-87	5.204	1	0-48	2.987	p = .004

*By two-tailed t test.

TABLE 2

Specific Medical Problems of Delinquent and Nondelinquent Children*

Specific Medical Problem	Delinquent Children		Nondelinquent Children		Analysis	
	Number	Percent	Number	Percent	Chi Square	Significance
Accident or injury	66	61.0	45	41.7	6.928	p = .009
Head or face trauma	39	35.9	24	21.6	4.475	p = .035
Perinatal difficulty	12	10.9	16	14.3	0.268	p > .500
Psychiatric symptom	19	17.1	9	8.0	3.085	p = .080
Child abuse	9	8.6	1	1.0	6.328	p = .012

*A number of children had more than one medical problem.

TABLE 3

Results of Two-Tailed t Tests of Cumulative Hospital Contacts and Medical Problems of Delinquent Versus Nondelinquent Children

Item	Age of Child (years)							
	2	4	6	8	10	12	14	16
Hospital								
t	2.462	3.001	2.610	2.296	2.345	2.615	2.518	2.787
Significance	p = .015	p = .004	p = .010	p = .023	p = .020	p = .010	p = .013	p = .004
Emergency room visits								
t	1.757	2.366	2.023	1.548	1.588	1.578	1.787	2.411
Significance	p = .081	p = .019	p - .045	p = .124	p = .114	p = .117	p = .078	p = .017
Clinic visits								
t	2.067	2.354	2.102	2.039	2.237	2.253	2.170	2.913
Significance	p = .041	p = .020	p = .037	p = .043	p = .027	p = .026	p = .032	p = .053
Ward admissions								
t	2.625	2.675	2.355	2.429	2.636	2.215	2.370	2.295
Significance	p = .010	p = .009	p = .020	p = .017	p = .010	p = .028	p = .019	p = .023
Accidents or injuries								
t	1.545	1.718	1.136	0.370	0.972	1.290	1.513	2.449
Significance	p = .124	p = .088	p = .258	p > .500	p = .332	p = .199	p = .132	p = .016
Respiratory illnesses								
t	1.458	1.632	1.222	1.238	1.161	1.184	1.273	1.620
Significance	p = .147	p = .105	p = .224	p = .217	p = .248	p = .238	p = .205	p = .107

TABLE 4

Results of Two-Tailed t Tests of Two-Year Interval Data on Hospital Contacts and Medical Problems of Delinquent Versus Nondelinquent Children

Item	Age of Child (Two-Year Intervals)							
	0-2	2-4	4-6	6-8	8-10	10-12	12-14	14-16
Hospital visits								
t	2.462	2.266	0.913	0.191	1.405	0.908	1.035	2.685
Significance	p = .015	p = .025	p = .363	p > .500	p = .162	p = .365	p = .392	p = .008
Emergency room visits								
t	1.757	2.209	0.431	0.899	1.070	0.489	1.165	2.754
Significance	p = .081	p = .029	p > .500	p = .370	p = .286	p > .500	p = .246	p = .007
Clinic visits								
t	2.067	2.206	0.656	0.789	1.819	0.747	0.632	2.158
Significance	p = .041	p = .029	p > .500	p = .431	p = .071	p = .456	p > .500	p = .033
Ward admissions								
t	2.626	1.402	0.009	0.990	1.125	0.722	0.226	0.330
Significance	p = .010	p = .163	p > .500	p = .324	p = .262	p = .472	p > .500	p > .500
Accidents or injuries								
t	1.545	1.267	0.287	1.474	1.617	1.397	1.080	2.717
Significance	p = .124	p = .207	p > .500	p = .142	p = .108	p = .164	p = .282	p = .008
Respiratory illnesses								
t	1.458	1.611	0.367	0.917	0.665	0.434	0.930	2.545
Significance	p = .147	p = .109	p > .500	p = .360	p > .500	p > .500	p = .354	p = .012

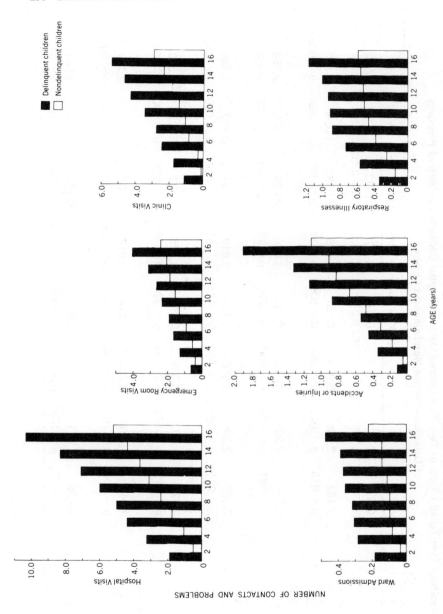

Figure 1. Cumulative hospital contacts and medical problems of delinquent and nondelinquent children throughout childhood.

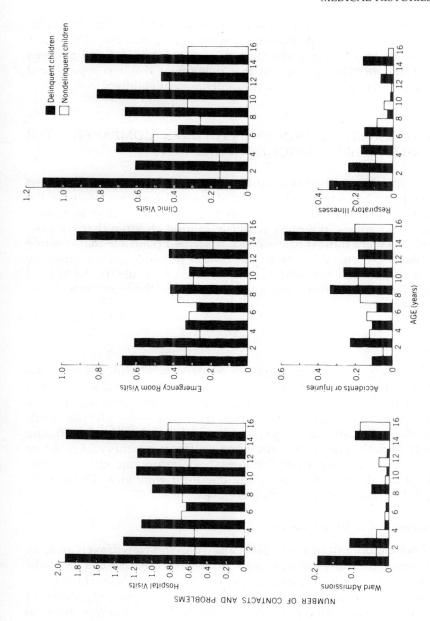

Figure 2. Two-year interval data on hospital contacts and medical problems of delinquent and nondelinquent children.

As shown in Figure 1 and Table 3, delinquent children made significantly more hospital visits than did nondelinquent children. Differences between the two groups were most striking before age 4 and between ages 14 and 16. Thus it seemed that delinquent children experienced more accidents and illnesses than nondelinquent children.

INCARCERATED DELINQUENT CHILDREN COMPARED WITH JUVENILE COURT DELINQUENT CHILDREN

We wondered whether an association existed between seriousness of delinquent behaviors and severity of medical histories. Many of the children seen at the court clinic who had committed offenses against person were among the most seriously injured children that we saw, having sustained trauma to the head. It seemed plausible that children who had experienced injury to the central nervous system might be more impulsive. They might have a decreased ability to control behaviors that could result in injury to others, be the injury intentional or unintentional.

Samples

Our study samples consisted of 84 delinquent children from the New Haven area, incarcerated at the regional correctional school, who were matched for age, sex, race and geographic area with a sample of nonincarcerated delinquent children, known only to the juvenile court. Although socioeconomic status could not always be ascertained, the majority of both groups were receiving welfare payments and could be categorized as coming from the lowest socioeconomic classes. Two-thirds of the samples were boys and one-third were girls. Of the children, 56% were white and 44% were black.

Assessment of Medical Status

Since children in both samples came from the New Haven area, an evaluation of their medical histories was made on the basis of a review of their hospital records at the major general hospital in New Haven.

As in our previous study, medical records were assessed in terms of numbers of visits, timing of visits, use made of different hospital services, and reasons for visits.

Degree of Violence

Of the incarcerated delinquents, complete juvenile court records were available on 80 children. Of the nonincarcerated delinquent sample, juvenile court records were available on 77 children. The average number of delinquent offenses in the incarcerated group was 11.9 compared with an average of 2.1 offenses in the nonincarcerated group. Of the 80 incarcerated children, 36.25% had committed violent offenses (*e.g.*, assault, threatening, arson, robbery), compared with 6.49% of the nonincarcerated group ($X_y^2 = 18.760$, p < .001). The nature of a child's behavior was not always reflected in the official designation of his offense, possibly as a result of plea bargaining and/or the court's wish to refrain from stigmatizing the child. For example, in eight cases assaultive behaviors were documented in charts but recorded as "breach of the peace" in official court records. Because of the discrepancy between official offense and actual behavior, we also compared the prevalence of documented actual violent behaviors in the two groups. We found that 50% of the incarcerated group were reported to have been involved in violent acts compared with 27.27% of the nonincarcerated group ($X_y^2 = 7.5997$, p < .01). Thus significantly more of the study group of incarcerated delinquents had performed aggressive delinquent acts than had their nonincarcerated delinquent peers.

Findings

Numbers of hospital visits were similar in the incarcerated and nonincarcerated delinquent samples. Incarcerated delinquents averaged 15.818 visits compared with 13.131 visits for nonincarcerated delinquents (t = 0.916, p = .362). There was a slight tendency for incarcerated delinquents to have made more emergency room visits than nonincarcerated delinquents. Incarcerated children averaged 8.974 emergency room visits compared with 5.714 emergency room visits for nonincarcerated delinquents (t = 1.949, p = .054). Clinic visits and ward admissions were almost identical in number in the two groups.

The greatest differences between the medical histories of the two groups emerged from an analysis of the reasons for hospital visits and from a study of the symptomatology noted in hospital charts. Although similar percentages of children in each group had been treated at one time or another for accidents or injuries (72.7% of the incarcerated delinquents versus 71.1% of nonincarcerated delinquents, $X_y^2 = .003$, p > .5), incarcerated children were significantly more likely to have sustained a head or face injury (62.3% versus 44.6%, X_y^2 = 4.371, p = .037). A measure of the severity of head injuries sustained by the two groups was reflected in the difference between the proportion of children who received skull X-rays. In the incarcerated group, 33.8% of the children had received a skull X-ray compared with 13.1% of the nonincarcerated group (X_y^2 = 8.566, p = .004). Numbers of visits for head and face injuries were also significantly greater in the incarcerated group (1.026 incarcerated versus .607 nonincarcerated, t = 2.072, p = .040). Of special note was the finding of a significant difference in numbers of head injuries before age 2 (.091 versus .012, t = 2.329, p = .022).

Child abuse was also noted more frequently in the medical charts of the incarcerated children (10.4% incarcerated versus 3.6% nonincarcerated (X_y^2 = 1.961, p = .162). It was our impression from previous clinical and epidemiological studies that abuse was under-recognized in both groups.

Of particular note was the finding that perinatal difficulties were significantly more prevalent in the histories of incarcerated delinquents than nonincarcerated delinquents. Information about pregnancy, delivery, and the immediate postnatal period was available in the charts of 41 incarcerated delinquents and 50 nonincarcerated delinquents. Of the incarcerated delinquents where any information was available, 36.6% had histories of perinatal difficulties, compared with 8.0% of nonincarcerated delinquents on whom information existed (X_y^2 = 9.480, p = .003). These perinatal difficulties ranged in quality from maternal syphilis to postnatal apnea requiring intubation.

Psychiatric symptoms were found more commonly in the medical records of incarcerated delinquents (44.2% children versus 26.2% nonincarcerated children, X_y^2 = 4.951, p = .027).

In an effort to determine which combination of the medical history variables investigated in this study best distinguished the incarcerated delinquent group from the nonincarcerated delinquent group, a multiple regression analysis was conducted, utilizing group member-ship (incarcerated vs. nonincarcerated) as the dependent variable. Predictor variables were: presence of perinatal difficulties, child abuse, psychiatric symptoms in the subjects, number of emergency room visits, clinic visits, ward admissions, accidents or injuries, head or face injuries, and visits for upper respiratory infections before age 16. It was found that two variables—presence of perinatal difficulties and number of head and face injuries—produced an R of .382, accounting for 14.6% of the total variance. Presence of perinatal difficulties accounted for 12% of the total variance and number of head and face injuries for another 2.6%.

We were also interested in determining whether there was a combination of variables that was especially effective in distinguishing the two groups relatively early in their lives. Consequently, another multiple regression analysis was conducted, utilizing group membership as the dependent variable and, as independent variables, presence of perinatal difficulties, number of emergency room visits, number of clinic visits, number of ward admissions, number of accidents and injuries, number of head and face injuries, and number of visits for upper respiratory infections, all before age four. The results of this analysis were remarkably similar to those reported above. The combination of presence of perinatal difficulties and number of head or face injuries before age four produced an R of .365, accounting for 13.3% of the total variance. Presence of perinatal difficulties accounted for 12% of the total variance and number of head and face injuries before age four for an additional 1.3%.

To summarize, perinatal difficulties and head and face injuries most importantly distinguished incarcerated from nonincarcerated delinquents, a pattern of findings as characteristic of the early childhood years as the later adolescent years. There were also tendencies for abuse to be more prevalent in the histories of incarcerated delinquents and for psychiatric symptoms to be noted more often in histories of incarcerated children.

On the basis of our clinical observations we were surprised that the presence of child abuse failed to distinguish the two groups at conventional levels of statistical significance. When we re-examined the medical records, we became convinced that the presence of child abuse was significantly under-recognized in the histories of the incarcerated group. When we reviewed the children's correctional school records, several cases where we suspected child abuse were confirmed. One child who, on two separate occasions was treated in the emergency room for spiral fractures of her right arm, was not recognized by the hospital as having been abused. Only when the child's correctional school record was reviewed did we learn that the child greatly feared her mother, who had broken her arm on two separate occasions. The medical record of another child only told of the child's frequent accidents. The chart failed to indicate that the child's older alcoholic brother routinely beat the child severely. Again, this documentation of abuse was found in the boy's correctional school record.

ESPECIALLY VIOLENT INCARCERATED DELINQUENT CHILDREN COMPARED WITH SIMPLY INCARCERATED DELINQUENT CHILDREN

During the course of our studies, a new secure unit for especially dangerous juveniles from all over Connecticut had been constructed at the correctional school in question. Over a 9-month period, 11 children from the New Haven area with histories of particularly violent offenses had been placed on this "secure unit." We decided to compare the medical histories of this especially aggressive group with the medical histories of the general correctional school population.

Because of the small number of secure unit children from the New Haven area, we did not attempt to match for age or race in our comparison sample. We decided rather to match only for sex and geographic area. That is, since all 11 secure unit children were male, we compared them with a random sample of 56 male delinquents from the New Haven area who had been incarcerated at the school but had not been placed in secure custody.

A comparison of secure unit boys and the simply incarcerated boys indicated that our secure population was significantly younger than our comparison group at the time of hospital record review (179 months versus 263 months, t = 5.654, p < .001). Of the secure unit boys, 40.0% were white compared with 62.5% of the incarcerated group. This difference was not significant (X_y^2 = 0.968, p = .326).

Although total numbers of hospital visits did not differ significantly between the groups (14.818 visits for secure children versus 15.923 visits for incarcerated children, t = 0.175, p > .500), ward admissions tended to be greater in number for secure unit children (1.000 versus 0.577, t = 1.457, p = .151). Of note, ward admissions before age two tended to be greater in number for secure unit children (0.182 versus 0.038, t = 1.788, p = .079). Secure unit boys tended to have more accidents and injuries before age 14 (3.636 versus 2.212, t = 1.444, p = .154). Secure unit boys also tended to have abuse or neglect and head and face injuries noted in their hospital charts more often than simply incarcerated boys, but differences again did not reach conventional levels of significance.

Of the six secure unit boys for whom perinatal data were available, five (83.3%) had perinatal difficulties compared with nine of 32 simply incarcerated boys (28.1%) for whom perinatal data were available (Fisher's exact test = p = .019). Thus significantly more violent offenders had experienced perinatal problems. Moreover, our sample of violent offenders tended to have more accidents and injuries, ward admissions, and abuse than their less violent incarcerated peers. Our findings suggest a continuum of physical trauma corresponding to a continuum of increasingly aggressive behaviors. That is, the nondelinquent children had the least serious medical histories; the juvenile court related delinquents the next most serious medical histories; the incarcerated boys extraordinarily adverse histories; and the violent incarcerated boys the most deleterious medical histories of all. Most noteworthy, since perinatal difficulties did not distinguish delinquent children known only to the juvenile court from nondelinquent children, was the fact that perinatal problems did differentiate the more serious delinquents from the less serious delinquents.

DISCUSSION

The results of our studies suggest that delinquents have significantly more numerous hospital contacts and significantly more accidents and injuries throughout childhood than do nondelinquents. The clustering of medical problems during the early years (0-2 and 2-4 years) and at the onset of adolescence (14-16 years) suggests that particular developmental factors may be operating. Both periods are thought to have in common increased physical (motor) capacities and an imbalance between inner behavioral controls and heightened impulses. In normal families the parents of very young children usually provide appropriate external controls, protecting and supporting the child until the child develops his own internal controls. If the parents, for whatever reason, are unable to provide this structure, there is a greater likelihood that immature impulsive behavior will result in frequent accidents and injuries. The parents of delinquents are often unable to provide adequate support and protection because of their own psychopathology and the adverse social situation in which they live. The evidence for psychopathology in parents of delinquents has often been documented (Glueck and Glueck, 1950: Lewis et al., 1976; Jonsson, 1967; Offord et al., 1978) and is evident in this study by the high prevalence of child abuse in the delinquent sample.

Early accidents and injuries, a consequence possibly of parental inadequacies, may contribute to central nervous system dysfunction which, in turn, further aggravates the child's difficulties with impulse control and social adaptation. The disappearance of striking differences between delinquents and nondelinquents in the interval between ages four and 14 years may in part be accounted for by the development of better internal controls during this period. Most likely it also reflects the support offered by a school setting. Between the ages of five and 14, most children are in school and receive a degree of protection and structure several hours each day.

With the onset of adolescence, the school becomes a less effective force as many delinquent children who have been held back over the years attend only sporadically or even drop out entirely. The burden of guidance, control, support, and protection once more falls squarely on the shoulders of the parents. Unfortunately, the continuing inadequacy of the parents again renders them ineffective when left to cope with their adolescent children. At the same time, the adolescent's heightened impulses and increased physical strength, along with access to weapons, cars, alcohol, and drugs make his impulsive behaviors most injurious to himself and to others. This may account in part for the increased usage of the hospital between ages 14 and 16 compared with the earlier years.

On the basis of our present studies of medical histories and our past work on the relationship of delinquency and psychopathology (Lewis and Balla, 1976), there would seem to be identifiable biopsychosocial factors that together contribute to violent delinquency. The combination of trauma to the central nervous system, either in the form of perinatal problems or head and face injuries; parental psychopathology, often expressed through incredible physical and psychological abuse of the child (Lewis et al., 1976); and social deprivation, manifested particularly by the failure of physicians to recognize and treat psychiatric illness and/or central nervous system dysfunction in lower socioeconomic children (Lewis et al., 1979) creates the kind of serious, often violent, delinquent child feared by our society today.

It should be stressed that we are not suggesting that a single factor (*e.g.*, brain damage, social deprivation, vulnerability to psychosis) is sufficient to engender violent delinquency. Rather, we would suggest that the combination of several factors—familial vulnerability, trauma to the central nervous system, physical and psychological abuse from a parent, and social deprivation—are sufficient to create the violent young offender.

Our findings also have implications for the prevention of serious delinquency. A history of frequent hospital contacts for a variety of different reasons and in the absence of a single medical disorder (*e.g.*, asthma), should alert the physician to the possibility of the development of delinquent behavior. Many of the disorders suffered by these children occur early, differences between delinquent and nondelinquent children emerging before the age of four. In particular, the child known to have experienced perinatal difficulties, who frequently comes to the emergency room at a young age with assorted accidents and illness should alert clinicians to the possible need for intensive ongoing psychological assistance as well as care for the immediate medical problem with which the child presents. It is the unfortunate practice of busy emergency rooms to treat each hospital contact as an isolated medical event, rather than to recognize a pattern of repeated hospital contacts for a multitude of unrelated disorders. It is, however, this very pattern that is often displayed by children who subsequently run afoul of the law. The recognition by the medical profession that delinquent children are often the same children who, during their early years, suffer from severe and numerous physical disorders, may be helpful in the prevention or at least the amelioration of serious maladaptive antisocial behaviors.

REFERENCES

Burt, C. (1925). *The Young Delinquent*. London: University of London Press.

Cantwell, R. J. (1974). The long-term neurological sequelae of anemia in infancy. *Pediat. Res.*, 8:342.

Carper, J. (1974). Medical care of delinquent adolescent boys. *Pediat. Clin. N. Am.*, 21:423–433.

Cravioto, J., and Delicardie, E. R. (1970). Mental performance in school age children: findings after recovery from early severe malnutrition. *Am. J. Dis. Child.*, 120:404–410.

Eilenberg, M. D. (1961). Remand home boys 1930-1955. *Brit. J. Crimin.*, 2:111–131.

Gibbens, T. N. C. (1963. The effects of physical ill health in adolescent delinquents. *Proc. Roy. Soc. Med.*, 56:1086–1088.

Glueck, S., and Glueck, E. (1950). Unraveling Juvenile Delinquency. New York: The Commonwealth Fund.

Hoekelman, M. D., Kelly, J., and Zinmer, A. W. (1976). The reliability of maternal recall: mothers' remembrance of their infants' health and illness. *Clin. Pediat.*, 15:261–265.

Hollingshead, A., and Redlich, F. (1958). *Social Class and Mental Illness: A Community Study*. New York: John Wiley & Sons, Inc.

Jonsson, G. (1967). Delinquent boys, their parents and grandparents. *Acta Psychiat. Scand.*, Supp. 195, Vol. 43.

Lewis, D. O., and Balla, D. A. (1976). *Delinquency and Psychopathology*. New York: Grune & Stratton.

Lewis, D. O., Balla, D. A., Shanok, S. S., and Snell, L. (1976). Delinquency, parental psychopathology and parental criminality: clinical and epidemiological findings. *J. Am. Acad. Child Psychiat.*, 15:665–678.

Lewis, D. O., and Shanok, S. S. (1977). Medical histories of delinquents and nondelinquents: an epidemiological study. *Am. J. Psychiat.*, 134:1020–1025.

Lewis, D. O., Shanok, S. S., Balla, D. (1979). Perinatal difficulties, head and face trauma, and child abuse in the medical histories of seriously delinquent children. *Am. J. Psychiat.*, 136:419–423.

Offord, D. R., Allen, N., and Abrams, N. (1978). Parental psychiatric illness, broken homes and delinquency. *J. Am. Acad. Child Psychiat.*, 17:224–238.

Pollitt, E., and Leibel, R. L. (1976). Iron deficiency and behavior. *J. Pediat.*, 88:372–381.

Read, M. S. (1975). Anemia and behavior: nutrition, growth and development. *Mod. Prob. Paediat.*, 14:189.

Winick, M., Meyer, K. K., and Harris, R. C. (1975). Malnutrition and environmental enrichment by early adoption. *Science*, 1970:1173–1175.

CHAPTER THIRTEEN

Nutrition, Cognition and Behavioral Adjustment; In Search of a Connection

ERNESTO POLLITT

In the last decade a causal connection between different forms of malnutrition secondary to a deficient diet, and delinquent or antisocial behavior have often been claimed in the so-called scientific literature. (See, for example, Hippchen, 1978.) Hypoglycemia (Yaryura-Tobias, 1978), vitamin B6 (Cott, 1978), niacinamide and ascorbic acid (Ware, 1978) deficits are identified, among others, as the culprits. A new syndrome of "subclinical pellagra" was described involving perceptual disturbances, hyperactivity, and aggressive behavior (Green, 1978). An hypothesis that human populations consuming corn-based diets may have reduced brain tryptophan and 5-HT levels and be prone to aggressive behaviors has also been postulated (Mawson and Jacobs, 1978). Yet, no published evidence has conclusively shown a causal connection between these two sets of variables. Reasons for this lack of evidence are presented in the following pages. Specifically, the purposes of this chapter are to: (1) identify some conceptual and methodological problems associated with the search for the role of nutrition factors in causality of delinquency behavior; (2) illustrate through a review of studies on the effects of iron deficiency, protein-calorie malnutrition and short term fasting the impact of dieting factors on behavior, and (3) establish hypothetical pathways to describe how nutrition may contribute to the causality of delinquency.

Short-term fasting, iron deficiency (sideropenia) and protein-energy malnutrition have different types of effects over psychological function and behavior. Consequently they offer the opportunity of discussing different ways in which dietary factors may be involved in complex social behaviors such as delinquency. A short-term abstinence from food (~ 12 to 24 hours) will probably affect behavior through short-term neurohormonal and metabolic changes. No alteration in neural tissue will be involved. Following feeding all behavioral effects will disappear and the subject will return to a usual level of performance or function. Sideropenia is a micronutrient deficiency which occurs in infants, children, and adults (primarily women). It usually is independent of any other nutrient deficiency; it is amenable to treatment through diet or iron repletion therapy; and it lasts from a few weeks to several months, possibly years. It has been claimed that it may produce neural structural changes if it occurs in early infancy (Cantwell, 1974). However, as discussed below, it is more reasonable to assume that its alleged behavioral effects are mediated by alteration in neurotransmitter metabolism. Finally, protein-energy malnutrition is a macro-nutrient deficiency generally secondary to a diet deficient both in quality and quantity. As a man-made disease, endemic in many developing countries, it is wedded with other complex forms of environmental deprivation; it is mostly prevalent among infants and young children. Before specifically probing into the effects of these three conditions on behavior, some analytical strategies in the search for a diet-delinquency connection should be discussed.

ANALYTICAL STRATEGIES: CONCEPTUAL AND METHODOLOGICAL PROBLEMS

Lack of evidence on the possible role of nutrition factors in delinquency is understandable. The general area of research on the influence of diet on behavior is in its infancy; serious problems still exist on both sides of the equation in variable definition and measurement. A few studies on the behavioral impact of macro- or micro-nutrient deficiencies (see Table 1) were available at the turn of the century. Clinical reports on pellagra and associated nervous system derangements, for example, date back to the first two decades of the century (Roe, 1973). However, systematic probes on both human and experimental animals on a diet-behavior connection began only in the early sixties. Pioneering efforts are found in the area of protein-calorie malnutrition and cognitive function and learning (Pollitt and Thomson, 1977). Within the recent past this area of research has blossomed, and impressive advances have occurred in the identification of dietary involvement in brain biochemistry and function (Wurtman and Wurtman, 1977, 1977a). Yet it is apparent that these gains represent only the onset of a lengthy but marvelous process of discovery.

Delinquency is a broad term including a wide variety of behaviors which violate the law. Because these behaviors deviate from an established social norm, delinquency may be considered a social illness. However, except for a few atypical cases, no identifiable morbid process with clear symptoms underlies or is associated with these behaviors. Therefore, delinquency can not be considered a disease entity. A search for a one-to-one antecedent-consequent relationship in causality of delinquency represents a misunderstanding of the variables involved and, perhaps more importantly, a misunderstanding of the principles of multiple causality.

TABLE 1
Classification of Malnutrition from (McLaren, 1976)

1.	Cause	primary (exogenous) secondary (endogenous)
2.	Type	excess, toxicity (overnutrition) deficiency (undernutrition)
3.	Nutrient	vitamins, elements, protein, energy sources
4.	Degree	mild, moderate, severe or alternatively depleted stores, biochemical lesion, functional change, structural lesion
5.	Duration	acute, sub-acute, chronic
6.	Outcome	reversible, irreversible

In a complex array of causal factors involved in delinquency there may be neither sufficient nor necessary causes (Hirschi and Selvin, 1966). Delinquency results from different sets of causal variables for different people in different circumstances. Yet this state of affairs does not negate that each of the particular factors involved within each individual case may be a component of a sufficient cause (Rothman, 1976). Malnutrition, secondary to a deficient diet, by itself need not produce delinquency; or many delinquents may not be malnourished; and still malnutrition may in some instances be an important component of causality in delinquent behavior. At issue, therefore, is not the call for proof of a diet-delinquency relationship. The point to be made is that diet-related factors may have adverse effects over behavior; these effects are of a kind that makes them suspect for a causal contribution to delinquency. Accordingly, the task ahead is to selectively review data and studies on the effects of highly prevalent diet-related nutritional deficiencies on behavior. Focus will be placed on short term fasting, iron deficiency, and protein-calorie malnutrition. Pertinent criticisms will be added to the review not only for the purposes of establishing validity of the data but also to illustrate the research problems in the area.

DIET AND BEHAVIOR

Short-Term Fasting

There is a scarcity of information on the effects of short-term abstinence of food on behavior and psychological function. The classical studies on starvation by Keys et al. (1950) cover a wider time span than our present concerns; therefore, we are limited to work focused on school feeding, morning hunger, and behavior. Selective attention will be given to studies that measured outcome variables of relevance to the issue at hand.

About fifty years ago it was postulated that hunger pangs and nervousness in children were correlated (Laird, Levitan and Wilson, 1931). In order to assess the validity of this contention 48 children from grades one, three, and five were studied for two consecutive weeks. On the basis of a behavior checklist completed by the teacher (unaware of the purpose of study) nervous children were divided into three groups. The first included those children receiving no special feeding (a control group given toys to play with); a second group included children receiving milk, and the remaining cases received milk plus a calcium supplement. The feeding was administered early in the morning (9:30 a.m.). The results showed a 6% reduction in nervousness among the children who received milk over the two week study period. The teachers reported improvement in behavior such as "less abstracted and more wide awake, more careful and less slovenly in thinking, and less easily fatigued." However, 50% of the milk-fed group showed no improvement or were worse at the end of the two week period.

The authors concluded that nervousness in elementary school children was related to hunger, and that mid-morning feedings of milk reduced nervousness. They also concluded that milk plus a calcium supplement decreased nervousness further, although no indication of baseline calcium nutrition was mentioned. Here it is important to note that there were a number of idiosyncrasies in the behavioral terminology used by the authors; and it is impossible to ascertain the theoretical framework which they used to select their outcome variables.

Kiester (1950) studied the effects of a mid-morning administration of fruit juice on hyperactivity, withdrawal, hostile behavior, and nervous habits of 133 children 27-60 months of age attending a nursery school. Each child was studied four times during the year—twice when receiving fruit juice and twice when receiving water. The behaviors were assessed by observation of each child for a 30-second interval after the 10:00 a.m. feeding of fruit juice or water.

The results indicate that the target behaviors appeared less frequently among children receiving fruit juice than among those receiving water. There were no significant age differences. Males, however, showed a greater reduction in the incidence of "negative" behaviors with administration of fruit juice than females.

Matheson (1970) assessed the value of a mid-morning orange juice feeding for 100 fifth grade students from three different schools. The study was conducted over a 10-day period, and performance on arithmetic (addition) and letter symbol decoding tests was the outcome variable studied. Because the children acted as their own controls, they were exposed to an experimental and a control situation on different days. The 10:30 a.m. orange juice supplementation was associated with significantly better performance at 9:15, 10:30, and 11:45 a.m. on tasks of decoding and addition. Tests taken after the orange juice feeding at 10:30 showed the most significant differences with respect to decoding tasks.

The time at which the arithmetic or decoding task was given (e.g., 9:15, 10:30, 11:45 a.m.) did not significantly affect the performance of children whose usual breakfast intake was poor or good (mid-morning orange juice feeding was not involved in these comparisons). However, breakfast intake data was not obtained on the day of testing; the quality of usual breakfast intake was determined by a three-day written food record collected several weeks after the experiment had been conducted.

Dwyer, Elias and Warren (1973) studied the effects of an instant breakfast (liquid meal) on 139 males in the first grade. The children were tested individually on tasks of attention (slow tapping test, digit test, block test) and for short periods on eye gaze (to assess attention maintenance within the classroom). One-half of the pupils were fed the liquid meal in the morning and one-half in the afternoon. The investigators found no between-group differences in performance on any of the tasks of attention measured between 9:30 a.m. and noon. Although home breakfast intake among the control group was obtained by dietary recall on the day of testing, results were reported in terms of "sporadic" breakfast eaters and "always eats breakfast" rather than in terms of intake of particular nutrients (*e.g.*, calories) on the day of testing.

Pollitt, Greenfield, and Leibel (1981) have also studied the co-variation between short-term food abstinence and performance in a series of problem solving, vigilance, and memory tasks. The subjects included in the study were 23 girls and 11 boys ranging from nine to 11 years of age. They were all well-nourished, healthy children. All were admitted twice to a Clinical Research Center; both admissions took place at about 4:00 p.m. and there generally was a seven-day interval between them. Dinner was served at 5:00 p.m. and included a hamburger and roll, french fries, applesauce, Kool Aid, and vanilla ice cream. The composition of the meal was as follows: 960 kcal; 40 g protein; 25 g fat and 145 g carbohydrate.

For half of the sample following the first admission, breakfast (BR) was served at 8:00 a.m. The other half received no breakfast (NBR) that morning. On second admission this order was reversed. Breakfast consisted of waffles and syrup, margarine, orange juice, and milk. The composition of breakfast was as follows: 535 kcal; 15 g protein; 20 g fat; and 75 g carbohydrate.

At about 9:00 p.m. on the night of admission preceding the NBR morning 15 cc of blood was obtained via venipuncture. On both testing days the behavioral battery was administered at 11:00 a.m. and thereafter an additional five cc of blood were obtained. Blood specimens were analyzed for glucose, lactate, and beta-hydroxybutyrate. Psychological testing battery included a problem-solving task [Matching Familiar Figure Test (MMFT)]; a vigilance test [Continuous Performance Task (CPT)]; and a short term memory test [Hagen Central Incidental task].

Among the sets of metabolite-behavioral relationships the only set that presented meaningful statistical findings were those including glucose. Accordingly, only these results are presented here.

The mean IQ for the group was 110.4 (Sd = 19.6). IQ correlated at a statistically significant level with the MFFT error ($r = .44$; $p = .005$), and latency scores ($r = .56$; $p = .001$) in the NBR condition. IQ did not correlate with any of the scores from the two other behavioral measures in either treatment condition.

Mean glucose value at NBR (noon time) was 77.6 mg/dl (SD = 9.0), which differed statistically ($t = 2.82$; $p < .01$) from the mean at 9:00 p.m. on the preceding night ($\overline{M} = 85.4$; Sd = 13.5). It did not differ at a statistically reliable level from the glucose mean ($\overline{M} = 80.1$; Sd = 10.7) obtained seven days apart at the BR condition (noon time) ($t = 1.41$; $p > .05$).

The distribution of glucose value at NBR was split by the median in order to compare the behavioral scores between the subgroups thus formed. Two two-way factorial ANOVAs were calculated including glucose (above and below the median) and IQ (above and below the median of the respective distribution) as treatment variables and the MFFT total error and latency scores as outcomes. In the ANOVA for errors the F values for both main effects, and for the IQ-glucose interaction, were not statistically significant.

In the case of the MFFT latency scores, the mean for the sub-group whose IQ and glucose values fell above their respective medians was 63.00s (sd = 268.0), and for the subgroup whose IQ and glucose fell above and below the medians, respectively, was 17.36s (sd = 123.8). Further, the average in the case of the subgroups falling below the median in both IQ and glucose was 27.59s (sd = 188.0), and for below the IQ and above the glucose medians was 33.43s (sd = 229.8). The main effect for IQ (F = 7.21; p < .01) was statistically significant. Both F values for the effect of glucose (F = 3.61) and for the IQ-glucose interaction (F = 3.72) showed a trend toward significance (p < .10). Because of this trend the MFFT data were analyzed further, breaking down the test into its four easy and four hard items. While the analysis of the former items yielded no statistical meaningful data, the analysis of the results on the four hard items showed particularly interesting statistical findings. The two-way ANOVA using glucose and IQ as treatment variables yielded significant F values for IQ (F = 7.46; p = .01) and for IQ-glucose interaction (F = 4.45; p < .05). The subjects with a high IQ and high glucose value had a latency mean of 45.05s (sd = 227.9); on the other hand, the subjects with similar high IQ but with a low glucose had a mean of 21.85s (sd = 176.9).

By contrast, the subjects with low IQs varied slightly from a mean latency score of 14.9s (sd 77.1) to 17.9s (sd = 148.5) as their glucose fell above and below the median, respectively. The two-way ANOVAs for errors in the four hard items yielded no statistically significant findings for either main or interactive effects.

A t-test comparison on the two runs of the CPT for the NBR condition yielded no significant differences between means of the subjects that fell above and below the glucose median. Likewise, there were no between-group differences in the means of the Hagen recall test. However, analyses of the correct responses to the probe on serial position 6 (recency effect) showed that the average score (M = 2.75; sd = .45) of the subjects with low glucose values was statistically higher (t = 5.44; p = .025) than that of the subjects with glucose values above the median. These findings suggest that the probability of recall error in serial position 6 was higher among the subjects with high, and not with low, glucose values.

Because this study used each subject as his/her own control, the most potent statistical analyses that can be made to determine treatment effects is that using difference scores. This analytical strategy minimizes covariate effects. Accordingly, the distribution of the glucose difference values (BR-NBR) was split by the median and the MFFT, CPT and Hagen difference scores (BR-NBR) of the two subgroups of subjects were compared by ANOVA with repeated measures.

The behavioral results showed that the difference MFFT error score of the subjects who fell above the median (M = .60; sd = 1.82) in the difference glucose value distribution were statistically different (F = 5.67; p = .02) than those who fell below the median (M = −1.20; sd = 2.2). This comparison indicated that those subjects whose glucose values dropped (negative sign) tended to have an increase (negative sign) in the number of errors in the MFFT. A similar comparison for latency showed a trend that may be expected given the error difference but without reaching statistical significance (F = 2.07; p = .11). The mean latency time of the subjects who fell below and above the median in glucose difference values was 26.8 (sd = 87.8) and −64.13 (sd = 22.8). This suggests that in comparison to those subjects whose values either did not drop or did not differ much from the BR to the NBR condition, there was an increase in the latency period of the subjects whose glucose values tended to fall.

The statistical analyses of the two CPT runs and of the Hagen recall task yielded findings of no statistical significance. However, in agreement with previous analyses on the same test, there was a statistical trend for the subjects to do better on S_6 of the Hagen recall task in the NBR ($\overline{M}$ = −.60; sd = .83) than in the BR condition ($\overline{M}$ = −.06; sd = .80) (F = 3.22; p = .08).

The data from this highly controlled study indicates that 19 hours of overnight-morning fasting may affect selective features of mental tempo and information processing. These effects, however, are not unidirectional. The data show that while in some cases problem solving competence is adversely affected, in other cases latency of response to problem solving is decreased without affecting accuracy. Moreover, it is also apparent that at least one feature of selective attention and short-term memory benefited.

The behavioral signs detected on the cognitive tests do not have to be taken as indication of a primary central nervous system central effect. Variations in arousal level associated with variations in peripheral factors may explain the findings. The metabolic states determined by the no-breakfast condition may have induced changes in peripheral neurophysiologic receptors. A behavioral response to these changes may, in turn, have affected performance in the tests administered.

SIDEROPENIA (IRON DEFICIENCY)

Iron deficiency in both animals and man may exist in the absence of anemia (Cook et al., 1976). In fact, iron kinetics are such that body iron stores, transferrin saturation, and even tissue level of essential heme-containing enzymes can be markedly diminished before the circulating mass of red cells is affected (Harris and Kellermyer, 1970). Moreover, tissue iron may be depleted in the early process of iron deficiency (Dallman, 1974).

Research on the behavioral impact of iron deficiency has focused on alterations in cognition, physical activity, and work productivity (Pollitt and Leibel, 1976). Reports on verbalization of children with sideropenia on cognitive-emotional experiences have also been published (Harris and Kellermyer, 1970). In the present chapter attention will be restricted to the data on cognition and clinical symptomatology (for recent references on work productivity, see Basta et al., 1979).

Clinical reports on patients with iron deficiency anemia indicate that they complain of fatigue, weakness, irritability, and a lack of ability to concentrate (Harris and Kellermyer, 1970; Werkman et al., 1964). However, patients are often asymptomatic, and the number and severity of symptoms does not appear to correlate with the degree of anemia (Berry and Nash, 1954; Wood and Elwood, 1966; Elwood et al., 1969). Furthermore, in one study at least, iron therapy and increased hemoglobin levels among previously anemic subjects did not ameliorate the symptoms (Morrow, et al., 1968).

It is important to note that the subjective response to iron therapy in anemic iron deficient patients may precede the rise in hemoglobin values (Harris and Kellermyer, 1970). Three to five days following the beginning of iron repletion therapy a return of strength and of appetite, as well as a feeling of well being were reported. These changes could not have been caused by alteration of red cell mass because of the timing of the change. Thus, it appears that the symptomatology often attributed to iron deficiency may not be dependent on the anemia but rather on some other metabolic correlates of iron depletion (Leibel et al., 1979; 1979a).

In adults, a serum iron level of less than 70 μg/dl (Hillman and Henderson, 1969) and/or transferrin saturation of less than 16 to 20% (Harris and Kellermyer, 1970) are well correlated with a failure to deliver to the marrow a quantity of iron sufficient for full proliferative capacity of the red cell line. Hunter and Smith (1972) showed that in 6- to 18-month-old children, a transferrin saturation of greater than 16% was virtually always associated with hematocrit and hemoglobin levels equal to or greater than 33% and 11 gm/dl, respectively. The converse, however, did not hold. Many children with hematocrit and hemoglobin levels greater than 33% and 11 gm/dl, respectively, had transferrin saturations of less than 16%. Thus, the iron deplete state, at least in its incipiency, is frequently not reflected in the Hgb or Hct levels. Therefore, studies using Hct and Hgb alone to identify the prospective iron-deficient individual must always under-estimate the prevalence of the iron-deficient state.

Webb and Oski (1973) investigated the scholastic achievement of adolescents with iron deficiency in Philadelphia. Twelve-to-fourteen-year-old, mostly black, junior high school students from an economically deprived population were the subjects for the study. Following a survey of 1,807 children, 96 of them were considered anemic based on hemoglobin values which ranged from 10.1 to 11.4 gm/dl. All anemic subjects had hypochromic, microcytic red cells and evidenced neither sickle cell hemoglobin nor red cell glucose-6-phosphate dehydrogenase deficiency. A control group of 101 students with hemoglobin values ranging from 14.0 to 14.9 gm/dl was also tested. A measure of scholastic performance was obtained from the composite score on the Iowa Tests of Basic Skills, Levels A-F/Form 3.

The scores of the anemic subjects were significantly lower ($P < 0.025$) than those of nonanemic students. Further, the older anemic male subjects displayed a progressive departure in performance from the non-anemic control subjects. The authors acknowledged that they had insufficient information to interpret the sex difference in the decline of scores as a function of age. The performance of both groups of children on a standard visual afterimage task was also investigated (Webb and Oski, 1973a). The subjects' reports on the visualization of an afterimage showed that the iron-deficient anemic children had a longer latency period than the nonanemic subjects.

A third study by Webb and Oski (Webb and Oski, 1974), on 74 of these 92 anemic children and 36 control subjects, employed a Behavior Problem Checklist. Observational ratings from 13 English teachers, who did not know the group in which each child belonged, were the basis for behavioral comparisons. The information provided by the checklist focused on: (a) conduct problems, (b) personality disturbances, and (c) inadequacy-immaturity. A nonsignificant between-group difference in the scores on personality disturbances and inadequacy-immaturity was observed. The difference in the conduct scale reached the 0.10 level of probability; this difference was interpreted to mean that the anemic subjects tended to have more conduct disturbances than the nonanemic subjects. In summary, the authors concluded that the scholastic performance of the anemic children was compromised by disturbances in attention and perception.

Pollitt, Greenfield and Leibel (1978) studied attention, learning, and memory in 23 preschool children with iron deficiency, and their controls. Both groups were matched for sex, race, and age. There were 17 boys and 6 girls in each group. Entry criteria included: (1) a gestational age of 38 weeks or more; (2) a birthweight of 2,500 grams or more; (3) no evidence of any chronic illness or hematologic disorder such as sickle cell trait disease, thalassemia trait or hereditary anemia that could affect body hemoglobin mass; (4) blood lead levels below 40 micrograms per cent. Table 2 summarizes the composition of the two groups at initiation of the study.

TABLE 2
Time One Status of Iron Deficient and Normal Group

Variable	Iron Deficient		Normal		p Value for t-Test Less Than
	Mean	S.D.	Mean	S.D.	
Hemoglobin (gm/dl)	11.54	.94	12.06	.5	.025
Hematocrit (%)	32.87	2.8	34.06	1.4	.05
Mean Cell Volume (fl.)	79.7	3.35	79.5	2.7	N.S.
SI/TIBC(%)	13.4	3.27	29.04	6.9	.001
Serum Iron (μg/dl)	35.0	10.0	77.7	17.1	.001
Age (months)	45.4	8.6	44.9	9.0	N.S.
Height (cm.)	101.2	6.9	100.8	6.4	N.S.
Weight (lbs.)	36.8	7.6	37.4	5.5	N.S.

Iron deficiency was defined at the initial period of the study by a serum iron to total iron binding capacity (SI/TIBC) ratio (per cent saturation) of 17% or less. Iron criteria for a control included a SI/TIBC ratio of 20% or above, and a hemoglobin greater than 11 grams per cent. Approximately 750 microliters of capillary blood were drawn via finger prick for biochemical and hematologic determinations.

Behavioral assessments took place on two consecutive days under optimal testing conditions. The experimenter had no knowledge concerning the iron status of the child during these evaluations.

A first set of three groups of two-choice discrimination learning tasks was given to the children. In each of these groups a correct response represents the choice of one of two stimuli defined as target by the experimenter. Once the child reaches learning criterion on each problem the correct stimulus is reversed and the solution to the new problem requires a shift of previously correct and incorrect responses.

In a first set of discrimination-learning tasks normal controls learned all three problems as well as all three reversal problems in fewer mean trials than iron-deficient children. These between-group comparisons were not statistically significant if analyzed independently. However, overall, normal children performed statistically superiorly (F = 4.5; p < .05) to iron-deficient children, and the trend was clearly indicative of superior performance on all problems by normal children.

The test battery also included a number of memory tasks. In the first such task a large number of two-choice discrimination learning problems were presented concurrently for a total of four trials each. Trials one and two of each problem were consecutive or massed. Trials two and three had either zero, four, or eight interpolated items separating them. Trial four did not appear until the next day of testing, 24 hours later.

Trial two and Trial three following zero interpolated items are a measure of attention and how much information enters the memory system. Figure 1 presents in diagrammatic form the results of the test. Performance on these two trials rises steadily from 50% or chance performance to approximately 80%. Trial three following either four or eight interpolated items shows decay in memory as a function of both time and item interference. This interference is indicated by a drop in performance to below 70% with four intervening items and performance near 60% correct with eight interpolated items. Iron-deficient and normal children did not differ in the amount of information lost through item interference and decay.

Following 24 hours, a large difference in favor of the normal group occurs on long-term memory retention following a long (eight trial) T2-T3 interval—72% vs. 57% correct. This difference is not indicative of a poorer long-term memory in the structural sense, but rather a differential rehearsal strategy on early trials. This task is designed to overload the short-term memory system by providing more information in the form of concurrent learning problems than the system can handle at one

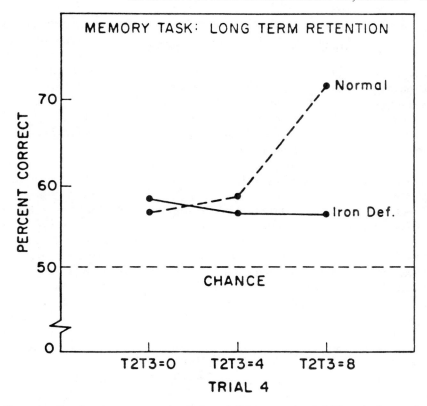

Figure 1.   Results of memory testing in iron deficient preschool children and controls.

time. A subject must, then, choose a rehearsal strategy to optimize memory retention.

The second memory task included in the test battery was a recognition memory task. Pictures pasted on 3″ × 3″ posterboard were presented to the child to look at, one at a time. Following presentation of the entire set, each picture was presented again, paired with a new picture and the child's task was to identify the picture he had just been shown. Sets of eight, sixteen, and thirty-two items were used. No consistent difference between the groups occurred, as normal children performed slightly better on the 16-item task, and iron deficient children performed slightly better on the eight- and thirty-two-item tasks.

An oddity learning task was also included in the test battery. Three stimuli, two of which were identical, were presented simultaneously on a 7" × 18" card and the child had to learn to choose the stimulus that was different from the other two. In this conceptual learning task, the specific makeup of the stimulus does not determine its correctness, but rather its relationship to other stimuli in the array.

Using new stimuli on every trial, 14 iron-deficient and 12 normal children were able to successfully reach a criterion of six in a row correct. On a more difficult task using the same stimuli on every trial varied in an AAB BBA manner, 10 iron-deficient and nine normal children obtained the same criterion. Neither of these differences reached statistical significance.

On the first trial of the oddity learning task each child has a choice between choosing a stimulus that was represented twice or one that appeared only once. From an attentional point of view, the single or odd stimulus has high salience, and is usually chosen on the first trial. While 67% of normal children chose the odd stimulus, only 38% of iron-deficient children did so. This difference was statistically significant ($t = 1.89$; $p < .05$). Moreover, when all 46 children were considered as a group, both initial hemoglobin level ($r = .37$; $p < .01$) and percent saturation ($r = .34$; $p < .02$) correlated with Trial 1 performance. This may indicate that level of arousal or attention may be influenced by these variables.

Fifteen of the 23 iron-deficient subjects received oral iron therapy for four months. Of the remaining eight subjects, four although untreated had saturations above 17% at the time of the second set of testing. Since the untreated and still-iron-deficient group had so few cases (four), only treated subjects were compared to normal children at time two. Each child who was iron deficient at time one and normal at time two, and his/her normal control, were used for making between-group comparisons.

The entire battery of behavioral tests was repeated following the four-months of iron therapy. Results from the analysis of the data indicate that following therapy, *iron-deficient children as a group perform equally well as their normal controls on all behavioral tests.*

The present data support the hypothesis that iron-deficient children are less able to selectively attend to relevant information and use less appropriate rehearsal strategies when their memory systems are overloaded. They also respond to salient stimuli less frequently than non-iron-deficient children. These deficits, however, appear to be eliminated once iron status is restored to normal.

The differences in hemoglobin and hematocrit between the index and their matched control children may be taken as an indication that few of the index children were anemic. However, these differences in hematology were numerically small; conversely, there were large statistical and numerical differences between groups in percent saturation. Accordingly, the index children should be primarily characterized as iron-deficient rather than anemic. The behavioral differences observed between groups were therefore most likely determined by the differences in levels of body iron.

Although a "lesion" in almost any of the iron-dependent metabolic pathways could provide a basis for the behavior changes attributed to iron deficiency, recent animal and human research has focussed on oxidative and neurotransmitter metabolism (Dallman et al., 1975; Dallman and Spirito, 1977; Woods et al., 1977; Voorhess et al., 1975). The rate-limiting enzymes in the pathways of catecholamine (Tyrosine hydroxylase) and serotonin (Tryptophan hydroxylase) synthesis are iron-dependent; monoamine oxidase, which catabolizes both compounds, and aldehyde oxidase (final oxidation of 5-hydroxy-indoleacetaldehyde to 5-hydroxyindoleacetic acid) are also apparently iron-dependent. Studies have recently appeared describing the in vitro function of these enzymes in brain tissue of iron-depleted animals and suggesting a correlative of behavior changes with changes in brain chemistry (Youdim and Green, 1977; Mackler et al., 1978).

In conclusion, the research reviewed on the effects of sideropenia suggests that iron deficiency has adverse effects over cognitive function, particularly control processes such as attention and memory rehearsal strategies. In addition, although it is far from conclusive, it appears that it may also interfere with school adjustment and achievement in adolescents. Both cognitive and behavioral disorders are not determined by reduced tissue oxygenation, and it appears that they are mediated by alterations in brain biochemical mechanisms. These mechanisms, however, remain unknown.

Protein-energy Malnutrition

Research on the behavioral effects of protein-energy malnutrition (PEM) face a serious methodological problem in the issue of disease definition. Except for severe forms of PEM, often no clear clinical signs or biochemical alterations can be detected in mild to moderate malnutrition, which are the most prevalent forms of this macro-nutrient deficiency.

In 1962 a joint Expert Committee on Nutrition from the Food and Agricultural Organization and from the World Health Organization was convened to establish a nomenclature and classification for protein-energy malnutrition (WHO Technical Report, 1962). The Committee deemed the task of classification extremely difficult, and the general term of Protein-Calorie (not protein-energy) Malnutrition remained without further refinement. A subsequent Expert Committee (WHO Technical Report, 1971) from the same organizations was formed in 1970 to once again grapple with the issue of classification. The Committee recognized Kwashiorkor and Marasmus as distinct pathologies but again suggested that the classification of PEM was a difficult problem for several reasons. Among them the following were specifically identified:

— There is no sharp dividing line between normal and pathological states of malnutrition, particularly when attempting to distinguish mild to moderate forms of protein-calorie malnutrition from the norms.
— Moderate to severe forms of protein-calorie malnutrition seldom exist in isolation. For example, complicating vitamin and mineral deficiencies would likely coexist with it. Thus, it is difficult to deduce whether moderate to severe forms of PCM is a clinical entity in itself.
— The presence of chronic infection may maintain a borderline nutritional deficiency which could precipitate into severe malnutrition in 24-48 hours.
— There is no specific relationship between failure to grow and nutritional intake, though growth is the best indicator of nutritional status, particularly in the mild to moderate forms of malnutrition.

The Committee report concluded that it was not feasible to devise a classification scheme that considered the age, severity, type, and duration of malnutrition. Furthermore, it was decided that for survey purposes attention be placed on systematic data collection rather than imposing data into categories.

In addition to the problem of disease definition there is one other serious methodological problem faced in establishing the impact of PEM on behavior. Protein-energy malnutrition secondary to a deficient diet almost always coexists with other forms of environmental deprivation which independently from or in conjunction with undernutrition have adverse effects over behavior. Economic impoverishment, low levels of education, large family size, poor hygienic and sanitary conditions, and high levels of morbidity and infection go hand-in-hand with PEM. These variables maintain complex feedback systems throughout the development of the affected children. Accordingly, it is simplistic to assume that each one of them independently shapes the development of the undernourished child.

Extensive and critical reviews of the literature on the effect of PEM on behavior recently published are available to the interested reader (Pollitt and Thomson, 1977; Cravioto and DeLicardie, 1979). For this reason one more review seemed redundant and therefore, the remaining part of this section is restricted to selective conclusions on the issue in question:

(1) Severe protein-energy deficiency occurring throughout most of the first 12 months of life among populations where malnutrition is endemic results in a severe deficit (one to two standard deviations below an average of 100) in intellectual function as compared to standards from the same population (Brockman and Ricciuti, 1971; Monckeberg, 1968; Pollitt and Granoff, 1967; Chase and Martin, 1970; Cravioto and DeLicardie, 1973; DeLicardie and Cravioto, 1974; Hertzig et al., 1972).

(2) Severe but acute protein-energy deficiency occurring during the second year of life among populations where malnutrition is endemic may, but generally does not, leave measurable retardation in intellectual function as compared to standards from the same population (Birch et al., 1971; Cravioto and Robles, 1965; Evans et al., 1971).

(3) There are no available data to determine whether severe but acute episodes of protein-energy malnutrition with an onset during the second year of life results in any impairment of intellectual function.

(4) Among populations where malnutrition is endemic, infants and young children of comparatively low stature (an indication of undernutrition) are likely to perform less well than average-size children from the sane community on aggregate tests of intelligence or on tests of specific cognitive process (Cravioto et al., 1966; Klein et al., 1972; Winick et al., 1975).

(5) Among populations where malnutrition is endemic, infants and young children of comparatively short stature are more likely to come from families found in the lowest strata of the socioeconomic structures of the population than children of similar age but of average size (Richardson, 1974; Mata, 1978; Levinson, 1974; Graham and Morales, 1963).

(6) Stature and graduated parameters of social structure (i.e., income, maternal education) explain significant parts of cognitive development test variance among infants and preschool children of populations where malnutrition is endemic. Their independent

contributions to test variance depend on the nature of the test construct in question. It is not currently possible to determine the constructs that are more amenable to the effects of one or the other sets of factors.

(7) Upgrading the quality of life throughout infancy and the preschool years improves the performance of children on aggregate scales of intelligence or on tests of specific cognitive factors as compared to their original performance before the change in life took place (Chavez et al., 1974; McKay et al., 1978).

HYPOTHETICAL PATHWAYS FOR THE CONNECTION OF NUTRITION AND BEHAVIOR ADJUSTMENT

Individually, most of the studies reviewed in the previous section cannot be used as the basis for conclusive inferences regarding specific effects of nutrition on behavior. However, as a group they strongly suggest that this is the case. The studies on overnight and morning fasting and morning feeding indicate that, at least among children, selective cognitive processes are likely to be altered following about 20 hours without food intake. Control processes involving attention are particularly vulnerable; and problem-solving abilities, under time constraints, are also amenable to alteration. Some features of short-term memory (*e.g.* recency effects in serial recall) are, however, apparently benefited by the short-term deprivation. In addition, few results from early studies on emotionality suggest that among children, morning snacks contribute to the maintenance of cooperative, emotionally stable behavior.

An interpretation of these findings is that fasting has incremental effects on behavioral arousal. This is apparent, for example, in the reduction in time-latency score (MFFT test) among the subjects with high IQ in the no-breakfast condition in the study by Pollitt et al. (1981). Behavioral arousal is also likely to be a reason why the performance of the subjects in this same treatment condition had a more noticeable recency effect, in the short-term memory task, than in the breakfast condition. Conceivably the data from the early reports on morning feeding and emotionality can also be taken as indicative of subtle adaptive changes in behavioral arousal.

The data on the behavioral effects of iron deficiency give no evidence of an arousal effect. Yet some of these results indicate that attention is also altered. Moreover, in contrast to the related data from the fasting studies, the experiments suggest that sideropenia may lessen the probabilities of accurate short-term recall—or, at least, affect the effective use of rehearsal strategies for recall. Further, data on adolescents in school show that iron deficiency may contribute to low school achievement and increase the chances of conduct problems. Cognitive and, possibly, behavioral deficiencies are apparently reversible following iron repletion therapy.

Finally, the data on protein energy malnutrition strongly suggest that in some circumstances at least (particularly in severe PEM), the nutritional deficiency may seriously retard not only control cognitive processes but general intellectual ability. However, PEM seems to act synergistically with other social deprivation factors in producing the adverse cognitive effects. Thus, the effects of the nutritional condition are potentiated (and perhaps become irreversible) by some of the other variables associated with the environmental deprivation that covaries with PEM. In fact it is probable (see Pollitt and Thomson, 1977) that the effects of PEM in cases of secondary malnutrition, and in the absence of economic impoverishment, may be easily reversible.

The cognitive effects of the three conditions analyzed are of different severity and have different development implications. They also represent different levels of threat to organismic homeostasis. By the same token, they must impact cognition through very different mechanisms. However, they do share a common element—their particular effect on cognitive function. Either through an interference with selective processes such as attention or memory rehearsal strategies, or through serious retardation of general mental ability the three conditions have an impact over the intellect. This is true independent from severity or of whether in one case the effect may last a few hours whereas in another case the effect may last over years. Accordingly, given an established level of severity, this impact partly restricts—at a time point—the chances of successful behavioral adjustment or performance. This means that the behavioral cost of the nutrition impact (at a given time) is a decrement of the potential an individual has of optimizing behavioral performance.

The nature of this relationship—from cognitive function to adjustment or performance—will surely not depend on the nutritional antecedent in question. It is now well accepted, for example, that under certain circumstances environmental influences play a remedial role in the behavior of children or adolescents with early nervous system trauma (see for example Richardson, 1974; Werner et al., 1971). Also, impoverished psychosocial settings potentiate the behavioral maladjustments associated with intellectual disabilities resulting from early neurological damage (Werner et al., 1971). The thesis then is that the nature of accompanying environmental factors will increase or decrease the probability that cognitive alteration (of short or long duration) resulting from nutrition factors will contribute to behavioral maladjustment.

Of importance here is to note that the contribution of the nutritional antecedent to behavioral maladjustment will not only vary as a function of severity but also of the frequency with which the factors that potentiate its effects appear. Thus, independent of severity, the probability of behavioral maladjustment associated with cognitive derangements in cases of PEM is high because PEM covaries with other variables that also contribute to such maladjustment. Conversely, the probability that abstinence of food for short term periods of time will contribute to behavioral maladjustments is very low because of its time span and the infrequency with which factors which potentiate its effects may present themselves. This holds true even if behavioral maladjustment is defined by one act or event.

The iron-deficient adolescents in the studies by Webb and Oski (1973, 1973a, 1974) are illustrative here. Given the sideropenia and the cognitive derangements thereof, the probabilities of conduct problems found in these subjects probably varied as a function of other factors. Specifically, it could be hypothesized that previous school achievement and social adaptation as well as home conditions would affect the probability of conduct problems. This state of affairs could then be presented in equation form as follows:

$$p(A) = f(_aI + _bG + _cS + _dH + e)$$

where p(A) = Probabilities of conduct problems
  I = Iron deficiency
  G = Grades in school before the onset of the iron deficiency
  S = School social adjustment before the onset of the iron deficiency
  H = Home environment (whether it fosters behavioral adjustment or not)
  a,b,c,d = coefficient
  e = error

Thus, given two subjects with the same level of iron deficiency (equal coefficient for I) their probabilities (p(A)) will vary as a function of the coefficients (a,b,c,d) found for each of the other variables (G,S,H) identified in the equation.

This mode of perceiving the contribution of nutrition factors is far removed from the conception of an antecedent-consequent relationship, and it falls in the center of a multifactorial model. It is in this direction which I think the search should go to establish the contribution of nutrition to delinquency.

ACKNOWLEDGMENTS

Supported in part by the Ford Foundation and by Grant No. HD09228-03 from the National Institute of Child Health and Human Development, Department of Health, Education and Welfare, United States Public Health Service.

REFERENCES

Basta, S. S., Soekirman, Karyadi, D., and Scrimshaw, N. S. (1979). Iron deficiency anemia and the productivity of adult males in Indonesia. *Am. J. Clin. Nutrition,* 32:916–925.

Berry, W. T. C., and Nash, F. A. (1954). Symptoms as a guide to anemia. *Brit. Med. J.,* 1:918.

Birch, H. E., Pineiro, C., Alcade, E., Toca, T., and Cravioto, J. (1971). Relation of kwashiorkor in early childhood and intelligence at school age. *Ped. Res.* 5:579–585.

Brockman, L. M., and Ricciuti, H. N. (1971). Severe protein-calorie malnutrition and cognition development in infancy and early childhood. *Dev. Psychol.* 4:312–319.

Cantwell, R. J. (1974). The long-term neurological sequelae of anemia in infancy. *Ped. Res.,* 8:342. (abstract)

Chase, H. P., and Martin, H. P. (1970). Undernutrition and child development. *N. Eng. J. Med.,* 282:933–939.

Chavez, A., Martinez, C., and Yaschine, T. (1974). The importance of nutrition and stimuli on child mental and social development. In: *Early Malnutrition and Mental Development,* J. Cravioto, L. Hambraeus, and B. Vahlquist (eds.). Uppsala: Almqvist & Wiksell.

Cook, J. D., Finch, C. A., and Smith, N. J. (1976). Evaluation of iron status of a population. *Blood,* 48:449–455.

Cott, A. (1978). The etiology of learning disabilities, drug abuse and juvenile delinquency. In: *Ecologic-Biochemical Approaches to Treatment of Delinquents and Criminals,* L. J. Hippchen (ed.). New York: Van Nostrand Reinhold Co.

Cravioto, J., and DeLicardie, E. (1973). Longitudinal study of language development in severely malnourished children. In: *Nutrition and Mental Functions,* G. Serban (ed.). New York: Plenum Press.

Cravioto, J., and DeLicardie, E. (1979). Nutrition, mental development, and learning. In: *Human Growth, Neurobiology and Nutrition,* Vol. 3, F. Falkner and J. M. Tanner (eds.). New York: Plenum Press.

Cravioto, J., DeLicardie, E., and Birch, H. (1966). Nutrition, growth and neurointegrative development: An experimental and ecological study. *Pediatrics (Suppl.),* 38:part II.

Cravioto, J., and Robles, B. (1965). Evolution of adaptive and motor behavior during rehabilitation from kwashiorkor. *Am. J. Orthopsych.,* 35:449–464.

Dallman, P. R. (1974). Tissue effects of iron deficiency. In: *Iron Biochemistry and Medicine,* A. Jacobs and M. Worwood (eds.). New York: Academic Press, Inc.

Dallman, P. R., Siimes, M. A., and Manies, E. C. (1975). Brain iron: Persistent deficiency following short-term iron deprivation in the young rat. *Brit. J. Haematology,* 31:209–215.

Dallman, P. R., and Spirito, R. A. (1977). Brain iron in the rat: Extremely slow turnover in normal rats may explain long-lasting effects of early iron deficiency. *J. Nutrition,* 107:1075–1081.

DeLicardie, E. R., and Cravioto, J. (1974). Behavioral responsiveness of survivors of clinically severe malnutrition to cognitive demands. In: *Early Malnutrition and Mental Development*, J. Cravioto, L. Hambraeus, and B. Vahlquist (eds.). Almqvist & Wiksell.

Dwyer, J. T., Elias, M. F., and Warren, J. H. (1973). Effects of an experimental breakfast program on behavior in the late morning. Department of Nutrition, Harvard School of Public Health, Cambridge, Mass. Unpublished.

Elwood, P. C., Waters, W. E., Greene, W. J. W., Sweetman, P., and Wood, M. M. (1969). Symptoms and circulating haemoglobin level. *J. Chronic Dis.*, 21:615–628.

Evans, D., Moodie, A., and Hansen, J. (1971). Kwashiorkor and intellectual development. *South African Med. J.*, 45:1413–1426.

Graham, G. C., and Morales, E. (1963). Studies in infantile malnutrition. I. Nature of the problem in Peru. *J. Nutrition*, 79:479–487.

Green, R. G. (1978). Treatment of penitentiary inmates. In: *Ecologic-Biochemical Approaches to Treatment of Delinquents and Criminals*, L. J. Hippchen (ed.). New York: Van Nostrand Reinhold Co.

Harris, J. W., and Kellermyer, R. W. (1970). *The Red Cell*. Cambridge, Mass: Harvard University Press.

Hertzig, M. E., Birch, H. G., Richardson, S. A., and Tizard, J. (1972). Intellectual levels of school children severely malnourished during the first two years of life. *Pediatrics*, 49:814–823.

Hillman, R. S., and Henderson, P. A. (1969). Control of marrow production by the level of iron supply. *J. Clin. Investigation*, 48:454–460.

Hippchen, L. J. (ed.) (1978). *Ecologic-Biochemical Approaches to Treatment of Delinquents and Criminals*. New York: Van Nostrand Reinhold Co.

Hirschi, T., and Selvin, H. C. (1966). False criteria of causality in delinquency research. *Social Problems*, 13:254–268.

Hunter, R. E., and Smith, N. J. (1972). Hemoglobin and hematocrit values in iron deficiency in infancy. *J. Ped.*, 81:710–713.

Keys, A., Brozek, J., Henschel, A., Mickelsen, O., and Taylor, H. L. (1950). *The Biology of Human Starvation*. Minneapolis, Minn: University of Minnesota Press.

Kiester, M. (1950). Relation of mid-morning feeding to behavior of nursery school children. *J. Am. Dietetics Assoc.*, 26:25–29.

Klein, R., Freeman, H., Kagan, J., Yarbrough, C., and Habicht, J. P. (1972). Is big smart? The relation of growth to cognition. *J. Health and Social Behav.*, 13:219–225.

Laird, D. A., Levitan, M., and Wilson, V. A. (1931). Nervousness in school children as related to hunger and diet. *Med. J. Record*, 134:494–499.

Leibel, R., Greenfield, D., and Pollitt, E. (1979). Biochemical and behavioral aspects of sideropenia. *Brit. J. Haematology*, 41:145–150.

Leibel, R. L., Greenfield, D., and Pollitt, E. (1979a). Iron deficiency: behavior and brain biochemistry. In: *Nutrition: Pre- and Post-Natal Development*, M. Winick (ed.). New York: Plenum Press.

Levinson, F. J. (1974): *Morinda: An Economic Analysis of Malnutrition Among Young Children in Rural India*. Cambridge, Mass: Cornell/MIT International Nutrition Policy Series.

Mackler, B., Person, R., Miller, L. R., Inamdar, A. R., and Finch, C. A. (1978). Iron deficiency in the rat. Biochemical studies of brain metabolism. *Ped. Res.* 12:217–220.

Mata, L. J. (1978). *The Children of Santa Maria Cauque: A prospective field study of health and growth*. Cambridge, Mass: MIT Press.

Matheson, N. E. (1970). Mid-morning nutrition and its effects on school type tasks. Ph.D. Dissertation, University of Southern California.

Mawson, A. R., and Jacobs, K. W. (1978). Corn consumption, tryptophan and cross-national homicide rates. *J. Orthomolecular Psych.*, 7:227–230.

McKay, H., Sinisterra, L., McKay, A., Gomez, H., and Lloreda, P. (1978). Improving cognitive ability in chronically deprived children. *Science*, 200:270–278.

McLaren, D. S. (1976). *Nutrition and its Disorders*. New York: Churchill Livingstone.

Monckeberg, F. (1968). Effect of early marasmic malnutrition on subsequent physical and psychological development. In: *Malnutrition, Learning and Behavior*, N. Scrimshaw and J. Gordon (eds.). Cambridge, Mass: MIT Press.

Morrow, J. J., Dagg, J. M., and Goldberg, A. (1968). A controlled trial of iron therapy in sideropenia. *Scottish Med. J.*, 13:78–83.

Pollitt, E., and Granoff, D. (1967). Mental and motor development of Peruvian children treated for severe malnutrition. *Revista Interamericana de Psicologia*, 1:93–102.

Pollitt, E., Greenfield, D., and Leibel, R. (1978). Behavioral effects of iron deficiency among preschool children in Cambridge, Mass. *Fed. Proc.*, 37:487.

Pollitt, E., and Leibel, R. L. (1967). Iron deficiency and behavior. *J. Ped.*, 88:372–381.

Pollitt, E., and Thomson, C. (1977). Protein-calorie malnutrition and behavior: A view from psychology. In: *Nutrition and the Brain*, Vol. 2, R. J. Wurtman and J. J. Wurtman (eds.). New York: Raven Press.

Pollitt, E., Leibel, R., and Greenfield, D. (1981). Brief fasting, stress and cognition in children. *Am. J. Clin. Nutrition*. (in press).

Richardson, S. A. (1974). The background histories of schoolchildren malnourished in infancy. *Advances in Pediatrics*, 21:167–195.

Roe, D. A. (1973). *A Plague of Corn; A Social History of Pellagra*. Ithaca: Cornell University Press.

Rothman, K. J. (1976). Causes. *Am. J. Epidemiol.* 104:587–592.

Voorhess, M. C., Stuart, M. J., Stockman, J. A., and Oski, F. A. (1975). Iron deficiency anemia and increased urinary norepinephrine excretion. *J. Ped.*, 86:542–547.

Ware, M. E. (1978). Some effects of nicotinic and ascorbic acids on the behavior of institutionalized juvenile delinquents. In: *Ecologic-Biochemical Approaches to Treatment of Delinquents and Criminals*, L. J. Hippchen (ed.). New York: Van Nostrand Reinhold Co.

Webb, T. E., and Oski, F. A. (1973). Iron deficiency anemia and scholastic achievement in young adolescents. *J. Ped.*, 82:827–830.

Webb, T. E., and Oski, F. A. (1973a). The effect of iron deficiency anemia on scholastic achievement, behavioral stability and perceptual sensitivity of adolescents. *Ped. Res.*, 8:294.

Webb, T. E., and Oski, F. A. (1974). Behavioral status of young adolescents with iron deficiency anemia. *J. Special Ed.*, 8:153–156.

Werkman, S., Shifman, L., and Shelley, T. (1964). Psychosocial correlates of iron deficiency in early childhood. *Psychosom. Med.*, 26:125–134.

Werner, E. E., Bierman, J. M., and French, F. E. (1971). *The Children of Kauai*. Honolulu: University of Hawaii Press.

Winick, M., Meyer, K., and Harris, R. (1975). Malnutrition and environmental enrichment by early adoption. *Science*, 190:1173–1175.

Wood, M. M., and Elwood, P. C. (1966). Symptoms of iron deficiency anemia: A community survey. *Brit. J. Prevent. Soc. Med.*, 20:117–121.

Woods, H. F., Youdim, M. B. H., Boullin, D., and Callender, S. (1977). Monamine metabolism and platelet function in iron-deficiency anemia. In: *Iron Metabolism*. Ciba Foundation Symposium 51. Amsterdam: Elsevier, p. 227.

World Health Organization. (1962). Joint FAO/WHO expert committee on nutrition: Sixth report. Geneva: WHO Technical Report Series 245.

World Health Organization. (1971). Joint FAO/WHO expert committee on nutrition: Eighth report. Geneva: WHO Technical Report Series 477.

Wurtman, R. J., and Wurtman, J. J. (eds.). (1977, 1977a). *Nutrition and the Brain,* Vols. 1 and 2. New York: Raven Press.

Yaryura-Tobias, J. A. (1978). Biologic research on violent behavior. In: *Ecologic-Biochemical Approaches to Treatment of Delinquents and Criminals,* L. J. Hippchen (ed.). New York: Van Nostrand Reinhold Co.

Youdim, M. B. H., and Green, A. R. (1977). Biogenic amine metabolism and functional activity in iron-deficient rats: Behavioral correlates. In: *Iron Metabolism,* Ciba Foundation Symposium 51. Amsterdam: Elsevier, p. 201.

CHAPTER FOURTEEN

Parents of Delinquents

DOROTHY OTNOW LEWIS, SHELLEY S. SHANOK,
DAVID A. BALLA

That parental behavior, attitudes, and mental health influence the behavior of their children has long been recognized. Sayings such as, "like father, like son" and "the apple falls not far from the tree" are commonplace and based on age-old observation. That the social adaptation of children often resembles closely that of their parents is readily apparent and needs little documentation. Less clear are the explanations for the similarities between the behaviors of sequential generations in particular families.

Explanations of the relationship between parental psychosocial states and the development of delinquency in children have often been simplistic as well as vague. They usually allude to ill-defined terms such as family disorganization. For example, the Gluecks reported the "under-the-roof" conditions existing in the households of delinquents to be especially chaotic and to fail to provide the child with the kind of discipline required in order to prevent delinquency (1950, 1970). Jenkins (1968) described the parents of "unsocialized aggressive" children as "depreciative, punitive (and) inconsistent" (p. 1440) and characterized the families of "socialized delinquents" as primarily neglectful of their children. According to Jenkins and Hewitt (1944), especially violent delinquents had suffered severe parental rejection. In a similar vein, Lukianowicz (1971) suggested that the most important single etiological factor influencing delinquent behavior in a group of incarcerated girls was "their disturbed family background" (p. 33). Cortes and Gatti (1972) concluded that "delinquents . . . receive at home less disciplinary control and less emotional support from their parents" (p. 3); ". . . the factors or

265

conditions that appear to be closest to the cause of delinquency are family disruption, particularly when the children are mesomorphic" (p. 21).

Others have called special attention to abusive parents. Redl and Wineman (1957) found parents of delinquents to exhibit "brutality, cruelty, and neglect" and to be narcissistically absorbed in their own interests to the exclusion of their children's needs. Similarly, Bandura and Walters (1959) noted that parents of delinquents were especially hostile to their children.

Closely related to the hypothesis that family disorganization causes delinquency is the idea that broken homes contribute significantly to antisocial behavior (Glueck and Glueck, 1950; Robins, 1966; Stephens, 1961; West, 1969). More recently, Rutter and Madge (1976) have found evidence to suggest that it is not so much the break-up of the home that leads to delinquency, but that it is rather the discord occurring within the family prior to marital dissolution. Offord and his colleagues (1978), in a study of a variety of factors associated with delinquency, stated, "It seems that broken homes play a major role in the production of delinquency in that the other factors do not further differentiate the groups when one looks at this already disadvantaged (nonintact) group" (p. 234).

Compassion has not characterized the studies or descriptions of the families of delinquents. On the contrary, many studies seeking explanations for the chaos within the households of delinquents have pointed accusing fingers at sociopathic, alcoholic, or downright criminal parents (Glueck and Glueck, 1950; Ferguson, 1952; Jonsson, 1967; McCord et al., 1959; West and Farrington, 1973).

A review of the literature since the time of Lombroso (1836-1909) reveals the difficulties scientific investigators have had freeing themselves from the Lombrosian idea that criminals represent a degenerative biological phenomenon and that amorality or immorality is passed genetically from generation to generation. As Schulsinger (1972) has observed, during the Third Reich, German psychiatric geneticists who studied the relatives of antisocial individuals concluded that heredity played a role in the etiology of antisocial behavior (Berlit, 1931; Riedel, 1937; Stumpfl, 1936).

More recent genetic studies of the families of antisocial individuals (Hutchings and Mednick, 1974; Mednick and Hutchings, 1978) have been more humane and more scientifically sophisticated in that they have attempted to explore possible inherited physiological responses to stress which might affect an individual's ability to acquire appropriate social behaviors through positive or negative reinforcement. Thus the more recent genetic studies have eschewed issues of inherent morality or immorality and, rather, have attempted to elucidate those neurophysiological factors that enhance or inhibit the ability to learn appropriate behaviors and function in socially acceptable ways. Consonant with this type of family study are the studies of the possible genetic transmission from parent to child of the hyperkinetic syndrome (Cantwell, 1975) and the relationship of this kind of vulnerability to the development of delinquency. In summary, the more recent genetic studies of the families of delinquents have focused on possible inherent neurophysiological sensitivities rather than on the transmission of delinquency or criminality.

Although many investigators have called attention to the fact that the parents of delinquents are often psychiatrically impaired, the diagnoses attributed to them have tended to fall into two categories: sociopathy (or its synonyms) and alcoholism (Jenkins, 1968; Cloninger and Guze, 1970; Guze et al., 1967; Bennett, 1959; Jonsson, 1967). Cloninger and Guze (1973), in a study of incarcerated females, adjudged that 55% of their fathers and 27% of their mothers suffered from alcoholism or sociopathy. Jenkins (1968) found that the mothers of his "socialized delinquents" themselves tended to be "prone to *delinquency* and *promiscuity*, the fathers to alcoholism" (p. 1444). In a lengthy review of the literature on parental alcoholism and the development of their offspring, El-Guebaly and Offord (1977) explored a variety of ways in which parental alcoholism may be associated with children's maladjustment.

Psychodynamic hypotheses regarding the effect of parental mental illness on development of delinquency have tended to focus on the transmission of values and characterologic traits. One of the most influential of these kinds of explanations was expounded by Johnson and Szurek (Johnson, 1949; Johnson and Szurek, 1952). They conceptualized the existence of "superego lacunae" in the personality structure of delinquents. The superego of the delinquent child was said to have become defective by virtue of the child's unconscious acting out of parental antisocial wishes. There was a tendency for psychiatrists and psychologists to view delinquent children—that is, children whose intrapsychic conflicts were evidenced by behavioral problems—as somehow quite different from children with intrapsychic problems that were manifested in less socially disruptive ways. Since delinquent children were viewed as "different," so their parents, too, must be viewed as different.

Bennett (1959) reported a tendency for delinquents to have "antisocial" or "morally unstable" parents in contrast to "neurotic" children, whose parents also tended to be "neurotic." Reiner and Kaufman (1959) characterized the majority of the parents of delinquents whom they studied as "impulse-ridden character disorders" who were "in a perpetual state of crisis" (p. 8) and had never "reached the oedipal level of development" (p. 19). Subsequently, Karson and Haupt (1968) reported the parents of children with conduct disorders to be more "extroversive" and less anxious than the parents of children with personality problems. In a later study (Karson and Markenson, 1973), mothers of children with conduct disorders were said to show less group conformity and to be less able to bind anxiety than mothers of children with personality problems. On the other hand, fathers in both groups were said to be similar, to suffer from low ego strength, strong feelings of guilt, and much free-floating anxiety.

More recently, concomitant with our greater understanding of some of the biological underpinnings of behavior, there has begun to develop an appreciation of the possibility that some of the more serious psychiatric disorders (*e.g.*, parental schizophrenia and/or mood disorders) may be associated not only with the development of similar disorders in their children, but may also be associated with the development of antisocial behaviors in children.

The studies of many investigators have begun to provide some other kinds of perspectives on the association of parental maladaptation and juvenile delinquency. These studies include Heston (1970) on the antisocial behavior of first degree relatives of schizophrenics; Cantwell (1975) on hyperactivity in the families of children with conduct disorders; Schuckit and Chiles (1978) on affective disorders and alcoholism in the parents of maladapted adolescents; and our own work (Lewis and Balla, 1976) on the prevalence of documented delinquency in the children of schizophrenics. This chapter will embrace our clinical and epidemiological findings to date about the parents of delinquents. We shall then explore some of the possible etiological and therapeutic implications of our work.

CLINICAL OBSERVATIONS

The comprehensive psychiatric evaluation of any child should include interviews with his parents. Whenever possible, whether working within a juvenile court clinic setting or within a correctional school setting, we made every effort to speak with the parents, guardians, or other relatives of the delinquent children we were evaluating.

When we began our clinical work with delinquent children and their families, we expected to be dealing primarily with social problems associated with life in a poverty-ridden environment. Familiar with much of the sociological and psychiatric literature, we were psychologically prepared to confront issues of overcrowding, poor housing, inadequate educational and recreational facilities, malnutrition, and racial and ethnic discrimination. Where psychiatric problems were concerned, the literature taught us to expect to encounter parental alcoholism and criminality. That these kinds of problems were prevalent became obvious quickly. Less immediately evident, however, were the kinds of parental psychiatric disorders that often underlay what on the surface presented as simply parental alcoholism, sociopathy, or overall inadequacy to the tasks of rearing children.

For example, early in our clinical work we were asked to evaluate a child who had been involved in a variety of sexual experiences with adult men. We were informed by the probation staff that the mother was a sociopath who had spent a considerable amount of time in prison, often for sexually-related antisocial acts. No wonder the youngster was sexually precocious if not downright promiscuous!

An interview with the child's mother revealed that she had a long antisocial record, dating back to childhood, when she had become pregnant out of wedlock. In the course of our interview, we learned that for many years the mother had been persecuted by voices which only she was able to hear but which caused her to behave in bizarre, inappropriate ways. She had been totally unable to sustain a relationship with a single individual, male or female, nor had she been able to care for her daughter, who became the sexual target of several of her mother's male acquaintances. In fact, the mother, recognizing her inability to care for her child, had placed the girl in the care of an elderly man who used the child sexually. When this mother was told that there might be effective treatment available to rid her of her auditory hallucinations, we inquired why she had never told anyone of her "voices."

The answer: "Nobody ever asked me."

Another mother, hospitalized on several occasions for symptoms consistent with the diagnosis of a bipolar mood disorder, had abandoned her children, including a seriously delinquent daughter, to her drug-addicted husband. When he was hospitalized, the children were placed in a variety of different foster homes.

Yet another mother, hospitalized several times with a diagnosis of schizophrenia, had all of her children placed in residential or correctional institutions and made her own home in a small car which she drove from town to town, occasionally sleeping in a motel for a night. Her son, a child incarcerated for having committed arson, was able to provide the names of motels where his mother sometimes stayed. Unfortunately, all efforts to locate this mother were fruitless, although some of the motels where she had slept could recall her occasional visits.

It was especially difficult to interview the parents of incarcerated children, some of whom had actually left the state, while others lived far from the correctional school and lacked transportation. Often the parent or relative willing and able to come to an interview proved to be the most psychiatrically intact adult family member. For example, one mother of an extremely violent, paranoid youngster was, herself, a competent, self-sufficient woman who had held a responsible job for several years. During the course of our interview we learned that she had placed her violently aggressive son in the care of a psychotic grandmother for the first several years of his life. There the boy had been warned of dangerous fumes penetrating the house and had been inculcated with a pervasive distrust of others. Supporting this child's psychotically paranoid orientation was a father who refused to permit his boy to be transferred from a correctional facility to a private psychiatric hospital, forcing the youngster to remain in a totally inappropriate setting, where his behavior continued to deteriorate. Although the father refused to be interviewed at the correctional school, he did appear at the psychiatric hospital to prevent his son's admission. He was described by hospital staff as inordinately suspicious and unable to comprehend his son's need for psychiatric care, thus foreclosing the possibility of treatment.

All available information, including interviews with those fathers willing and able to meet with us, suggested that the fathers of the delinquents we saw were as disturbed as the mothers. Unfortunately, they often manifested their problems in especially physically violent ways. For example, one father (with the help of a relative) tied his boy to a bed and burned the soles of his feet. Another psychotically impaired father refused medical treatment for his son but rather beat his epileptic boy to exorcise the devil, then sent the boy to church daily. Another father not only beat his wife and children severely, but also threatened them with guns, occasionally shooting bullets through walls and windows. Many of the fathers and mothers described had spent periods of time in prisons, psychiatric hospitals, and drug and alcohol abuse treatment facilities.

PSYCHIATRIC HOSPITALIZATION and/or CRIMINALITY IN PARENTS OF DELINQUENTS

As evidenced by our review of the literature and our clinical descriptions, it is very difficult to translate these parental problems into quantitative terms that have social relevance. One psychiatrist's diagnosis of paranoid psychosis may be another's diagnosis of sociopathic violence. Our initial epidemiological study of the interrelationships of delinquency, parental psychopathology, and parental criminality was an effort to deal with the ambiguities in interpretation of much of the previous literature related to antisocial children and their parents by using measures independent of our own clinical assessments. We therefore chose as our measures of parental psychiatric disorder, parental antisocial behavior, and delinquency, actual contact with the psychiatric system, the adult criminal justice system, and the juvenile court.

Four groups of subjects were selected for study.

1. All identifiable parents of children referred to the court clinic during its first year of operation (n = 273, first-year clinic group).
2. All identifiable parents of children referred to the court clinic during its second year of operation (n = 205, second-year clinic group).
3. A random sample of parents of children referred to the juvenile court but not to the court clinic during the same years as the clinic samples (n = 261, court comparison group).
4. A random sample of persons residing in a predominantly lower socioeconomic sector of the community (n = 938, community comparison group).

Sample 3, "court comparison," was chosen in order to ascertain whether or not the parents of clinic-referred children were similar to the parents of the general population of delinquent children coming through the court.

Subjects from the first three samples were preponderantly, but not exclusively, from lower socioeconomic backgrounds. That is to say, these samples were typical, socioeconomically, of the population of delinquents in this community. Court records, however, were not uniform enough to make definitive social-class assignments. In the two clinic groups, approximately 77% of the subjects were white, and 23% black—proportions similar to those reported to exist in the juvenile court system in this community. In the third sample, the court comparison sample, the racial composition was unknown because, for reasons of civil rights, race was not uniformly recorded. We assumed, because of the random sampling procedure, that the racial composition would be representative of the court at large.

Of the fourth sample, the vast majority of individuals (75%) came from classes IV and V (Hollingshead and Redlich, 1958). Approximately 85% were white and 15% were black. Thus the fourth community sample was similar to, but not identical with, the delinquent samples; however, socioeconomically it was as comparable a group on which data could be obtained as was possible in the New Haven community at the time of the study.

Dependent Measures—Psychiatric Disorder

We used two different measures of parental psychiatric disorder, depending on the specific comparisons to be made. For all internal comparisons involving only the three delinquent groups, and for comparisons of the delinquent groups with the general population of Connecticut, our criterion of psychiatric disorder was the fact of having received psychiatric treatment and/or hospitalization at one of the six major state psychiatric facilities. In comparisons of the three delinquent samples with the fourth lower SES community group, we used as our criterion on psychiatric disorder the fact of having received treatment and/or hospitalization at one or both of the two major state facilities serving the New Haven community.

Definitions of Psychiatric Impairment

The choice of these criteria raised issues of the definition of psychiatric disorder. It has been well documented that psychiatric treatment rates are not synonymous with the prevalence of serious psychiatric disorder (Srole et al., 1962). We assumed that psychiatric treatment or hospitalization was a reasonable, but extremely conservative, index of the true prevalence of psychiatric impairment in these groups. In addition, while treatment rates excluded those individuals who through psychiatric interviews could have been identified as psychiatrically impaired, treatment rates have the distinct advantage of having been measured independently of any clinical biases of the investigators.

Issues of Case Loss

In addition to the definitional question of the true prevalence of psychiatric disorder, there were several questions of case loss. We made no attempt to identify treatment at several municipal and all private institutions in the state. Because comparison figures for the New Haven population would have been difficult to ascertain, we did not include the fact of treatment at the regional Veterans Administration facility, although we were able to ascertain that many of the parents of delinquents were known to have received psychiatric treatment there. No attempt was made to identify treatment by private psychotherapists. Finally, no attempt was made to ascertain treatment of persons who had moved from the state or who had received treatment prior to moving to Connecticut.

Our criteria were so limited on several grounds. First, the demographic characteristics of the samples mentioned above made it extremely likely that the vast majority of persons remaining in the area and seeking psychiatric help would be treated at one of the state facilities. Conversely, it was unlikely that any significant proportion would receive treatment on a private, and therefore expensive, basis.

Treatment data from the Veterans Administration facility, though gathered, were not utilized because of the difficulty in ascertaining prevalence rates of such treatment for the state population at large or, more importantly, for the lower SES population. Finally, failure to identify cases treated by facilities other than the state institutions mentioned above would have the consequence of making any prevalence figures gathered on parents of delinquents conservative estimates of psychiatric disorders. Consequently, any case loss would work against, rather than for, the demonstration of the extent of psychiatric disorder in these groups.

Dependent Measures—Criminality

While the primary focus of the study was on parental psychopathology, we felt that it was impossible to ignore the factor of parental antisocial behavior in relation to the picture of delinquency in the children. Whatever the limitations of our clinical judgments of psychopathology, clinical judgments of antisocial behavior are still more difficult to make. As mentioned above, many investigators have emphasized the rationality and class appropriateness of behavior that is seen as deviant from a middle-class perspective. Because of the possibility of biases and distortions in our clinical judgments of what constituted antisocial behavior, we chose an objective measure of criminality: the fact of having a criminal record in the files of the state police. It is well known that such data are class- and race-related, but at least they had the advantage of being open to independent verification. As with the data on psychiatric treatment, the names, addresses, and birthdates of the parents in the two clinic groups and the court comparison groups were cross-matched with state police files.

While it would have been desirable to obtain criminal data not only on the parents of delinquents, but also on the lower SES community sample, this kind of information could not be obtained. Hence data on the relationship of parental psychiatric treatment and parental criminality will be restricted to parents of delinquents only.

RESULTS OF PSYCHIATRIC COMPARISONS OF THE THREE COURT GROUPS

Of the population of 273 parents of the first-year clinic group, 44 (16.1%) had been known to one or more of the six psychiatric facilities in this study: 30 (10.99%) as inpatients and 14 (5.1%) as outpatients. Of the 205 parents in the second-year clinic group, 27 (13.17%) were known: 18 (8.78%) as inpatients and 9 (4.39%) as outpatients. Of the 261 comparison group parents, 27 (10.34%) were known: 19 (7.28%) as inpatients and 8 (3.06%) as outpatients. The proportion of parents receiving psychiatric treatment in the first-year clinic group did not differ significantly from the proportion of parents receiving treatment in the second-year clinic group $(X_y^2 = .80, p > .10)$. The proportion of parents receiving inpatient treatment in these two groups also did not differ significantly $(X_y^2 = .63, p > .10)$. Consequently, the first- and second-year clinic groups were combined. The analyses to be reported below are therefore based on the combined groups.

Of considerable surprise to us was the finding that the proportion of clinic parents having received psychiatric treatment and/or hospitalization (14.85%) did not differ significantly from the proportion of court comparison group parents receiving such treatment (10.34%) $(X_y^2 = 2.98, p > .05)$. The proportion of clinic group parents who received inpatient treatment (10.04%) also did not differ significantly from the proportion of court comparison group parents receiving such treatment (7.28%) $(X_y^2 = 1.56, p > .10)$. These results suggested that the two groups of clinic parents were probably similar to the general juvenile court parental population in terms of having received psychiatric treatment.

Comparison of Psychiatric Treatment of Parents of Delinquents with the General and Lower SES Population

While the proportions of parents of delinquents who had received psychiatric treatment are, in and of themselves, important indicators of the psychiatric status of the groups, it was essential to investigate whether or not such an occurrence differed from that in the general population. As in our previous report (Lewis and Balla, 1976), we compared the rates of hospitalization in the parent samples with two independent estimates of rates of hospitalization in the general and lower SES populations. Such multiple comparisons are necessary because of the inadequacy of any single estimate of psychiatric treatment rates in the general population as compared with the population of parents of children referred to the juvenile court.

Our first comparison involved a contrast of the incidence of inpatient psychiatric hospitalization during a single year, July 1, 1971-June 30, 1972, for the state of Connecticut (52/10,000 or 0.0052), with incidence figures for our three court groups for the same year. That year was chosen for study because it was the one in which the majority of offenses by clinic children occurred. In the first-year clinic group, there were 8 hospitalizations in a population of 273 persons (0.0293). In the second-year clinic group there were 8 hospitalizations in a population of 205 persons (0.0390). In the court comparison group there were 3 hospitalizations in a population of 261 persons (0.0115). Comparison of the state proportions with ours yielded a Z of 5.605 (p < .001) for the first-year clinic group, and a Z of 6.760 (p < .001) for the second-year clinic group, demonstrating a significantly greater incidence of hospitalization for both clinic groups than for the general population of Connecticut during that year. A comparison of the incidence of psychiatric hospitalization of the comparison group with the incidence of the state's general population yielded a Z of 1.432 (p < .10, p > 05). Thus, while the comparison group had a higher incidence of hospitalization for that year than the general population, it was not as striking as in the clinic groups. This may be related in some way to the fact that 1971-72 was not the modal year for the delinquent offenses in this comparison group.

We next compared the occurrence of psychiatric in- and outpatient treatment in the three court parent groups with the occurrence of psychiatric in- and outpatient treatment in the community comparison sample of 938 persons mentioned above. Workers at the Connecticut Mental Health Center had determined that a total of 37 individuals in this sample had made use of one or both of the two psychiatric facilities serving the local community at some point during their lifespan above the age of 16. We found that 39 of the first-year clinic group, 24 of the second-year clinic group, and 23 of the court comparison group parents had made use of one or both of these facilities during their lifespan above age 16. Thus, in the combined clinic groups 63 of 478 individuals had made use of one or both of the two state psychiatric facilities serving the area. When this proportion (63/478) was compared with the proportion of users of the facilities in the community group (37/938), a X_y^2 of 39.753 (p < .001) was yielded. A similar comparison of proportions of the court comparison sample (23/261) and the community sample yielded a $X_y^2 = 9.18$ (p < .01). Since the court clinic and court comparison samples were not significantly different ($X_y^2 = 2.74$, p > .05), we compared the three court groups with the community group ($X_y^2 = 34.868$, p < .001). In all cases significantly greater use of these two major psychiatric facilities was found by parents of children identified as delinquent than by a random sample of the lower SES New Haven population.

Criminal Histories in Parents in the Three Court Samples

Of the 219 fathers of clinic children, 38 (17.3%) were found to have a criminal record. Of the 127 court comparison group fathers, 25 (19.7%) had criminal records. The difference between these proportions was not statistically significant ($X_y^2 = 0.158$, p > .10). Of the 259 clinic group mothers, 23 (8.9%) had criminal records. Of the 134 court comparison group mothers, 6 (4.5%) had criminal records. This difference was also not significant ($X_y^2 = 1.902$, p > .10).

It is therefore reasonable to conclude that the clinic parents and court comparison parents did not differ significantly from the point of view of criminality. Consequently, in all further studies, the court clinic and court comparison groups were pooled. Considering the clinic and court comparison groups combined, 14.4% of delinquent children had a father with a criminal history; and 7.2% of delinquent children had a mother with a criminal history.

Associations of Parental Criminality and Psychiatric Treatment

Of the 63 criminal fathers, 14 (22%) had received some form of psychiatric treatment, while of the 283 noncriminal fathers, 18 (6.4%) had received such treatment ($X_y^2 = 13.614$, p < .001). Of the 63 fathers with a criminal history, 9 (14.2%) had been psychiatrically hospitalized. Of the 283 fathers without a criminal history, 10 (3.5%) had been psychiatrically hospitalized. These proportions are significantly different ($X_y^2 = 9.500$, p < .01). Thus a highly significant association of paternal criminality and paternal psychiatric treatment was found.

Turning to the mothers, we found that of 29 criminal mothers, 7 (24.1%) had been psychiatrically hospitalized, while of the 364 noncriminal mothers, 39 (10.7%) had been hospitalized ($X_y^2 = 3.474$, .05 < p < .10). Of the 29 mothers with criminal histories, 8 (27.6%)

had received some form of therapy, compared with 55 (15.11%) of the 364 noncriminal mothers (X_y^2 =2.248, .10 < p <.20). It would seem that there also might be an association between maternal criminality and psychiatric treatment, although this was not as striking as in the case of the fathers.

Patterns of Intermarriage Among Parents in the Three Court Groups

While there appeared to be an association of criminality and psychiatric treatment in individual parents in the three court groups, we were interested also in possible patterns of intermarriage. Questions remained as to whether psychiatrically treated men were married to similarly treated women, whether men with criminal histories were married to women with criminal histories, and whether men or women with psychiatric histories married partners with criminal histories.

Of the 63 psychiatrically treated women, 13 (20.63%) were married to psychiatrically treated men. Of 330 nontreated women, 22 (6.67%) were married to treated men. The difference between these proportions was significant, $X_y^2 = 11.06$, p < .001. Of the 35 treated men, 13 (37.14%) were married to treated women, whereas of the 311 nontreated men, 50 (16.08%) were married to treated women ($X_y^2 = 8.03$, p < .01).

We found no tendency for men with criminal histories to marry women with criminal histories. However, of 63 criminal men, 20 (31.75%) had married women with histories of psychiatric treatment, while 43 (15.19%) of the 283 noncriminal men had married women with histories of psychiatric treatment ($X_y^2 = 8.4$, p < .01). Nor did we find anything to suggest a greater likelihood that criminal women would be married to psychiatrically treated men.

DISCUSSION

Considerable support was found for our clinical observations that in many instances delinquency and parental criminality and psychopathology represented a common underlying difficulty in adaptation on the part of an entire family. The prevalence of psychiatric treatment was greater both in the parents of clinic-referred and the parents of nonclinic-referred delinquent children than in the general population of the state of Connecticut or in a socioeconomically comparable sample of persons in New Haven. Secondly, an association between individual parental psychiatric treatment and parental criminality was found in both the mothers and fathers of the delinquent children. Our final hypothesis was only partially confirmed. Fathers with psychiatric histories tended to marry mothers with psychiatric histories, and fathers with criminal histories also tended to marry mothers with psychiatric histories. From these data, two marital constellations emerged of parents of delinquents: psychiatrically treated males married to psychiatrically treated females, and criminal males married to psychiatrically treated females. It was not true, however, that criminal mothers and fathers tended to marry each other. Furthermore, criminal mothers did not, on the whole, marry psychiatrically treated fathers.

It might be argued that our emphasis on adaptive failures at the level of the individual and the family is erroneous, and that our findings represent nothing more than the application of social control through the labeling process. According to this view, both the state criminal justice system and the state psychiatric system are used interchangeably to control troublesome elements in a lower SES population. Apart from our impression that this position represents an unduly conspiratorial view of society, it is incongruent with our clinical observations. Many of the parents that we saw were unquestionably severely psychiatrically disturbed, as illustrated in the case vignettes presented earlier.

It would be difficult to reconcile such aberrant behaviors simply with theories of social control and labeling. We must emphasize that our epidemiological studies sprang from our clinical observations and should be interpreted in the light of them.

The findings of this study also suggest that there exists a subset of delinquent children whose behavior is not entirely explained through the application of sociological theories. It would seem more reasonable to interpret the delinquent behavior of this subgroup as reflecting (1) an inability of the parents to provide adequate socialization and supervision because of their own pervasive psychiatric disturbance; (2) a possible intrinsic vulnerability within some of these children (the result, perhaps, of early physical and psychological buffetings) that makes them less able to withstand the stresses of an unsupportive family and social environment.

Finally, while it is possible to conceive of two separate entities, psychopathology and criminality, our clinical observations and epidemiological findings suggest an alternative picture. Delinquency, childhood psychiatric disturbance, adult criminality, and the need for psychiatric treatment as an adult are in many instances different manifestations of a common underlying severe problem of adaptation. The juvenile justice system, criminal justice system, and the psychiatric treatment system have not yet learned to deal with these kinds of adaptive failures. At times, they are regarded as evidence of sickness; at other times, as evidence of criminal proclivities. Many of these people have been known to both systems, and it almost seems that the system which is asked to cope with a given individual at a given time is determined by the system which is being impinged upon and therefore takes note of maladaptive behavior.

DELINQUENCY IN THE CHILDREN OF PSYCHOTIC PARENTS

Having found, clinically and epidemiologically, that the parents of delinquents had an especially high prevalence of serious psychopathology and of psychiatric hospitalization, we decided to explore further the question of the association of parental psychosis and delinquency. We had explored the prevalence of psychiatric hospitalization in the parents of known delinquents. We focused our next epidemiological study from a different perspective. We decided to study the question of whether psychotic and psychiatrically treated individuals were more likely than their nontreated (presumably healthier) socioeconomically comparable peers to have a delinquent child.

For several reasons, we chose the diagnosis of schizophrenia as our measure of parental psychosis. First, schizophrenia, no matter how defined, is commonly recognized as a seriously disabling psychiatric disorder. Patients so diagnosed usually have at one time or another manifested psychotic symptoms such as auditory or visual hallucinations, delusions, and/or extreme paranoia. Second, our clinical experience with delinquents and their parents often revealed that parents, children, or both had from time to time experienced or demonstrated psychotic thought processes or behaviors considered characteristic of the diagnosis schizophrenia. Finally, there is a growing body of literature suggesting a relationship between parental schizophrenia and a multiplicity of maladaptive disorders in children. For example, Mednick and Schulsinger (1968) reported a tendency for the children of schizophrenic mothers to pose disciplinary problems at school and to be aggressive. Similarly, Beisser and colleagues (1967) reported, "More children growing up in a home with a schizophrenic mother show evidence of emotional and behavioral disorder than do children growing up in homes of 'normal' mothers" (p. 440).

These kinds of findings, while suggestive of a possible link between schizophrenic parents and the development of antisocial behaviors in children, did not specifically investigate parental psychosis and officially documented delinquency. We therefore decided to try to determine the prevalence of officially recorded delinquency in the children of schizophrenic parents compared with the prevalence of delinquency in the children of socioeconomically similar but nonpsychiatrically treated individuals.

The methodology of this study has been described in detail elsewhere (Lewis and Balla, 1976, pp. 136-159), and we shall therefore concentrate here on the results of the work. It is worthwhile to note here, however, that the sample of schizophrenic parents consisted of individuals between the ages of 30 and 65 seen at a community mental health center during a given period of time who had received the diagnosis of "schizophrenia" on two or more separate occasions, often by two or more different clinicians. Thus, determination of parental psychosis was completely independent of the investigators. Of the total number of patients treated during the period in question, 223 met the criteria for inclusion in the schizophrenic group.

The comparison sample consisted of socioeconomically comparable individuals from the same community who, by virtue of their address and low socioeconomic status, were eligible for treatment at the same psychiatric facility. There were 491 individuals in the comparison sample.

The criterion for delinquency was that at least one child in a family have a delinquent record at the local juvenile court.

The proportion of delinquent children of schizophrenics compared with the proportion of delinquent children of nonschizophrenics is presented in Table 1. As can be seen from the table, 17% of schizophrenics had a child known to court compared with 6% of nonschizophrenics. When the samples were subdivided by sex, by race, and by sex and race, differences between groups were similar, although X_y^2 values were at varying levels of significance, depending on sample size.

However, schizophrenia alone did not seem to account entirely for some of the differences between schizophrenics and nonschizophrenics. Of special concern were findings that black schizophrenic parents were far more likely than white schizophrenic parents to have court-involved children: 31% of black schizophrenics compared with 13% of white schizophrenics had a child known to court ($X_y^2 = 7.324$, $p < 0.01$). Differences between black and white comparison groups did not reach conventional levels of significance.

It would have been tempting to conclude that findings concerning race simply reflected social inequalities in this country at the time of the study. Such an explanation, however, did not account for the striking differences within the black community itself between the prevalence of delinquency in the children of black schizophrenics compared with black nonschizophrenics (31% compared with 10%) ($X_y^2 = 6.908$, $p < 0.01$). Thus the fact of a parent's being schizophrenic greatly increased the chance of his child's becoming delinquent. Simply being black only

TABLE 1
Delinquency in Children of Schizophrenic Parents Versus Comparison Parents with Respect to Parental Sex and Race

	Schizophrenics with Delinquents / Total Schizophrenics	Comparison Parents with Delinquents / Total Comparison	Schizophrenics with Delinquents (%)	Comparison Parents with Delinquents (%)	X^2	p
Are schizophrenics parents more likely to have delinquent children than comparison parents?	37 / 223	29 / 491	17	6	19.618	<0.001
Schizophrenics by sex vs. comparison group						
Male schizophrenics/male comparisons	12 / 56	14 / 212	21	7	9.486	<0.01
Female schizophrenics/ female comparisons	25 / 167	15 / 279	15	5	10.631	<0.01
Schizophrenics by race vs. comparison group						
Black schizophrenics/ black comparisons	14 / 45	8 / 77	31	10	6.908	<0.01
White schizophrenics/ white comparisons	23 / 178	21 / 414	13	5	10.035	<0.01

slightly increased the chances of the child's coming into conflict with the law. However, being both black *and* schizophrenic greatly increased the likelihood that one's child would become delinquent.

The explanations for the greater likelihood of schizophrenics, particularly black schizophrenics, having court-involved offspring are not obvious or easy to discover. That social factors play a role in this phenomenon is extremely likely. Our own work, clinical and epidemiological (Lewis et al., 1979), indicates that seriously psychologically disturbed black children and their parents are less likely to be recognized as in need of medical or psychological treatment and more likely to be considered delinquent or criminal than are white children and their families. Bender (1959) has noted that during adolescence the psychotic borderline child tends to appear merely sociopathic. We would add that this is especially the case where the black child is in question.

In spite of the fact that race bias plays a role in determining who is designated delinquent and who is considered psychiatrically ill, the most striking differences in the prevalence of delinquency were the differences between the children of schizophrenics and nonschizophrenics. It seems reasonable therefore to conclude that something about serious parental mental illness (perhaps specifically schizophrenia) brings about the conditions within a family and creates the vulnerabilities within a child conducive to the development of delinquency in certain children. This particular study, while suggestive of an association between parental schizophrenia and children's delinquency, must be interpreted with caution in that it fails to establish whether other kinds of serious parental psychiatric illnesses (such as manic-depressive disorders) also predispose to delinquency in certain children. However, this study suggests that a predisposition for a schizophrenic disorder, combined with environmental factors, some of which are known and others of which are yet to be understood, are in many instances related to the development of delinquency in the children of schizophrenics.

FATHERS OF JUVENILE DELINQUENTS

Considering the genetic, psychodynamic, social, and physical influence of fathers on their children, surprisingly little is understood about the paternal role in child development (Lamb, 1976). This dearth of information is especially true in regard to fathers of delinquents. Mothers have, for the most part, been the major focus of attention, receiving credit for raising successful offspring and, of course, blame when things have gone awry.

Another explanation for the dearth of information about fathers of delinquents is that fathers of delinquents are often difficult to find. That delinquent children tend to come from broken homes has frequently been documented (Glueck and Glueck, 1950; Robins, 1966; Stephens, 1961; West, 1969). When separations occur, delinquent children tend to remain with their mothers (Gardner, 1959), making it especially difficult to study their fathers. Even when the father of a delinquent child remains in the home, he is less likely to come to an informal clinical or probation review than to an official court hearing where a definitive judgment is to be made.

There are, we believe, certain psychodynamic, medical, and perhaps even genetic reasons for learning more about the fathers of delinquents. From a psychodynamic point of view (particularly from a Freudian standpoint), the presence of the father or even the fantasied attributes of an absent father affect the child. Moreover, the development of the conscience (*i.e.*, superego) is considered dependent on the internalization of parental values. Since males are hypothesized to be of especially strong moral fiber compared to females (Freud, 1925), one might assume that the father would be especially important for superego formation. Looking at possible negative psychodynamic influences, a particularly aggressive father could engender in the son an identification with violence and impulsivity. Similarly, unconscious rage against such an individual could be displaced onto other authority figures, causing the child to flout teachers and other perceived authority figures.

From a purely physical point of view, the presence or absence of the father often has much to do with a child's health and well-being. The kind of nutrition, protection, and general health that the child experiences is often dependent on the father's presence. Also, the physical effects of an assaultive father on a child may be as important in determining the child's adjustment to society as the psychological effects of living with such a father.

Finally, one cannot ignore the genetic influence of fathers, since every child receives half of his genes from his father. Investigators have in recent years looked at the transmission of certain vulnerabilities from one generation to the next. Genetic studies focusing on the schizophrenic continuum of disorders (Heston, 1970; Rosenthal, D., et al., 1968; Reider, 1973), the genetic transmission of certain kinds of central nervous system dysfunction (Wender, 1972; Cantwell, 1975), and on the heritability of alcoholism (El-Guebaly and Offord, 1977) may all be relevant to the study of delinquent children and their fathers.

There have been attempts to delineate particular personality traits in fathers which contribute to their children's delinquent behaviors. Descriptions of fathers' personalities have ranged from their being called excessively passive to exceptionally authoritarian (Duncan, 1971; McCord and McCord, 1959; Milebamane, 1975; Rosenthal, M.J., et al., 1962). Jenkins (1966; 1968) related different parental personality types to different kinds of delinquent behaviors. These kinds of descriptions have in common a nebulous quality, that of groping to describe characteristics that are hard to document or quantify.

Attempts to collect "harder" data have often resulted in restricting inquiry to certain circumscribed areas of paternal behavior and functioning. Jenkins (1966, 1968), Robins (1966), Jonsson (1967), the Gluecks (1950), and others have called attention to the high prevalence of alcoholism in the fathers of delinquents. Similarly, Guze and his colleagues (1967) found alcoholism to be especially prevalent in the histories of fathers of convicted criminals.

One of the more common "hard data" approaches to the gathering of information about the fathers of delinquents is the study of the prevalence of paternal criminality. This kind of study springs from two different premises: first, that delinquent behavior is a learned response to parental influences, and second, that the tendency toward criminality may be inherited from generation to generation. Another explanation for the relative abundance of such studies is that criminality is one of the few phenomena that lend themselves to quantification by virtue of official, publicly available arrest and conviction records. For this kind of study, fathers themselves need not be seen!

West (1969) reported that 38% of boys with serious antisocial behavior had a father with a criminal record. Jonsson (1967) reported that 29% of the fathers of delinquents studied had criminal records. In our own studies (Lewis and Balla, 1976; Lewis et al., 1976), 19.7% of a random sample of delinquent children had a father with a known criminal record in the state police files. Robins and her colleagues (1975) reported that a father's arrest was the most common predictor of a child's delinquency. Taking into account considerations of heredity and environment, Hutchings and Mednick (1974) studied the prevalence of registered criminality in the biological and adoptive fathers of male criminal adoptees. They found that if the biological father was not criminal, criminality in the adopting father did not influence the child toward criminality. The combination of both a biologically and an adopting criminal father, however, were associated with the child's criminality. Kirkegaard-Sorensen and Mednick (1975) reported the combination of a criminal father and a schizophrenic mother to be especially criminogenic for the child. The significance of this finding will be explored following the presentation of our own findings.

The great problem in studying paternal alcoholism and/or criminality is that both conditions cover not only a multitude of sins, but also a multitude of different kinds of behaviors, family interactions, and psychiatric disorders, only some aspects of which may have a bearing on the etiology of a child's delinquency. Clearly, most of the children of alcoholics do not become delinquent and, by anyone's statistics, most delinquents do not have a criminal father. If paternal alcoholism and/or criminality affects the development of a child's delinquent behavior, it is necessary to determine which psychological or biological aspects of alcoholism or criminality produce their deleterious effects and what other factors, environmental and/or biological, may interact with these particular paternal characteristics to produce antisocial behavior in a child. Until meticulous social, family, psychiatric, and neurological studies of the fathers of delinquents are undertaken, the significance of such factors as paternal criminality and alcoholism will remain elusive.

Clinical Observations

Our own clinical observations of the fathers of delinquents, while indicative of severe psychopathology (*e.g.*, the father who chained and burned his son, the father who beat his son to exorcise the devil, the father who threw his infant across the room), were too subjective to form the basis of definitive conclusions. Furthermore, relatively few fathers were available for evaluation and much information had to be gathered from court and social service records.

Because so few fathers were actually personally interviewed and information from court records was not uniform, it would make no sense to try to quantify our clinical impressions. Nevertheless, certain kinds of clinical pictures emerged. First, many fathers were indeed out of the picture, having moved to other parts of the country, started new families, or wound up in prisons and/or hospitals.

Of the fathers remaining, only a few were described as well-functioning, competent individuals, supporting their families through steady employment. These individuals were definitely the exceptions. Far commoner was information clearly indicative of serious paternal psychopathology. While excessive alcohol ingestion was frequently mentioned, it was usually accompanied by descriptions of extreme violence, often toward the delinquent child. Several fathers were actually jailed for child abuse.

Many fathers who were physically abusive had histories of psychiatric disorders other than alcoholism. One such father, in addition to his brutality toward the family, was known to have tried to hang himself. Another father, who disciplined his children by locking them in their room and filling it with tear gas, was known to have been psychiatrically hospitalized as early as age 12. One father was known to burn his children with cigarette butts at night when their mother was sleeping. Several fathers had been jailed for sexually molesting their children. The multiplicity of ways in which such paternal disorders and behaviors may contribute to the antisocial behavior of a child will be considered at the conclusion of this chapter. Suffice it to say, here, that such terms as "alcoholism" and "criminality" do not begin to convey the kinds of brutal, frightening experiences many delinquent children have endured at the hands of their fathers.

Epidemiological Findings

Aware that our clinical observations might have been skewed by the fact that many of the fathers we evaluated had delinquent children with known psychopathology, we embarked on a number of more objective epidemiological studies of paternal mental health and also of paternal criminality. The epidemiological findings reported below are drawn from several studies regarding delinquency, parental psychopathology, parental criminality, and the medical histories of delinquent and nondelinquent children.

In one study of samples of 109 delinquent and 109 nondelinquent children from the same socioeconomic class matched for age, sex, and race, we found that 7.3% of the delinquent children had a father known to one of the two major psychiatric facilities serving the area, compared with 0.9% of nondelinquent children. The difference between these two proportions was significant ($X_y^2 = 5.795$, $p < .05$). Many treated fathers had been inpatients. Since outpatient therapy was available to this group, hospitalization can be seen as a measure of severity of psychopathology.

As previously mentioned, in another study of the parents of delinquents (Lewis and Balla, 1976; Lewis et al., 1976), we found that 19% of fathers of delinquents had criminal records in the central files of the state police, compared with 7% of the mothers, a significant difference ($X_y^2 = 25.91$, $p < .001$).

From the above data one could determine whether an association existed between paternal psychiatric treatment and paternal criminality. Indeed, we found that of the fathers of delinquents with criminal records, 22% also had received psychiatric treatment as compared with 6.45% of the noncriminal fathers of delinquents ($X_y^2 = 13.614$, $p < .001$).

Clearly, an association existed within individuals between paternal criminality and paternal psychopathology as measured by treatment prevalence.

Up to this point, we might assume that paternal behaviors are transmitted to the child either in terms of a lack of judgment, poor reality testing, etc., or more directly in terms of role models for antisocial behavior. We wondered whether there was a less obvious linkage of paternal maladaptation and delinquency in children. In a previous study (Lewis and Shanok, 1977), we found that delinquent children had more serious and extensive medical histories than did a matched sample of nondelinquent children. Was it possible that paternal maladaptation might be related in some way to the physical well-being of delinquent children? In order to investigate this possibility, we compared the numbers of hospital visits of a sample of delinquent children with psychiatrically treated fathers and the numbers of visits of delinquent children with untreated fathers. We found that the delinquents with treated fathers averaged 18.88 hospital visits through age 16, contrasted with 9.55 visits for delinquents with nontreated fathers ($t = 1.678$, $p = .097$). Visits to hospital clinics were highly correlated with paternal psychiatric treatment, delinquents with treated fathers averaging 15 clinic visits compared with only 4.86 visits for delinquents with fathers untreated ($t = 2.655$, $p = .010$).

Of particular interest was the finding that there was no excess of hospital visits for delinquent children of psychiatrically treated mothers. Thus, paternal psychopathology was more closely associated with the physical well-being of the child than was maternal psychopathology.

We wondered whether paternal maladaptation as reflected by the fact of having a criminal record was related to a child's medical status through age 16. We found that delinquent children with criminal fathers averaged 21.4 hospital visits compared with 10.42 visits for delinquent children with noncriminal fathers. The difference between these numbers of visits was highly significant ($t = 2.519$, $p = .014$). Of special interest was the finding that 66.7% of delinquent children with criminal fathers had received a head or face injury before age 12 as recorded in the hospital record, whereas only 22.2% of delinquents without criminal fathers had experienced such injury. The difference between these proportions was also significant ($X^2_y = 10.362$, $p = .002$).

To our surprise, no significant association was found between maternal criminality and children's medical histories. Again, the maladaptation of the father seemed more closely related to the child's health problems than that of the mother.

It might be assumed, from the above data, that paternal maladaptation was sufficient in and of itself to predispose a child to delinquency and/or a poor medical history. Such an explanation would be valid only if the wives of criminal and/or psychiatrically disturbed fathers were themselves well-functioning individuals. We found, however, as already noted, that there was a significant association between paternal and maternal maladaptation; deviant men married deviant women (Lewis et al., 1976).

Given our emphasis to this point on parental maladaptation and poor health histories in delinquent children, we wondered whether the combination of paternal and maternal maladaptation was especially associated with children's poor health histories. While the number of families with documented paternal and maternal maladaptation in this sample was too small to make statistical findings more than suggestive, one striking finding should be noted. Children with both criminal fathers and psychiatrically treated mothers averaged 13.00 visits to the hospital before age four, while the average number of visits before four for children without this parental combination was 2.95 visits ($t = 2.59$, $p = .011$). The same pattern of multiple early hospital visits was evident in the medical histories of delinquents with both psychiatrically treated fathers and mothers.

IMPLICATIONS OF PARENTAL MALADAPTATION

Our clinical and epidemiological studies of the parents of delinquents strongly suggest that the previously recognized "under the roof" disturbance, poor ability to provide discipline, sociopathy, alcoholism, and broken homes are but superficial indicators of far more serious psychopathology in many of the parents of delinquents. Fathers of delinquents are more likely to go to jail than are mothers, whose psychopathology shows itself in less violent aggressive ways. It would seem that society is more willing to recognize certain social aberrations performed by women as signs of sickness, while equally disturbed men are treated more punitively. This is particularly true, we believe, in the case of members of racial or ethnic minorities.

We have learned from our epidemiological work that disturbed and/or criminal fathers tend to gravitate toward seriously disturbed women. These women are rarely emotionally strong enough to control their husbands' behavior and protect their children adequately. Frequently, the mothers of delinquents are themselves physically abusive to the children and are unable to counterbalance the effects of the fathers' impulsive violent behavior. A not uncommon family history of delinquents is that of a physically abusive father who after several years abandons the household, leaving the already battered children to the care of a distraught, emotionally disturbed, inadequate mother.

It would seem that many of the parents of delinquent children are indeed a psychiatrically disturbed group whose frequent violence, when directed toward their children, has physical and psychological consequences relating to the etiology of delinquency. By setting an example of impulsivity and violence, by engendering chronic rage in the child, and sometimes by inflicting actual central nervous system damage, such parents contribute to their children's delinquent behaviors.

The kinds of psychological and physical traumata experienced by many delinquent children often engender behaviors which appear to be genetically transmitted because of their resemblance to parental behaviors. We would suggest that if genetic factors play any role at all in delinquency, they are more likely to involve the inheritance of special vulnerabilities to maladaptive behavior in the nature of susceptibility to disorganized thought processes or to attentional and perceptual disorders. Only when such diverse kinds of vulnerabilities are environmentally influenced toward an antisocial set of behaviors may delinquency result. This kind of speculation is in keeping with the work of such investigators as Heston (1970) and Rosenthal, D., et al. (1968), who hypothesized a schizophrenic spectrum of disorders, one manifestation of which was delinquent behavior.

Similarly, there is some evidence that certain forms of perceptual-motor and attentional disorders may in some cases be inherited. Again, should specific central nervous system sensitivities be inherited, it must be stressed that this is not the same as the inheritance of potential criminality. Rather the vulnerable child may simply be more susceptible to malignant social and psychological forces within his family or environment than the child without such sensitivities. Our previous research suggests that delinquency per se is not heritable, but that the child of psychotic parents or the neurologically impaired child may be more susceptible to the kinds of family and social stresses that engender antisocial behaviors than is the ordinary child of well-functioning parents.

REFERENCES

Bandura, A., and Walters, R. H. (1959). *Adolescent Aggression*. New York: Ronald Press.

Beisser, A. R., Glasser, N., and Grant, M. (1967). Psychological adjustment in children of schizophrenic mothers. *J. Nerv. Ment. Dis.*, 145:429–440.

Bender, L. (1959). The concept of pseudopsychopathic schizophrenia in adolescents. *Am. J. Orthopsychiat.*, 29:491–512.

Bennett, I. (1959). *Delinquent and Neurotic Children*. London: Tavistock Publications.

Berlit, B. (1931). Erblichkeitsuntersuchungen bei Psychopathen. *Zeitschrift für die gesamte Neurologie und Psychiatrie.*, 134:382.

Cantwell, D. P. (1975). *The Hyperactive Child: Diagnosis, Management and Current Research.* New York: Spectrum Publications.

Cloninger, C. R., and Guze, S. B. (1970). Female criminals. *Arch. Gen. Psychiat.*, 23:554–558.

Cloninger, C. R., and Guze, S. B. (1973). Psychiatric illnesses in the families of female criminals: a study of the 288 first degree relatives. *Brit. J. Psychiat.*, 122:697–703.

Cortes, J. B., and Gatti, F. M. (1972). *Delinquency and Crime: A Biopsychosocial Approach.* New York: Seminar Press.

Duncan, P. (1971). Parental attitudes and interactions in delinquency. *Child Development.* 42:1751–1765.

El-Guebaly, N., and Offord, D. R. (1977). The offspring of alcoholics: a critical review. *Am. J. Psychiat.*, 134:357–365.

Ferguson, T. (1952). *The Young Delinquent in His Social Setting.* London: Oxford University Press.

Freud, S. (1925). Some psychical consequences of the anatomical distinction between the sexes. *Standard Edition*, 19:243–258. London: Hogarth Press, 1961.

Gardner, G. E. (1959). Separation of the parents and the emotional life of the child. In: *Problem of Delinquency*, S. Glueck (ed.). Boston: Houghton Mifflin, pp. 138–143.

Glueck, S. and Glueck, E. (1950). *Unraveling Juvenile Delinquency.* New York: Commonwealth Fund.

Glueck, S., and Glueck, E. (1970). *Toward a Typology of Juvenile Offenders.* New York: Grune & Stratton.

Guze, S. B., Wolfgram, E. D., McKinney, J. K., and Cantwell, D. P. (1967). Psychiatric illness in the families of convicted criminals: a study of 519 first degree relatives. *Dis. Nerv. Syst.*, 28:651–659.

Heston, L. (1970). The genetics of schizophrenia and schizoid disease. *Science*, 167:249–256.

Hollingshead, A. B., and Redlich, F. C. (1958). *Social Class and Mental Illness.* New York: John Wiley & Sons.

Hutchings, B., and Mednick, S. A. (1974). Registered criminality in the adoptive and biological parents of registered male adoptees. In: *Genetics, Environment, and Psychopathology*, S. A. Mednick et al. (eds.). Netherlands: North Holland Publications, pp. 215–227.

Jenkins, R. L. (1966). Psychiatric syndromes in children and their relation to family background. *Am. J. Orthopsychiat.*, 36:450–457.

Jenkins, R. L. (1968). The varieties of children's behavioral problems and family dynamics. *Am. J. Psychiat.*, 124:1440–1445.

Jenkins, R. L., and Hewitt, L. (1944). Types of personality structure encountered in child guidance clinics. *Am. J. Orthopsychiat.*, 14:84–94.

Johnson, A. M. (1949). Sanctions for superego lacunae of adolescents. In: *Searchlights on Delinquency*, K. R. Eissler (ed.). New York: International Universities Press, pp. 225–234.

Johnson, A. M., and Szurek, S. A. (1952). The genesis of antisocial acting out in children and adults. *Psychoanal. Quart.*, 21:323–343.

Jonsson, G. (1967). Delinquent boys, their parents and grandparents. *Acta Psychiat. Scand.*, 43: Suppl. 195, 1967.

Karson, S. & Haupt, T. D. (1968). Second order personality factors in parents of child guidance clinic patients. *Multivariate Behav. Res.*, Special Issue: 97–106.

Karson, S., and Markenson, D. J. (1973). Some relations between parental personality factors and childhood symptomatology. *J. Pers. Assess.*, 37:249–254.

Kirkegaard-Sorensen, L., and Mednick, S. A. (1975). Registered criminality in families with children at high risk for schizophrenia. *J. Abnorm. Psychol.*, 84:197–204.

Lamb, M. E. (1976). The role of the father: an overview. In: *The Role of the Father in Child Development*, M. E. Lamb (ed.). New York: Wiley Interscience, pp. 1–63.

Lewis, D. O., and Balla, D. A. (1976). *Delinquency and Psychopathology*. New York: Grune & Stratton.

Lewis, D. O., Balla, D. A., Shanok, S. S., and Snell, L. (1976). Delinquency, parental psychopathology, and parental criminality: clinical and epidemiological findings. *Am. J. Child Psychiat.*, 15:665–678.

Lewis, D. O., Balla, D. A., and Shanok, S. S. (1979). Some evidence of race bias in the differential diagnosis and treatment of the juvenile offender. *Am. J. Orthopsychiat.*, 49:53–61.

Lewis, D. O. and Shanok, S. S. (1977). Medical histories of delinquents and nondelinquents: an epidemiological study. *Am. J. Psychiat.*, 134:1020–1025.

Lukianowicz, N. (1971). Juvenile offenders: a study of 50 remand home and training school girls in Northern Ireland. *Acta Psychiat. Scand.*, 47:1938.

McCord, W., McCord, J., and Zola, I. K. (1959). *Origins of Crime: A New Evaluation of the Cambridge-Somerville Youth Study*. New York: Columbia University Press.

Mednick, S. A., and Hutchings, B. (1978). Genetic and psychophysiological factors in asocial behavior. *J. Am. Acad. Child Psychiat.*, 17:209–223.

Mednick, S. A., and Schulsinger, F. (1968). Some premorbid characteristics related to breakdown in children with schizophrenic mothers. *J. Psychiat. Res.*, 6:267–291.

Milebamane, B. M. M. (1975). Perception des attitudes et pratiques educatives du pere par les delinquants et les normaux. *Canad. Psychiat. Assn.*, 20:299–303.

Offord, D. R., Allen, N., and Abrams, N. (1978). Parental psychiatric illness, broken homes, and delinquency. *J. Am. Acad. Child Psychiat.*, 17:224–238.

Redl, F., and Wineman, D. (1957). *The Aggressive Child*. New York: Free Press.

Reiner, B. S., and Kauffman, I. (1959). *Character Disorders in Parents of Delinquents*. New York: Family Service Association of America.

Riedel, H. (1937). Zur empirischen Erbprognose der Psychopathie. *Zeitschrift für die gesamte Neurologie und Psychiatrie*, 159:648.

Rieder, R. O. (1973). The offspring of schizophrenic parents: a review. *J. Nerv. Ment. Dis.*, 157:200–211.

Robins, L. N. (1966). *Deviant Children Grown Up*. Baltimore: Williams & Wilkins.

Robins, L. N., West, P. A., and Herjanic, B. L. (1975). Arrests and delinquency in two generations: a study of black urban families and their children. *J. Child Psychol. Psychiat.*, 16:125–140.

Rosenthal, D., Wender, P. H., Kety, S. S., Schulsinger, F., Welner, J., and Ostergaard, L. (1968). Schizophrenic offspring reared in adoptive homes. In: *Transmission of Schizophrenia*, Rosenthal, D. and Kety, S. S. (eds.). Oxford: Pergamon Press, pp. 377–391.

Rosenthal, M. J., Ni, E., Finkelstein, M., and Berkowits, G. K. (1962). Father-child relationships and children's problems. *Arch. Gen Psychiat.*, 7:360–373.

Rutter, M., and Madge, N. (1976). *Cycles of Disadvantage*. London: Heinemann.

Schuckit, M. A., and Chiles, J. A. (1978). Family history as a diagnostic aid in two samples of adolescents. *J. Nerv. Ment. Dis.*, 166:165–176.

Schulsinger, F. (1972). Psychopathy, heredity and environment. *Int. J. Ment. Health*, 1:190–206.

Srole, L., Langer, T. S., Michael, S. T., Opler, M. K., & Rennie, T. A. C. (1962). *Mental Health in the Metropolis: The Midtown Manhattan Study*. New York: McGraw-Hill.

Stephens, W. N. (1961). Judgment by social workers on boys and mothers in fatherless families. *J. Gen. Psychol.*, 99:59–64.

Stumpfl, F. (1936). Erbanlage und Verbrechen. *Charakterologische und Psychiatrische Sippenunter suchungen*. Berlin: Julius Springer.

Wender, P. H. (1972). The minimal brain dysfunction syndrome in children. I. The syndrome and its relevance for psychiatry. II. A psychological and biochemical model for the syndrome. *J. Nerv. Ment. Dis.*, 155:55–71.

West, D. J. (1969). *Present Conduct and Future Delinquency*. New York: International Universities Press.

West, D. J., and Farrington, D. P. (1973). *Who Becomes Delinquent*. London: Heinemann.

Part III

Some Social Factors

CHAPTER FIFTEEN

Racial Factors Influencing the Diagnosis, Disposition, and Treatment of Deviant Adolescents

DOROTHY OTNOW LEWIS, SHELLEY S. SHANOK

This chapter will report clinical and epidemiological evidence of the operation of race bias in the diagnosis, disposition, and treatment of aggressive, psychiatrically disturbed adolescents. Our systematic study of factors affecting the placement and care of deviant adolescents sprang from clinical observations.

In the course of our work, first in a juvenile court setting, then in a correctional school, we noted that many black children who had previously been evaluated in child guidance clinics, schools, and even psychiatric hospitals, had been dismissed as simply characterologically impaired or as reacting purely to social and intrafamilial stresses in spite of what we considered to be clear evidence of psychotic and/or organic disorders.

We found a tendency of other clinicians to dismiss recurrent hallucinations in black children as culturally expectable and appropriate. Pervasive paranoid ideation leading to irrational aggressive acts was often dismissed as healthy adaptation to a hostile society. Extreme grandiosity was interpreted as streetwise bravado. And clear evidence on psychoeducational testing of minimal brain dysfunction or of specific learning disabilities was frequently ascribed simply to cultural deprivation. Even the most bizarre behaviors, when manifested by black children, were dismissed as manipulative or attention-getting devices.

For example, one black child had been psychiatrically hospitalized for four years between the ages of eight and 12 because of bizarre and dangerous behaviors starting in early childhood. An electroencephalogram performed when he was nine years old was reported to be "abnormal with features indicative of a seizure disorder focus present." He was discharged from the psychiatric hospital as he approached adolescence. Shortly after discharge he was arrested for grabbing and fondling breasts of three different women whom he passed in the street. When efforts were made to rehospitalize this youngster, he was refused readmission. A psychiatrist who saw him once in detention without benefit of access to his hospital record stated, "Even without any background information, I feel I can make a psychiatric judgment about him. . . . If he committed an unlawful act for which he is now in detention and cannot remember it, I do not see this as a brain disturbance for which an extensive work-up would be necessary." The staff at the psychiatric unit that had been his home for four years interpreted the boy's inappropriate behaviors while in the street as calculated devices intended to gain readmission to the hospital. Unwilling to be so obviously manipulated, the staff concluded that the boy needed "to learn about the consequences of his behavior" and dispatched him post haste to the correctional school.

Another black youngster who had a longstanding practice of swallowing items ranging from rat poison to razor blades was transferred from a psychiatric hospital to the correctional school after his ninth hospital admission. This boy had a history of serious head trauma which was followed by seizures and transitory hemiparesis. Subsequent to this injury the boy suffered from periodic hallucinations and delusions resulting in multiple hospitalizations. The transfer from hospital to corrections occurred following an episode at the hospital when the boy cut his wrists. Transfer to the correctional school was possible because of a previous adjudication of delinquency and commitment to the state. In addition to having been adjudicated a runaway, he had also been arrested and declared delinquent for walking through a store naked but for an outer coat, impersonating a female, and propositioning a police officer by flashing his nudity. The judge deemed the boy's behavior bizarre and, while adjudicating him delinquent, sent him to a psychiatric hospital. The hospital staff, however, considered the boy's self-mutilation and swallowing of sharp objects to be conscious manipulative acts performed for purposes of remaining hospitalized.

Of note, during the course of psychological testing just prior to his ninth hospitalization, this youngster was observed to rest his head against the telephone on the examiner's desk and begin "slowly licking the plastic on the phone case. At another point he placed his mouth level to the table and put the edge of the table between his lips." The psychological examiner concluded, "Obviously someone who is capable of swallowing rat poison and who licks telephones and bites on table edges has some pretty serious oral 'hang-ups.' " Rationalization for transferring this boy from the hospital to the correctional school was provided by a hospital psychologist who concluded that the boy had "grown accustomed to doing bizarre things in order to get out of situations he finds undesirable." The psychologist's parting words provide a clear example of the capacity of white professionals to dismiss grossly bizarre behaviors performed by black children as evidence of social rather than psychological disturbance. He stated in his transfer examination, "This is most assuredly a youngster with a troubled life style. He displays no evidence of psychotic thinking disorder, and admits to no distressing emotional problems."

Even when seriously disturbed delinquent black children were accepted at psychiatric hospitals, it seemed to us, from the vantage point of a correctional school, that they were quick to be discharged from both private and state institutions and transferred to corrections if their psychopathology manifested itself in aggressive ways. For example, one black boy, an intelligent, severely paranoid youngster, had been admitted to a private psychiatric institution after threatening a cab driver with a gun. He had a history of two head injuries in early childhood, and he had been raised by a psychotic grandmother. Psychological testing at the hospital revealed "visual-motor difficulties, hyperactive and distractible behavior, and behavior alternating between regressive and quite infantile, such as lying on the floor." Previous test records described him as "volatile, unpredictable, slightly bizarre . . . schizoid personality with unpredictable aggressivity and minimal brain dysfunction."

While in this private hospital, the boy experienced what was described in his chart as "a severe episode of aggressive and somewhat bizarre behavior . . . lying on the floor clutched in a fetal position, complaining of abdominal pain . . . relatively uncommunicative . . . followed by much belligerent destructive action including breaking of windows [and] biting a police officer." The psychiatrist on duty diagnosed a psychomotor epileptic attack. An encephalogram confirmed this diagnosis, revealing a "right posterior temporal spike abnormality." In spite of this clear evidence of a seizure disorder, this boy was transferred to a state hospital with a diagnosis of "Depressive Neurosis 300.40" and "Explosive Personality 301.30." He was subsequently transferred from the state hospital to a correctional setting because of erratic behaviors ranging from seclusiveness and suicidal ideation to provocative threatening behaviors and suspected fire setting.

At the state hospital he was diagnosed as paranoid with a possible "underlay of schizophrenia." Thus, at both psychiatric hospitals, potentially treatable psychiatric disorders were recognized (*i.e.*, epilepsy and schizophrenia) but he was transferred nevertheless to a correctional setting.

Private and state hospitals both often were reluctant to attempt to treat psychiatrically or neurologically impaired black youngsters if the children had delinquent histories and behaved aggressively. Thus children with potentially treatable diagnoses such as psychomotor epilepsy and schizophrenia at the time of transfer tended to be reassessed and given less promising diagnoses such as explosive personality, antisocial personality, or acting out aggressive reaction.

Since all of the children we evaluated who were transferred from psychiatric hospitals to corrections had committed delinquent acts, it was possible that these children were actually more aggressive than other psychiatrically hospitalized adolescents. Conceivably, their behaviors rather than their race were the major factors contributing to their transfer. It was also possible that the many psychiatrically disturbed children sent to the correctional school who had never been hospitalized were indeed more violent than the average psychiatrically hospitalized adolescent.

We had, in previous studies, found an unusually high prevalence of neuropsychiatric disorders and medical problems in a sample of violent incarcerated delinquents (Lewis et al., 1979a, 1979b; Lewis and Shanok, 1979). We wondered whether degrees of aggressiveness, nature of psychopathology, or nature of medical problems might influence whether a child were sent to a psychiatric hospital or to a correctional setting. We hypothesized that the behaviors of incarcerated children would be characterized by aggression, whereas the behaviors of psychiatrically hospitalized adolescents would be more introverted and/or self-destructive.

Having experienced difficulties gaining psychiatric hospitalization or residential treatment for several of our most disturbed black students, we also wondered whether particular demographic factors, specifically race, affected the disposition of seriously disturbed delinquent children. We therefore embarked on the following study.

A COMPARISON OF INCARCERATED ADOLESCENTS AND PSYCHIATRICALLY HOSPITALIZED ADOLESCENTS

Samples and Settings

We decided to compare two populations of children, all adolescents from a particular urban area in Connecticut who, in a given year, were sent to the only correctional school in the state, and all adolescents from the same area who, in that same year, were admitted to the adolescent unit of the state psychiatric hospital serving that catchment area.

The correctional school sample consisted of 63 children, 52 boys and 11 girls. The adolescent unit sample consisted of 34 children, 21 boys and 13 girls. Six children had been placed at both institutions. These were included in the correctional school sample because they had first been hospitalized, then transferred to corrections. An additional 19 of the 63 incarcerated children had been in psychiatric hospitals and/or residential treatment centers prior to incarceration.

At the time of the study, approximately one year after the adolescents in each group had been institutionalized, the average age of the correctional school sample was 15.560 years, whereas the average age of the adolescent unit children was 17.009 years. Ages were thus significantly different (t = 6.151, p < .001). The difference in ages was possibly a result of the fact that the hospital had a children's unit for children under 14 years of age and that the adolescent unit accepted children between ages 14 and 17 years. The correctional school, on the other hand, had to accept all children sent there and ages on admission ranged from 11 years to 16 years of age. Once committed, however, children could remain there until their eighteenth birthdays. In order to correct for possible bias resulting from age differences between the two groups, data regarding medical histories were analyzed before age four years and before age 16 years.

The two institutions were, at the time of the study, situated in the same town, approximately 25 miles from New Haven and only minutes from each other by car. Both institutions had open and closed facilities and were, theoretically, equipped to care for aggressive children. The adolescent unit had 16 beds reserved for boys, 12 for girls. The correctional school had six cottages of 30 beds each. At the time of the study, four were reserved for boys and two for girls.

Sources of Data

Data were gathered from the records of the adolescent unit of the state hospital, the records of the correctional school, and from the records of the largest general hospital serving the urban area in question. This hospital was used by 83.9% of the correctional school sample and 88.2% of the adolescent unit sample.

The following factors were explored: violent and nonviolent behaviors influencing institutionalization; psychiatric symptomatology; numbers of general hospital visits; usage of particular services (*i.e.*, emergency room, clinics, wards); the nature of medical problems (*e.g.*, perinatal difficulties, anemia, accidents and injuries, respiratory infections); age; sex; and race. Although socioeconomic class could not always be established from records, the great majority of children in both groups came from the lowest socioeconomic sectors of the population of the urban area in question.

For purposes of assessing the presence or absence of violent behaviors, violence was defined as any mention in the records of physical violence directed against other people and/or arson.

FINDINGS

Behaviors

Our assumption that the psychiatrically hospitalized adolescents would be demonstrably less violent than their incarcerated peers was refuted by the data available. Of the 33 hospitalized adolescents about whom information regarding behaviors was available (one record could not be obtained), 25 (76%) had performed extremely violent acts against others. Nineteen of these children were, according to their charts, known to the police or to the courts for a variety of more or less violent acts although the courts had not sent them to the correctional institution.

Examples of violence performed by subjects in the psychiatrically hospitalized group were as follows: one boy had been arrested for sexual assault, vandalism, indecent exposure, and beating an aged relative; another had committed armed robbery, had sold drugs, and had a multiplicity of minor charges against him; one boy had knifed another boy and had stated, "I get real violent. I don't stop until I see they're bleeding"; one boy had threatened his mother's life and was released on $2,500 bail and sent to the adolescent unit after injuring a policeman; another boy, charged with burglary, firesetting, larceny, and reckless endangerment, had allegedly homosexually attacked a small child and had taken his father's gun and tried to kill him; another boy had attempted to choke a younger sibling, had subsequently been ejected from a Salvation Army shelter when he assaulted another patron, and had a gun confiscated at one hospital, bullets confiscated at another.

Violence was characteristic of hospitalized girls as well as hospitalized boys. One girl had been expelled from a residential school because of violent behaviors and had subsequently assaulted a hospital staff member; another had a history of assaultiveness since second grade, had punched another patient in the mouth, and had threatened to harm staff; and another girl, also expelled from school because of assaultiveness, had slapped around a child for whom she was babysitting and physically assaulted the child's mother.

Of the eight remaining hospitalized adolescents about whom behavioral information existed, five had histories either of violence toward property (*e.g.*, smashing furniture, breach of the peace) and/or threatening others with violence. Counter to our prediction, only three of the hospitalized adolescents were characterized primarily by self-destructive behaviors.

Although it is not possible to compare exactly the prevalence and degree of violence in the two samples since the assessment of violence is inexact, a review of correctional school records indicated that 46 (77%) of the incarcerated sample had committed violent acts comparable in severity to the 25 most violent hospitalized adolescents (*e.g.*, assault, armed robbery, sexual assault). Thus, as far as we could determine, violence was as characteristic of the hospitalized sample as it was of the incarcerated sample.

Psychopathology

Adolescent unit and correctional school records were maintained for clinical purposes and not for research. Therefore information regarding psychopathology was not uniform. This lack of uniformity was especially true of correctional school records because not all children had been evaluated psychiatrically. Most, however, had had psychological testing and a probation or social work interview recorded in the chart.

Of the 33 adolescent unit children for whom clinical data existed, 13 were described as psychotic and 10 were described as evidencing borderline or equivocal manifestations of psychosis. Of the 60 incarcerated children for whom some clinical data existed, 14 were described as demonstrating grossly psychotic symptoms and 17 were said to evidence equivocal signs of psychotic disorder.

During the year in question, not all adolescent unit youngsters and very few incarcerated youngsters received neurological evaluations. It was not possible, therefore, to compare the neurological status of youngsters in the two groups.

Because of the variable nature of the available clinical data, we felt that it made little sense to make statistical comparisons between the prevalences of psychosis or borderline psychosis in the two groups.

A more uniform source of data was available in the records of the general hospital. We found that 38.9% of the correctional school sample and 45.7% of the adolescent unit sample had psychiatric problems noted in their hospital charts before age 17 years ($X_y^2 = 0.175$, p > .5). Of the correctional school sample, 32.1% of the children received psychiatric and/or social work consultations at the general hospital before age 17, compared with 25.7% of the adolescent unit sample ($X_y^2 = 0.161$, p > .5). Thus similar proportions of each sample were identified at the general hospital as in need of psychosocial services and provided with them.

Medical Histories

Medical histories of the correctional school sample as reflected in general hospital records were more adverse than the histories of adolescent unit children. Correctional school children averaged 12.5 hospital contacts through age 16, compared with 9.382 visits for adolescent unit children. They used the emergency room more frequently, averaging 7.621 ER visits through age 16, compared with 4.706 ER visits for adolescent unit children (t = 1.936, p = .056). Clinic visits were similar in number for both samples through age 16 (4.224 vs. 4.941); however, correctional school children tended to have more ward admissions through age 16 (0.672 vs. 0.265, t = 1.985, p = .051). They also suffered more accidents and injuries through age 16 (3.932 vs. 1.882, t = 2.747, p = .008), particularly head and/or face injuries (1.288 vs. 0.559, t = 2.341, p = .022). Anemia was also more prevalent in the correctional school sample (71.4% vs. 21.1%, $X_y^2 = 9.568$, p = .003).

Similarly high proportions of children in each sample had experienced perinatal difficulties (61.3% correctional school vs. 60.0% adolescent unit), and similar proportions were mentioned in hospital records as having been abused (27.1% vs. 20.6%).

Comparison of Medical Histories of Children from Each Sample Born at the General Hospital

Although the correctional school children appeared to have more adverse medical histories than did the adolescent unit children, it was possible that differences in numbers of visits and numbers of injuries through age 16 reflected length of residence in the area rather than actual numbers of medical events. A greater proportion of the correctional school children had been born at the general hospital than had the adolescent unit children (47.5% vs. 26.5%, $X_y^2 = 3.13$, p =

.077). This difference could conceivably have skewed our findings. We therefore decided to compare the medical histories of children in each sample who had been born at the general hospital in question.

Of the correctional school children, 28 had been born at the general hospital, while 9 of the adolescent unit children had been born there. Correctional school children averaged only slightly more hospital contacts through 16 years of age (19.074 vs. 13.444). Emergency room visits through age 16 averaged 11.444 compared with 7.222, and average number of ward admissions were somewhat greater in number (0.926 vs. 0.444). Clinic visits through age 16 were similar in number for the two samples, (4.704 vs. 3.778).

Of note, although actual numbers of hospital contacts did not differ significantly between the two groups born at the hospital, correctional school children averaged significantly more accidents and injuries through age 16 than did adolescent children (5.464 vs. 1.889, t = 2.733, p = .010). Head and face injuries specifically were greater in number through age 16 for the incarcerated group (2.107 vs. 0.667, t = 2.059, p = .048). Of note, 82.1% of incarcerated children had been treated for a head or face injury prior to their seventeenth birthday, compared with 22.2% of adolescent unit children (Fisher's Exact Test = p = .003). Anemia was more commonly noted in the charts of incarcerated children (82.4% vs. 40.0%, Fisher's Exact Test = p = .101). Perinatal difficulties were exceptionally high in both groups (60.7% vs. 75.0%). The prevalence of recognized abuse in both groups through age 16 was identical (33.3% vs. 33.3%).

Medical Histories Before Age Four Years of Children Born in the General Hospital

We were particularly interested in early trauma because of the vulnerability of the immature nervous system and the possible influence of early trauma on future development. We therefore compared the medical histories of our two groups before age four years. We found that our correctional school group had made significantly greater numbers of hospital visits by four years of age (6.037 vs. 1.667, t = 1.667, p = .019). The mean number of accidents and injuries during this period of development and the mean number of head and face injuries were slightly greater in the incarcerated group, but differences did not reach conventional levels of significance. The mean number of visits for respiratory infections during the first four years of life were greater in the incarcerated group; however, again, differences did not reach conventional levels of significance.

Thus the correctional school children had more adverse medical histories than did adolescent unit children. Early frequent hospital visits in particular distinguished the two groups.

Sex and Race of Entire Samples

Of correctional school sample, 17.5% were female, compared with 38.2% of the adolescent unit sample ($X^2_y = 4.064$, p = .044).

One of the most striking differences between these two samples concerned race. Of the correctional school sample, 67.2% were black, in contrast to the adolescent unit sample, of whom 29.4% were black ($X^2_y = 11.072$, p < .001).

Sex and Race of Children Born at the Hospital

Only 14.3% of the correctional school sample born at the hospital were female, compared with 44.4% of the adolescent unit group (Fisher's Exact Test = p = .079). Race also distinguished the two groups. Of the correctional school sample born at the hospital, 60.7% were black, in contrast to 11.1% of the adolescent unit group (Fisher's Exact Test = p = .012).

Multiple Regression Analysis

Having found the quality and prevalence of violence to be similar in the two groups of children, we wondered which of the medical or demographic variables that we were able to investigate distinguished the correctional school sample from the adolescent unit sample most clearly. We therefore conducted a multiple regression analysis, using group membership as the dependent variable (*i.e.*, correctional school sample born at the hospital vs. adolescent unit sample born at the hospital) and the following independent variables: perinatal problems; number of ER visits through age 16; number of ward admissions through age 16; number of accidents and injuries through age 16; number of head and face injuries through age 16; number of respiratory infections through age 16; sex; and race.

The most powerful variable distinguishing the groups was race, which accounted for 18.1% of the variance. Numbers of accidents and injuries through age 16 years accounted for 11.0% of the variance, the correctional school sample having the greater number. Sex accounted for 6.8% of the variance. Perinatal difficulties accounted for 4.0% of the variance, the adolescent unit sample having more perinatal problems. The above factors together accounted for 40.0% of the entire variance (R = .632).

When we repeated the multiple regression analysis changing the variables accidents and injuries from continuous to discontinuous variables (*i.e.*, accident or injury through age 16, yes/no, and head or face injury through age 16, yes/no) the picture changed. That is, the most powerful factor distinguishing the two groups was the fact of having received a head or face injury prior to age 17 years. This factor accounted for 30.2% of the variance, a greater proportion of correctional school children having at one time or another sustained a head or face injury requiring hospital care. Race accounted for 16.7% of the variance. Perinatal difficulties accounted for 6.1% of the variance, adolescent unit children having a greater prevalence of perinatal problems. Sex was the fourth most powerful predictor, accounting for 4.8% of the variance. These four factors accounted for 57.8% of the variance (R = 0.760).

Factors Distinguishing Incarcerated from Hospitalized Adolescents Before Age Four

We wondered whether a constellation of medical and demographic factors existed that distinguished the two groups early in life. We therefore conducted the same kinds of multiple regression analyses using age four as the cutoff point. That is, our dependent variable, again, was group membership (*i.e.*, correctional school sample born at the hospital vs. adolescent unit sample born at the hospital), and our independent variables were: perinatal problems; number of ER visits before age four years; number of ward admissions before age four years; number of accidents and injuries before age four years; number of head and face injuries before age four years; number of respiratory illnesses before age four years; sex; and race.

We found that, again, race was the most powerful predictor of group membership, accounting for 18.1% of the variance. Sex predicted 8.8% of the variance, and number of ER visits 6.4% of the variance, correctional school children having more ER visits. These three factors accounted for 33.3% of the total variance (R = 0.577).

When accidents and injuries before age four years and head and face injuries before age four years were treated as discontinuous variables (*i.e.*, accident or injury before four years, yes/no, head or face injury before four years, yes/no), the following findings emerged. Race accounted for 18.1% of the variance, sex for 8.8% or the variance, and having had a hospital-treated accident or injury before age four years accounted for an additional 7.2% of the variance, incarcerated adolescents being more likely to have been treated at the hospital before age four for an accident or injury. These three factors together accounted for 34.1% of the total variance (R = 0.584). Thus, the two groups could be distinguished from each other before their fourth birthdays.

RACE BIAS IN PERSPECTIVE

Counter to one of our major hypotheses, the results of our present study suggested that the majority of adolescents hospitalized in the state psychiatric facility were as violent as their incarcerated peers. Whether or not the two samples were equally psychiatrically disturbed was difficult to ascertain, although our clinical and epidemiological findings suggested that both samples were similarly psychiatrically impaired. Consonant with these findings was the fact that both groups had similarly adverse medical histories. However, incarcerated children were significantly more likely to have sustained head injury requiring hospital care, an ironic finding since one might assume that injured children would be recognized as such and treated therapeutically, either out of need or out of societal compassion. Needless to say, such was not the case. Either professionals knew nothing of the injuries or dismissed them as insignificant. Early accidents and injuries and emergency room visits in particular also characterized the incarcerated group, findings consistent with our earlier studies of medical histories of delinquents. Such traumata may have been a contributing factor to the expression of subsequent social maladaptation. Coupled with a history of having been abused, the combination of neurological vulnerabilities and psychological mistreatment undoubtedly contributed to maladaptation.

One of the most striking factors distinguishing the two groups was neither behavior nor psychopathology. It was race. In brief, violent, disturbed adolescent blacks were incarcerated; violent, disturbed whites were hospitalized. Even when black children were initially considered to be psychiatrically disturbed and were hospitalized, they often were subsequently transferred to corrections. At this time in Connecticut, a child committed to the state because of delinquency and placed in a hospital can, at the discretion of the Department of Children and Youth Services, be transferred to a correctional setting for indeterminate periods of time, reviewed after two years. The reverse, however—the transfer of children from correctional to hospital setting for more than 15 days—requires extensive legal and administrative procedures. Thus it is easier for a clinician to gain and maintain residential placement for a child at the correctional school than it is to obtain psychiatric treatment at a hospital or residential treatment setting.

Given the clinical and epidemiological evidence of racial bias in the diagnosis and treatment of black adolescents, we must ask why such a phenomenon might occur. Throughout the history of modern psychiatry there has been a reluctance on the part of white psychiatrists to see that white people and black people, despite certain social and cultural differences, are basically alike, that they think in similar ways, that they feel the same kinds of pain, and that they suffer from the same kinds of psychiatric disorders.

In the early years of this century, the psychiatric literature describing the differences between blacks and whites was more obviously racist than today. In the very first volume of the *Psychoanalytical Review*, psychiatrists were cautioned to distinguish between the psychotic behavior of blacks and whites and to avoid mistaking primitive thought processes in blacks for psychosis (Evarts, 1914). Lind (1914), in a purported analysis of the differences between the dreams of black and white patients, concluded that the dreams of black people were "of a juvenile type" and that "their psychology is of a primitive type." In an article in the *American Journal of Insanity*, Mary O'Malley (1914) asserted, "Like a child, the negro dwells in the visionary and the immaterial." Following this line of reasoning, she went on to provide her assessment of a black prisoner:

> One colored woman, a criminal who murdered a fellow prisoner, placed in solitary confinement was constantly troubled at night by this woman's "ghosts." After admission to this hospital these visions continued at times, especially on dark or stormy nights, although she had no actual hallucinatory experience. (p. 316).

Clearly, visual misperceptions in black patients (perhaps especially black prisoners) were considered to be culturally normal and not evidence of psychotic thought processes. According to O'Malley:

> A psychosis in an obviously lower race, such as the colored race, really must necessarily offer some features from a mental standpoint which distinguish it in a general way from a psychosis of a higher race. This is so apparent that it requires no further discussion. (pp. 310–311).

This kind of racially biased perspective persisted in the psychiatric literature. The very first volume of the *American Journal of Psychiatry* contained an article by a Dr. Bevis (1921) which stated unequivocally that blacks as a group suffered from psychic inferiority. Blacks were called jolly, careless, and easily amused. Fear, credulity, intellectual poverty, and childlike imagination coupled with superstitions were considered sufficient to occasionally bring about optical illusions. Again, superstition, not illness, was thought to account for certain hallucinatory phenomena.

According to Bevis, Evarts, O'Malley, Lind, and even such world-renowned psychiatrists as Jung (1928), blacks were inherently different from whites and their psychopathology had to be judged by different criteria from the criteria used to assess psychopathology in whites. In essence, those behaviors and beliefs which for whites were considered to be signs of severe psychopathology were considered by white clinicians to be normal for blacks.

Racially biased rationalizations were also expounded for the exclusion of blacks from certain psychiatric facilities in the North. According to Thomas and Sillen (1972), a superintendent of the Hartford Retreat explained the low admission rate of blacks to his facility as a reflection of their constitutional cheerfulness which made them less vulnerable to insantiy. Once again, blacks were depicted as essentially different beings from whites, beings with different moods as well as different thought processes.

More recently, psychiatrists and sociologists have perpetuated the myth that blacks and whites are psychologiclly different and that behaviors and beliefs which for whites would be deemed "crazy" are normal for blacks. For example, Fischer (1969) has stated: ". . . what is called sick or deviant behavior for one group may actually be adaptive—or functional—in another (p. 442)." White, as recently as 1970, asserted: ". . . what the dominant culture deems deviant or anti-social behavior might indeed be the functioning of a healthy black psyche which objectively recognizes the antagonisms of the white culture and develops mechanisms for coping with them (p. 52)." In other words, White would have us believe that behaviors and thought processes that are clearly abnormal for whites, such as seriously antisocial acts, are culturally appropriate for blacks. As Comer (1972) stated so well:

> Well-meaning social scientists . . . attempting to explain the circumstances in the black community have sometimes reinforced the stereotypes instead of demolishing them (p. 173).

The modern psychiatrist has been warned against the error of using his own social, economic, or cultural status and values as the norm. He continues to be taught that he must guard against the tendency to diagnose psychosis in a racially or ethnically different population from his own. He is taught that different standards should be used.

The condescending quality of this double standard for diagnosis has by and large been overlooked because of what appears at first to be a broadminded approach to mental health. This prevailing point of view must also be recognized as a reaction to what may have been an overestimation of psychopathology in the black population during the 1940s and 1950s. In the 1960s, psychiatrists were sensitized to a tendency of epidemiological investigators to overestimate the prevalence of mental illness, especially psychosis, in the black population. Frumken (1954), Malzberg (1940; 1953; 1963), and Wilson and Lantz (1957) were taken to task by such critics as Pasamanick (1963) and Fischer (1969) for their overestimation of mental illness in the black population compared to the white population. While some of these studies were discredited because of their unsound methodology, others, such as Malzberg's, were criticized because in spite of ". . . methodological care . . . [and] . . . a good deal of accuracy . . . they have been influential in maintaining the notion of inferior Negro mental health" (Fischer, 1969, p. 430–431).

In light of the overtly racist literature, and in light of the recent emphasis on the possible misinterpretation of cultural differences, the reticence of white mental health professionals to diagnose serious psychopathology and abusive behaviors in black delinquent patients or their parents probably reflects in part a deliberate effort to avoid even the semblance of racism. To diagnose a black delinquent or his parent as psychotic or abusive may seem judgmental to the white professional who would have fewer qualms about so labeling a white individual.

It has been our experience that, as a result of efforts to avoid possible over-diagnosis, black delinquent children and their parents must demonstrate flamboyantly psychotic behavior before they are recognized as being in need of treatment. Our observations are consistent with those of Pasamanick and of Schleifer. Pasamanick (1963) commented on the likelihood that whites in Virginia suffering from alcoholism were more likely to be placed in treatment facilities while the Negro alcoholic was committed to jail. Schleifer and his colleagues (1968) also stated:

> Our findings suggest that Negroes need to display greater behavioral disorganization before police relinquish control and turn the individual over to a hospital for treatment. (p. 45).

We can only add that, if psychiatrically disorganized black adults need to demonstrate severe behavioral disorganization in order to receive treatment, black juvenile delinquents are required to evidence still greater psychopathology in order to obtain treatment. This may be in part because the economically deprived environment from which the black delinquent often comes, the behaviors with which he is charged, and his adolescent stage of development encourage the white diagnostician to dismiss even the most bizarre and illogical acts as manifestations of normal ghetto behavior, signs of characterologic disorder, or evidence of adolescent adjustment difficulties. That this behavior is usually considered deviant and inappropriate by his own family and even by his peers is often disregarded.

Our findings regarding violent females call attention to one of the few instances in our society of the operation of reverse sex bias. Girls are expected to be gentle and to adapt gracefully to society. When they manifest their psychiatric disturbance through aggressive behaviors, they are more likely than their male counterparts to be considered psychologically aberrant and in need of treatment rather than punishment.

Clearly, the psychiatric profession is not solely responsible for the essential segregation of black and white violent adolescents that we have documented to exist in Connecticut. Adolescent unit charts indicated that the choice of disposition was often made by police, probation staff, and judges. Many violent white adolescents were apprehended by police, then diverted from the courts to the hospital. Thus the psychiatric, judicial, and law enforcement sectors of our society must share the responsibility for creating the situation we have documented.

If genuine differences in sociocultural orientation and adaptive patterns and norms can be demonstrated to exist between blacks and whites, boys and girls, then of course they must be taken into consideration for purposes of accurate diagnosis. Unfortunately, at present inaccurate stereotyping often passes for sophisticated appreciation of ethnic and sexual differences.

The stereotyped notion of paranoid blacks, reluctant to work with white professionals, has sometimes led to a lowering of training standards for individuals assigned to the treatment of lower socioeconomic class blacks. The assumption prevails that blacks and whites are basically psychologically different and that black children and families are best diagnosed and treated by black mental health workers. Unfortunately this kind of reasoning is frequently used to rationalize and justify providing black patients with partially trained paraprofessionals while white patients receive care from more rigorously trained professionals. At present there are no uniform standards for the qualification and training of paraprofessionals comparable to standards set for the training of professional mental health workers. Although many paraprofessionals are talented in their work, often some of the most psychiatrically impaired black children and families are treated by some of the least experienced workers in the mental health field.

We must share our clinical experience, which indicates that lower socioeconomic class blacks, children and parents, are usually pleased to have the opportunity to receive the undivided, uninterrupted attention of well-trained competent professionals whatever their color or background. When candor on the part of the professional is obvious, and when the purpose and nature of the evaluation are clarified, fruitful working relationships will exist.

While the reluctance or inability of many white mental health professionals to recognize severe psychopathology in many of their seriously disturbed black delinquent patients may be motivationally benign, the results of a failure to diagnose accurately are usually malignant. Stated simply, white mental health professionals dealing with a black delinquent population are often, in their efforts to avoid labeling, allowing human suffering to go untreated or mistreated.

Another inescapable implication of our findings is that many seriously psychiatrically disturbed, abused, neglected black children are being channeled to correctional facilities while their white counterparts are more likely to be recognized as in need of help and directed toward therapeutic facilities. The failure of white mental health professionals to recognize and treat serious psychopathology when it exists in the black delinquent population accounts in part for the fact that our adult correctional facilities as well as our children's correctional facilities are becoming disproportionately filled with members of minority groups.

REFERENCES

Bevis, W. (1921). Psychological traits of the southern Negro with observations as to some of his psychoses. *Am. J. Psychiat.*, 1:69–78.

Comer, J. (1972). *Beyond Black and White*. New York: Quadrangle Books.

Evarts, S. (1914). Dementia praecox in the colored race. *Psychoanal. Rev.*, 1:388–403.

Fischer, J. (1969). Negroes and whites and rates of mental illness: reconsideration of a myth. *Psychiatry*, 32:438–446.

Frumkin, R. (1954). Race and minor mental disorders. *J. Negro Ed.*, 23:97–98.

Jung, C. (1928). *Contributions to Analytical Psychology*. New York:Harcourt, Brace and World.

Lewis, D. O., and Shanok, S. S. (1979). A comparison of the medical histories of incarcerated delinquent children and a matched sample of nondelinquent children. *Child Psychiat. Human Dev.*, 9:210–214.

Lewis, D. O., Shanok, S. S., Pincus, J. H., and Glaser, G. H. (1979a). Violent juvenile delinquents: psychiatric, neurological and abuse factors. *J. Am. Acad. Child Psychiat.*, 18:307–319.

Lewis, D. O., Shanok, S. S., and Balla, D. A. (1979b). Perinatal difficulties, head and face trauma, and child abuse in the medical histories of seriously delinquent children. *Am. J. Psychiat.*, 136:419–423.

Lind, J. (1914). The dream as a simple wish fulfillment in the Negro. *Psychoanal. Rev.*, 1:295–300.

Malzberg, B. (1940). *Social and Biological Aspects of Mental Disease*. Utica, N.Y.: State Hospital Press.

Malzberg, B. (1953). Mental disease among Negroes in New York State, 1939–41. *Ment. Hyg.*, 37:450–476.

Malzburg, B. (1963). Mental disorders in the United States. In: *Encyclopedia of Mental Health*, Vol. 3, A. Deutsch (ed.). New York: Franklin Watts.

O'Malley, M. (1914). Psychosis in the colored race: a study in comparative psychiatry. *Am. J. Insanity.*, 71:309–337.

Pasamanick, B. (1963).Some misconceptions concerning differences in the racial prevalence of mental disease. *Am. J. Orthopsychiat.*, 33:72–86.

Schleifer, C., Derbyshire, R., and Martin, J. (1968). Clinical change in jail-referred mental patients. *Arch. Gen. Psychiat.*, 18:42–46.

Thomas, A., and Sillen, S. (1972). *Racism and Psychiatry*. New York: Brunner/Mazel.

White, J. (1970). Guidelines for black psychologists. *Black Scholar* (March): 52–57.

Wilson, D., and Lantz, E. (1957). The effect of culture change on the Negro race in Virginia as indicated by a study of state hospital admission. *Am. J. Psychiat.*, 114:25–32.

CHAPTER SIXTEEN

Treatment Programs for Delinquent Children: Implications of the Psychobiological Vulnerabilities to Delinquency

DOROTHY OTNOW LEWIS

Not so long ago the notion that any biological predisposition or vulnerability to psychopathology was immutable prevailed. This belief in the unalterable nature of biological characteristics was especially strong when applied to criminality. "The apple falls not far from the tree" was accepted as though its meaning sprang from laws as well established as the Newtonian law of physics from which the metaphor derived.

Lombroso's theory that criminals represented a degenerate biological phenomenon influenced psychiatry and later criminology. Criminality was thus considered to be a specific endowment capable of transmission in toto from generation to generation. So influential was this theory that to this day terms such as "defective delinquent" remain in the statutes of many states, a grim reminder of Lombrosian attitudes toward social deviance.

The morally abhorrent theories of Lombroso were followed by a lengthy period of time when psychodynamic and social theories dominated the literature on delinquency and criminality. Partially in reaction to Lombrosian theory, partially in response to social optimism based on a rejection of the Calvinist notions of social immutability, and partially in tune with the exciting new theories of psychoanalysis permeating western culture, psychiatrists turned their attention to the study of psychodynamic factors influencing or associated with delinquency. Freud (1916) focused on the unconscious wish of the criminal to be caught. Aichhorn (1935) explored the concept of a "defective superego" in delinquents. Johnson and Szurek (Johnson, 1949; Johnson and Szurek, 1952) conceptualized the existence of "superego lacunae." And as late as 1962, Grossbard blamed "ego deficiencies" for the behaviors of delinquent children who, he believed, acted out unconscious fantasies. The question was reduced to that immeasurable, unanswerable conundrum: was the id too strong, the ego too weak, or the superego riddled with holes through which parental unconscious impulses leaked? During the first half of the twentieth century there were only a few investigators such as Healy and Bronner (1926; 1936) and Lauretta Bender (1937; 1959) who called attention to the severe psychopathology, sometimes psychotic, sometimes of an organic nature, underlying some delinquency.

Concomitant with the psychiatric emphasis on psychodynamics alone (and perhaps in reaction to it), sociologists studied theories of deviance based on the effects of social structure and class differences. Merton (1938; 1957) influenced a generation and more of sociologists with his theory that deviance in socioeconomically deprived individuals resulted from the experience of living in an affluent society in which legal access to material wealth and prestige was forever blocked. The poor (and they do make up the majority of incarcerated children and adults) were said to turn to crime when they could not obtain wealth and status by legitimate means open to more affluent members of society. Other investigators and theoreticians such as Shaw and McKay (1942) explained away social deviance in the lower socioeconomic classes as manifestations of different cultural values. Delinquency and crime were not related to psychopathology at all. They were, one might say, alternative life styles. (The patronizing quality of such an explanation was obviously not apparent in spite of the fact that most poor people and most members of minorities did not indulge in criminal behaviors.) Variations on Merton's theory were expanded by Sutherland and Cressey (1969), Cloward and Ohlen (1960), Cohen (1955), and Becker (1963). Society was blamed for labeling as "delinquent" behaviors that were said to be culturally sanctioned in the lower socioeconomic sectors of our society (Nye and Short, 1957; Wheeler and Cottrell, 1966). That delinquency was characteristic of a minority of the minority population and was often viewed as deviant by the rest of the minority population was beside the point.

When psychotherapy alone proved ineffective in modifying seriously delinquent behaviors, this form of deviance came to be viewed as a separate diagnostic entity, "sociopathy." Since psychotherapy alone was not helpful, and for many years psychiatrists lacked other treatment modalities, "sociopathy" came to be considered a syndrome difficult if not downright impossible to cure. This pessimism was communicated to the legislative and judicial sectors of society. Sociopathy came to be considered an untreatable psychiatric disorder. However, its existence was deliberately excluded in courts of law from other exculpatory psychiatric diagnoses. That such a negative attitude continues to exist was brought abruptly to my attention when, during the course of my testimony in the Juvenile Court, a judge referred to another psychiatrist's previous psychiatric evaluation in which he called a particular child "sociopathic." Thumbing through the case record, the judge exclaimed, "Sociopathy! Dr. Jones calls this child sociopathic. That's not treatable, is it, Dr. Lewis?"

Fortunately, although the first seventy years of the twentieth century were not exactly the Golden Age of research in delinquency, they were years in which important advances in general psychiatry were occurring, advances which would eventually have implications for the treatment of delinquent children. To mention but a few advances, insulin shock and electroconvulsive therapy were discovered to be effective in certain psychotic states. With the development of diphenylhydantoin, many epileptic conditions hitherto resistant to the barbiturates could be treated effectively. In fact, diphenylhydantoin proved especially useful for the treatment of psychomotor epileptic symptoms which did not respond to phenobarbital alone. Recently carbamazepine (Tegretol®) has also been found to be useful in the treatment of some psychomotor seizures. Penicillin effectively destroyed the spirochete, a cause of hitherto untreatable syphilitic dementia. And, of course, the phenothazines, in the 1950s, were found to reduce the psychotic symptoms of many schizophrenics and, indeed, to be effective in ameliorating the psychotic symptoms of other kinds of psychiatric disorders. Similarly, the monoamine oxydase inhibitors, tricyclic antidepressants, and lithium carbonate were discovered to be extremely effective in ameliorating the symptoms of many of the mood disorders. Finally, many of the attentional disorders referred to by a variety of terms such as hyperkinesis, minimal brain dysfunction, perceptual-motor disturbance, central processing disorders, conduct disorder, and attention deficit disorder have been responsive to the recently introduced (and often abused) methylphenidate.

Concomitant with relatively effective medical treatment for hitherto resistant psychiatric disorders has come a renewed willingness on the part of psychiatrists and social scientists to explore possible inherent or acquired biological vulnerabilities. Thus, behaviors in children previously looked upon as purely psychogenic as well as annoying and maladaptive have been recognized at times to spring from some sort of as yet ill-defined central nervous system dysfunction. Although in most cases no organic lesions have been found, the fact that certain symptoms are identical to those of patients with known CNS injury and are responsive to some pharmacologic agents has led to the conceptualization of a biological dysfunction with psychological and behavioral manifestations.

The schizophrenias, a variety of disorders previously thought to result primarily from impaired family interactions, have been recognized to be an inherited vulnerability to disorganized thought processes. Similarly, the severe depressions, formerly ascribed to introjected rage and/or to early loss, have also been recognized often to result from fluctuations in neurotransmitters. And certain forms of epilepsy have been discovered to be inherited. Thus, the mood disorders, the schizophrenias, and epilepsy are recognized as predispositions or vulnerabilities that tend to run in families.

The most important evolution in psychiatric thinking that followed these discoveries was the documentation of the interaction of biological vulnerabilities and environmental factors. Thus depression and mania are now recognized as mood states that depend not only on biological predispositions but also on life events that trigger emotional and biological responses. The phenomenon of impending discharge from a psychiatric hospital precipitating an exacerbation of mania or depression is a good example of this interaction. Similarly, studies of monozygotic twins discordant for schizophrenia have enhanced our awareness that, although schizophrenia may represent an inherent vulnerability, a variety of environmental factors will often determine whether or not this vulnerability is ever expressed. The overt expression of epilepsy too is often environmentally influenced.

In spite of the truly revolutionary advances in the understanding of the etiology and treatment of some of the major psychiatric disorders, delinquent and criminal behaviors have, by and large, remained areas of ignorance. In spite of the fact that antisocial behaviors have been reported to be characteristic of a disproportionate number of the first degree relatives of individuals suffering from schizophrenia, hyperkinesis, and even depression, antisocial maladaptation has rarely been recognized as a possible manifestation of vulnerabilities to these very disorders.

The preceding chapters strongly support the hypothesis that antisocial behavior manifested by children and adults is frequently the final common pathway of the interaction between environmental factors and a variety of different potentially treatable neuropsychiatric vulnerabilities. Perhaps the explanation for the failure of society to identify and treat these biological vulnerabilities lies in the fact that the majority of individuals who manifest their vulnerabilities in antisocial ways also suffer from almost insurmountable social vulnerabilities. They tend to come, for the most part, from chaotic, seriously psychiatrically impaired families. Their parents usually lack the sophistication as well as the financial and emotional resources to recognize the early signs of their children's disturbance and to obtain assistance for themselves and their children. Furthermore, the question arises whether we have not created a rising population of biologically vulnerable children by virtue of the partial treatment of psychotic individuals who are discharged from hospitals with inadequate supports and are expected to raise their own families. We thereby increase not only the numbers of genetically vulnerable children, but we also place the children of these individuals at enormous environmental risk. That is, many psychiatrically disturbed, distraught parents resort to extremes of brutality as they attempt to cope with the responsibilities of parenting. Still more tragic is the fact that even when assistance is sought, these children and their families are especially vulnerable to the effects of entrenched prejudice that cause them to be dismissed as merely lazy, incorrigible, or socially disadvantaged.

Coming from the lowest socioeconomic sectors of society, often from racial and ethnic minorities, delinquents and criminals rarely receive the kind of careful diagnostic attention they require. The kinds of vulnerabilities underlying manifestly antisocial acts are often multiple and subtle. Were they more obvious (as in the case of grossly psychotic, epileptic, or brain-damaged children), they would undoubtedly have been recognized so early that the children never would have reached the court's attention.

The diagnostic evaluation of seriously delinquent children, if it is to be of any use at all, is detailed and time-consuming. It includes a careful family history, interviews with parents and relatives, a social evaluation, a lengthy medical history, and then, of course, an unhurried psychiatric, neurological, general medical, and psychoeducational evaluation. Each of these procedures may indicate further exploration necessitating the gathering of old medical and school records, specific medical tests such as an electroencephalogram, or more detailed perceptual-motor testing. This kind of assessment is expensive.

When a seriously delinquent child has the benefit of this kind of multifaceted evaluation, it is extremely likely that multiple, longstanding problems will come to light. Whatever the individual child's constellation of problems, one can be fairly certain that they will not prove to be the kind that can be "cured" in a few months or even a few years. Central nervous system dysfunction, epilepsy, psychotic symptomatology—like diabetes—are chronic disorders requiring ongoing care. Moreover, in the case of seriously delinquent, violent youngsters, these kinds of vulnerabilities are complicated by the fact that many of the youngsters in whom they exist have also been abused (one might better say tortured) by their families. The psychological effects of such treatment on biologically vulnerable children are sometimes more difficult to treat than are the biological problems. However, when biological vulnerabilities are overlooked and untreated, it is doubtful a child will be able to respond well to psychotherapeutic intervention.

It is clear from the preceding chapters and discussion that any treatment program that focuses on a single aspect of a delinquent child's biopsychosocial vulnerabilities will almost surely fail. Programs based exclusively on the belief that a psychotherapeutic or behavior modification modality of treatment will cure seriously delinquent children are likely to fail. Similarly, treatment approaches that rely exclusively on psychopharmacologic interventions, such as programs that give all antisocial children antiepileptics, stimulants, antipsychotics, or lithium without attention to individual differences and to psychodynamic and environmental factors will also fail to be effective in many cases.

Programs designed to meet the needs and alter the behaviors of seriously delinquent youngsters must be able to provide a wide variety of different kinds of therapeutic interventions. They must have psychotherapeutic, educational, and medical components. They must be equipped to assess a child's need for psychopharmacologic treatment, to individualize such treatment, and, above all, to monitor responses carefully. Programs, to be effective, must be flexible enough to be able to provide the child with the care he requires in his own home whenever possible, but must also be able to provide residential care for a child in his own community should his own household be unable to meet his needs. A program that separates a child for lengthy periods of time from his family, such as the programs at training schools, will often engender resentment and depression in the child that make it impossible for him to take advantage of important psychotherapeutic and educational aspects of a program. No sophisticated program can ignore the intense attachment of many children to even the most physically and emotionally abusive of parents. And it is, after all, this attachment to family that must form the basis of empathy with other individuals.

No matter how rich, diversified, and individualized a program may be, if it terminates its investment in a given child at the time of the child's sixteenth or eighteenth birthday, it will most likely fail. A commitment to help that is limited in time is, of course, not a true commitment. Any child knows that. Looked at another way, the majority of readers of this book had the benefit of more or less structured settings and supportive individuals (teachers as well as parents) throughout their adolescent years and on into their twenties. College, medical school, law school, graduate school provided us with the kind of physical and emotional supports that enabled us to plan and train for future independence. To expect multiply handicapped youngsters, often totally lacking the support of parents, to require less than we did is unrealistic if not naive. The underlying vulnerabilities to delinquency, like diabetes and heart disease, are chronic in nature and demand ongoing care. Therefore, if we fail to provide sufficient ongoing opportunities for emotional and intellectual growth and support, many seriously delinquent children will be forced as young adults to obtain support of one sort or another in public institutions. Since psychiatrically impaired violent individuals, especially those from racial or ethnic minorities, are unwelcome in hospitals, they will be forced to seek supports in prisons, the only institutions that cannot refuse them admission.

Juvenile delinquents are even more disenfranchised than are other children in our society. This is because, as we have documented, their parents tend to have such overwhelming social and psychiatric problems that they often cannot function as effective advocates for their multiply handicapped children. They stand in marked contrast to, say, the parents of autistic children who tend to be healthy, competent individuals and thus effective spokesmen for their children's needs. Thus therapeutic programs for autistic children, a syndrome that affects about 4 in 10,000 children, are more likely to receive legislative attention and adequate support than are therapeutic programs for seriously delinquent children who constitute a far larger proportion of the population of handicapped children.

At first glance, it may seem as though the kinds of ongoing, community-based, multifaceted programs required to help seriously delinquent children would be exorbitantly expensive. A cost-benefit analysis of the failure to institute such programs, however, must take into account not only the cost of probable lengthy imprisonment for untreated children, but also the cost of damage to persons and property, and the moral cost of failure to provide scientifically available treatment to children. All things considered, the implementation of community-based, ongoing, multifaceted programs for seriously delinquent children that provide for increasing levels of independence may prove to be a social, moral, and perhaps even financial bargain.

Finally, the data in the previous chapters must be regarded as tentative. It represents the beginning of systematic research into the causes of antisocial behavior in children. It has implications for prevention as well as treatment. If advances are to be made in the understanding of social deviance, research in the area must be encouraged and supported. Clearly, the greatest promise for the diminution of delinquency in our society lies in the area of primary prevention.

REFERENCES

Aichhorn, A. (1935). *Wayward Youth*. New York: Viking Press.

Becker, H.S. (1963). *Outsiders: Studies in the Sociology of Deviances*. New York: Free Press.

Bender, L. (1937). Behavior problems in children of psychiatric and criminal parents. *Psychol. Monogr.*, 19:22–247.

Bender, L. (1959). The concept of pseudopsychopathic schizophrenia in adolescents. *Am. J. Orthopsychiat.*, 29:491–509.

Cloward, R.A., and Ohlen, L.E. (1960). *Delinquency and Opportunity: A Theory of Delinquent Gangs*. New York: Free Press.

Cohen, A.K. (1955). *Delinquent Boys: The Culture of the Gang*. New York: Free Press.

Freud, S. (1916). Criminals from a sense of guilt. *Standard Edition*, 14:332–333, 1957.

Grossbard, H. (1962). Ego deficiency in delinquents. *Soc. Casework*, 43:171–178.

Healy, W., and Bronner, A.F. (1926). *Delinquents and Criminals, Their Making and Unmaking: Studies in Two American Cities*. New York: Macmillan.

Healy, W., and Bronner, A.F. (1936). *New Light on Delinquency and Its Treatment*. New Haven: Yale University Press.

Johnson, A.M. (1949). Sanctions for superego lacunae of adolescents. In: *Searchlights on Delinquency*, K.R. Eissler (ed.). New York: International Universities Press, pp. 225–245.

Johnson, A.M., and Szurek, S.A. (1952). The genesis of antisocial acting out in children and adults. *Psychoanal. Quart.*, 21:323.

Merton, R.K. (1938). Social structure and anomie. *Am. Soc. Rev.*, 3:672–682.

Merton, R.K. (1957). *Social Theory and Social Structure, Rev. Ed.* New York: Free Press.

Nye, F.I., and Short, J.F. Jr. (1957). Scaling delinquent behavior. *Am. Soc. Rev.*, 22:326–331.

Shaw, C.R. and McKay, H.D. (1942). *Juvenile Delinquency and Urban Areas*. Chicago: University of Chicago Press.

Sutherland, E.H. and Cressey, D.R. (1969). A sociological theory of criminal behavior. In: *Delinquency, Crime and Social Process*, D.R. Cressey and D.A. Ward (eds.). New York: Harper & Row, pp. 426–436.

Wheeler, S. and Cottrell, L.S. Jr. (1966). *Juvenile Delinquency: Its Prevention and Control*. New York: Russell Sage Foundation, pp. 22–27.

Index